LOTUS 1-2-3

HEATH LABORATORY COURSE SERIES

A Laboratory Course in DOS, WordPerfect 5.0, Lotus 1-2-3, and dBASE IV

A Laboratory Course in DOS, WordPerfect 5.0, Lotus 1-2-3, and dBASE III PLUS

A Laboratory Course in DOS, WordPerfect 4.2, VP-Planner Plus, and dBASE III PLUS

A Laboratory Course in WordPerfect 5.0

A Laboratory Course in WordPerfect 4.2

A Laboratory Course in Lotus 1-2-3

A Laboratory Course in VP-Planner Plus

A Laboratory Course in dBASE IV

A Laboratory Course in dBASE III PLUS

A LABORATORY COURSE IN
LOTUS 1-2-3

ERNEST S. COLANTONIO

D. C. HEATH AND COMPANY
LEXINGTON, MASSACHUSETTS   TORONTO

Acquisitions Editor: John Carter Shanklin
Developmental Editor: Katherine T. Pinard
Production Editor: Kathleen A. Savage
Designer: Cornelia L. Boynton
Production Coordinator: Mike O'Dea
Composition and pre-press: Graphic Typesetting Service
Photo Researcher: Martha L. Shethar
Cover: John D. Kramer/ImageSet Design

Published simultaneously in Canada.

Printed in the United States of America.

International Standard Book Number: 0–669–21749–2

10 9 8 7 6 5 4 3 2 1

PREFACE

The microcomputer has become standard equipment in most schools, offices, and businesses. A wealth of exceptional software is available to apply this versatile tool to a wide range of tasks. *A Laboratory Course in Lotus 1-2-3* has been written for the novice end-user of microcomputers and application software.

Many microcomputer users work with operating systems and spreadsheet software. This text teaches students how to use such software in their everyday lives. In particular, this text concentrates on DOS 3.3 and 4.0 and Lotus 1-2-3 Releases 2.01, 2.2, and 3.0.

Text Content and Organization

A Laboratory Course in Lotus 1-2-3 has been carefully designed for use in any first course in microcomputer application software.

Computer Skills   he text is designed for use in courses with microcomputer laboratory facilities. Specifically, the text teaches DOS 3.3 and 4.0 and Lotus 1-2-3 Releases 2.01, 2.2, and 3.0. We assume that students have access to these software packages and a computer that can run them.

Appendixes   The text's three appendixes provide additional material that may be of interest to students and instructors. Appendix A, Selecting a System, provides valuable tips for those individuals faced with the daunting task of purchasing hardware and software. Appendix B, Software Installation, briefly summarizes how to set up DOS and Lotus 1-2-3 on a computer. Appendix C presents comprehensive command summaries for DOS and Lotus 1-2-3.

■ Text Learning Aids

A Laboratory Course in Lotus 1-2-3 combines a relaxed writing style with an outstanding array of pedagogical features to facilitate understanding and encourage reader enthusiasm.

Chapter Outline   Each chapter opens with *In This Chapter*, an outline of the chapter's headings.

Chapter Preview   Students learn more effectively if they are presented with clear learning objectives. Each chapter's *Preview* section introduces the material and provides learning objectives.

Readability   The text's engaging writing style ensures that concepts are explained clearly and simply. Editors, course instructors, and reviewers have carefully monitored the reading level to maintain accessibility for students.

Design and Illustrations   Students prefer a textbook that will hold their interest. We have created a design that is simple, but that effectively presents the material. High-resolution computer screen views are liberally inserted throughout each chapter to help illustrate major topics.

End-of-Chapter Materials   A carefully graded set of review materials is provided at the end of each chapter. First, the *Summary* briefly reviews the information that parallels the learning objectives stated in the chapter's *Preview*. Next, the *Key Terms* presents all of the chapter's boldfaced glossary terms. Twenty *Multiple Choice* and twenty *Fill-In* questions test students' understanding of the material. Ten *Short Problems* and ten *Long Problems* provide computer exercises that let students apply their new skills.

Glossary   A complete glossary includes clear definitions for all the boldfaced terms in the text.

Command Summaries   Appendix C contains comprehensive command summaries for DOS and Lotus 1-2-3 that serve as quick-reference guides to the software packages.

Keyboard Templates   Color-coded keyboard templates for DOS and Lotus 1-2-3 are included just inside the back cover of the book. Designed to be detached from the book and placed on top of the keyboard, these invaluable reminders list the important keyboard commands of each software product. The color-coding indicates at a glance whether the Shift, Control, or Alternate key should be pressed in conjunction with another key to execute a command.

■ Acknowledgments

Many people helped make *A Laboratory Course in Lotus 1-2-3* possible. I would like to thank Robert Hendersen and Nancy Sampson of the University of Illinois Department of Psychology Instructional Computer Laboratory for the use of various microcomputer hardware and software. Paul W. Ross of Millersville University provided many helpful suggestions throughout the development of this project. In addition to her work as copyeditor, Ann Hall helped extensively with the *Insight* and *Real World* features.

I would like to thank all of my colleagues who reviewed the manuscript:

- Professor Harvey Blessing, Essex Community College
- Professor Walter Bremer, California Polytechnic University
- Professor Frank S. Butash, University of Hartford
- Dr. William J. Engelmeyer, Anne Arundel Community College
- Professor Clinton P. Fuelling, Ball State University
- Professor C. Brian Honess, University of South Carolina
- Professor Susan Karian, Denison University
- Professor Gladys Norman, Linn-Benton Community College
- Dr. J. Douglas Robertson, Bentley College
- Professor Jerry Sitek, Southern Illinois University at Edwardsville
- Professor Karen Watterson, Shoreline Community College

Thanks also to the Lotus Development Corporation for their support of student and faculty by supplying us with their new software.

Finally, my special gratitude and appreciation go to all the people at D. C. Heath who worked long hours and sweated endless details to make this text the best that it could be, especially Kathleen Savage, Cia Boynton, and Mike O'Dea.

E.S.C.

About the Author

Ernest S. Colantonio brings combined teaching, technical, and writing skills to this textbook. He received his undergraduate degree in psychology and completed several semesters of graduate work in computer science at the University of Illinois at Urbana-Champaign. While in graduate school, he taught introductory courses in computer science for nontechnical majors. Since 1982, Mr. Colantonio has developed microcomputer software for various organizations, including the Illinois State Geological Survey, the University of Illinois Department of Psychology, the Office of Naval Research, Psychology Software Tools Corporation, and SubLOGIC Corporation. He is the author of several data processing and microcomputer textbooks. Currently, Mr. Colantonio spends most of his time writing new textbooks from his home north of Green Bay, Wisconsin. He also develops and teaches introductory computer courses for Lakeland College and Northeast Wisconsin Technical College.

4   Beginning Lotus 1-2-3   123

5   Intermediate Lotus 1-2-3   173

Summary ● Key Terms ● Multiple Choice ● Fill-In ● Short Problems ● Long Problems

6 Advanced Lotus 1-2-3   219

Summary ● Key Terms ● Multiple Choice ● Fill-In ● Short Problems ● Long Problems

A LABORATORY COURSE IN
LOTUS 1-2-3

THE MICROCOMPUTER SYSTEM

In This Chapter

Preview

We begin this first chapter by introducing IBM and IBM-compatible microcomputers, their hardware components, and popular types of software. (By *IBM-compatible* we mean any computer that works like a comparable IBM model and can run the same software.) Then we discuss a few helpful hints for working with microcomputers.

After studying this chapter, you will understand

- what is meant by the term *microcomputer*.
- the basic operations performed by all computers.
- the four major hardware components of a typical microcomputer system.
- the major components inside a microcomputer's system unit.
- the three major types of microcomputer displays.
- how the various special-purpose keys on a microcomputer keyboard are used.
- the four most popular types of microcomputer printers.
- the three major categories of microcomputer software.
- how to turn on a microcomputer.
- how to operate a microcomputer printer.
- how to care for floppy disks.

What Is a Microcomputer?

Its very name tells us that a **microcomputer** is a small computer. A **computer** is an electronic device that performs calculations and processes data. Most people think of a microcomputer as being small enough to fit on top of a desk. Although some powerful models can serve several users simultaneously, most microcomputers are used by only one person at a time. For this reason, microcomputers are also often called **personal computers.**

Another characteristic of microcomputers is that their "brain" or **central processing unit (CPU)** consists of a single electronic device known as a **microprocessor.** This device, a marvel of miniature engineering, controls the microcomputer, performs its calculations, and processes data. A microprocessor is just one type of **integrated circuit chip,** which is a thin slice of semiconductor material, such as pure silicon crystal, impregnated with carefully selected impurities. These chips are commonly used in computers and many other modern electronic devices.

One way to define microcomputers is by what they do. They can be used to help accomplish many different tasks. At the lowest level, however, a microcomputer performs the same basic operations as all computers. This can be summed up as *input, processing,* and *output* (see Figure 1).

First, a **program** is needed to tell the computer what to do. This is a set of instructions that controls a computer's operation. The program lets you enter raw **data,** which can consist of numbers, text, pictures, and even sounds. These data entered into the computer are called **input.** The program instructs the computer to process the data by doing calculations, comparisons, and other manipulations. The final result is processed data or **information,** hopefully a more organized and useful form of the original input. This information produced by the computer is called **output.** Keep in mind that there is no magic here—a program is needed to tell the computer what to do and the output information is only as valid as the original input data.

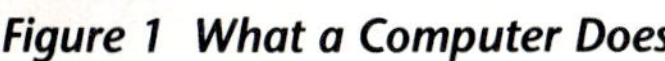

Figure 1 What a Computer Does

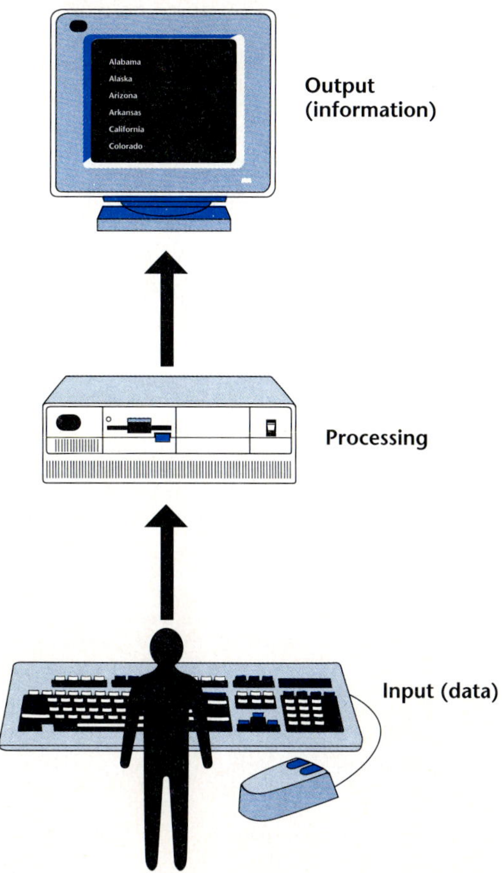

Although microcomputers perform the same basic operations as larger computers, they differ in speed and capacity. Larger computers can generally process data faster than microcomputers. They can also internally store more data at a time than microcomputers. These factors make larger computers better for performing lots of extremely complex and time-consuming computations. Microcomputers are also less adept than larger computers at handling several different users or tasks at the same time. On the other hand, microcomputers are superbly adapted to help with many work-a-day tasks like typing papers, figuring taxes, maintaining mailing lists, sending messages, drawing charts, managing finances, and even playing games.

Finally, microcomputers generally fall within a given price range. This can be as little as $100 or as much as $15,000. Today the average price of a typical microcomputer used in business is around $2500. This is, however, a good deal less than the cost of much more powerful computers, which may run into many thousands or millions of dollars. Although microcomputers are by no means cheap, their prices have been generally dropping even as their capabilities have increased. For example, in late 1983 the list price of a basic IBM Personal Computer XT was $5675. The list price of its successor, a similarly-equipped IBM Personal System/2 Model 30, was only $2545 when first released in mid-1987. Even though the newer Model 30 costs less than half as much as the old XT, it still has more than twice the speed and storage capacity, along with many other improvements.

Hardware

The **hardware** of a computer system is the electronic and mechanical equipment that make it work. Like a stereo system, microcomputer hardware generally consists of several distinct components connected by cables. Although there are several possible arrangements and many different models, Figure 2 shows a typical microcomputer system, the IBM Personal System/2 Model 30 and an IBM Personal Pageprinter. The four major parts are the system unit, display, keyboard, and printer. In this figure, you also can see the power switch, a floppy disk drive, and a mouse, all of which will be discussed later.

System Unit

From the outside, the system unit looks like a shallow box about the size of a portable typewriter. Figure 3 shows what the system unit of an IBM Personal System/2 Model 50 looks like on the inside. This central component houses important elements such as the computer's motherboard, microprocessor, memory, disk drives, and power supply.

Motherboard   The main circuit board of a computer is called the **motherboard** or **system board** (see Figure 4). Among other components, the motherboard holds the computer's CPU, some memory, and much of its control circuitry. In addition, the motherboard contains the **bus,** a set of wires and connectors that link the CPU to memory and other computer components.

Figure 2 A Microcomputer System

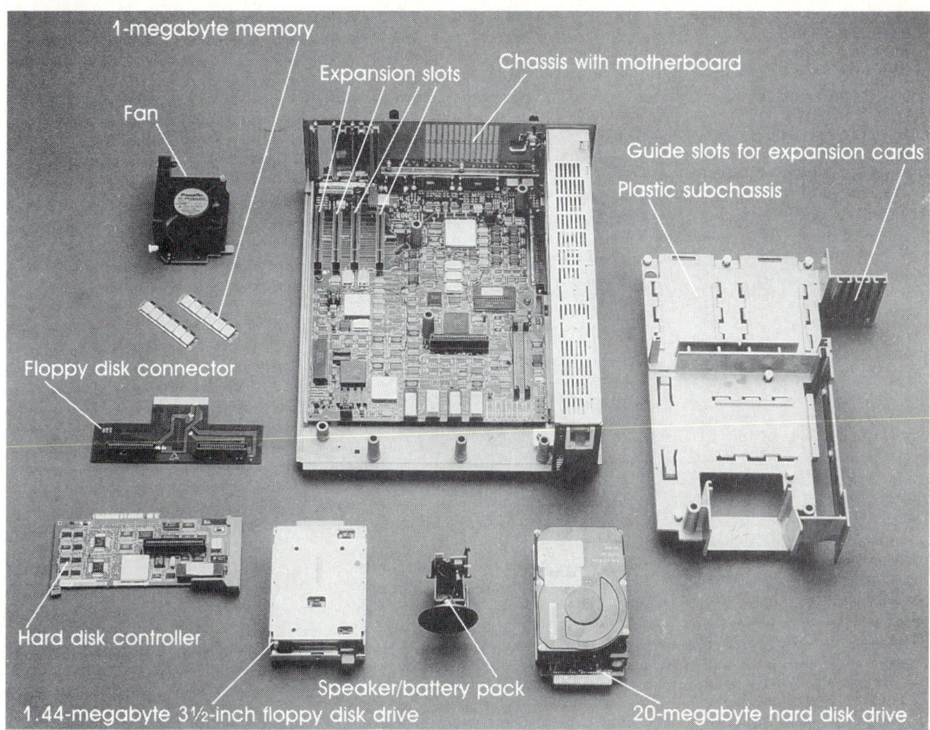

Figure 3 Inside the System Unit

In most microcomputers, the bus is accessible through a series of **expansion slots.** Each expansion slot is an internal connector that allows you to plug an additional circuit board into the motherboard. The IBM Personal System/2 Model 50, for example, has four expansion slots, which can be seen in Figure 4. Some computers come with eight or more expansion slots. A circuit board that plugs into an expansion slot is called an **expansion board, card,** or **adapter.** Such circuit boards make it possible to connect a wide variety of extra equipment to a computer, thus *expanding* its capability.

The motherboard or expansion boards also contain device controllers. A **device controller** is a set of chips or a circuit board that operates a piece of computer equipment such as a disk drive, display, keyboard, mouse, or printer. Recently, there has been a trend toward building device controllers onto microcomputer motherboards. The IBM Personal System/2 Model 50 shown in Figure 4, for example, has most of its device controllers on the motherboard.

Microprocessor   As we said, the microprocessor is a microcomputer's central processing unit (CPU). It consists of a single integrated circuit chip that is usually soldered or plugged into a socket on the motherboard (see Figure 4). IBM and IBM-compatible microcomputers use microprocessors from the Intel 8088 family, which includes the 8088, 8086, 80286, 80386, and 80486 chips. The 8088 is used in older IBM and IBM-compatibles such as the original IBM Personal Computer and PC/XT. The slightly more efficient 8086 chip is used in IBM's newer low-end models, such as the IBM Personal System/2 Models 25 and 30. The more capable 80286 chip is used in mid-range microcomputers, such as the original IBM Personal Computer AT and the newer IBM Personal System/2 Models 50 and 60.

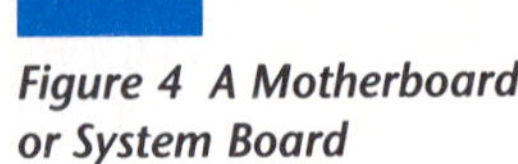

Figure 4 A Motherboard or System Board

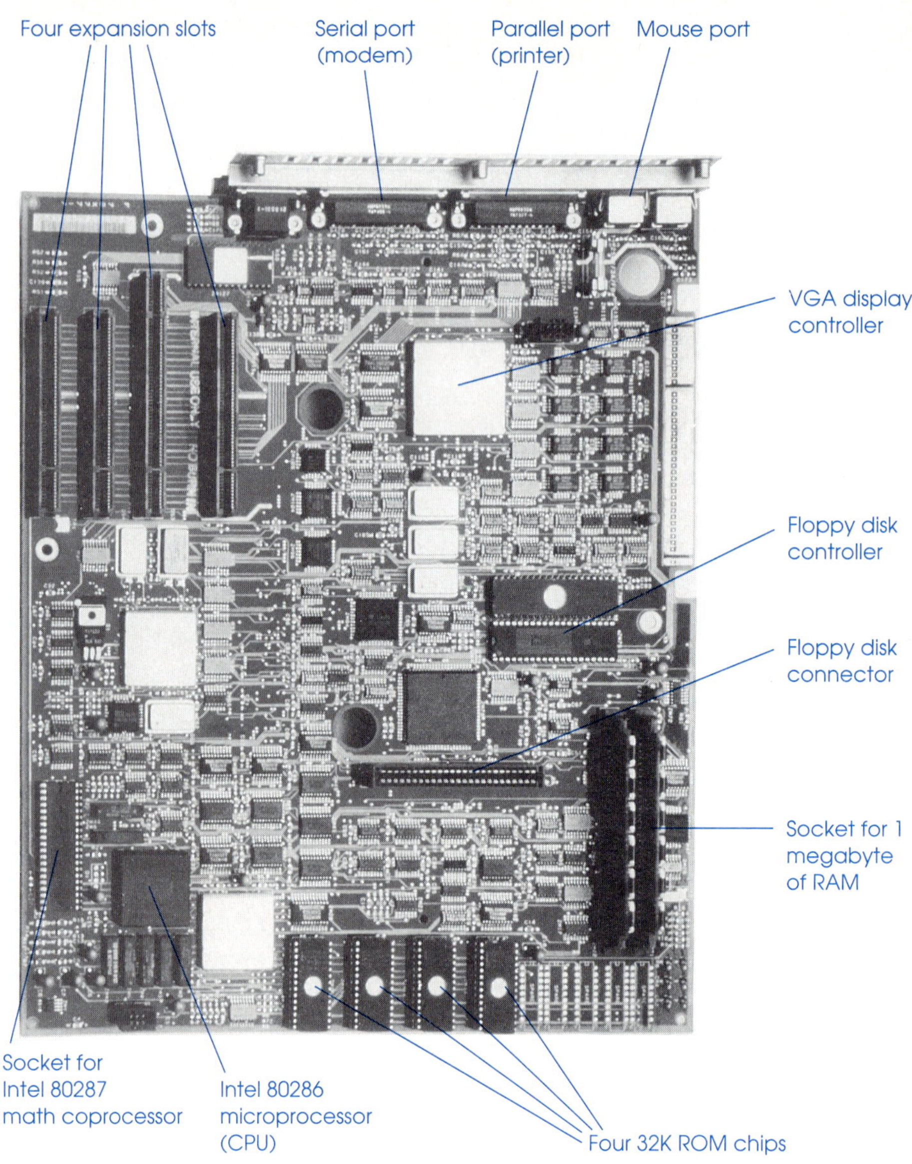

The fast and powerful 80386 chip is used in high-end models, such as the IBM Personal System/2 Models 70 and 80. Finally, the faster and even more powerful 80486 is used in IBM's Power Platform upgrade for the Personal System/2 Model 70 and high-performance computers such as the Apricot VX FT Server and the Hewlett-Packard Vectra 486 PC.

Memory   **Memory** is a computer's internal storage, used to hold programs and data. Also called **primary storage,** memory is measured in bytes. A **byte** is the amount of storage needed to hold a single character, such as the letter *A*, or a number between 0 and 255. Since computers can store thousands, millions, or even billions of bytes, the terms kilobyte, megabyte, and gigabyte are often used. One **kilobyte (K)** is equal to 1024 bytes, one **megabyte (M)** is equal to 1,048,576 bytes, and one **gigabyte (G)** is equal to 1,073,741,824 bytes. In general, microcomputer memory is made up of two types of integrated circuit chips: RAM and ROM.

RAM, which stands for **Random Access Memory,** is temporary storage. Programs and data can be kept there while they are being used and then overwritten by other programs and data later. When the computer is turned off, RAM loses its contents. Most microcomputers can now have at least 640K of RAM on the motherboard. Many can have much more installed on expansion boards. For example, the IBM Personal System/2 Model 80 can be equipped with up to 16 megabytes of RAM.

ROM, which stands for **Read Only Memory,** is permanent storage. The contents of ROM chips, which are encoded at the factory, remain intact when the computer is turned off. The programs and data permanently stored in ROM can be read and used, but never erased, changed, or augmented. Many microcomputers use ROM to store programs and data that are used frequently but need never be changed, such as portions of the operating system. Most microcomputers contain at least one ROM chip as part of their primary storage. The IBM Personal System/2 Model 50, for example, uses four 32K ROM chips on the motherboard to store essential programs and data (see Figure 4).

Disk Drives   A **disk drive** is a piece of equipment that can read and write programs and data on magnetic disks. A **magnetic disk** is a semi-permanent storage medium that can be erased and rewritten over and over again. Most microcomputers can be equipped with two basic kinds of disk drives: floppy disk drives and hard disk drives.

A **floppy disk drive** works with **floppy disks** (also called **diskettes**), which are inexpensive, flexible magnetic disks encased in plastic (see Figure 5). Floppy disks can be inserted and removed from their disk drives. The IBM Personal System/2 Model 50, for example, comes standard with one floppy disk drive. This drive accepts a 3½-inch floppy disk which can hold up to 1.44 megabytes

Figure 5 Floppy Disks

Figure 6 Hard Disk Drive

of programs and data. Although most newer microcomputers now come with 3½-inch floppy disk drives, many microcomputers still use 5¼-inch floppy disk drives. A typical 5¼-inch floppy disk holds 360K, but many drives can use 5¼-inch disks that hold 1.2 megabytes.

A **hard disk drive** uses one or more rigid, magnetic platters to hold programs and data (see Figure 6). Most hard disk drives have their magnetic disks permanently sealed inside. These disks spin much faster and have much greater capacity than floppy disks. Hard disk drives come in sizes ranging from 10 megabytes to several hundred megabytes. The most popular sizes are now 20, 30, and 40 megabytes. The IBM Personal System/2 Model 50, for example, comes standard with a 20-megabyte internal hard disk. On a microcomputer with a hard disk, programs are usually run from the hard disk. The floppy disk drive is generally relegated to copying software to or from the hard disk and making backup copies of important programs and data.

Display

A **display,** also called a **monitor,** is similar in many ways to an ordinary television screen. The display is used to present text and **graphics,** which are simply any kind of pictures, drawings, charts, or plots. Almost all computer monitors create text and graphics on the screen with tiny dots called **pixels** (short for picture elements). The number and size of these pixels determine a monitor's sharpness or **resolution.** There are three basic types of displays:

- **Monochrome Text** These monitors can display only letters, numbers, punctuation, and a limited set of other symbols in just one color, usually green on black, amber on black, white on black, or black on white.
- **Monochrome Graphics** In addition to text, these monitors can also display graphics on the screen. Only one color can be presented, but different shades of that color may be used.
- **Color Graphics** These monitors can display text and graphics in more than one color.

The capabilities of a particular display system are dependent on both the monitor itself and its device controller. The device controller for a display is called a **display adapter.** Several display adapters are available for IBM and IBM-compatible microcomputers:

- **Monochrome Display Adapter (MDA)** This is the controller used with early low-end IBM microcomputers. It can display only text on a monochrome screen, but it generates crisp, easy-to-read characters.
- **Color Graphics Adapter (CGA)** This is IBM's first microcomputer color graphics adapter. It can produce color graphics, but the quality is rather poor. In other words, its low resolution makes text and graphics look rather fuzzy. Furthermore, the CGA is limited to a maximum of only 16 different colors, of which only four can be on the screen at the same time.
- **Hercules Graphics Adapter** This adapter, made by Hercules Computer Technology, acts as a monochrome display adapter, but adds monochrome graphics capability.
- **Enhanced Graphics Adapter (EGA)** This color graphics adapter from IBM can do everything the CGA can do, yet is much better than the CGA. The resolution is significantly higher and the maximum number of different colors on the screen is 16 out of 64 possible choices.
- **Multi-Color Graphics Array (MCGA)** This is the display adapter built onto the motherboards of the IBM Personal System/2 Models 25 and 30. It can be used with either a monochrome graphics or color graphics monitor. Its maximum resolution is better than the EGA and can display a maximum of 256 different colors on the screen at once out of 262,144 possible choices.
- **Video Graphics Array (VGA)** This is the display adapter built onto the motherboards of the IBM Personal System/2 Models 50, 60, 70, and 80. It can also be purchased as a separate expansion board for other types of IBM and IBM-compatible computers. Slightly more advanced than the MCGA, the VGA can also do everything the EGA can do.

Keyboard

The keyboard is the primary device for entering text and telling the computer what to do. It is similar, in many respects, to a typewriter keyboard. Many microcomputers also have an auxiliary input device known as a **mouse.** This little box, which is slid across the table top, allows the user to manipulate objects on the display screen, draw pictures, and select actions to be performed by pressing one or more buttons.

Three basic keyboard designs are used on IBM and IBM-compatible microcomputers: the original IBM Personal Computer keyboard, the original IBM Personal Computer AT keyboard, and the new IBM Enhanced keyboard. Figure 7 shows all three of these keyboards. Besides the usual letters and punctuation marks found on any typewriter, a computer keyboard has other important keys:

- **Enter** (or **Return**) Analogous to the carriage return on a typewriter, this key is used to signal the end of an entry. Basically, it tells the computer to go ahead and process what was just typed.
- **Backspace** Like the Backspace key on a typewriter, this key is used to go back and type over a previously typed character.
- **Shift** Located at either side of the keyboard, one of the Shift keys is held down while pressing another key to produce a capital letter or the symbol shown on the top part of the key.

Figure 7   IBM Keyboard Designs
*(top) Original IBM PC Keyboard,
(center) "AT-Style" Keyboard, and
(bottom) IBM Enhanced Keyboard*

- **Caps Lock** This key is like the Caps Lock key on a typewriter, except that it works for only letter keys. When the Caps Lock key is pressed, capital letters will appear when you press letter keys. When Caps Lock is pressed again, small letters will appear when their keys are pressed.
- **Tab** Like the Tab key on a typewriter, this key is used to advance to the next tab stop.
- **Escape** The Escape key (abbreviated **Esc**) is often used to cancel a previously typed entry or to prematurely end a program.

- **Break** This key is much like the Escape key and is used by some programs in a similar fashion.
- **Control** Somewhat like a Shift key, the Control key (abbreviated **Ctrl**) is pressed in conjunction with other keys. It's used to control a program's actions by sending certain codes to the computer.
- **Alternate** Similar to the Control key, the Alternate key (abbreviated **Alt**) is also pressed in conjunction with other keys. It's used to give an alternate meaning to the keys pressed along with it.
- **Insert** This key (abbreviated **Ins**) is often used to insert a new entry between existing entries.
- **Delete** This key (abbreviated **Del**) is often used to erase an entry or a single character.
- **Function Keys** These are keys that are pressed to activate frequently used operations within a program. They are used differently by different programs. IBM-compatible keyboards have either 10 function keys along the left side or 12 function keys across the top. The function keys are labeled with an F followed by a number, like this: F1, F2, F3, and so on.
- **Cursor Movement Keys** Most programs use these keys to let you move the **cursor** (a little blinking underscore or box) around the screen. In a word processing program, for example, the cursor marks the place where text is inserted, deleted, or otherwise manipulated. The cursor movement keys include Up Arrow, Down Arrow, Left Arrow, Right Arrow, Home, End, Page Up, and Page Down.
- **Numeric Keypad** This is an array of keys at the right side of a keyboard that resembles the layout of a calculator's keys. It includes the ten digits and other symbols that facilitate the entry of numbers and formulas. On the IBM PC and AT keyboards, the numeric keypad is superimposed on the cursor movement keys.
- **Num Lock** This key is used to switch the function of the numeric keypad. In one state, the numeric keypad acts as number keys. In the other state, the numeric keypad acts as cursor movement keys. You press the Num Lock key to switch between these two states.
- **Print Screen** If you have a printer, this key is pressed to send a copy of the current screen to your printer. On some keyboards, it is abbreviated **PrtSc.**
- **Pause** This key is used to temporarily suspend the operation of the current program.
- **Scroll Lock** This key is used by few programs and it has no standard function. Some programs use it to switch the Cursor Movement keys into a state in which they can move (or scroll) the whole screen up, down, left, or right.

Printer

A **printer** is a device that produces permanent copies of text and graphics on paper. Although a printer is not absolutely necessary to run most programs, it is handy because microcomputers are commonly used to produce letters, reports, books, tables, figures, charts, graphs, diagrams, maps, and pictures. Paper output, or *hard copy*, is a convenient medium for distributing text and graphics to others. The four kinds of printers most frequently used with microcomputers are dot-matrix printers, daisy-wheel printers, ink-jet printers, and laser printers.

Dot-Matrix Printers   A **dot-matrix printer** is an output device that uses tiny dots to create text and graphics on paper (see Figure 8). Just as graphics monitors use pixels to construct characters and pictures on a screen, dot-matrix printers

Figure 8 Dot-Matrix Printer
*(a) The printhead of a dot-matrix printer,
(b) The process of printing a dot-matrix character, (c) The pattern of dots within the matrix
that form the character, and (d) The IBM Proprinter XL24, a dot-matrix printer*

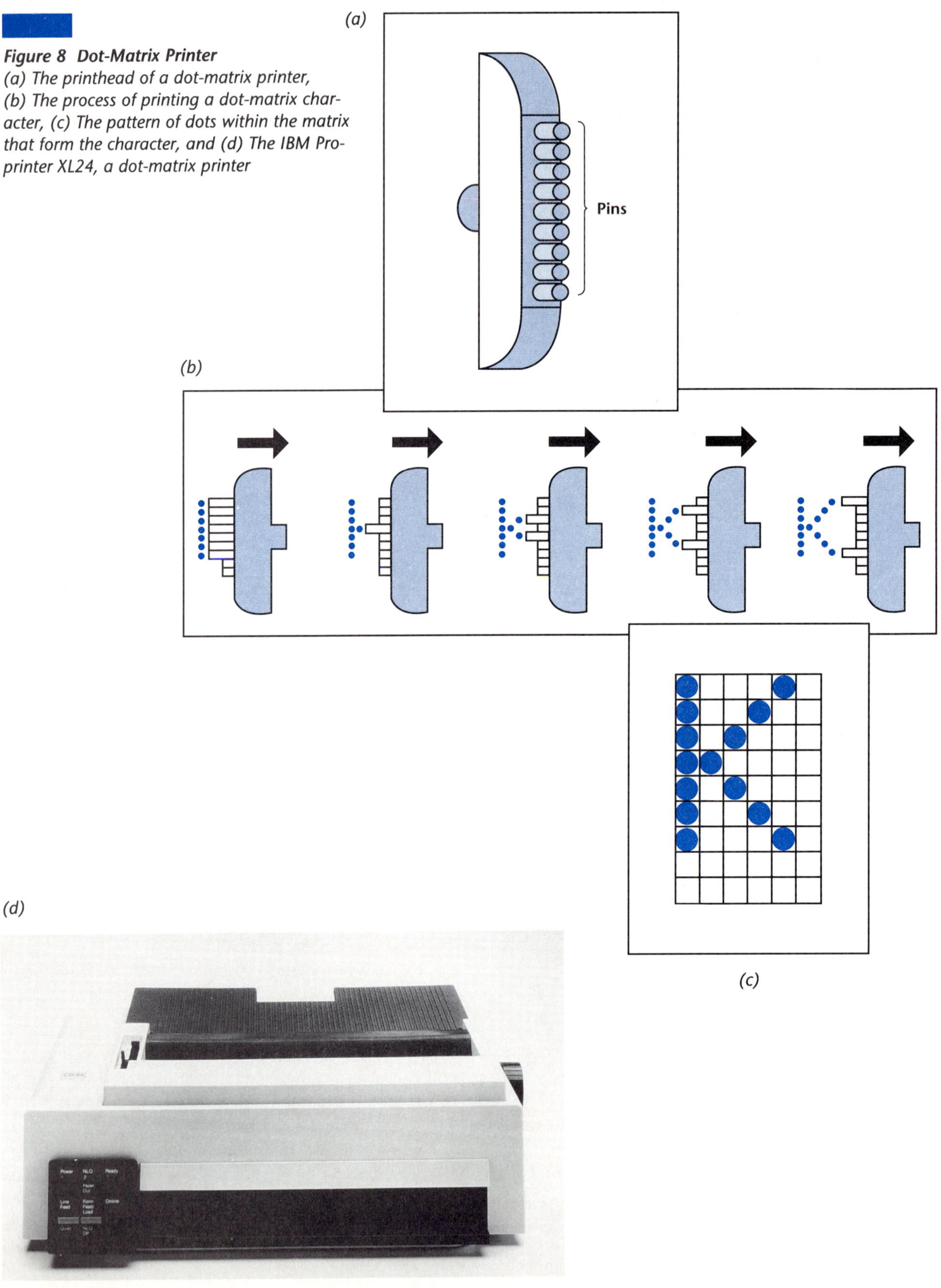

similarly use dots of ink on pages of paper. Inside the dot-matrix printer a **print-head** is moved across the paper from left to right, and sometimes also from right to left (see Figure 8). This printhead may contain anywhere from 7 to 27 pins arranged in a vertical column. While most dot-matrix printers use 9 pins, more expensive printers with 24 pins are also common. As the printhead moves horizontally, it constructs a character by repeatedly striking these pins against an inked ribbon and the paper. Electrical signals cause the appropriate pins to be thrust out at the proper moment to form the successive columns of dots that make up a character's image. Each column of the character is struck in turn against the ribbon and paper until the complete image has been formed. Dot-matrix printers are sometimes described as being impact printers because of the way the pins hit the ribbon and paper. This printing mechanism is most often used for text, but dot-matrix printers can usually produce graphics, too.

Dot-matrix printers are the most popular type of microcomputer printer. They are reasonably priced, fairly quick, and pretty reliable. Prices range between $150 and $3000, but the typical cost of a 9-pin dot-matrix printer is about $500. The speed of a dot-matrix printer depends upon what print mode it is using. The fastest mode is called **draft mode,** in which characters are formed by just a single pass of the printhead. Some expensive dot-matrix printers are able to achieve speeds of 400 characters per second in draft mode. Many dot-matrix printers also have a **near letter-quality (NLQ) mode.** In this mode, the printhead makes two or more passes over each character, slightly shifting its position each time. This tends to fill in the gaps between the dots and makes text appear more like it was produced by an electric typewriter. Using NLQ mode may slow some printers down to only 15 characters per second. Generating graphics with a dot-matrix printer can also be time-consuming. Depending upon how dark the images are, it may take several minutes per page to produce graphics on a dot-matrix printer.

Daisy-Wheel Printers   A **daisy-wheel printer** uses a circular printing mechanism called a **daisy wheel.** Solid, raised characters are embossed on the ends of little "arms" arranged in a circle like the spokes of a wheel or the petals of a daisy. As this daisy wheel spins, a tiny, stationary hammer strikes the back of the proper character when it passes (see Figure 9). This impact drives the character pattern, which is embossed in reverse, against an inked ribbon and the paper. Daisy-wheel printers are true **letter-quality** printers because they produce well-defined text just like electric typewriters. Their prices are comparable with that of dot-matrix printers. Unlike dot-matrix printers, however, daisy-wheel printers cannot produce graphics. They are also noisier and slower than dot-matrix printers. The typical daisy-wheel printer can only print about 10 characters per second, and even the most expensive models generally cannot do better than 100 characters per second. Daisy-wheel printers are still common, but they are being supplanted by 24-pin dot-matrix printers and laser printers.

Ink-Jet Printers   An **ink-jet printer** has a mechanism that squirts tiny, electrically-charged droplets of ink out of a nozzle and onto the paper (see Figure 10). No pins or hammers strike the paper, so ink-jet printers are classified as non-impact printers. Ink-jet printers are fast, quiet, and can produce high-quality print, but they are slightly more expensive than dot-matrix printers. Some ink-jet printers require special paper to avoid smearing. On the other hand, many ink-jet printers can print in color, a capability most other types of printers lack.

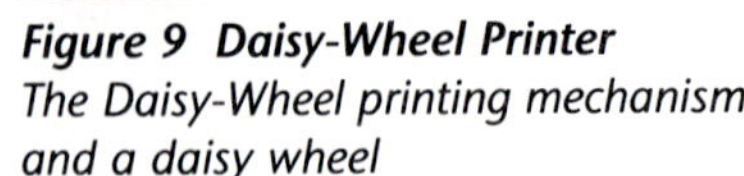

Figure 9 Daisy-Wheel Printer
*The Daisy-Wheel printing mechanism
and a daisy wheel*

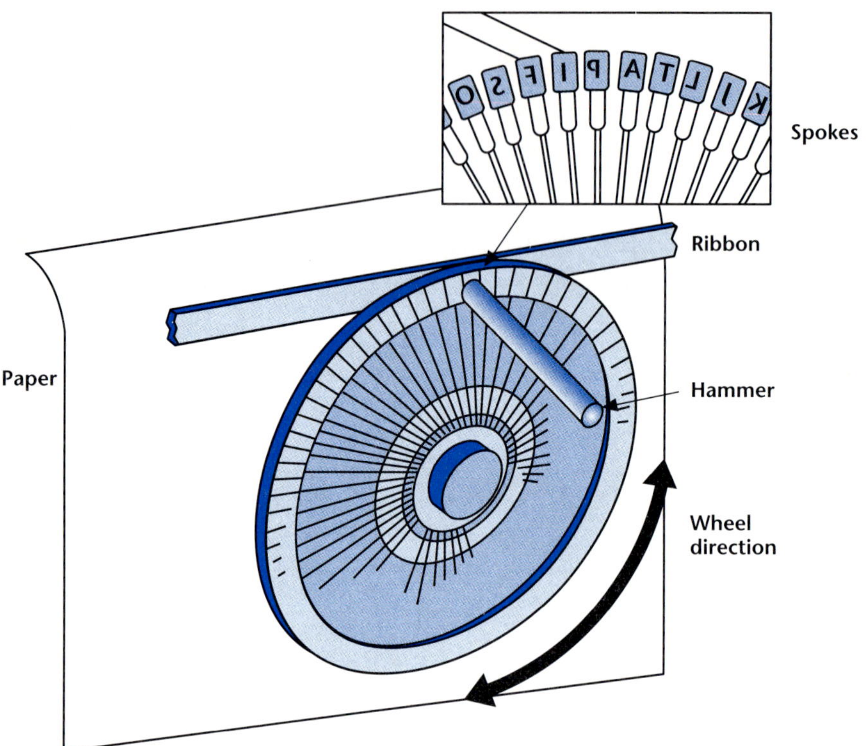

Laser Printers   A **laser printer** is an output device that uses tightly focused beams of light to transfer images to paper (see Figure 11). A tiny laser emits pulsating pinpoint bursts of light that are reflected off a special spinning mirror. This mirror reflects light onto a rotating drum. Light striking the drum causes it to become charged with electricity. An inklike toner is attracted to the drum in these electrically charged spots. When the drum is rolled over a piece of paper, the toner is transferred to the paper and an image is permanently fixed through a combination of heat and pressure. This image transfer process is similar to that found in a plain-paper photocopy machine. The result is high-quality text and graphics that almost look as if they were typeset. Like ink-jet printers, laser printers are classified as nonimpact printers.

Laser printers represent the most advanced printing technology. Although the images they produce are made up of dots, these dots are much smaller and more densely packed than the dots created with a dot-matrix printer. The typical microcomputer laser printer is capable of printing at a resolution of 300 dots per inch, both horizontally and vertically. This means 90,000 dots per square inch. Besides printing high-quality images, laser printers are also fast and quiet. The

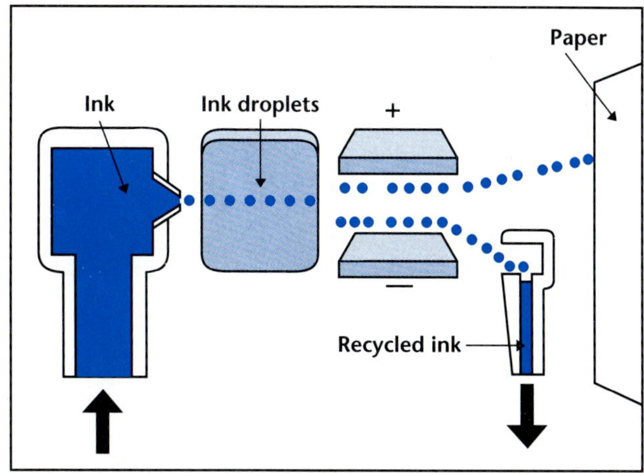

Figure 10 Ink-Jet Printer
*(above) Ink jet printing, and (below)
the Hewlett-Packard PaintJet color
graphics printer*

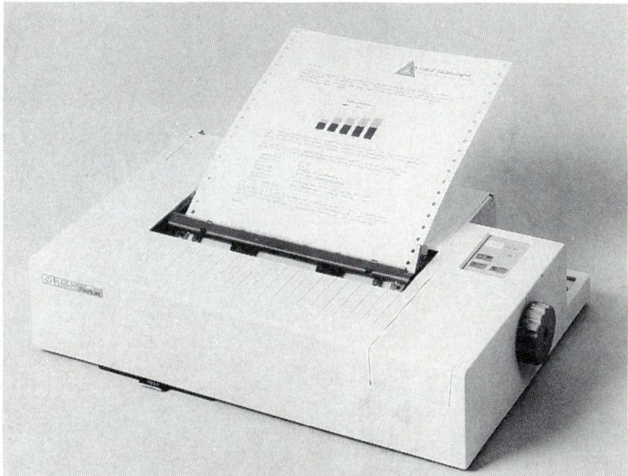

average speed of most laser printers is 8 pages per minute. This is equivalent to about 400 characters per second. Because laser printers don't use impact methods like dot-matrix and daisy-wheel printers, they are very quiet by comparison. The major disadvantage to laser printers is their cost. Prices generally start at around $1000. Despite the cost, more and more laser printers are being used with microcomputers every year. They are especially popular in office situations where the printer can be shared among several users.

Software

By itself, computer hardware is useless. Programs are needed to operate the hardware. As we mentioned earlier, a program is simply a sequence of instructions that tells a computer what to do. **Software** is a general term that refers to any single program or group of programs. In contrast to hardware, which is

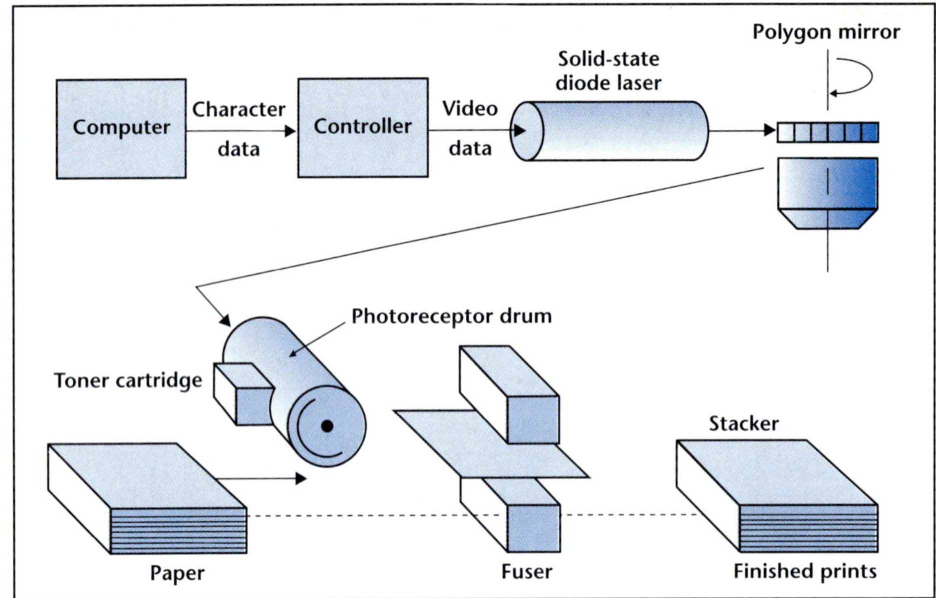

Figure 11 Laser Printer
(above) The laser printing mechanism, and (below) the Hewlett-Packard LaserJet Series II laser printer

constructed from physical materials like metal and plastic, software is built from knowledge, planning, and testing. A person who creates programs is called a **programmer.** Programmers use their knowledge of how a computer works to plan sets of instructions that accomplish useful tasks. These instructions are entered into the computer and repeatedly tested and modified until they achieve the desired results. Programs and data are generally kept on magnetic disks, where they can be accessed and used over and over again. Note that the disks themselves aren't the software, they are just the medium on which software is stored.

As an analogy, think of a stereo system. The amplifier, compact disc player, and speakers are the hardware. The amplifier is like the central processing unit and memory, the compact disc player is like a disk drive, and the speakers are like the display, except they present audio instead of video output. The music, which is stored on compact discs, is like software, which is stored on floppy disks. Just as you can amass a huge music collection by buying more compact discs, you can build a bigger software library by purchasing additional programs on floppy disks. The stereo system is of little use without the compact discs and the compact discs are useless without the stereo system. Similarly, a computer system is useless without software and software is useless without a computer system on which to run it.

Just as there are different types of hardware, there are also different types of software. Basically, there are three major categories: system software, programming languages, and application software.

System Software

System software handles the many details of managing a computer system. A computer's **operating system** makes up most of its system software. This is the set of programs that controls a computer's hardware and manages the use of software. One small part of the operating system, for example, is a program that identifies which key you've pressed, determines the character that corresponds to that key, and forms that character on the display screen. Another example is a program that lets you erase the contents of a magnetic disk. Some system software is built into a computer's ROM chips, while other system software comes on magnetic disk and must be purchased separately.

Programming Languages

Computer programs are developed with programming languages. A **programming language** is simply a set of symbols and rules to direct the operations of a computer. There are many different programming languages in common use, each designed to develop certain types of programs. A few of the most popular programming languages are BASIC, Pascal, C, FORTRAN, COBOL, and Ada. Although it can be helpful to learn a programming language for some very specific applications, most people who use computers don't actually program them. They just use programs, such as operating systems and application software, that have been developed by professional programmers.

Application Software

Application software is the software that applies the computer to useful tasks such as helping you create documents, figure your taxes, maintain mailing lists, and draw charts. Also called **application packages** or simply **applications,** these programs are the real reason most people buy and use microcomputers. The three most widely used applications are word processing, spreadsheet, and data base management.

- **Word Processing** A **word processing package** is software that helps you prepare documents by letting you enter, store, modify, format, copy, and print text.
- **Spreadsheet** A **spreadsheet package** is software that lets you manipulate tables of columns and rows of numbers, text, and formulas. It is an extremely flexible tool that can be used to handle typical accounting chores, monitor investments, balance a checkbook, and work out a budget.
- **Data Base Management** A **data base** is an organized collection of one or more files of related data. A **file** is a mass of individual data items kept together on

a disk. A **data base management package** is software that lets you create, add to, delete from, update, rearrange, select from, print out, and otherwise administer data files such as mailing lists and inventories.

Besides these "big three" application packages, there are many other types of popular software, including the following:

- **Communications** Using an auxiliary device called a **modem,** a computer can transmit and receive programs and data over ordinary telephone lines. Communications software makes it possible for a computer to use a modem to call other computers and access on-line information services.
- **Graphics** Graphics packages let you use a computer to create all kinds of pictures including graphs, charts, maps, paintings, drawings, diagrams, blueprints, simulated slide shows, and animated presentations.
- **Desktop Publishing** Combining the results of word processing and graphics, desktop publishing or page layout software lets you use a computer and laser printer to produce near-typeset quality documents.
- **Integrated Software** Integrated software combines word processing, spreadsheet, data base management, communications, and graphics applications in a single package.
- **Windowing Environment** Working closely with the operating system, a windowing environment allows you to divide your screen into a number of different boxes, or *windows*, and run a separate program in each one.
- **DOS Shell** A DOS shell is a program that enhances PC-DOS or MS-DOS, the operating system used with IBM and IBM-compatible microcomputers. Basically, it is an easy-to-use front-end to DOS that helps you execute commands and manage disk files.
- **Utilities** There are a host of small, specific programs called utilities that add handy features and functions to a particular operating system or application package. These include disk and file utilities, printer utilities, keyboard utilities, and desk accessories such as calculators, calendars, and address books.
- **On-Line References** Software to help you check your spelling, find a synonym, or look up a word's definition are all examples of on-line references.
- **Statistics and Math** Many programs exist for performing statistical analyses and helping solve mathematical equations.
- **Project Management** A project management package is software that helps you formally plan and control complex undertakings, such as the construction of a building, the development of a new product, or the installation of a large computer system.
- **Accounting** Accounting software lets you use a computer to record, analyze, and report business transactions.
- **Personal Finance and Taxes** Many programs exist for helping you manage your money and prepare your federal and state income tax returns.
- **Education** There is a wide range of programs for teaching skills and concepts, from learning the alphabet to designing physics experiments.
- **Entertainment** An amazing variety of microcomputer software exists for playing games, simulating cars and planes, and playing music.
- **Hypertext** A hypertext package is software that lets you store and retrieve all kinds of information in a nonsequential manner. In other words, you can randomly jump from topic to related topic, accessing any kind of information the computer can store, including text, graphics, audio, and video.
- **Expert System** An expert system is a computer program that contains a collection of facts and a list of rules for making inferences about those facts. Such software can use these facts and rules in a particular field to advise, analyze, categorize, diagnose, explain, identify, interpret, and teach.

Helpful Hints for Using a Microcomputer

Now that we've covered the general topics, let's go over a few specific details that can help prepare you for using a microcomputer.

Turning on the Computer

Sometimes, just turning on the computer can be an adventure. It seems that some manufacturers are fond of "hiding" the **power switch.** This has the practical purpose of making it difficult to turn off the computer by accident while in the middle of some critical task. Not being able to find the power switch, however, can make you feel lost before you even begin.

On the new IBM Personal System/2 computers, the power switch is a big red toggle right up front on the system unit. No problem here. On other computers, if the switch isn't immediately obvious up front, then it is probably on the right side of the system unit toward the rear. This is the case in IBM PCs, XTs, and ATs. Some models from other companies have the power switch mounted somewhere on the back of the system unit or monitor.

Many color graphics displays have a separate power switch that must also be turned on, otherwise you will be looking at a permanently blank screen. The on/off switch is usually the top knob of three on the front of the monitor and is turned on by rotating it to the right. The other two knobs are the contrast and brightness controls, just like the ones on many television sets. If these three controls aren't right up front, they may be present as slightly protruding little disks located just under the bottom front edge of the monitor or on the back of the monitor.

Operating the Printer

Like the system unit and monitor, the printer also has a power switch that must be turned on. This power switch is frequently positioned at the rear on the left or right side. In addition, there are at least three other buttons on most printers. Usually stationed on the top or front of the printer, these three buttons may be labeled *On Line, Line Feed,* and *Form Feed.* The **On Line button** is very important and is usually paired with an indicator light. When the On Line light is on, the printer is connected to and controlled by the computer so that printing can occur. Make sure the On Line button is pressed so that the On Line light is on before attempting to print. The **Line Feed** and **Form Feed** buttons let you advance the paper in the printer, usually only when the printer is off line.

Caring for Floppy Disks

Although floppy disks are quite durable and can take quite a bit of punishment, here are a few guidelines you should follow in their handling:

- Don't touch the exposed surfaces on 5¼-inch disks. Don't open the metal shutter on 3½-inch disks.
- Don't bend or fold 5¼-inch floppies.
- Don't expose disks to extreme heat.

- Keep 5¼-inch disks in their sleeves when not in use.
- Don't write on 5¼-inch disks with pencils or hard point pens.
- Keep disks dry.
- Don't expose disks to strong magnetic fields (keep them away from magnets and powerful motors).
- Always try to keep at least one backup copy of all important disks.
- Carefully insert and remove disks from disk drives. Wait until the drive's red access light is off before changing disks.

Summary

- *What is meant by the term microcomputer.* A microcomputer has a microprocessor as its CPU, is small enough to fit on a desk, is used by one person at a time, and costs between $100 and $15,000.

- *The basic operations performed by all computers.* A computer program lets you enter input, processes data, and produces output.

- *The four major hardware components.* A typical microcomputer has a system unit, a keyboard and perhaps a mouse, a display, and a printer.

- *The major components inside the system unit.* The system unit contains the motherboard, microprocessor, memory, and disk drives.

- *The three major types of displays.* Monochrome text, monochrome graphics, and color graphics are the three basic types of displays.

- *How the various special-purpose keys are used.* Enter signals the end of an entry; Backspace and Delete erase characters; Alternate, Control, and Shift keys are pressed along with other keys; Escape and Break keys cancel or stop actions; Tab advances to the next tab stop; Insert adds a new entry; function keys perform common operations; cursor movement keys move the cursor; the numeric keypad resembles the keys on a calculator; Num Lock switches the function of the numeric keypad; Print Screen prints the screen; and Pause suspends the current program.

- *The four most popular types of printers.* Dot-matrix, daisy-wheel, ink-jet, and laser are the four most popular types of microcomputer printers.

- *The three major categories of software.* System software, programming languages, and application packages are the three major categories of microcomputer software.

- *How to turn on a microcomputer.* Flip the power switch located on the front, side, or rear.

- *How to operate a printer.* Flip the power switch and make sure the On Line indicator is lit.

- *How to care for floppy disks.* Don't touch exposed disk surfaces; don't expose disks to temperature extremes, dust, or water; don't bend, fold, or write on 5¼-inch disks; keep disks away from magnets; keep backup copies of important disks; and carefully insert and remove disks only when the drive's access light is off.

Key Terms

As an extra review of this chapter, try defining the following terms.

application package (application)
bus
byte
central processing unit (CPU)
computer
cursor
daisy wheel
daisy-wheel printer
data
data base
data base management package
device controller
disk drive
display (monitor)
display adapter
dot-matrix printer
draft mode
expansion board (card, adapter)
expansion slot
file
floppy disk (diskette)
floppy disk drive
Form Feed button
gigabyte (G)
graphics
hard disk drive
hardware
information
ink-jet printer
input
integrated circuit chip

kilobyte (K)
laser printer
letter-quality
Line Feed button
magnetic disk
megabyte (M)
memory
microcomputer (personal computer)
microprocessor
modem
motherboard (system board)
mouse
near letter-quality (NLQ) mode
On Line button
operating system
output
pixel
power switch
primary storage
printer
printhead
program
programmer
programming language
random access memory (RAM)
read only memory (ROM)
resolution
software
spreadsheet package
word processing package

Multiple Choice

Choose the best selection to complete each statement.

1. A microcomputer is a computer in which the central processing unit consists of
   (a) a RAM chip.
   (b) a ROM chip.
   (c) a microprocessor chip.
   (d) a device controller chip.

2. A set of instructions that controls a computer's operation is
   (a) a program.
   (b) data.
   (c) input.
   (d) output.

3. The main circuit board of a computer is called the
   (a) expansion board.
   (b) device controller.
   (c) bus.
   (d) motherboard or system board.

4. IBM and IBM-compatible microcomputers use microprocessors from the
   - (a) Motorola 68000 family.
   - (b) Intel 8088 family.
   - (c) Zilog Z80 family.
   - (d) GTE G65SC816 family.

5. A byte is the amount of storage needed to hold a
   - (a) single character.
   - (b) single page.
   - (c) single line.
   - (d) single file.

6. Which of the following does NOT describe random access memory (RAM)?
   - (a) It is temporary storage.
   - (b) It loses its contents when the power is turned off.
   - (c) It is permanently encoded at the factory.
   - (d) It can be read and written over again and again.

7. The two most popular floppy disk sizes are
   - (a) 3½-inch and 8-inch.
   - (b) 5¼-inch and 8-inch.
   - (c) 3½-inch and 5¼-inch.
   - (d) 3-inch and 12-inch.

8. Which of the following types of display systems can present text and pictures on the screen, but only in a single color?
   - (a) monochrome text display
   - (b) monochrome graphics display
   - (c) color graphics display
   - (d) monochrome display adapter

9. Which of the following microcomputer keyboard keys is used to tell the computer to go ahead and process what was just typed?
   - (a) Enter key
   - (b) Escape key
   - (c) Control key
   - (d) Function key

10. The most advanced and expensive type of printer in the following group is the
    - (a) dot-matrix printer.
    - (b) daisy-wheel printer.
    - (c) ink-jet printer.
    - (d) laser printer.

11. A set of programs that controls a computer's hardware and manages the use of software is called
    - (a) an operating system.
    - (b) a programming language.
    - (c) an application package.
    - (d) a data base management package.

12. Which of the following types of software lets you manipulate tables of numbers, text, and formulas?
    - (a) word processing package
    - (b) spreadsheet package
    - (c) data base management package
    - (d) operating system

13. Which of the following types of software lets you use a modem to transmit and receive programs and data over ordinary telephone lines?
    - (a) communications package
    - (b) graphics package
    - (c) desktop publishing package
    - (d) windowing package

14. Which of the following types of software lets you use a computer to record, analyze, and report business transactions?
    - (a) graphics package
    - (b) accounting package
    - (c) DOS shell
    - (d) utilities

15. Small, specific programs that add handy features and functions to a particular operating system or application package are called
    (a) on-line references.   (b) hypertext programs.
    (c) spreadsheets.   (d) utilities.

16. Which of the following types of software would be the best choice for maintaining a mailing list?
    (a) word processing package   (b) spreadsheet package
    (c) data base management   (d) accounting package
        package

17. Which of the following types of programs would you use to help plan and control the construction of a new office building?
    (a) word processing package   (b) spreadsheet package
    (c) integrated software package   (d) project management package

18. Which of the following types of software lets you store and retrieve all kinds of information in a nonsequential manner and then randomly jump from topic to related topic?
    (a) word processing package   (b) spreadsheet package
    (c) hypertext package   (d) expert system

19. Which printer button determines whether the printer is connected to and controlled by the computer?
    (a) Power   (b) On Line
    (c) Line Feed   (d) Form Feed

20. Which of the following should you NOT do to a floppy disk?
    (a) Keep it in its sleeve when not   (b) Keep it away from extreme heat.
        in use.
    (c) Keep it near a magnet when   (d) Keep it dry.
        not in use.

Fill-In

1. An _______ microcomputer works like a comparable IBM model and can run the same software.

2. At the lowest level, the basic operations of all computers can be summed up as input, _______, and output.

3. The _______ of a computer system is the electronic and mechanical equipment that make it work.

4. A microcomputer's motherboard contains the _______, which is a set of wires and connectors that link the CPU to memory and other computer components.

5. _______ is temporary storage for programs and data, which can be used and then overwritten by other programs and data. _______, on the other hand, is permanent storage encoded at the factory with frequently used programs and data that need never be changed.

6. Most microcomputers can be equipped with two basic types of disk drives: floppy disk drives and _______.

7. The number and size of a monitor's _______ determine its sharpness, or resolution.

8. The _______ is the display adapter that comes built onto the motherboards of high-end IBM Personal System/2 microcomputers.

9. Many microcomputers have an auxiliary input device known as a _______, which is a little box with one or more buttons that is slid across the table top.

10. On an IBM keyboard, the _______ Movement keys include Up Arrow, Down Arrow, Left Arrow, Right Arrow, Home, End, Page Up and Page Down.

11. _______ printers are by far the most popular type of microcomputer printer.

12. _______ is a general term that refers to any single program or group of programs.

13. BASIC, Pascal, C, FORTRAN, COBOL, and Ada are all examples of popular programming _______.

14. _______ software is the software that applies the computer to useful tasks such as helping you create documents, prepare a budget, or maintain a mailing list.

15. _______ packages let you use a computer to create all kinds of graphs, charts, maps, paintings, drawings, diagrams, slide shows, and presentations.

16. Combining the results of word processing and graphics software, _______ software lets you use a computer and laser printer to produce near-typeset quality documents.

17. _______ software combines word processing, spreadsheet, data base management, communications, and graphics applications in a single package.

18. A _______ environment allows you to divide your screen into a number of different boxes and run a separate program in each one.

19. A _______ management package is software that helps you formally plan and control complex undertakings.

20. An _______ system is a computer program that contains a collection of facts and a list of rules for making inferences about those facts.

BEGINNING DOS

In This Chapter

Preview

According to *Business Week,* some 10 million IBM and IBM-compatible micro-computers were being used in businesses around the world by the middle of 1987. Joseph R. (Rod) Canion, president of Compaq Computer Corporation, figures that customers have spent $80 billion on IBM PCs, IBM-compatibles, and the hardware and software that work with them. IBM sold approximately 2.7 million microcomputers in 1988. Compaq, the leading "clone" manufacturer and number 2 business computer maker in the United States, sold around 500,000 that same year. The number 3 business computer manufacturer is Apple, which makes machines that are not IBM-compatible unless they are fitted with special equipment. Frederic E. Davis, editor-in-chief of *MacUser* magazine, estimates that IBM and IBM-compatibles outnumber Apple Macintoshes in the marketplace six to one. Clearly, IBM and IBM-compatibles are by far the most popular class of microcomputer. The overwhelming majority of these machines are running DOS.

After the original IBM Personal Computer was unveiled in 1981, DOS quickly became popular in offices, large corporations, and other businesses where IBM has traditionally wielded a great deal of influence. As soon as various hardware manufacturers started selling lower cost IBM-compatible computers, DOS also began popping up in small businesses, organizations, and institutions, as well as in schools, libraries, and homes. Because of this "hardware explosion," many software developers began to write application packages to run under DOS. This attracted even more users, who attracted still more software developers. At the same time, hardware manufacturers began to develop expansion boards and peripheral devices to be used with computers that run DOS. Today, a huge body of application software and a multitude of hardware devices are devoted to DOS microcomputers. Despite more advanced operating systems, such as OS/2 and XENIX, designed for high-end IBM and IBM-compatible machines, DOS is still the most popular microcomputer operating system in the world. In 1988 alone, IBM and Microsoft shipped 9.8 million copies of DOS, and approximately 75 percent of all microcomputers sold used DOS. This percentage is expected to increase until at least 1991.

After studying this chapter, you will know how to

- start up DOS with the computer turned off.
- start up DOS with the computer turned on.
- obtain a directory of the files on a disk.
- use the special DOS keys.
- change the default disk drive.
- obtain a disk and memory status report.
- clear the display screen.
- format a diskette.
- format a system diskette.
- copy files.
- copy an entire diskette.
- change file names.
- erase files.
- protect a diskette from accidental erasure.
- display on the screen and print text files.
- run an application package.

DOS Versions

DOS stands for **Disk Operating System.** It was originally written for IBM by Microsoft, which kept the right to sell DOS under its own name. Today, DOS is developed jointly by both IBM and Microsoft. When it is sold by IBM for IBM microcomputers, it is called PC-DOS or IBM DOS. When it is sold by Microsoft for IBM-compatibles, such as those made by Compaq, Tandy, or Zenith, it is called MS-DOS. Although a few minor differences exist between the system software sold by IBM and Microsoft, from the user's standpoint PC-DOS and MS-DOS are almost identical. So, they are often both referred to generically as DOS.

Computer technology advances quickly. To remain popular, an operating system must be continually upgraded to accommodate new computers and new capabilities for existing models. Several versions of DOS have been released by IBM and Microsoft. In each release, bugs have been worked out and improvements have been made to previous versions. The driving force behind each new version of DOS, however, has been new hardware capabilities, usually related to disk drives.

It is important to know which version of DOS you are using, because some hardware and software can only be used with more recent releases. Fortunately, each new DOS version is **upwardly compatible** with former versions. This means, at least in theory, that every official command that worked with previous versions should work with the new version. In most cases, this is so. However, there always seems to be at least one command that doesn't work quite the same in the new release. Nevertheless, for the most part you probably don't have to change the way you did things before unless you want to take advantage of the added capabilities of a new DOS version.

If you don't need these additional capabilities, you don't have to buy the latest version of DOS each time a new release is issued. As long as the version you have works well with your hardware and software, you can continue using it. Keep in mind that although a new DOS version may add certain capabilities, you must pay for the upgrade and that new DOS versions typically use more memory and more disk space. In many cases, upgrading is simply not worth it. Unless you're buying a new machine or adding a different disk drive, you may not need the latest DOS version.

DOS versions are identified by numbers such as 1.00, 3.30, and 4.01. The number to the left of the decimal point reflects a major classification; the numbers to the right represent more minor differences. The larger the number, the more recent the version. This table summarizes the major DOS versions that have been released so far, along with the primary reason for each upgrade:

Version	Date	Reason for Upgrade (New Capabilities)
1.00	8/81	5¼" 160K single-sided floppy disk drives
1.10	5/82	5¼" 320K double-sided floppy disk drives
2.00	3/83	5¼" 360K floppy, 10M hard disk drives
2.10	10/83	5¼" 360K half-height floppy drives
3.00	8/84	5¼" 1.2M floppy, bigger hard disk drives
3.10	3/85	Network disks and file sharing
3.20	12/85	3½" 720K floppy disk drives
3.30	3/87	3½" 1.44M floppy disk drives
4.00	7/88	Hard disks larger than 35M, DOS Shell
4.01	10/88	Corrected errors in version 4.00

We will be using MS-DOS 4.01 for the examples. Most of what we cover, however, also applies to DOS 2.00 and newer versions. Versions 1.00 and 1.10 are now considered obsolete. If you are using a version of DOS other than 4.01, the screens you see on your computer may be slightly different than the ones shown in this book.

Getting Started

Although DOS is a powerful microcomputer operating system, you can easily learn its most commonly used features. DOS might be set up at your particular computer site in any of several different ways. You are most likely to use DOS in one of the following arrangements:

1. On a microcomputer with two floppy disk drives and DOS installed on one or more diskettes.

2. On a microcomputer with a hard disk drive and DOS installed on the hard disk.

3. On a microcomputer connected to a local area network with DOS installed on the network file server. Some DOS commands do not work over a network, as we will point out.

You may need additional direction from your instructor to run DOS at your computer installation. You should then be able to complete the following lessons. If DOS has not already been installed on your hard disk (with a path to the DOS subdirectory) or on floppy disks for you, see Appendix B.

Lesson 1: Booting DOS

DOS stands for Disk Operating System. Although some low-level parts of the operating system programs are stored in ROM chips, the higher level programs of the operating system are kept on a floppy or hard disk. Like any program, the operating system must be loaded into the computer's memory before it can start working. The operating system, however, is what loads programs into memory and sets up the computer to execute them. If this is so, how does the operating system itself get started? Does it load itself? In a way, yes. Basically, a small program in ROM is automatically invoked every time the computer is turned on or reset. After loading itself into memory, this program then loads the rest of the operating system into memory and begins execution. In a sense, the computer pulls itself up by its own bootstraps. The process of initially loading and executing the operating system is often called **booting up.** In the particular case of IBM and IBM-compatibles, this is also called booting DOS, loading DOS, or simply starting DOS. At this point, your computer should be turned off.

Step 1: Insert the DOS Startup Disk

If your computer has a hard disk, skip this step and go directly to Step 2. If your computer is connected to a local area network, you may have to complete this step. If your computer does not have a hard disk and is not connected to a network, you must insert a diskette containing DOS before you can turn it on. In most cases, this diskette will be labeled "DOS Startup."

If your computer has two or more floppy disk drives, the A drive is the one on top or to the left. This is the floppy disk drive from which you boot DOS.

If drive A accepts 5¼-inch diskettes, grasp the DOS Startup disk by the label and remove it from the paper sleeve. Be careful not to touch the exposed parts around the oval slot and circular hole. Hold the disk with the label side up and the oval slot pointing toward the computer. Slide the diskette all the way into the drive slot, where it may click into place, and close the door or lever (see Figure 1).

If drive A accepts 3½-inch diskettes, grasp the DOS Startup disk with the label up and the metal shield pointing toward the computer. The arrow embossed or printed on the disk should point toward the computer. Slide the diskette all the way into the drive slot, where it will click and drop into place (see Figure 1).

*Figure 1 Inserting and
Removing Diskettes*

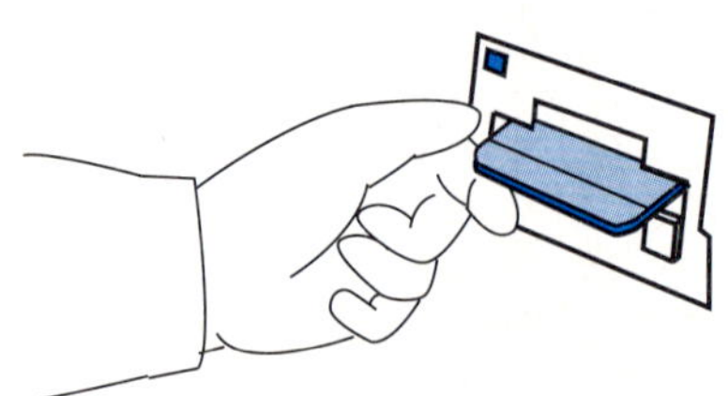

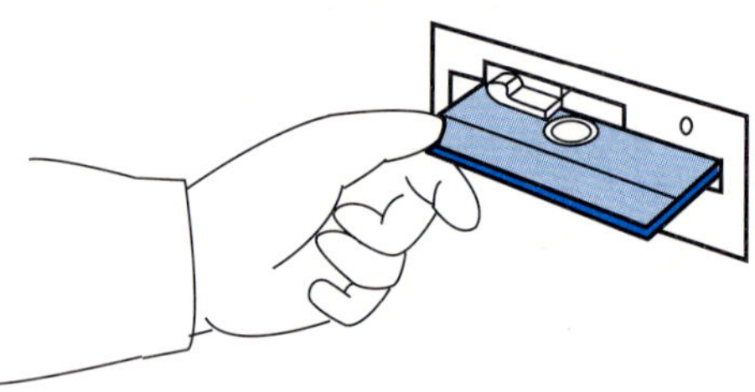

Insert diskette with arrow side up and arrow pointing to diskette drive. Press gently on diskette until it clicks and drops into place.

Remove by pressing eject button on lower right of diskette drive.

Insert diskette into drive until it clicks into place; label must be facing up with write-protect notch on left. Close drive door.

Remove by opening drive door and gently pulling out diskette.

Step 2: Turn On the Computer

If your display has its own power switch, turn it on first. Then turn on the computer. Older IBM microcomputers have a big red toggle switch on the right side of the system unit toward the rear; the newer Personal System/2 models have the switch right up in front (see Figure 2). Some IBM-compatibles have the power switch on the back side of the system unit. Flip the power switch. On many computers you will hear the cooling fan begin to hum.

Step 3: Watch the Display and Wait

After the power has been turned on, the computer completes some self-tests to ensure that it is working properly. One of these tests checks out all of the memory installed in the computer. This test could take several minutes, so don't be alarmed if nothing seems to be happening. After the power-on self-tests are complete, the computer will beep and check drive A to see if it contains the DOS Startup disk. If your computer has a hard disk and no diskette in drive A, it will boot up from the hard disk. Assuming the computer is in working order, the Startup diskette has been inserted correctly (if you need it), and DOS has been correctly installed on the Startup diskette or hard disk, you will see a message on the display screen. The exact contents of this message will depend on the type of computer and the way DOS was installed on the disk. If your computer does not have a built-in battery-maintained clock, DOS may ask you to enter the current date and time.

Step 4: Enter the Date and Time

If you don't see the following message on your screen, skip this step:

```
Current date is Tue 01-01-1980
Enter new date (mm-dd-yy):
```

Type today's date in the form of mm-dd-yy or mm/dd/yy. In other words, type in the month number, a dash or slash, the day of the month, another dash or slash, and the last two digits of the year.

Figure 2 The Power Switch

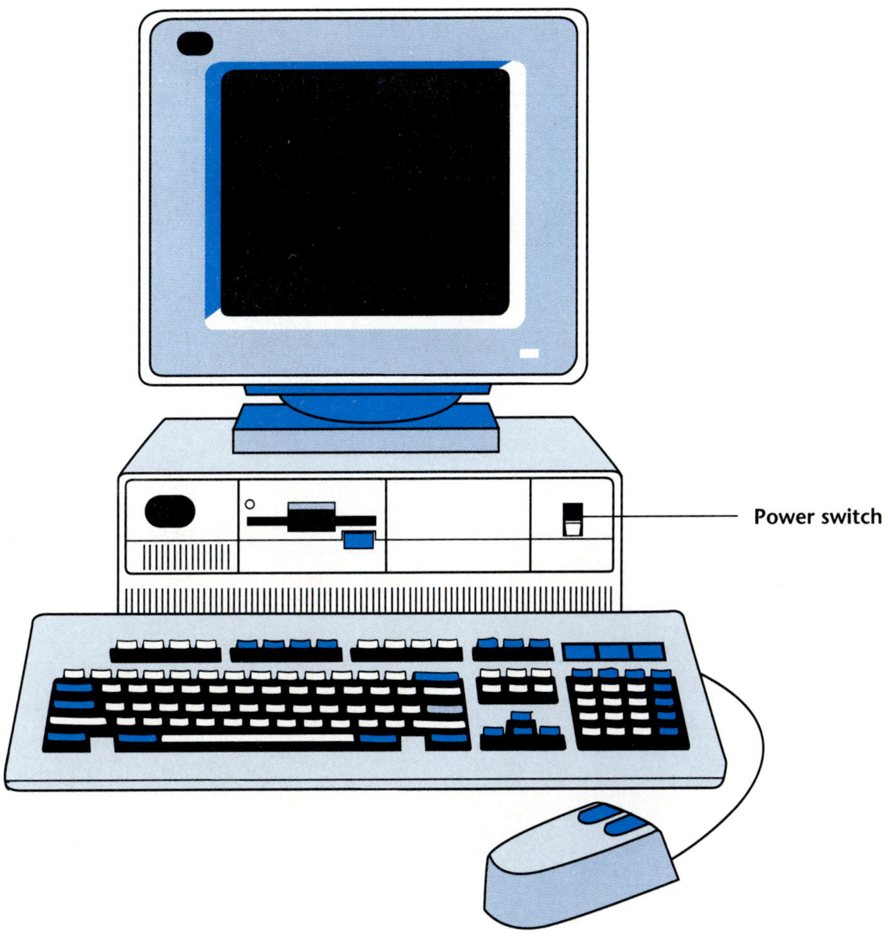

Press   **Enter**

Next, a message like this may appear:

```
Current time is 12:00:39.05a
Enter new time:
```

Type the hour, a colon, and the minute. If it is afternoon, add twelve to the hour as in the 24-hour clock format. For example, if it is 2 P.M., you would enter 14:00. You can also enter the second and hundredths of a second if you happen to carry a stop watch and feel so inclined. Just the hour and minute are sufficient, however.

Press   **Enter**

At this point, your screen may look like Figure 3. The C> on the last line is the **DOS prompt.** In this case, it indicates that disk drive C, the hard disk, is the default drive. The **default drive** is the disk drive that DOS assumes you want to use unless you specify otherwise. If you booted up from drive A, then drive A would be your default drive and the DOS prompt would be A>. The prompt tells you that DOS is waiting for a command.

Practice   Turn off the computer. Wait ten seconds. Turn it back on again. If it asks you to enter a new date, just press **Enter** without typing a date. If it asks you to enter

Figure 3 Booting Up

```
Current date is Tue 01-01-1980
Enter new date (mm-dd-yy): 7-10-89
Current time is 12:00:39.05a
Enter new time: 12:42


Microsoft(R) MS-DOS(R) Version 4.01
            (C)Copyright Microsoft Corp 1981-1988

C>_
```

a new time, just press **Enter** without typing a time. You don't have to enter a new date and time, but if your computer doesn't have a battery-maintained clock, it is best to enter the correct date and time when you boot up.

Lesson 2: Rebooting DOS

Occasionally, something goes wrong in a program and the computer may seem to be "stuck." Or after working with a program you may have to "reinitialize," or bring the computer back to the way it was when you first turned it on. You could, of course, just turn off the computer and boot it up as you learned in Lesson 1. There is another way to reboot the computer without shutting it off, however.

Step 1: Press Ctrl-Alt-Del

DOS has a special combination of keypresses that will reboot the computer without having to shut it off first. All you have to do is press the keys marked Control (or Ctrl), Alternate (or Alt), and Delete (or Del), and hold them down at the same time for a moment.

Press   **Ctrl-Alt-Del**

Step 2: Watch the Display and Wait

In most cases, the screen will go blank, the computer will beep, and the disk drive will spin and blink its red access light just as it did when you first turned it on. If all this doesn't happen, a serious program error has probably overwritten a crucial part of DOS in memory, and you will have to turn off the computer and boot it up as you did in Lesson 1. If all is well, DOS will again ask you to supply the date and time if your computer does not have a battery-maintained clock.

Step 3: Enter the Date and Time

If DOS asks you to enter a new date and time, do so as you did in Lesson 1. DOS will once again display its copyright message and the prompt, as shown in Figure 3.

Practice　　Reboot your computer without turning it off. Enter the correct date and time if asked to do so.

Lesson 3: Listing a Disk File Directory

In most cases, you tell DOS what to do by entering commands or responding to prompts that ask you to supply more information. Some DOS commands are loaded into memory when the computer is booted up and kept there until the power is turned off. These **internal commands,** also called **resident routines,** are kept in memory because they are the most essential or most frequently used parts of the operating system. For example, one of the simplest and most commonly used DOS internal commands is DIR, which displays a file directory. After you boot up, internal commands are always available from any disk. The remaining DOS commands are called **external commands** or **transient routines,** because they are kept in disk storage and temporarily loaded into memory only when they are needed or specifically requested. CHKDSK, for example, is an external DOS command that displays information about a disk and the memory installed in your computer.

Programs, data, and text are kept on disks in files. Every file has a name, size, creation date, and creation time associated with it. The DIR command lets you see what files you have on a particular disk or in a particular subdirectory. A **subdirectory** is a group of files on a disk organized under a single name.

Step 1: Enter DIR

To execute the DIR command:

Type　**dir**
Press　**Enter**

It doesn't matter whether you type DOS commands in lowercase letters, uppercase letters, or a combination of both. For example, DIR, dIr, and Dir are all equivalent.

DIR, which is short for DIRectory, displays information about the files on a disk or in a subdirectory. When the command is entered by itself, it will produce a directory listing on the screen of the default disk or current subdirectory. Figure 4 shows the screen after executing the DIR command. Your screen is probably different because your default disk most likely has different files on it.

Step 2: Examine the Directory Listing

Examine the screen in Figure 4. First it reveals the volume label of the disk. The volume label is just the name of the disk, which in this case is HARD DISK. Next is the volume serial number, which is just a code number assigned to the disk when it is formatted. DOS versions prior to 4.00 do not have volume serial numbers. Then DOS says that this is a directory of the disk in drive C, and it

```
C>dir

 Volume in drive C is HARD DISK
 Volume Serial Number is 3324-07CC
 Directory of  C:\

CONFIG   SYS        146 07-09-89   1:22p
AUTOEXEC BAT        145 07-09-89   1:22p
COMMAND  COM      37557 12-19-88  12:00a
DOS          <DIR>       07-09-89   1:23p
        4 File(s)   19701760 bytes free

C>_
```

lists the names, sizes, dates, and times of the files. Notice that the first three file names have two parts. We'll have more to say about this file name format shortly. The last file name in the list, DOS, is the name of a subdirectory. The <DIR> designation next to the name tells you that it is a subdirectory and not an ordinary file. This subdirectory, which we'll look at later, contains the files that make up most of DOS. It was created when DOS was installed on the hard disk.

Each file name, except for the DOS subdirectory, has a number to its immediate right. This is the size of that file in bytes. A byte, you'll recall, is basically equivalent to a single character. Finally, listed to the right of each file size is the date and then the time at which the file was created or last changed. The first file in the list, for example, is named CONFIG.SYS, occupies 146 bytes, and was created on July 9, 1989, at 1:22 P.M.

At the bottom of the listing, the DIR command tells you that four files are in this directory and there are 19,701,760 "bytes free." This means that 19,701,760 bytes of storage are still unused on the disk. Since it's important to know what files are on a disk and how much room is left, DIR is one of the most frequently used DOS commands.

Step 3: Examine Another Disk's Directory

The DIR command can also be used to list the directory of a disk in a drive other than the current default drive. You can do this by specifying the disk drive letter after DIR. For example, if your computer has a hard disk, you can examine the directory of a disk in floppy drive A. If you have a diskette with files on it, insert the diskette into drive A.

Type **dir a:**
Press **Enter**

The **a:** is the designation for the A disk drive. If you have a computer with two floppy drives, you can examine a disk in the second drive by entering DIR B:. Note that the hard disk is usually referred to as the C drive, regardless of whether a B floppy drive is installed.

Step 4: Examine the Contents of a Subdirectory

The DIR command can also be used to list the files in a subdirectory. All you have to do is type the name of the subdirectory after the DIR. For example, if your computer has a hard disk with a subdirectory named DOS, try the following command:

Type   **dir dos**
Press   **Enter**

Figure 5 shows the result. Since 68 files are in this directory listing but only 25 lines can be shown on the screen, many of the names have moved up and disappeared off the top of the screen. Figure 5, therefore, shows only the bottom part of the listing. For the rest of this chapter, we will assume you have a computer with a hard disk that has a DOS subdirectory.

Step 5: Look For a Specific File

Frequently, you'd like to be able to check if a particular file is on a disk or in a subdirectory without having to look at the entire directory listing. The DIR command can do this for you if you give it the name of the file you're looking for. All you have to do is enter the name of the file after the DIR. If you want to look in a subdirectory, type the subdirectory name, a backward slash (\), and then the name of the file. DOS will either list an abbreviated directory with only that file in it or tell you the file is not there. For example, if your computer has a DOS subdirectory, execute this command:

Type   **dir dos\format.com**
Press   **Enter**

This command tells DOS to look in the DOS subdirectory for a file named FOR-MAT.COM. Figure 6 shows the result. If your computer doesn't have a DOS subdirectory, try this command instead:

Type   **dir format.com**
Press   **Enter**

Figure 5 Looking at a Subdirectory

```
GRAPHICS COM     16693 10-06-88   12:00a
GRAPHICS PRO      9397 10-06-88   12:00a
HIMEM    SYS      6261 10-06-88   12:00a
MODE     COM     22960 10-06-88   12:00a
NLSFUNC  EXE      6878 10-06-88   12:00a
PRINTER  SYS     18914 10-06-88   12:00a
RECOVER  COM     10588 10-06-88   12:00a
4201     CPI      6404 10-06-88   12:00a
4208     CPI       720 10-06-88   12:00a
5202     CPI       370 10-06-88   12:00a
README   TXT     14148 10-12-88    9:13p
BACKUP   COM     36880 10-06-88   12:00a
EGA      CPI     49068 10-06-88   12:00a
LCD      CPI     10703 10-06-88   12:00a
RESTORE  COM     36946 10-06-88   12:00a
PCIBMDRV MOS       263 10-06-88   12:00a
SHELL    CLR      4406 10-06-88   12:00a
SHELL    HLP     66527 10-06-88   12:00a
SHELL    MEU      4588 10-06-88   12:00a
SHELLB   COM      3894 10-06-88   12:00a
SHELLC   EXE    153855 10-06-88   12:00a
DOSUTIL  MEU      6660 10-06-88   12:00a
       68 File(s)    19701760 bytes free

C>_
```

*Figure 6 Looking for a
Specific File*

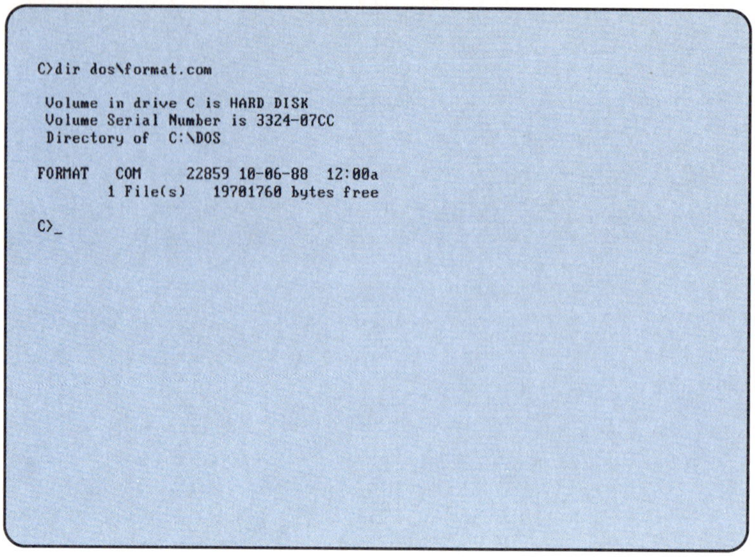

```
C>dir dos\format.com

 Volume in drive C is HARD DISK
 Volume Serial Number is 3324-07CC
 Directory of  C:\DOS

FORMAT   COM    22859 10-06-88  12:00a
         1 File(s)   19701760 bytes free

C>_
```

For the rest of this chapter, we will assume you have a DOS subdirectory on your default disk. If you do not, omit the dos or dos\ designations from the instructions given.

DOS File Names   This is a good time to digress a bit and discuss DOS file names in more detail. First of all, notice that each file in the directory you listed has a unique name. No two files in the same directory can have the same name because DOS wouldn't be able to tell them apart. Two files on different disks or in different subdirectories, however, can have the same name. A file name can consist of two parts: a primary filename and an optional extension. The first part, or **filename** as IBM calls it, can be from one to eight characters long. It can include any of the characters you see on the keyboard except for the following, which are considered invalid in filenames:

. " / \ [ ] : | < > + = ; ,

The second part, an optional short name, is called an **extension.** It is separated from the primary filename by a period and has from one to three characters in it. These characters also can be any of the keyboard characters except those we just listed. If a file's name does have an extension, you may have to use both parts when telling DOS to do something with that file. Extensions are most often used to classify files. For example, here are some of the more common file name extensions, along with the types of files they usually designate:

COM	DOS external command or an executable program
EXE	DOS external command or an executable program
BAT	Batch file
SYS	System setup file
ASM	Assembly language program
BAS	BASIC language program
PAS	Pascal language program
TXT	Text file
BAK	Backup copy of some other file
DOC	Document file of some word processing programs
WKS	Worksheet file of some spreadsheet programs
DBF	Data base file of some data base managers

Finally, a file name can be prefaced with the designation of its disk drive and subdirectory. For example, C:\DOS\FORMAT.COM is the full specification for the file FORMAT.COM on the hard disk C in the DOS subdirectory. Note that the colon must be used after the disk drive letter and the backslash must be used before and after the subdirectory name. If you don't enter part of the specification, such as the disk drive letter or subdirectory, DOS will assume you mean the default drive or current subdirectory.

Step 6: Look for a Specific Group of Files

Not only can the DIR command find a single file on a disk, it can also be used to list a group of files if their names have some characters in common. The DOS **global file name characters,** * and ?, can be included in a filename or extension to give you greater flexibility in designating DOS files. The * character can be used in a file specification to symbolize any character or group of characters. For example, *.SYS means "any file with an extension of SYS." The ? character is used to symbolize any single character. For example, MO?E.COM means "any file that has an extension of COM and a four-letter filename beginning with MO and ending with an E." Both global file name characters can be used together in the same specification, too. For example, ????.* means "any file with at most four characters in its first part." Try each of the following commands:

Type	**dir dos*.sys**
Press	**Enter**
Type	**dir dos\mo?e.com**
Press	**Enter**
Type	**dir dos\????.***
Press	**Enter**

Figure 7 shows what you should see on your screen after entering the command DIR DOS*.SYS.

Figure 7 Looking for a Group of Files

```
C>dir dos\*.sys

 Volume in drive C is HARD DISK
 Volume Serial Number is 3324-07CC
 Directory of  C:\DOS

COUNTRY  SYS     12806 10-06-88   12:00a
DISPLAY  SYS     15692 10-06-88   12:00a
KEYBOARD SYS     23328 10-06-88   12:00a
EMM386   SYS     87776 10-06-88   12:00a
RAMDRIVE SYS      8235 10-06-88   12:00a
SMARTDRV SYS     10224 10-06-88   12:00a
XMA2EMS  SYS     29211 10-06-88   12:00a
ANSI     SYS      9105 10-06-88   12:00a
DRIVER   SYS      5241 10-06-88   12:00a
HIMEM    SYS      6261 10-06-88   12:00a
PRINTER  SYS     18914 10-06-88   12:00a
       11 File(s)   19701760 bytes free

C>_
```

Practice

1. List a directory of your default disk drive.

2. List a directory of the DOS subdirectory.

3. Try this command:

   Type   **dir *.***
   Press   **Enter**

   What does it do?

4. Try this command:

   Type   **dir dos*.exe**
   Press   **Enter**

   What does it do?

5. Create a listing of the DOS subdirectory that shows only those files that begin with the letter S.

6. Create a listing of the DOS subdirectory that shows only those files with primary filenames less than four characters long.

7. Notice that subdirectory names have no extensions. Try this command (follow the asterisk with a period):

   Type   **dir *.**
   Press   **Enter**

   What does it do?

Lesson 4: Using Special DOS Keys

Like most software, DOS assigns special meanings to certain keys and combinations of keypresses. You've already learned some of these. For example, you know that you must press the Enter key after typing in a command. This tells DOS to go ahead and process that command. The Backspace key can be used to correct typing errors on a line before the Enter key has been pressed. In Lesson 2 you learned that pressing the Control (Ctrl), Alternate (Alt), and Delete (Del) keys at the same time will reboot DOS without having to shut off the power and turn it back on. Let's explore some of the other keys DOS uses (see Figure 8).

Step 1: Press the Escape Key to Cancel a Line

As you've probably already discovered, it's pretty easy to make typing mistakes when using a keyboard. If the command you're typing is short and you haven't pressed the Enter key yet, the easiest way to fix a mistake is to backspace over it and retype it. If the command is long or if you really messed it up, you can cancel the entire line and start over. To do this, press the Escape (Esc) key. For example, type the following line at the DOS prompt (but don't press the Enter key):

   Type   **This line is really messed up!**

Suppose what you really meant to type in was DIR DOS, and you realized your mistake before you pressed the Enter key.

   Press   **Escape**

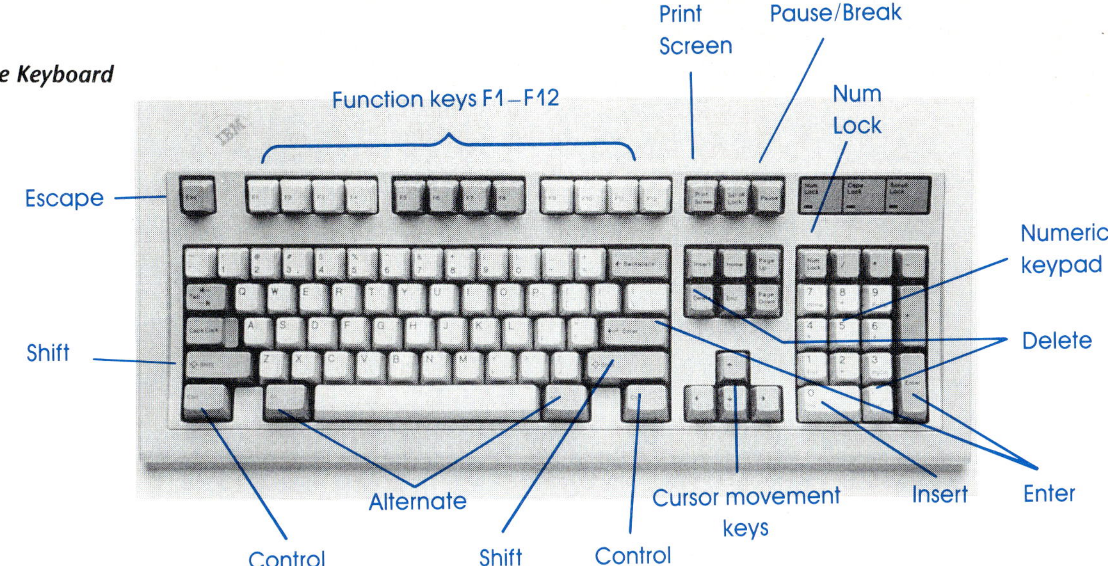

Figure 8 *The Keyboard*

Pressing the Escape key cancels the current line. When you do this, DOS will display a / (slash) to signal that the line has been canceled, and it will skip down to the next line so you can start over. Now execute the following command to see the familiar DOS directory:

Type   **dir dos**
Press   **Enter**

Step 2: Press Ctrl-Num Lock to Pause Screen Scrolling

As you watch the DOS directory scroll by on the screen, the first part of it disappears off the top. Sometimes, information scrolls by before you get a chance to read it all. It would be nice if you could temporarily stop the screen so that you wouldn't have to take speed-reading lessons to use the computer. Fortunately, DOS will pause for you if you hold down the Control key and press the Num Lock key. On the newer IBM Enhanced-style keyboards, you press the Pause key instead of Ctrl-Num Lock. In either case, this action will immediately pause any screen that is scrolling by. To resume scrolling, press any key (except a Shift, Lock, Ctrl, or Alt key). For example, execute the following commands:

Type   **dir dos**
Press   **Enter**
Press   **Ctrl-Num Lock** (or **Pause**)

Figure 9 shows what can happen. You can pause and resume scrolling as many times as you wish.

Step 3: Press Ctrl-Break to Cancel a Command

Suppose that you've entered DIR DOS or DIR by mistake and you don't want to wait for the whole directory to scroll by on the screen. Or perhaps you've seen enough and you just want to stop it. You can cancel a DOS command by pressing

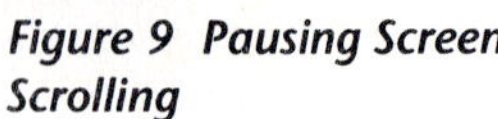

*Figure 9 Pausing Screen
Scrolling*

```
C>dir dos

 Volume in drive C is HARD DISK
 Volume Serial Number is 3324-07CC
 Directory of  C:\DOS

 .              <DIR>       07-09-89    1:23p
 ..             <DIR>       07-09-89    1:23p
 DOSSHELL BAT        196 07-09-89    1:22p
 COMMAND  COM      37557 12-19-88   12:00a
 COUNTRY  SYS      12806 10-06-88   12:00a
 DISKCOPY COM      10396 10-06-88   12:00a
 DISPLAY  SYS      15692 10-06-88   12:00a
 FDISK    EXE      60935 12-19-88   12:00a
 FORMAT   COM      22859 10-06-88   12:00a
 KEYB     COM      14727 10-06-88   12:00a
 KEYBOARD SYS      23328 10-06-88   12:00a
 REPLACE  EXE      19415 10-06-88   12:00a
 SYS      COM      11456 10-06-88_
```

the Control and Break keys at the same time. This stops a command from finishing its job. In many cases, Ctrl-Break will also terminate programs other than just DOS commands. To see how this works, follow these directions:

Type   **dir dos**
Press   **Enter**
Press   **Ctrl-Break**

Pressing Ctrl-Break will terminate the directory command before it finishes. Figure 10 shows how this might appear on your screen. The ^C at the bottom stands for Ctrl-C, which means that the command has been canceled.

On IBM PC- and AT-style keyboards, the Break key is right next to the Num Lock key, and is also labeled Scroll Lock. On the newer IBM Enhanced-style keyboards, the Break key is the same as the Pause key. On all types of keyboards, you can also cancel a command by holding down the Control key and typing a C. Note that Ctrl-Break (or Ctrl-C) is different from the Escape key. Escape will cancel a line typed at the DOS prompt before the Enter key is pressed. Ctrl-Break cancels a command after the Enter key has been pressed and while the command is executing.

Step 4: Press Shift-PrtSc to Print the Screen

Frequently there is a sequence of commands or some information on the screen that you would like to save. If you have a printer connected to your computer, DOS can produce a hard copy of everything that is currently on the display screen. On IBM PC- and AT-style keyboards, you press one of the Shift keys along with the key marked PrtSc (Print Screen). On the newer IBM Enhanced-style keyboards, you simply press the key labeled Print Screen. If you have a printer, make sure it's turned on.

Press   **Shift-PrtSc** (or **Print Screen**)

You should get a copy of what's on your screen right now.

Figure 10 Canceling a Command

Step 5: Press Ctrl-PrtSc to Echo to the Printer

The printout you got from the previous step contains only one screen of text. This output would not help much if you wanted a hard copy of the entire DOS directory, because the whole directory doesn't fit on the screen at once. Pressing Control and PrtSc (or Control and Print Screen on the Enhanced-style keyboards), however, will cause whatever you type and the computer's responses to be displayed both on the screen and sent to the printer. This echoing will continue until you press Ctrl-PrtSc again. So, you could, for example, get a hard copy of your entire computer session.

To get a hard copy of the DOS disk directory, follow these directions:

Press   **Ctrl-PrtSc**
Type   **dir**
Press   **Enter**

You should see the directory information being displayed on the screen a bit slower as it is also being sent to the printer. When it's finished and you see the DOS prompt, execute this command again to turn off printer echoing:

Press   **Ctrl-PrtSc**

Practice

1. Create a hard copy listing of this Practice session if you have a printer.

    Press   **Ctrl-PrtSc (or Ctrl-Print Screen)**

2. Start typing a command, but don't press the Enter key:

    Type   **dir a:**

    Suppose you meant to type just **dir**, but made a mistake. Cancel the command:

    Press   **Escape**

    Now execute the command you meant to enter:

    Type   **dir**
    Press   **Enter**

3. Generate a directory listing of your DOS subdirectory or Startup disk. Pause and restart the screen scrolling at least twice before the command is finished.

4. Again, generate a directory listing of your DOS subdirectory or Startup disk. This time, however, cancel the command before it finishes by using Ctrl-Break or Ctrl-C.

5. Turn off printer echoing.

6. If you have a printer, make sure it is turned on.

Type   **dir**
Press   **Enter**

Create a hard-copy listing of just the current contents of your screen.

Lesson 5: Changing the Default Disk Drive

IBM and IBM-compatible computers without hard disks boot up from the diskette in drive A, which is the default disk drive. Computers that have a hard disk with DOS installed on it boot up from drive C, which is considered the default drive. You will recall that the current default drive is indicated by the DOS prompt, for example, A> or C>. This means that whenever you enter a command that doesn't explicitly specify a particular disk drive, the current default drive is assumed. For example, when you enter DIR by itself, you get the directory of the current default drive. If your computer has more than one disk drive, like most IBM and IBM-compatible computers, you may occasionally want to change your default drive from A or C to another installed drive. This is a common procedure, sometimes called **switching drives.** Let's look at how and why you would change the default disk drive.

Step 1: Enter the Designation of the New Default Drive

If you have a computer with a hard disk and one floppy drive, put a disk with files on it into drive A. Then execute this command to change your default drive from C to A:

Type   **a:**
Press   **Enter**

If you have a computer with two floppy disk drives, put a disk with files on it into drive B. Then execute this command to change your default drive to B:

Type   **b:**
Press   **Enter**

DOS will respond with a prompt indicating the new default drive.

Step 2: Use the New Default Drive

Now when you execute a command, DOS will assume you are referring to the new default drive unless you specify otherwise. For example, try this command:

Type   **dir**
Press   **Enter**

You will get a directory listing of the new default drive, A or B (see Figure 11). Although this might not seem terribly exciting at the moment, being able to

```
A>dir

 Volume in drive A has no label
 Volume Serial Number is 0E1E-1BE0
 Directory of  A:\

COMMAND  COM     37557 12-19-88  12:00a
AUTOEXEC BAT        39 10-06-88  12:00a
CONFIG   SYS        96 10-06-88  12:00a
COUNTRY  SYS     12806 10-06-88  12:00a
DISKCOPY COM     10396 10-06-88  12:00a
DISPLAY  SYS     15692 10-06-88  12:00a
FDISK    EXE     60935 12-19-88  12:00a
FORMAT   COM     22859 10-06-88  12:00a
KEYB     COM     14727 10-06-88  12:00a
KEYBOARD SYS     23328 10-06-88  12:00a
REPLACE  EXE     19415 10-06-88  12:00a
SELECT   COM      3642 10-06-88  12:00a
SELECT   HLP     28695 10-06-88  12:00a
SELECT   PRT      1329 10-06-88  12:00a
SYS      COM     11456 10-06-88  12:00a
        15 File(s)     18432 bytes free

A>_
```

change the default drive enables you to make full use of all of your installed disk drives. As you become more proficient with DOS and application packages, you'll find yourself switching disk drives often. For example, on systems with two floppy drives, you may leave the DOS Startup disk in drive A and a disk containing a particular application package in drive B. Then, after booting up, you could switch to drive B to run your application program.

Step 3: Switch Back to the Original Default Disk Drive

If your computer has a hard disk, execute this command to switch back to it:

Type   **c:**
Press   **Enter**

If your computer has no hard disk, execute this command to make A your default drive:

Type   **a:**
Press   **Enter**

1. If your computer has a hard disk, put a diskette with files on it in drive A. If your computer has no hard disk, put a diskette with files on it in drive B. Change your default disk drive to A or B. Use the DIR command to generate a directory listing. Now switch back to your original drive.

2. Try switching to a disk drive that doesn't exist, such as Z. What happens?

3. Try switching to your current drive. For example, if C is your default drive, do this:

Type   **c:**
Press   **Enter**

What happens?

 ## Lesson 6: Checking Disk and Memory Status

You've already learned how one DOS command, DIR, can be used to list information about the files on a disk or in a subdirectory. Another DOS command, CHKDSK, can be used to display further information about a disk and the memory installed in your computer. CHKDSK is an external command, which means that it is kept in a separate file named CHKDSK.COM in the DOS subdirectory on a hard disk. External commands are available only when they are located on your default disk or in your current subdirectory, or when a path has been set up to the subdirectory that contains them. You will learn about paths in the next chapter. If DOS has been installed correctly on your hard disk, a path should already be set up to the DOS subdirectory so that the DOS external commands are always available. Note: the CHKDSK command does not operate when DOS is running on a local area network.

Step 1: Enter CHKDSK

To check the disk in your default drive, execute this command:

> Type   **chkdsk**
> Press   **Enter**

Your screen should look like Figure 12, although the numbers probably will be different.

Step 2: Examine the Status Report

The CHKDSK status report supplies several useful items of information. First, it tells you that the total capacity of the hard disk is 21,204,992 bytes (a little more than 20 megabytes). This is roughly equivalent to about 6,575 pages of single-spaced typewritten text. **Hidden files** are special files used by DOS and some other programs. They're hidden because they do not appear in the disk directory so that you won't rename, change, or delete them. Next the CHKDSK command tells you how many subdirectories and ordinary user files are on the disk and how much space they occupy. It will also say whether any bytes on the disk are in "bad sectors," although there aren't any on the disk shown in Figure 12. Bad sectors occur when some of the disk is unusable due to manufacturing flaws—a fairly common occurrence with hard disks. The unusable areas are discovered when the disk is formatted and are marked so that DOS won't use them. The disk shown in Figure 12 has 19,701,760 bytes of empty space.

The CHKDSK command also reveals information about **allocation units,** which relate to how DOS assigns disk space to files. This is technical information that most users don't really need to know. Finally, CHKDSK reports that this particular computer has 655,360 bytes (or 640K) of RAM installed, of which 521,248 bytes are free to be used by application programs. The difference between these two figures, 134,112 bytes, is the amount of RAM taken up by the parts of DOS that remain in memory, such as the internal commands, and any memory-resident programs that have been loaded.

Like many DOS commands, CHKDSK can be used on a disk other than the default disk. Put a diskette with files on it into drive A. Then execute this command:

> Type   **chkdsk a:**
> Press   **Enter**

Figure 12 The CHKDSK Report

```
C)chkdsk

Volume HARD DISK   created 01-01-1980 12:20a
Volume Serial Number is 3324-07CC

 21204992 bytes total disk space
    73728 bytes in 3 hidden files
     4096 bytes in 1 directories
  1425408 bytes in 69 user files
 19701760 bytes available on disk

     2048 bytes in each allocation unit
    10354 total allocation units on disk
     9620 available allocation units on disk

   655360 total bytes memory
   521248 bytes free

C)_
```

Lesson 7: Clearing the Screen

By now, you've probably accumulated quite a collection of commands and directory listings on your screen. Although this does no harm, it can be a bit distracting. Or, perhaps you want to type a sequence of commands and then do a print screen, and you would like to start off with a clean slate. It's easy to tell DOS to clear the screen with an internal command called CLS.

Step 1: Enter CLS

To clear the screen, execute the clear screen command:

Type   **cls**
Press   **Enter**

DOS will erase everything from the screen and start you off again with the system prompt on the first line in the upper left corner.

Practice Use the DIR command to generate a directory listing of your default disk drive. Now clear the screen.

Lesson 8: Formatting a Diskette

Every new disk must undergo an initial preparation known as formatting before it can be used to store programs and data files. Many manufacturers and retailers format the hard disks that are installed in the computers they sell. This initialization for diskettes, however, is not commonly done at the factory, so generally you must format each new floppy you're going to use with your own computer. You also can reformat a previously formatted disk to completely erase all the files that are stored on it. But you should be very careful whenever you format a previously used disk. Make sure that it doesn't hold any files that you want to save. Basically, DOS performs the following procedures when you format a disk:

- Checks the disk for bad or damaged spots that cannot reliably store data and marks these as unusable
- Completely erases any programs and data that might be on the disk
- Builds a directory to hold information about the files that eventually will be stored on the disk
- Marks off the empty space on the disk into equal-sized portions called **sectors**
- Creates a DOS startup disk if instructed to do so

The DOS FORMAT command, which is an external command, performs all of these functions. Note: the FORMAT command does not operate when running DOS on a local area network. This is a safety precaution to prevent users from reformatting shared hard disks.

Step 1: Get a Floppy Disk to Format

The most common and simplest use of the FORMAT command is to set up diskettes that will not be used to boot up the computer. Since the operating system is not installed on these diskettes, they can devote all of their space to holding programs and data files. For this lesson you'll need a new floppy disk or a previously used disk that can be completely erased. If you are going to format a diskette that's not new, double-check to make sure it doesn't have any programs or data files on it that you want to keep. Formatting a disk erases everything on it.

Step 2: Enter the FORMAT Command

To format a diskette in the A drive, execute the following command:

    Type   **format a:**
    Press   **Enter**

Step 3: Insert the Disk to Be Formatted

The FORMAT command will then tell you to insert the new diskette into drive A. Insert the disk as indicated, and then press the Enter key.

    Press   **Enter**

Step 4: Enter a Volume Label

The procedure takes about a minute for a 5¼-inch double-sided, double-density diskette, during which time DOS displays a percentage that shows how much it has formatted so far. When it is finished, the FORMAT command will prompt you to enter a volume label, or name, for the newly formatted disk. (Older versions of DOS don't automatically ask you to do this.) You can choose any name you like, but it must be no longer than eleven characters. If you don't want to enter a name, you can just press the Enter key. Name your disk like this:

    Type   **my disk**
    Press   **Enter**

Step 5: Examine the Screen

After you enter a volume label, FORMAT will tell you how much room is on the disk and whether it contains any bad sectors (see Figure 13). If the diskette has no bad sectors and DOS has not been installed on it, these two numbers will be the same: 362,496 bytes for a 5¼-inch double-sided, double-density diskette. The FORMAT command also displays information about the disk's allocation units and reports the volume serial number.

Step 6: Terminate the FORMAT Command

Finally, the FORMAT command asks you if you want to format another diskette. You can answer "no" like this:

Type   **n**
Press   **Enter**

You'll then get the DOS prompt back again, as shown in Figure 13.

Format another blank diskette or reformat the disk you have just formatted. This time, however, press **Enter** without typing a volume label.

Lesson 9: Formatting a System Diskette

The diskette you formatted in Lesson 8 can be used to store programs and data files. It cannot, however, be used to boot up the computer, because it doesn't have DOS installed on it. If you want to format a DOS startup diskette that can be used to boot up your computer from drive A, you must follow a slightly different procedure.

Figure 13 Formatting a Diskette

```
C>format a:
Insert new diskette for drive A:
and press ENTER when ready...

Format complete

Volume label (11 characters, ENTER for none)? my disk

    362496 bytes total disk space
    362496 bytes available on disk

      1024 bytes in each allocation unit
       354 allocation units available on disk

Volume Serial Number is 354B-0BD4

Format another (Y/N)?n
C>_
```

Step 1: Use the /S Parameter

A **parameter** is a specification that designates an alternate action for a command. Many DOS commands can be given one or more parameters to specify a slightly different way of performing their tasks. The FORMAT command, for example, can be instructed to install the operating system on the disk it's preparing. To do this, you add the /S parameter after the specification of the disk to be formatted. The /S tells FORMAT to put the DOS internal commands and the command processor on the disk being formatted. You can try this out by reformatting the disk you formatted in Lesson 8. To prepare a DOS startup disk, execute this command:

> Type **format a:/s**
> Press **Enter**

Step 2: Insert the Disk to Be Formatted

The FORMAT command will then tell you to insert the new diskette into drive A. Insert the disk you formatted in Lesson 8 into drive A and then press the Enter key.

> Press **Enter**

Step 3: Enter a Volume Label

When the formatting procedure is complete, the FORMAT command will report that the system has been transferred to the disk. It will then prompt you to enter a volume label for the disk. Name your disk like this:

> Type **startup**
> Press **Enter**

Step 4: Examine the Screen

After you enter a volume label, FORMAT will tell you how much room is on the disk, whether the disk contains any bad sectors, and how much space is being used by DOS. Figure 14 shows a 5¼-inch double-sided, double-density diskette with MS-DOS 4.01 installed on it. The disk holds 362,496 bytes, DOS takes up 109,568 bytes, and 252,928 bytes of empty space are available. The FORMAT command also displays information about the disk's allocation units and reports the volume serial number.

Step 5: Terminate the FORMAT Command

Finally, the FORMAT command asks you if you want to format another diskette. You can answer "no" like this:

> Type **n**
> Press **Enter**

You'll then get the DOS prompt back again.

Step 6: Examine the Disk's Directory

Now, let's look at the directory of the disk you just formatted. Execute this command:

Figure 14 Formatting a System Diskette

```
C>format a:/s
Insert new diskette for drive A:
and press ENTER when ready...

Format complete
System transferred

Volume label (11 characters, ENTER for none)? startup

    362496 bytes total disk space
    109568 bytes used by system
    252928 bytes available on disk

      1024 bytes in each allocation unit
       247 allocation units available on disk

Volume Serial Number is 0308-07D1

Format another (Y/N)?n
C>_
```

Type **dir a:**
Press **Enter**

Your screen should look like Figure 15. Notice that only the file COM-MAND.COM is on the new system disk. It does not contain any of the external command files that are on the DOS disk. So, although you could boot up with this new disk and you could execute internal commands such as DIR, you could not use any external commands such as CHKDSK or FORMAT unless you copied their command files onto it.

Hard Disks The FORMAT command also works for hard disks. Once a hard disk is initially formatted, however, it may seldom, if ever, be formatted again. Since computers with hard disks often have many important and sometimes irreplaceable files on them, you should be extremely cautious with them. Don't

Figure 15 Directory of the New System Diskette

```
C>dir a:

Volume in drive A is STARTUP
Volume Serial Number is 0308-07D1
Directory of  A:\

COMMAND  COM     37557 12-19-88  12:00a
        1 File(s)    252928 bytes free

C>_
```

attempt to format a hard disk unless you know exactly what you're doing and you're sure that all files on the hard disk have backup copies on other disks. As we said, many computers now come with their hard disks already formatted by the manufacturer or retailer.

Practice

1. Try booting up from your new system diskette. Make sure the newly formatted diskette is in drive A. If the drive has a door or lever, make sure it is closed.

   Press   **Ctrl-Alt-Del**

   Skip entering the date and time:

   Press   **Enter**
   Press   **Enter**

2. Use DIR to list a directory of your default disk, which should be the new system diskette in drive A. As you can see, internal commands like DIR always work after you boot up because they are kept in a hidden DOS file and auto-matically loaded into memory, where they remain.

3. Use CHKDSK to try to get a status report of your default disk. DOS will say "Bad command or file name." CHKDSK does not work on your new system disk because it is an external command, stored in its own file named CHKDSK.COM, and it has not been copied to the new disk. Similarly, FOR-MAT will not work from your new system disk either unless its file is copied to the disk first.

4. Remove the new system diskette from drive A. If your computer does not have a hard disk, put the original DOS Startup diskette back into drive A. Reboot your computer:

   Press   **Ctrl-Alt-Del**

   Enter the correct date and time if necessary.

Lesson 10: Copying Files

One of the reasons computers are so useful is that they make it simple to copy programs and data. Once information is entered into a computer, any number of copies usually can be made very easily and quickly. An important function of any operating system is duplicating files. DOS provides several methods of copy-ing files. One of the most popular DOS commands is COPY, which reproduces one or more individual files.

Step 1: Copy a Single File (the Long Way)

Once a diskette has been formatted, it can be used to store program and data files. Let's use the COPY command to copy a single file from the DOS subdirec-tory onto your newly formatted diskette. First, we'll do it the longhand way, and then we'll show you a shortcut. To copy the file FORMAT.COM from the DOS subdirectory onto your formatted diskette, make sure the diskette is in drive A. Then execute this command:

```
Type   copy c:\dos\format.com a:format.com
Press  Enter
```

The first file specification after the COPY command is the **source,** or what you're copying from—the file FORMAT.COM on the hard disk C in the DOS subdirectory. The second file specification is the **target,** or what you're copying to—a file named FORMAT.COM on the diskette in drive A. The source and the target can have the same name because they are on separate disks. After you execute the COPY command, DOS will tell you that one file was copied. Now execute this command to see the contents of the diskette:

>Type **dir a:**
>Press **Enter**

You should see the file FORMAT.COM in the directory of the diskette in drive A, as shown in Figure 16.

Step 2: Copy a Single File (the Short Way)

In most cases, if you omit certain information from a command, DOS will make an assumption about what you mean. For example, if you don't supply a disk drive or subdirectory designation in front of a file name, DOS will assume that you mean the default drive and current directory. Similarly, if you don't specify a name for the target file, the COPY command will assume that it is to use the same name as the source. This assumption will work as long as the source and the target files are on different disks or in different subdirectories. Now try this shorter command to copy FORMAT.COM to the diskette:

>Type **copy dos\format.com a:**
>Press **Enter**

This command tells DOS to copy the file FORMAT.COM on the default disk in the DOS subdirectory to the diskette in drive A and give it the same name.

Note that you have just copied the FORMAT.COM in the DOS subdirectory to the FORMAT.COM that already existed on the diskette in drive A from the copy operation performed in Step 1. If you choose a name that already exists on the target, DOS will simply copy over it, destroying whatever was in that file

Figure 16 Copying a File

```
C>copy c:\dos\format.com a:format.com
        1 File(s) copied

C>dir a:

 Volume in drive A is STARTUP
 Volume Serial Number is 0308-07D1
 Directory of  A:\

COMMAND  COM     37557 12-19-88  12:00a
FORMAT   COM     22859 10-06-88  12:00a
        2 File(s)     229376 bytes free

C>_
```

before. Since you copied the same file, there's no problem here. As a rule, however, you should be very careful about the name you choose for a target file. If it already exists on the disk you're copying to, the original version will be overwritten. Make sure you no longer need any file on the target disk or subdirectory with the same name as a copy to be created.

Step 3: Copy a Group of Files

By using the global file name characters * and ? introduced in Lesson 3, you can copy several files at once with a single COPY command. For example, execute this command:

Type   **copy dos*.com a:**
Press **Enter**

This command will try to copy every file in the DOS subdirectory with an extension of COM to the diskette in drive A. If you have only a 360K diskette in drive A, it will probably run out of room, as shown in Figure 17. Nevertheless, DOS will copy as many files as it can to the diskette.

Step 4: Copy a File to the Same Directory

You cannot have two files in the same directory with identical names. The COPY command simply will not allow you to duplicate a file in the same directory unless you provide a different name for the target file. So, the COPY command can reproduce a file on the same disk or in the same subdirectory, but the source and the target must have different names.

A common reason for duplicating a file in the same directory is for backup purposes. Let's say that you're going to change an existing file. If that file is especially important, you might want to keep a copy of the original version before you make any alterations. Then if some problem occurs, you will still have the original version intact. So, before you change a file, it might be a good idea to make a copy of it, but with a slightly different name. For example, suppose you

Figure 17 Copying a Group of Files

```
C>copy dos\*.com a:
DOS\COMMAND.COM
DOS\DISKCOPY.COM
DOS\FORMAT.COM
DOS\KEYB.COM
DOS\SYS.COM
DOS\ASSIGN.COM
DOS\CHKDSK.COM
DOS\COMP.COM
DOS\DEBUG.COM
DOS\DISKCOMP.COM
DOS\EDLIN.COM
DOS\LABEL.COM
DOS\MORE.COM
DOS\TREE.COM
DOS\PRINT.COM
DOS\GRAFTABL.COM
DOS\GRAPHICS.COM
DOS\MODE.COM
DOS\RECOVER.COM
DOS\BACKUP.COM
Insufficient disk space
        19 File(s) copied

C>_
```

wanted to somehow change the file AUTOEXEC.BAT, but wanted to keep a copy of the original. You could make a backup copy of the original version on the same disk if you change its name slightly. For example, execute these commands:

Type   **copy autoexec.bat autoexec.bak**
Press   **Enter**
Type   **dir**
Press   **Enter**

The COPY command creates a copy of the AUTOEXEC.BAT file on the default disk and names it AUTOEXEC.BAK (the BAK is for backup), as shown in Figure 18. Now you could go ahead and safely make modifications to AUTOEXEC.BAT, because you've retained a copy of the original file in AUTOEXEC.BAK.

Practice

1. You can use the COPY command to duplicate every non-hidden file on a disk or in a subdirectory. For example, execute this command:

   Type   **copy dos*.* a:**
   Press   **Enter**

   You will probably quickly run out of room on the diskette in drive A, but this command would work if the target disk were large enough.

2. To see how the COPY command will not allow you to duplicate a file with the same name in the same directory, try this command:

   Type   **copy autoexec.bak**
   Press   **Enter**

   Because you omitted the target file name, DOS assumed you meant the same name as the source. Since two files in the same directory cannot have the same name, DOS aborts the command and displays the error message, "File cannot be copied onto itself."

Figure 18 Copying a File to the Same Directory

```
C>copy autoexec.bat autoexec.bak
        1 File(s) copied

C>dir

 Volume in drive C is HARD DISK
 Volume Serial Number is 3324-07CC
 Directory of  C:\

CONFIG   SYS       146 07-09-89   1:22p
AUTOEXEC BAK       256 01-01-80   5:52a
COMMAND  COM     37557 12-19-88  12:00a
DOS      <DIR>        07-09-89   1:23p
AUTOEXEC BAT       256 01-01-80   5:52a
        5 File(s)   19699712 bytes free

C>_
```

3. You should be careful with the COPY command. It is up to you to make sure you are copying the file you want and that the target name is correct. For example, execute this command (be sure you type *.bak* and not *.bat*):

Type   `copy command.com autoexec.bak`
Press   **Enter**

DOS will copy the file COMMAND.COM to the file AUTOEXEC.BAK, over-writing the previous contents of AUTOEXEC.BAK. It does not ask you if this is really what you want to do.

Lesson 11: Copying an Entire Diskette

DOS has a more specific copy command that lets you duplicate an entire diskette all at once. The DISKCOPY command formats the target diskette, if necessary, and copies all files, hidden or otherwise, exactly as they are on the original source diskette. DISKCOPY may be used to duplicate only floppy disks, not hard disks. Furthermore, DISKCOPY works only if the source and target are the same type of diskette. For instance, you cannot use the DISKCOPY command to duplicate the contents of a 5¼-inch diskette on a 3½-inch diskette. Fortunately, you can use DISKCOPY even if you have only one floppy drive. To see how the DISK-COPY command works, you can make an exact copy of the formatted system diskette you've been working with. You will need another diskette of the same type, either new and unformatted, or containing files you are sure you no longer need. Note: the DISKCOPY command does not operate when running DOS on a local area network.

Step 1: Execute the DISKCOPY Command

If your computer has two identical floppy disk drives, execute this command:

Type   `diskcopy a: b:`
Press   **Enter**

If your computer has only one floppy drive or two drives that are of different types, such as a 5¼-inch drive and a 3½-inch drive, execute this command instead:

Type   `diskcopy a: a:`
Press   **Enter**

Step 2: Follow the Directions

The DISKCOPY command will tell you which drive to put your source and target diskettes into and when to do so. Remember: the diskette you want to copy is the source, and the new diskette is the target. If your computer has only one floppy drive, you may have to swap the source and target diskettes in drive A several times, depending on how much memory is installed.

Step 3: Terminate the DISKCOPY Command

When it is finished, DISKCOPY will ask you if you want to copy another diskette. If the answer is no, do this:

Type   `n`
Press   **Enter**

If you have only one floppy drive, Figure 19 shows what you should see on your screen when DISKCOPY is finished.

DISKCOPY is a very useful command for making backup copies of important diskettes. In fact, the documentation that comes with many software packages suggests that you use the DISKCOPY command to duplicate all of your original diskettes as soon as you get them. Furthermore, you should put the originals away for safekeeping and only use your copies. Then, if you accidentally erase something or if a diskette you use daily becomes damaged or wears out, you will still have your original diskettes from which to make additional copies. These are good suggestions, and DISKCOPY will work fine as long as your software is not copy-protected.

Practice   Use DISKCOPY to duplicate some other diskette that you have.

Lesson 12: Changing File Names

When you create a file, either using a DOS command such as COPY or from within an application package such as a word processor, you assign it a name. This name need not be permanent, however. DOS lets you change file names very easily. There are several reasons why you might want to change an existing file name. Perhaps you've thought of a more appropriate name or maybe you would like to shorten the name. You may want to copy a file onto a disk that already contains another file with the same name. In this case, you could change the name of the file already on the disk so that its contents will not be overwritten by the file you want to copy. The RENAME command, which is an internal command, lets you change the name of one or more files.

Step 1: Rename a Single File

Changing a single file's name is quite easy. Just type RENAME (or its abbreviation, REN), followed by the file name you want to change and then the new

*Figure 19 Copying an
Entire Diskette*

```
C>diskcopy a: a:

Insert SOURCE diskette in drive A:

Press any key to continue . . .

Copying 40 tracks
9 Sectors/Track, 2 Side(s)

Insert TARGET diskette in drive A:

Press any key to continue . . .

Volume Serial Number is 08E3-3224

Copy another diskette (Y/N)? n

C>
C>_
```

name that file is to have. For example, suppose you want to copy a new version of the file FORMAT.COM to the system diskette you created in Lesson 9, but you want to keep a copy of the original FORMAT.COM. You could rename the original FORMAT.BAK and then copy the new FORMAT.COM to your disk. Make sure your formatted system diskette is in drive A. Then execute these commands:

Type   **a:**
Press   **Enter**
Type   **rename format.com format.bak**
Press   **Enter**
Type   **dir format.***
Press   **Enter**

Your screen should look like Figure 20. The directory shows that you've successfully changed the name of FORMAT.COM to FORMAT.BAK.

Before you go on, change FORMAT.BAK back to FORMAT.COM to restore your disk to the way it was. This time, however, try using the abbreviated form of the RENAME command:

Type   **ren format.bak format.com**
Press   **Enter**

Step 2: Rename Several Files at Once

Using the global file name characters * and ?, you can rename several files at once. For example, with a single command you can rename each file on your system diskette with an extension of COM and give it an extension of BAK. Make sure the system diskette you formatted in Lesson 9 is in drive A and that drive A is your default drive. Then execute this command:

Type   **ren *.com *.bak**
Press   **Enter**

Figure 20 Renaming a File

```
C>a:

A>rename format.com format.bak

A>dir format.*

 Volume in drive A is STARTUP
 Volume Serial Number is 0308-07D1
 Directory of  A:\

FORMAT    BAK     22859 10-06-88  12:00a
        1 File(s)       2048 bytes free

A>_
```

Now execute this directory command to see what you've done:

Type   `dir *.bak`
Press   **Enter**

Your screen should look something like Figure 21. There are now no files on your disk with COM extensions. They all have BAK extensions instead. Before you go on, change them all back to the way they were with this command:

Type   `ren *.bak *.com`
Press   **Enter**

Practice   Change the name of the file AUTOEXEC.BAK, which you created in Lesson 10, to JUNK. Remember, this file is on your hard disk or DOS Startup disk.

Lesson 13: Erasing Files

Just as you accumulate old memos, notes, letters, clippings, and other scraps of paper on your desk, disks also can become cluttered with files that are no longer needed. Occasionally, you may have to clean up a disk and discard unnecessary files. Once you erase a file, however, it may be difficult or even impossible to retrieve its contents. In fact, DOS includes no utility for "unerasing" files, although such programs are sold by some independent software publishers. Before you erase any file, make sure you no longer need it. DOS makes it very easy to erase files, so you should be careful. Many instances of people losing files can be attributed to accidents or carelessness with the DOS ERASE command, also known as DEL. ERASE (or DEL) is an internal command.

Step 1: Erase a Single File

To erase a single file, just type ERASE or DEL (for delete) and follow it with the name of the file you want to erase. Make sure that the system diskette you

Figure 21 Renaming a Group of Files

```
    Volume Serial Number is 0308-07D1
    Directory of  A:\

    COMMAND  BAK     37557 12-19-88   12:00a
    FORMAT   BAK     22859 10-06-88   12:00a
    DISKCOPY BAK     10396 10-06-88   12:00a
    KEYB     BAK     14727 10-06-88   12:00a
    SYS      BAK     11456 10-06-88   12:00a
    ASSIGN   BAK      5753 10-06-88   12:00a
    CHKDSK   BAK     17787 10-06-88   12:00a
    COMP     BAK      9459 10-06-88   12:00a
    DEBUG    BAK     21574 10-06-88   12:00a
    DISKCOMP BAK      9857 10-06-88   12:00a
    EDLIN    BAK     14069 10-06-88   12:00a
    LABEL    BAK      4458 10-06-88   12:00a
    MORE     BAK      2134 10-06-88   12:00a
    TREE     BAK      6302 10-06-88   12:00a
    PRINT    BAK     14131 10-06-88   12:00a
    GRAFTABL BAK     10239 10-06-88   12:00a
    GRAPHICS BAK     16693 10-06-88   12:00a
    MODE     BAK     22960 10-06-88   12:00a
    RECOVER  BAK     10588 10-06-88   12:00a
            19 File(s)      2048 bytes free

    A>_
```

formatted in Lesson 9 is in drive A and that drive A is your default drive. Because you know this diskette holds only copies of DOS files that you have on the hard disk or on the original DOS Startup disk, you can safely erase files from it. Nevertheless, you should always be careful when erasing files. Data and programs are more frequently lost as the result of an accidentally or carelessly entered ERASE command than from any other cause. Suppose you want to erase the file FORMAT.COM from the diskette. Execute this command:

> Type   **`erase format.com`**
> Press   **Enter**

Now execute this directory command to see what you've done:

> Type   **`dir format.com`**
> Press   **Enter**

The file is now gone, so your screen should look like Figure 22.

Step 2: Erasing Several Files All at Once

By using the global file name characters * and ?, you can tell DOS to erase several files with a single ERASE command. In fact, you can even wipe out every file on a disk. Although this is often done to clear off a disk, it should be used with care. Make sure that the system diskette you formatted in Lesson 9 is in drive A and that drive A is your default drive. Then execute this command:

> Type   **`erase *.*`**
> Press   **Enter**

Because this is a potentially disastrous command if entered by mistake, DOS will ask if you are sure you want to do this. If you answer yes, DOS will go ahead and erase everything. If you answer no, DOS will immediately cancel the ERASE command. You will get this chance to back out, however, only if you use the *.* designation. If you enter ERASE *.EXE, for example, DOS will not ask if you are sure and will immediately delete all files with an extension of EXE. So again, *be*

Figure 22 Erasing a File

```
A>erase format.com

A>dir format.com

 Volume in drive A is STARTUP
 Volume Serial Number is 0308-07D1
 Directory of  A:\

File not found

A>_
```

careful with the ERASE command! Answer yes and then list a directory to see what you have done:

> Type **y**
> Press **Enter**
> Type **dir**
> Press **Enter**

Your screen should look like Figure 23.

Switch back to the hard disk or the DOS Startup disk you used to boot up the computer. Remember the AUTOEXEC.BAK file you created in Lesson 10 and that you renamed JUNK in the Practice section of Lesson 12? Erase it, but this time use DEL instead of ERASE. DEL and ERASE are two names for the same DOS command.

Lesson 14: Protecting Diskettes

In certain situations, commands such as FORMAT, COPY, DISKCOPY, RENAME, and ERASE won't work. Most diskettes have a feature that prevents them from being altered. This feature, called **write-protection,** is similar to the tabs on audio and video cassette tapes that you can remove to prevent accidentally recording over material you want to save.

Step 1: Write-Protect a 5¼-inch Diskette

Most 5¼-inch diskettes have a small rectangle cut out of one side, called the **write-protect notch** (see Figure 24(a)). This notch can be covered with a gummed tab or tape to write-protect the diskette. Files on a diskette protected in this manner can be read but not written or altered as long as the notch remains covered. Diskettes that are write-protected cannot be formatted, have files renamed

Figure 23 Erasing All the Files

```
A>erase *.*
All files in directory will be deleted!
Are you sure (Y/N)?y

A>dir

 Volume in drive A is STARTUP
 Volume Serial Number is 0308-07D1
 Directory of  A:\

 File not found

A>_
```

Figure 24 Write-Protecting Diskettes

(a)

5 ¹/₄ - inch diskette

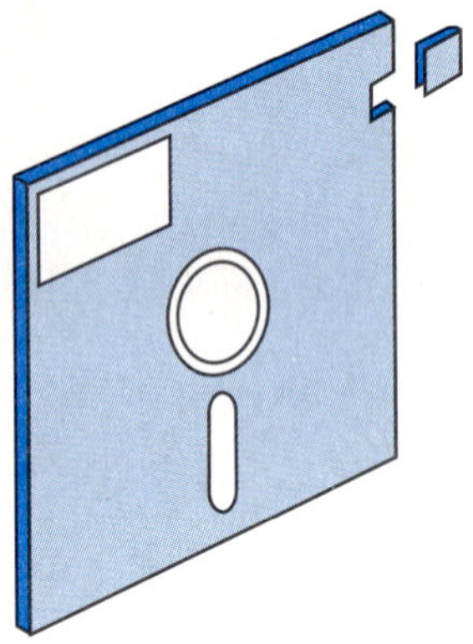

(b)

3 ¹/₂ - inch diskette

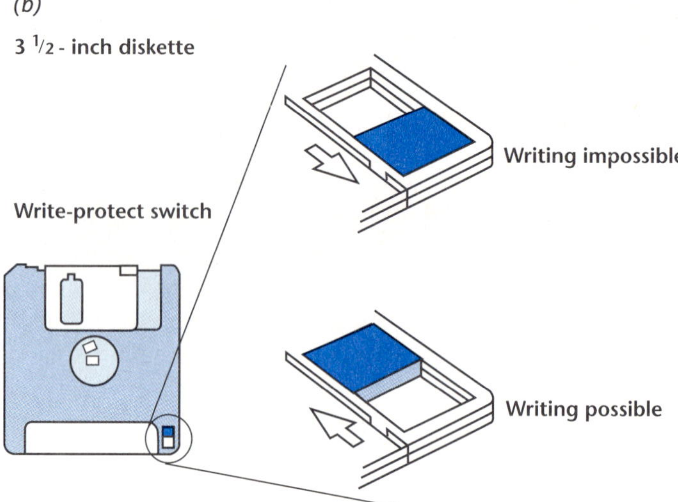

on them, have files copied onto them, or have files erased from them. If you attempt to do so, DOS simply issues a write-protect error message. Some 5¼-inch diskettes don't have a write-protect notch. These diskettes are permanently write-protected.

If you have a gummed tab or piece of tape, try write-protecting a 5¼-inch diskette. Then try copying a file to the diskette, or renaming or erasing a file already on the diskette.

Step 2: Write-Protect a 3½-inch Diskette

The smaller, 3½-inch diskettes also can be write-protected, but the mechanism is slightly different. These diskettes have a **write-protect switch** on the reverse side in the lower right corner (see Figure 24(b)). This switch is a tab that can be slid to open or close a little hole in the disk's plastic case. When the hole is open, the diskette is write-protected. When it is closed, files can be written and altered on the diskette.

If your computer uses 3½-inch diskettes, try write-protecting one. Then try copying a file to the diskette, or renaming or erasing a file already on the diskette.

Copy-Protection   With write-protection, you can safeguard programs and data that are stored on diskettes from accidental erasure. Some software developers use **copy-protection** to discourage you from duplicating their packages and illegally selling or giving away copies. Copy-protected diskettes are prepared in a manner that makes it difficult or impossible to copy them with ordinary DOS commands such as COPY and DISKCOPY. Since it is so easy to duplicate diskettes, some manufacturers feel that they must copy-protect their software to prevent widespread distribution to people who don't rightfully pay for it. Unfortunately, copy-protected software is often inconvenient for rightful owners to use or back up. Although manufacturers of most major application packages have since dropped copy-protection from their products, many game programs are still copy-protected.

If you try to use COPY or DISKCOPY on a diskette that is copy-protected, any one of several results might occur. The attempt could simply fail and cause an error message to be displayed. In other cases, the copy procedure might seem to successfully complete, but when you try to run the software it just won't work. Trying to duplicate copy-protected diskettes can be an effort in futility; to spare the user unnecessary frustration, manufacturers should clearly state whether their packages are copy-protected. The safest course is to follow the instructions for using and making backup copies of original diskettes.

Practice   Write-protect a new diskette or one containing files you don't need. Then try to format it.

Lesson 15: Displaying and Printing Text Files

So far, you've learned quite a bit about manipulating files with DOS. You haven't, however, looked inside one. The DOS TYPE command, which is an internal command, lets you display the contents of a file on the screen. The DOS PRINT command, which is an external command, lets you send the contents of a file to the printer. Although TYPE and PRINT will work with almost any file, unless it's a text file all you'll see is gibberish. A **text file** contains only ordinary letters, numbers, and punctuation marks. It is usually produced by a text editor or word processing program. AUTOEXEC.BAT and CONFIG.SYS, which we will explain further in the next chapter, are text files that tell DOS how to set up your computer when you boot up. Although these files are not absolutely necessary for booting up, they are created on most hard disks and DOS Startup diskettes when DOS is installed. If you don't have AUTOEXEC.BAT or CONFIG.SYS on your hard disk or DOS Startup disk, just read through this lesson.

Step 1: Execute the TYPE Command

Make sure the disk you booted up from is your default disk. Use the DIR command to see if AUTOEXEC.BAT and CONFIG.SYS are present on the disk. To examine the contents of the AUTOEXEC.BAT and CONFIG.SYS text files on your screen, execute these commands:

```
Type    type autoexec.bat
Press   Enter
Type    type config.sys
Press   Enter
```

DOS will display the contents of the files, as shown in Figure 25, although your screen will probably look somewhat different. The exact contents of the AUTO-EXEC.BAT and CONFIG.SYS files may vary quite a bit, depending on how DOS was installed and what options are being used. In the next two chapters, you will learn what all of the statements in these two files mean.

Step 2: Prepare the Printer

Many text files eventually wind up on paper, especially if they are produced by a word processing or text editing program. The DOS PRINT command lets you send a text file directly to the printer instead of displaying it on the screen.

Figure 25 Displaying Text Files

```
C>type autoexec.bat
@ECHO OFF
SET COMSPEC=C:\DOS\COMMAND.COM
VERIFY OFF
PATH C:\DOS
APPEND /E
APPEND C:\DOS
C:\DOS\GRAPHICS
VER
PRINT /D:LPT1

C>type config.sys
BREAK=ON
BUFFERS=20
FILES=20
LASTDRIVE=E
SHELL=C:\DOS\COMMAND.COM /P /E:256
DEVICE=C:\DOS\ANSI.SYS
INSTALL=C:\DOS\FASTOPEN.EXE C:=(50,25)

C>_
```

Before you can print a file, your printer must be turned on. Make sure that the power is on and that the printer is on-line, that is, connected to your computer.

Step 3: Execute the PRINT Command

To use the PRINT command, type PRINT followed by the name of the file you want to print. Print the AUTOEXEC.BAT file by executing this command:

Type   **print autoexec.bat**
Press   **Enter**

DOS may ask you to supply the following (if it doesn't, don't worry):

    Name of list device [PRN]:

This rather cryptic request allows you to tell DOS which printer to use if you have more than one connected to your computer. The expression [PRN] means that unless you tell it otherwise, DOS will send the output to the default printer, which has the device name PRN. If you have only one printer, then it is the default printer. All you have to do is press the Enter key.

Press   **Enter**

DOS will ask you to supply the list device only the first time you use PRINT for any given computer session. After you do so, DOS will tell you the file is currently being printed.

To print the CONFIG.SYS file, execute this command:

Type   **print config.sys**
Press   **Enter**

DOS will tell you the file is currently being printed and will present the DOS prompt again (see Figure 26). From the printer you will get copies of the AUTO-EXEC.BAT and CONFIG.SYS files, each on their own page.

Figure 26 Printing Text Files

```
C>print autoexec.bat

  C:\AUTOEXEC.BAT is currently being printed
C>print config.sys

  C:\CONFIG.SYS is currently being printed
C>_
```

Practice

1. You can use TYPE to display nontext files, although what you see on the screen won't make much sense. For example, execute this command and see what happens:

   Type   **type command.com**
   Press   **Enter**

2. Get a directory listing of your DOS subdirectory or Startup disk and examine it for any files with the extension BAT or TXT. If you are running MS-DOS 4.01, for example, the files DOSSHELL.BAT and README.TXT may be in your DOS subdirectory. Examine the contents of these files, or any others from the DOS subdirectory or Startup disk, with the TYPE command. You can preface the file name with the disk drive or subdirectory specification. For example, execute this command to view the README.TXT file from the DOS subdirectory:

   Type   **type dos\readme.txt**
   Press   **Enter**

3. Use the PRINT command to get a hard copy of the files you just examined.

Lesson 16: Running a Program

This lesson won't really teach you anything new, because you've been running programs throughout this chapter. Every time you used an external DOS command, you were running a program. Remember: files with an EXE or COM extension are stand-alone, executable programs that you can run.

Step 1: Switch to the Appropriate Disk

First, you must make sure a program you want to run is stored on a disk in one of your drives when you want to run the program. For example, to run an application program such as WordPerfect, Lotus 1-2-3, or dBASE IV, you must

Real World

Microsoft Branches Out

Microsoft Corp., one of the patriarchs of the software industry, believes there's strength in numbers.

The Redmond, Washington-based company could have sat back and watched profits roll in from its highly successful MS-DOS operating system software, but founder Bill Gates decided the company needed more than one star product.

After developing PC-DOS and OS/2 in conjunction with IBM, Microsoft moved into the UNIX field by buying a stake in The Santa Cruz Operation, Inc. and working to bring graphical applications to the UNIX environment.

Microsoft has been heavily involved in applications software for the Macintosh, as well. Gates saw something in the Macintosh long before other software developers did. The result was that Microsoft became the number one software company for Macintosh products. It has three Macintosh best sellers: Excel, a spreadsheet package; Word, a word processor; and Works, an integrated software package.

Microsoft is also pushing its Windows operating environment, which has been described as a "halfway house for DOS users not ready to move to OS/2." Windows uses the experience that Microsoft's programmers gained from working with the Macintosh.

But the road has not been completely smooth for Microsoft. Apple sued Microsoft in 1988 over similarities between Windows and the Macintosh operating system. The court case could drag on for years.

Delayed shipping is another bump in Gate's road. Both Microsoft Word 4.0 for the Macintosh and Microsoft Word 5.0 for DOS were not shipped when promised. The glitches haven't hurt Microsoft's profits, however. In 1988, they jumped almost 63 percent, to $151 million. Diversity apparently pays well.

Source: "New Conquests for the MS-DOS Master," *Datamation,* June 15, 1989, p. 131.

have it installed in a subdirectory on your hard disk or have it on a diskette in a floppy drive. If your computer is connected to a local area network, you could run the program if it's stored on your network's file server disk. DOS must be able to find a program before it can run it. You may have to change your default drive to the one containing the program to be run. An alternative is to preface the program name with the disk drive letter.

Step 2: Switch to the Appropriate Subdirectory

Some programs stored in a subdirectory may need to be run from inside that subdirectory. You will learn how to switch subdirectories in the next chapter. An alternative to switching subdirectories is to preface the program name you enter with the drive and subdirectory in which the program's file is stored.

Step 3: Type the Program Name and Press the Enter Key

As you now know, you invoke an external DOS command by entering its name along with any necessary file names and other information. In this sense, application programs such as WordPerfect, Lotus 1-2-3, and dBASE IV are the same as DOS external commands; all you have to do to run them is type the name of the EXE or COM file in which they're stored and press the Enter key. So, for example, to run WordPerfect from your default drive, you would execute this command (don't do it now):

Type   **wp**
Press   **Enter**

When you do this, DOS will load the WordPerfect program into primary memory and begin executing it.

Practice   Running an application package is just like running a DOS external command such as CHKDSK. You can run a program from a disk other than the one in your default drive. For example, copy the CHKDSK.COM file from your DOS sub-directory to a formatted diskette in drive A. With the hard disk as your default drive, execute this command:

Type   **a: chkdsk**
Press   **Enter**

Summary

- *Starting up DOS with the computer turned off.* Insert the DOS Startup diskette in drive A if the computer has no hard disk and then turn the computer on.

- *Starting up DOS with the computer turned on.* Press Ctrl-Alt-Del.

- *Obtaining a directory of the files on a disk.* Use the DIR command.

- *Using the special DOS keys.* Press Escape to cancel a line. Press Ctrl-Num Lock or Pause to interrupt screen scrolling. Press Ctrl-Break to cancel a command. Press Shift-PrtSc to print the screen. Press Ctrl-PrtSc to echo to the printer.

- *Changing the default disk drive.* Enter the new drive letter followed by a colon.

- *Obtaining a disk and memory status report.* Use the CHKDSK command.

- *Clearing the display screen.* Use the CLS command.

- *Formatting a diskette.* Use the FORMAT command.

- *Formatting a system diskette.* Use the FORMAT command with the /S parameter.

- *Copying files.* Use the COPY command.

- *Copying an entire diskette.* Use the DISKCOPY command.

- *Changing file names.* Use the RENAME (REN) command.

- *Erasing files.* Use the ERASE (DEL) command.

- *Protecting a diskette from accidental erasure.* Cover the notch with a gummed tab or piece of tape on a 5¼-inch disk. Slide open the write-protect switch on a 3½-inch diskette.

- *Displaying and printing text files.* Use the TYPE command to display text files on the screen and the PRINT command to send them to the printer.

- *Running an application package.* Switch to the proper disk drive and subdirectory, if necessary, and then enter the name of the program.

Key Terms

As an extra review of this chapter, try defining the following terms.

allocation unit
booting up
copy-protection
default drive
Disk Operating System (DOS)
DOS prompt
extension
external command (transient
  routine)
filename
global file name character
hidden file
internal command (resident
  routine)

parameter
sector
source
subdirectory
switching drives
target
text file
upwardly compatible
write-protect notch
write-protect switch
write-protection

Multiple Choice

Choose the best selection to complete each statement.

1. An operating system is a(n)
   - (a) hardware component of a mainframe computer system.
   - (b) application program that produces text files.
   - (c) set of programs that lets you use your computer's hardware and software resources.
   - (d) system of procedures for operating a computer.

2. Transient routines or external commands are
   - (a) kept in primary memory until the computer is shut off.
   - (b) kept on disk and loaded into memory only when needed.
   - (c) kept in ROM (read-only memory) chips.
   - (d) used once then deleted.

3. The driving force behind each new DOS release has usually been
   - (a) the addition of a new disk drive capability.
   - (b) an effort to improve the user interface.
   - (c) an attempt to eliminate all bugs.
   - (d) an effort by IBM and Microsoft to make more money.

4. Upwardly compatible means that
   - (a) you cannot take advantage of the new version's abilities.
   - (b) all old software versions must be upgraded.
   - (c) new hardware must be purchased to use the new version.
   - (d) operations that worked with former versions work with the new version.

5. A command is a(n)
   - (a) combination of hardware switch settings.
   - (b) operating system directive issued to a user.
   - (c) application package instruction.
   - (d) word or abbreviation that tells DOS to run a program.

6. To boot DOS with the power off

    (a) insert the DOS Startup disk (if necessary) and turn on the power.

    (b) hold down the Control, Alternate, and Delete keys at the same time.

    (c) turn the power on and issue the boot command.

    (d) turn the power on and kick the computer.

7. Pressing Ctrl-Alt-Del will

    (a) invoke a DOS transient routine.

    (b) delete a file.

    (c) reboot DOS without having to shut off the computer.

    (d) execute an application program.

8. The DOS directory command is

    (a) DIRECT.

    (b) LIST.

    (c) DIR.

    (d) CATALOG.

9. The two parts of a DOS file name are

    (a) a disk drive designation and a disk sector number.

    (b) a primary filename and an optional extension.

    (c) a primary filename and a creation date.

    (d) a primary extension and the size in bytes.

10. Files with COM and EXE extensions usually designate

    (a) external commands and executable program files.

    (b) command files and extension files.

    (c) configuration files and batch files.

    (d) BASIC and FORTRAN files.

11. Pressing Ctrl-Num Lock or Pause will

    (a) echo input and output to the printer.

    (b) print the screen.

    (c) cancel a command.

    (d) temporarily halt screen scrolling.

12. To change the default disk drive

    (a) put a new disk in drive A.

    (b) type the new disk drive designation and press Enter.

    (c) open up the computer and replace the faulty drive.

    (d) issue the DIR command.

13. To display a disk and memory status report, use

    (a) STATUS.

    (b) DIR.

    (c) CHKDSK.

    (d) DISKCOPY.

14. Formatting a diskette does not do the following:

    (a) check the diskette for bad sectors.

    (b) wipe out all data on the diskette.

    (c) mark off the space into sectors.

    (d) sort files in the directory.

15. To format a system diskette you must

    (a) reboot the system.

    (b) use the /S parameter with the FORMAT command.

    (c) enter the COPY command.

    (d) purchase a master diskette from IBM.

16. Which command would you use to copy every file from disk drive A to B?

    (a) COPY A:*.* B: (b) DIR A: B:

    (c) COPY A: B: (d) REN

17. To make an exact copy of an entire diskette, use

    (a) COPY. (b) DISKCOPY.

    (c) DIR. (d) Ctrl-Alt-Del.

18. Entering the command DEL *.* will

    (a) reboot the system. (b) copy all files to the disk in the default drive.

    (c) rename all files on the disk in the default drive. (d) erase all files from the disk in the default drive.

19. To display a text file on your screen, use the

    (a) PRINT command. (b) DISKCOPY command.

    (c) TYPE command. (d) Ctrl-Num Lock key.

20. To run a program you must

    (a) type its filename and press the Enter key. (b) reboot DOS.

    (c) press Ctrl-Break. (d) first make a backup copy.

Fill-In

1. A disk operating system has many utilities for dealing with the _______ that are stored on disks.

2. _______ is usually used with IBM computers while _______ is usually used with compatible computers such as those made by Compaq, Tandy, and Zenith.

3. Booting DOS refers to the process of loading the disk operating system into _______.

4. In some cases, when you first boot DOS it asks you to enter the _______ and the _______.

5. The _______ command can be used to list the names, sizes, and creation dates and times of all the files on a disk.

6. A file's primary filename can have from one to _______ characters in it.

7. File name extensions are often used to _______ files.

8. You can press the _______ key to cancel a command if you haven't pressed the Enter key yet.

9. You can press _______ to cancel a command before it finishes executing.

10. The DOS _______ indicates the current default disk drive.

11. The _______ command can tell you how much memory is installed in your computer.

12. A diskette must be _______ before it can be used to store program and data files.

13. The _______ command can be used to duplicate one or more files on the same or on different disks.

14. _______ file name characters can be used to refer to several files at the same time.

15. The DISKCOPY command will automatically _______ the target diskette if it's brand new.

16. The REN command can be used to _______ one or more file names.

17. To remove a file from a disk, you would enter _______ or _______ followed by the file's name.

18. The TYPE command lets you display _______ files on your screen.

19. You could use the _______ command to produce a hard copy of a text file.

20. To run a program, you must type its _______ and then press _______.

Short Problems

1. If you have access to a diskette other than DOS Startup, produce a directory listing of the files on it. If you have a printer, try using Ctrl-PrtSc to turn on printer echoing before you issue the directory command so that you can get a hard copy.

2. When you booted DOS, you may have been asked to supply the date and time. Two DOS commands, DATE and TIME, tell you the current date and time and let you change these settings. Try the DATE and TIME commands. If you don't want to change the date and time settings, just press the Enter key when asked for the new date or time. Notice how DOS automatically figures out and displays the day of the week.

3. Use the * global file name character to produce a directory listing of all the files in the DOS subdirectory or on the DOS Startup disk with an EXE extension.

4. Use the * global file name character to produce a directory listing of all the files in the DOS subdirectory or on the DOS Startup disk whose names begin with the letter K.

5. Use the ? global file name character to produce a directory listing of all the files in the DOS subdirectory or on the DOS Startup disk that have an *E* as the second letter of their primary filename.

6. DOS versions 3.0 and newer have a command that lets you supply or change a volume label without having to reformat a disk. If you have DOS 3.0 or newer try using the LABEL command on a diskette that you have formatted for a lesson in this chapter.

7. If you don't know what DOS version you have, enter **ver**. This command displays the number of the DOS version you are using.

8. Another way to find out the volume label of a disk is to use the VOL command. Enter **vol**. This command displays the volume label (if there is one) of the default disk.

9. It is possible to display a text file on your screen by using the COPY command instead of the TYPE command. In certain cases, DOS can refer to its peripheral devices as if they were files. There are several file names that have a special meaning to DOS. These are called DOS device names. For example, CON refers to the console, or the keyboard and screen. If your disk has a file named AUTOEXEC.BAT on it, execute this command:

    Type   **copy autoexec.bat con**
    Press **Enter**

    You should see the text of file AUTOEXEC.BAT displayed on your screen just as if you used the TYPE command.

10. Just as CON is a DOS device name that refers to the keyboard and screen, PRN is a DOS device name that refers to the printer. Try using the COPY command to get a printout of the AUTOEXEC.BAT file.

11. The DIR command has two optional parameters that can be useful when looking at disks with lots of files on them. The /P parameter will automatically pause the display when the screen is full and let you press a key to continue. The /W parameter will display the directory in a wide format across the screen, omitting the sizes and creation dates and times so that more file names will fit at once. Obtain a directory listing of the DOS subdirectory or DOS Startup disk using these options:

    Type   **dir /p**
    Press   **Enter**
    Type   **dir /w**
    Press   **Enter**

INTERMEDIATE DOS

In This Chapter

Preview

In the previous chapter you learned the basics of DOS, the operating system used on millions of IBM and IBM-compatible microcomputers. This chapter continues your exploration of DOS with slightly more advanced topics.

After studying this chapter, you will know how to

- use the DOS editing and function keys.
- set the BREAK option.
- work with subdirectories.
- use the PATH and APPEND commands.
- change the DOS prompt.
- back up and restore disks and files.
- recover files from damaged disks.
- use the prompt option when erasing files.
- append files and copy files to devices.
- set the VERIFY option.
- change file attributes.
- copy groups of files.
- update sets of files.
- transfer the DOS system files.
- compare files and disks.
- change volume labels.
- change the current date and time.
- display a memory report.
- reassign, join, and substitute drives.
- print multiple files.

Getting Started

You've already learned how to start DOS and use its most common features and commands. This chapter assumes you have completed all of the lessons and exercises in Chapter 2. Furthermore, it assumes that you have a computer with a hard disk and DOS 3.30, 4.00, or 4.01 installed on it in a subdirectory named DOS. All of the screens in the following lessons were created with MS-DOS 4.01. To work the following lessons, boot up or reboot your computer if you have not already done so.

Lesson 1: Using the DOS Editing and Function Keys

As you learned in Chapter 2, DOS assigns special meanings to certain keys. By now you should know how to use Enter, Ctrl-Alt-Del, Escape, Ctrl-Num Lock (or Pause), Ctrl-Break, Shift-PrtSc (or Print Screen), and Ctrl-PrtSc. In addition, DOS has other key presses that can help you enter commands and save time. These are known as the DOS editing and function keys.

Step 1: Retrieve the Previous Command

Every time you enter a command, DOS saves what you have typed in a special area of memory. You can retrieve the previous command by pressing the F3 function key. For example, follow these instructions:

Type   **dir**
Press   **Enter**
Press   **F3**

When the directory command is finished, DOS will copy the previous command, which was DIR, to your screen at the cursor location, as if you had typed it again.

Press   **Enter**

DOS will execute the DIR command again. The F3 command is especially convenient for repeating the same command several times in a row, or for repeating an especially long command.

Step 2: Edit the Command Line

When you press F3, DOS only copies the previous command to the command line. You still have to press Enter to actually execute the command. You can, however, alter the command line if you like. For example:

Press   **F3**
Press   **Space Bar**
Type   **c:**
Press   **Enter**

This sequence of actions will retrieve the previous command, which was DIR, and add the disk drive specification C: onto the end. Once the previous command is retrieved, you can also use the Backspace or Left Arrow key to delete characters to the left of the cursor.

Step 3: Copy the Next Character from the Previous Command

Pressing F3 retrieves all of the previous command and presents it on your screen. You can also retrieve one character at a time from the previous command by pressing the F1 key. For example:

Press   **F1** (3 times)
Press   **Enter**

This sequence of commands will retrieve and then execute only the first three characters (DIR) of the previous command. The F1 key allows you to retrieve some of the previous command or make modifications to it.

Step 4: Retrieve Some of the Previous Command

Put a formatted diskette in drive A if it does not already contain one. Execute this command:

Type   **dir a:**
Press   **Enter**

Suppose you now want to examine disk drive C or B.

Press   **F2**
Type   **a**

This tells DOS to retrieve the previous command, but only up to the *a* character you've specified. So, now you can type a different end to the command:

Type   **c:**
Press   **Enter**

Step 5: Examine the Other Editing Keys

The editing and function keys we have discussed are probably the most frequently used. A few other keys, however, are available. The following table lists all of the DOS editing keys.

Key	*Action*
F1	Retypes one character at a time from the previous command.
F2	Retypes all characters up to the next character you type from the previous command.
F3	Retypes all of the previous command.
F4	Deletes all the characters from the previous command up to the next character you type.
F5	Saves the contents of your current command line as if it were the previous command.
F6	Inserts an end-of-file code (Ctrl-Z).
Delete	Skips over a character from the previous command.
Insert	Switches insert/overwrite mode in the command line.
Escape	Cancels the current line.

Practice

1. Try the F4 function key.

   Type   **garbage dir**
   Press   **Enter**

   Don't worry about the error message. To throw out the garbage, and execute the remaining DIR command, do this:

   Press   **F4**
   Type   **d**
   Press   **F3**
   Press   **Enter**

2. Try the F5 function key. Suppose you are typing a long command and realize you have made an error. You have not yet pressed the Enter key. For example, do this (but don't press Enter):

   Type   **ytpe autoexec.bat**
   Press   **F5**

   Pressing F5 will save what you have typed as if it were the previous command. Now, follow these instructions to correct your error, retrieve the rest of the command, and execute the correct TYPE command:

   Type   **ty**
   Press   **F3**
   Press   **Enter**

3. Try the Del editing key.

   Type   **xxdir**
   Press   **Enter**

Suppose you meant to type *dir*. To fix your mistake, do this:

Press　**Del** (2 times)
Press　**F3**
Press　**Enter**

4. Try the Ins editing key.

Type　**dir os**
Press　**Enter**

Suppose you meant to type *dir dos*. To fix your mistake, follow these instructions:

Press　**F1** (4 times)
Press　**Ins**
Type　**d**
Press　**F3**
Press　**Enter**

Lesson 2: Setting the BREAK Option

In Chapter 2 you learned that you can press Ctrl-Break to cancel a program that is running. Normally, Ctrl-Break works only when DOS is checking the keyboard or sending characters to the screen or printer. You can also tell DOS to check whether Ctrl-Break has been pressed during disk reads and writes.

Step 1: Execute the BREAK Command

The BREAK command allows you to check or change the status of the BREAK option, which controls when Ctrl-Break will cancel a program. To see the current setting of the BREAK option, execute this command:

Type　**break**
Press　**Enter**

DOS will tell you whether BREAK is on or off.

Step 2: Change the BREAK Option

You can change the current setting of BREAK by entering the BREAK command followed by ON or OFF. For example, if BREAK is OFF, turn it on with this command:

Type　**break on**
Press　**Enter**

Now check what you have done:

Type　**break**
Press　**Enter**

Your screen should look like Figure 1.

Practice　Switch the BREAK option back to the way it was before you changed it.

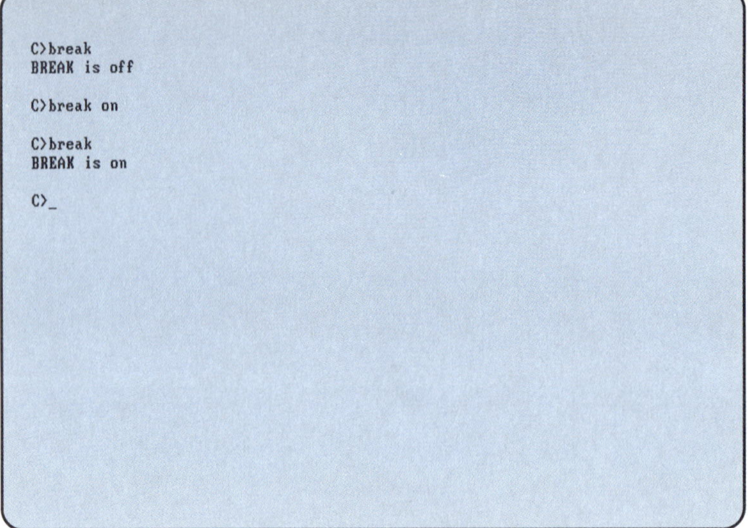

Figure 1 Setting the BREAK Option

Lesson 3: Working with Subdirectories

As you can imagine, people who use microcomputers extensively often generate large numbers of files. Before hard disks became common, users stored their files in many different floppy disks. Organizing files meant physically organizing diskettes by keeping them well-labeled and storing them in subdivided boxes, racks, or cabinets. Once hard disks became common, however, operating systems had to devise a better method of organizing large numbers of files. Even a modest 20-megabyte hard disk can store thousands of different files. Looking for a particular file among hundreds or thousands of files is time consuming and tedious. Consequently, most microcomputer operating systems, including DOS, have evolved a **hierarchical** method of organizing files into groups. A hierarchical system allows you to cluster files into orders or ranks, each subordinate to the one above. These groups of files, called subdirectories, are like file folders that can be nested within one another. Disks can be organized into subdirectories, each of which can contain files and other subdirectories.

Subdirectories are an invaluable tool for organizing programs and data files on high-capacity storage devices. In addition, subdirectories make it easier for the operating system to locate a particular file, because large numbers of files are divided into smaller groups. Although subdirectories are most often, indeed almost always, found on hard disks, they are occasionally used on floppy disks, too. DOS includes commands that let you create, access, and remove subdirectories.

With DOS, every disk has a single main directory, known as the **root directory.** DOS automatically creates a root directory on every disk you format. This is the directory you are in when you first boot up DOS or when you first change your default drive. The root directory itself has no name, but it's represented by a backslash (\).

Step 1: Create a Subdirectory

The internal DOS command MD or MKDIR (short for "make directory") is used to create a new subdirectory. It is followed by the **path** of the new subdirectory. A path is an optional disk drive specifier followed by a list of subdirectory names, separated by backslashes. The rules for naming subdirectories are the same as the rules for naming files. The simplest path is a single backslash \, which represents the root directory of your current default drive. Let's create a new subdirectory on your hard disk. Execute this command:

> Type   **md c:\myfiles**
> Press   **Enter**

The command you just entered creates a subdirectory named MYFILES on the hard disk C. This subdirectory is one level below the root directory. To see the result, execute this command:

> Type   **dir**
> Press   **Enter**

You should see MYFILES followed by the <DIR> designation in the directory listing as shown in Figure 2.

Step 2: Change to the Subdirectory

Think of the subdirectory as a separate "sub-disk" on your disk. You use the change directory (CD or CHDIR) command, which is an internal command, to move into your new subdirectory. Execute these commands:

> Type   **cd c:\myfiles**
> Press   **Enter**
> Type   **dir**
> Press   **Enter**

Your screen should look like Figure 3, showing the directory listing inside the MYFILES subdirectory.

Figure 2 Using MD to Create the MYFILES Subdirectory

```
C>md c:\myfiles

C>dir

 Volume in drive C is HARD DISK
 Volume Serial Number is 3324-07CC
 Directory of  C:\

CONFIG   SYS       146 07-09-89    1:22p
MYFILES      <DIR>     07-12-89    2:10p
COMMAND  COM     37557 12-19-88   12:00a
DOS          <DIR>     07-09-89    1:23p
AUTOEXEC BAT       256 01-01-88    5:52a
        5 File(s)   19699712 bytes free

C>_
```

Figure 3 Using DIR Inside the MYFILES Subdirectory

Step 3: Copy a File to the Subdirectory

Right now, the MYFILES subdirectory has no ordinary user files in it. You can, however, copy files into this subdirectory just as if it were a separate disk. For example, let's copy the AUTOEXEC.BAT file from the root directory into the MYFILES subdirectory. Execute this command:

> Type   **copy c:\autoexec.bat**
> Press **Enter**

This command copies the file AUTOEXEC.BAT from the root directory of the hard disk C into your current subdirectory, which happens to be MYFILES. Execute this command to see the contents of your subdirectory:

> Type   **dir**
> Press **Enter**

A copy of AUTOEXEC.BAT now also exists in the MYFILES subdirectory. It's important to realize that there are two separate copies of AUTOEXEC.BAT now on the disk: one in the root directory and one in the MYFILES subdirectory.

Step 4: Display the Directory Structure

A hard disk can hold a great many subdirectories and files. DIR will list the subdirectories and files of only one directory at a time; it cannot show the structure beneath that level. TREE, an external DOS command, can list all of the subdirectories on a disk. It can also list all of the files in each subdirectory. With DOS versions 4.00 and newer, TREE depicts the structure of the disk graphically. Older DOS versions simply list the paths and subdirectories. Execute this command to get a TREE listing of the root directory of your hard disk:

> Type   **tree c:**
> Press **Enter**

Figure 4 shows the result. You can also tell the TREE command to list all files in all directories by using the /F parameter. Execute this command to see how it works:

> Type   **tree c: \ /f**
> Press   **Enter**

Step 5: Remove the Subdirectory

Once you are in a subdirectory, you can almost think of it as a separate disk. You can run programs from within a subdirectory. Many DOS commands that deal with files will operate only on the files in your current subdirectory unless you specify otherwise. For example, you can delete every file in a subdirectory without affecting any of the files in the root directory or any other subdirectory. For example, make sure you are in the MYFILES subdirectory and then execute these commands:

> Type   **erase *.***
> Press   **Enter**
> Type   **y**
> Press   **Enter**
> Type   **dir**
> Press   **Enter**

DOS will erase every file in your current directory, the MYFILES subdirectory. The DIR command should reveal that this is true. Now change back to the root directory and check its contents by executing these commands:

> Type   **cd c: **
> Press   **Enter**
> Type   **dir**
> Press   **Enter**

As you can see, the AUTOEXEC.BAT file in the root directory is still intact.

Figure 4 Using TREE to Display the Directory Structure

Just as you must occasionally delete unneeded files, sometimes you must remove subdirectories too. Suppose that you are finished with the MYFILES subdirectory and you want to remove it from your disk. To do this you must first erase any files inside the subdirectory and move out of the subdirectory. You have already done this. Now execute the remove directory command (RD or RMDIR) to remove the empty MYFILES subdirectory from your disk:

Type `rd c:\myfiles`
Press **Enter**
Type `dir`
Press **Enter**

You will see that the MYFILES subdirectory has indeed been removed, and your disk is the same as it was when you began this lesson. Like MD and CD, RD is an internal DOS command.

1. Create a new subdirectory on your disk and name it after yourself (eight characters or less). Change to your new subdirectory. Now create three additional subdirectories inside your new subdirectory and name them ONE, TWO, and THREE. Change to the ONE subdirectory and copy the AUTOEXEC.BAT file from the root, or some other file from the DOS subdirectory into the ONE subdirectory.

2. Use the DIR command to examine the contents of your ONE subdirectory. Notice the first two entries in the directory listing. The . (single period) is a special DOS designation that symbolizes your current directory. The .. (double period) symbolizes the directory above your current directory. For example:

   Type `dir .`
   Press **Enter**

   See what happens. Now try this command:

   Type `dir ..`
   Press **Enter**

   You will get a listing of the directory above ONE.

3. DOS pros often use the . and .. designations as shortcuts. The . is equivalent to *.*. Use it to erase all the files in your current subdirectory, which should be ONE. Now, change back to the subdirectory above ONE, the subdirectory you named after yourself:

   Type `cd ..`
   Press **Enter**

   Try using the .. designation again to return to the root directory.

4. Remove the ONE, TWO, and THREE subdirectories and then remove the subdirectory you named after yourself, leaving your disk the way it was before this practice session.

Lesson 4: Using the PATH and APPEND Commands

In many ways, a subdirectory is like a separate disk. Unless you give DOS special instructions, you can access the files within a subdirectory only when you have switched to that subdirectory with the CD command. In order to fully realize the benefits of DOS subdirectories, you must also understand the PATH and APPEND commands.

Step 1: Execute the PATH Command

By default, you cannot gain access to the programs or data files in a subdirectory unless you are in that subdirectory. Alternatively, you can precede the name of every command or data file with its full path. For example, if you want to use the CHKDSK command (which is an external command kept in the file CHKDSK.COM), and you are not in the DOS subdirectory on the hard disk C, you could enter the command this way:

>   Type   **c:\dos\chkdsk**
>   Press   **Enter**

Typing the disk drive and path before every command, however, can be tiresome. Fortunately, the PATH command can eliminate the need to do this.

Use the PATH command to tell DOS which subdirectories to search through if it cannot find a program or batch file you request in your current directory. (You will learn about batch files later in this chapter.) For example, in most cases you want the commands in the DOS subdirectory to be accessible no matter which disk or directory you are using. Usually, DOS is installed so that a PATH command granting access to the DOS subdirectory is executed every time the computer is booted up. As you will learn later in this chapter, this is typically done by putting a PATH command in the AUTOEXEC.BAT file.

Execute the following command to see the current command search path that has been set up for you:

>   Type   **path**
>   Press   **Enter**

You can also use the PATH command to change the command search path. For example, suppose you want programs and batch files in the root directory and the DOS subdirectory to be accessible from any disk or directory. To set this up, execute the following PATH command:

>   Type   **path c:\; c:\dos**
>   Press   **Enter**

The PATH command is followed by a list of paths you want DOS to search whenever it cannot find the command you have entered. The paths are separated by semicolons. This PATH command has two search paths, c:\, the root directory of the hard disk C, and c:\dos, the DOS subdirectory beneath the root directory on the hard disk C. To see what you have done, execute this command again:

>   Type   **path**
>   Press   **Enter**

Your screen should look like Figure 5.

You need only enter the PATH command once, unless you want to change the list of subdirectories. Consequently, it is usually placed in the AUTO-EXEC.BAT file to be executed every time you boot up your computer.

Step 2: Execute the APPEND Command

The PATH command works only for files with extensions of BAT, COM, or EXE. In other words, PATH will allow DOS to find only programs and batch files in other directories. Users of DOS 3.3 and newer versions, however, can use the APPEND command, which can find other types of files.

*Figure 5 Using the PATH
Command*

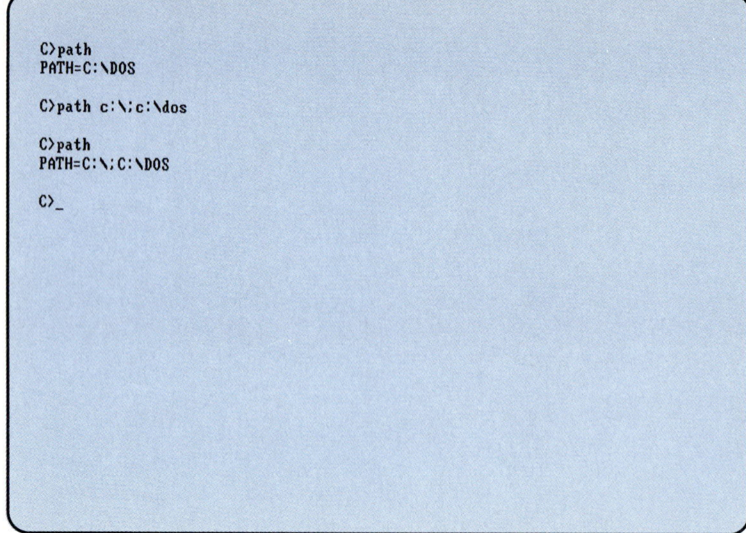

For example, create a subdirectory called LESSONS on your hard disk and change to it with these commands:

Type   **md c:\lessons**
Press **Enter**
Type   **cd c:\lessons**
Press **Enter**

Now, execute these commands to create a sample text file you can use:

Type   **copy con sample.txt**
Press **Enter**
Type   **This is a sample text file.**
Press **Enter**
Press **F6**
Press **Enter**

To see what you have created, execute this command:

Type   **type sample.txt**
Press **Enter**

The text file you have just created should be presented on your screen. As you can see, it is accessible from within the LESSONS subdirectory. Now, move back to the root directory and try to type the file by executing these commands:

Type   **cd c:**
Press **Enter**
Type   **type sample.txt**
Press **Enter**

DOS should say "File not found," as shown in Figure 6, because you are at the root and the file SAMPLE.TXT is in the LESSONS subdirectory.

Now suppose that you want data files in the root directory, the DOS subdirectory, and the LESSONS subdirectory to be accessible from all other disks and directories. Like the PATH command, APPEND can be followed by a list of sub-

Figure 6 SAMPLE.TXT Is Not Found in the Root Directory

```
C>md c:\lessons

C>cd c:\lessons

C>copy con sample.txt
This is a sample text file.
^Z
          1 File(s) copied

C>type sample.txt
This is a sample text file.

C>cd c:\

C>type sample.txt
File not found - SAMPLE.TXT

C>_
```

directories separated by semicolons. Execute the following APPEND command:

> Type   **append c:\;c:\dos;c:\lessons**
> Press   **Enter**

This command tells DOS the directories you want to search for files that have extensions other than BAT, COM, and EXE. Now try this command again:

> Type   **type sample.txt**
> Press   **Enter**

The file should be displayed on your screen, as shown in Figure 7. DOS was able to find SAMPLE.TXT because the APPEND command you entered told it where to search.

Like PATH, the APPEND command is usually put in the AUTOEXEC.BAT file to set up the search paths for data files every time the computer is turned on.

Practice 1. You can also use the APPEND command to see the current search path for data files.

> Type   **append**
> Press   **Enter**

If you enter this command without a list of subdirectories, DOS will display the search paths, if any, that have been established by the most recent APPEND command on your computer.

2. Use the TYPE command to examine the AUTOEXEC.BAT file in the root directory of your disk. Does it contain a PATH and APPEND statement?

Lesson 5: Changing the DOS Prompt

By default, the DOS prompt consists of the current drive letter followed by a > (greater than sign). For example, if hard disk C is your current drive, then the default DOS prompt is

> C>

Figure 7 APPEND Enables DOS to Find SAMPLE.TXT

```
C>md c:\lessons

C>cd c:\lessons

C>copy con sample.txt
This is a sample text file.
^Z
         1 File(s) copied

C>type sample.txt
This is a sample text file.

C>cd c:\

C>type sample.txt
File not found - SAMPLE.TXT

C>append c:\;c:\dos;c:\lessons

C>type sample.txt
This is a sample text file.

C>_
```

You can, however, change the appearance of the DOS prompt with the PROMPT command.

Step 1: Change the Prompt to a Text String

Suppose you want your DOS prompt to be Hello> instead of A> or C>. Execute this command:

Type   **prompt Hello$g**
Press **Enter**

As soon as you enter this command, the DOS prompt will be changed to Hello>. The $g in the command is a special code that stands for the > (greater than sign).

Step 2: Change the Prompt to Show the Disk and Directory

You can probably think of any number of cute prompts such as Hello>. A more useful prompt would show your current disk drive and directory. This is especially handy if you frequently use subdirectories, because it's easy to forget your current path. To change your prompt to display your current path, execute this command:

Type   **prompt pg**
Press **Enter**

If you are at the root directory of your hard disk, the prompt will immediately change to C:\>. Now change to your LESSONS subdirectory by executing this command:

Type   **cd \lessons**
Press **Enter**

Your DOS prompt should now be C:\LESSONS>.

Step 3: Explore the Other Prompt Options

The PROMPT command allows several options besides $g and $p. The following table lists all of the special codes you can use with the PROMPT command. These codes can be combined and mixed with text to create an unlimited number of prompts.

Prompt Code	*Action*
$q	Presents the = (equal sign) character.
$$	Presents the $ (dollar sign) character.
$t	Presents the current time of day.
$d	Presents today's date.
$p	Presents the current path.
$v	Presents the version of DOS being used.
$n	Presents the current drive letter.
$g	Presents the > (greater than sign) character.
$l	Presents the < (less than sign) character.
$b	Presents the | (vertical bar) character.
$_	Starts a new line.
$e	Presents a left arrow symbol.
$h	Performs a Backspace.

Try as many of the prompt options in the preceding table as you like. When you are finished experimenting, execute the following command to change the DOS prompt to the current disk drive and directory:

Type   **prompt pg**
Press   **Enter**

Lesson 6: Backing Up and Restoring Disks and Files

Floppy disks and hard disks, though quite reliable, are not infallible. Eventually, every disk or disk drive will fail. In addition, almost every computer user mistakenly erases important programs or data on occasion. It is essential, therefore, to keep backup copies of all files that may be difficult, if not impossible, to replace. DOS includes two external commands, BACKUP and RESTORE, that help you keep extra copies of your software and data files.

Step 1: Back Up the Entire Hard Disk

Although the DOS BACKUP command can be used to make extra copies of floppy disks on other floppy disks, it is most often used to back up all or part of a hard disk onto floppy disks. BACKUP is better than using the COPY command to back up a hard disk, because most hard disks contain too many files to fit on a single floppy disk. Unlike COPY, the BACKUP command will automatically use as many diskettes as needed to save the files from a hard disk. The BACKUP command will fill each diskette as much as possible, even if it means splitting a single file between two disks. Then, BACKUP will prompt you to insert additional floppy disks until it copies all of the files. Furthermore, the BACKUP command of DOS versions 3.3 or newer will even format the backup floppy disks if necessary.

Suppose you want to make a backup copy of your entire hard disk. Assume that you have never backed up your hard disk before. First, you would switch back to the root directory and use DIR or CHKDSK to estimate how many floppy disks you will need. For example, if your hard disk contains 10 megabytes of files, you would need 29 or 30 360K floppy disks. Don't do this on your computer (it might require too many diskettes and take too long), but here is the command you would enter:

backup c: a: /s

This command tells DOS to back up the C drive onto the floppy disks that you will put into drive A. The /S parameter tells DOS to back up all the subdirectories as well. If you are using DOS 4.00 or newer, the BACKUP command can automatically format new diskettes if necessary. If you are using DOS 3.3, you should tell the BACKUP command to format new diskettes (if yours are not already formatted) by including the /F parameter after the /S parameter. Finally, if you are using a DOS version previous to 3.3, you have to format all of your backup diskettes *before* you execute the BACKUP command.

The BACKUP command will then beep and present the message shown in Figure 8. It is up to you to make sure that the floppy disks you use for the backup do not contain any files you need. You would insert the first diskette into drive A, close the door, and press any key. DOS will then list the files as it copies them to the first diskette. When no more room is left on the diskette, DOS will beep and prompt you to enter the second diskette. This will continue until all the files are backed up. As DOS fills the diskettes, you should label them consecutively as backup disk 1, backup disk 2, and so on.

Step 2: Do an Incremental Backup

If you make it a practice of backing up your hard disk at regular intervals, say every day or week, there is no need to copy those files that have not changed. You do, however, want to make sure that you back up any new or modified files.

Figure 8 Using the BACKUP Command

```
C:\>backup c: a: /s

Insert backup diskette 01 in drive A:

WARNING! Files in the target drive
A:\ root directory will be erased
Press any key to continue . . .
```

This is known as an **incremental backup.** Fortunately, you can tell DOS to do an incremental backup with two additional parameters to the BACKUP command. The /M parameter tells the BACKUP command to copy only new or changed files. The /A parameter tells the BACKUP command to add the selected files to the existing backup diskettes and not erase their contents. So, this would be the command you enter to do an incremental backup (don't do it now):

```
backup c: a: /s/m/a
```

DOS would then tell you to insert the last backup diskette into drive A and press any key when you are ready. Any new or changed files would then be added to this diskette, and additional diskettes, if needed.

In addition to /S, /M, /A, and /F (for DOS 3.3), the BACKUP command also accepts the following parameters:

/D:*date*	Backs up only those files that were created or modified on or after the specified *date*.
/T:*time*	Backs up only those files that were created or modified at or after the specified *time*.
/L:*file*	Creates a backup log in the specified *file*.

Step 3: Restore the Backed Up Disk

Hopefully, you'll never have to use the backup diskettes of your hard disk. Suppose the worst has happened, however, and you must copy the files from your backup diskettes back onto your hard disk. This is done with the RESTORE command. First, you would make sure that you are at the root directory of the hard disk. Again, don't do this now, but the command to restore the entire hard disk would be:

```
restore a: /s
```

This command will restore the files from the backup diskettes in drive A to your current directory, which should be the root directory of the hard disk C. It will prompt you to insert the backup diskettes in the same order in which they were created. The /S parameter tells DOS to restore subdirectories as well.

Step 4: Back Up a Subdirectory

It is also possible to use the BACKUP command to save a copy of a single subdirectory. This is often done when the contents of a hard disk subdirectory will not fit on a single floppy disk. Although your LESSONS subdirectory is very small, let's create a backup of it to illustrate the procedure. Get a formatted floppy disk that is either empty or contains files that can be erased. Then execute this command:

```
Type   backup c:\lessons a: /s
Press  Enter
```

Insert the floppy disk into drive A and press any key. DOS will back up the contents of the LESSONS subdirectory onto the diskette in drive A. Your screen should look like Figure 9.

*Figure 9 Backing Up the
LESSONS Subdirectory*

```
C:\>backup c:\lessons a: /s

Insert backup diskette 01 in drive A:

WARNING! Files in the target drive
A:\ root directory will be erased
Press any key to continue . . .

*** Backing up files to drive A: ***
Diskette Number: 01

\LESSONS\SAMPLE.TXT

C:\>_
```

Step 5: Restore a Subdirectory

Suppose that you accidentally erased the contents of the LESSONS subdirectory. Simulate this accident by executing this command:

> Type   **erase c:\lessons*.***
> Press   **Enter**
> Type   **y**
> Press   **Enter**

Now, execute the following command to restore the LESSONS subdirectory from the backup diskette:

> Type   **restore a: c:\lessons*.* /s**
> Press   **Enter**

DOS will ask you to insert backup diskette 1 in drive A and press any key when you are ready. After you do this and the RESTORE command is finished, your screen should look like Figure 10.

In addition to /S, which ensures the restoration of subdirectories, the RESTORE command also accepts the following parameters:

/P	Prompts you for permission to restore files.
/B:*date*	Restores only those files that were last modified on or before the specified *date*.
/A:*date*	Restores only those files that were last modified on or after the specified *date*.
/E:*time*	Restores only those files that were last modified at or earlier than the specified *time*.
/L:*time*	Restores only those files that were last modified at or later than the specified *time*.
/M:*file*	Restores only those files modified since the last BACKUP.
/N	Restores only those files that no longer exist on the target disk.

*Figure 10 Restoring the
LESSONS Subdirectory*

```
C:\>restore a: c:\lessons\*.* /s

Insert backup diskette 01 in drive A:
Press any key to continue . . .

*** Files were backed up 07-13-1989 ***

*** Restoring files from drive A: ***
Diskette: 01
\LESSONS\SAMPLE.TXT


C:\>_
```

Step 6: Back Up and Restore One or More Files

BACKUP and RESTORE can also be used for individual files and groups of files specified with the DOS global file name characters ? and *. Simply insert the file specification instead of just the drive letter or subdirectory of the disk to be backed up. For example, suppose you wanted to back up only those files with an extension of TXT on your hard disk. Make sure you are at the root directory of hard disk C and execute this command:

Type   **backup c:*.txt a: /s**
Press   **Enter**

Insert your floppy disk into drive A and press **Enter** again. All TXT files in all subdirectories on disk C will be backed up to drive A. To restore the files, enter this command:

Type   **restore a: c:*.txt /s**
Press   **Enter**

1. If you have several blank diskettes you can use, backup the DOS subdirectory from your hard disk onto them. If you have only one diskette available, back up only one file or a group of files (such as *.SYS) that will fit on a single diskette.

2. Use the DIR command to examine the backup diskette you have created.

Lesson 7: Recovering Files from Damaged Disks

Every hard disk and floppy disk will eventually wear out or become physically damaged or magnetically corrupted in some way. When one of these unfortunate events occurs, DOS may not be able to read the files stored in or around the bad spots. This is one reason why you should try to maintain up-to-date backup copies of all of your important files and disks. If you don't do this, however, and DOS cannot read one of your files or perhaps even an entire disk, the RECOVER command may be able to help. This external command should be used only as a last resort. RECOVER does not work when DOS is run from a local area network.

Step 1: Recover a Single File

Suppose you try to retrieve a file from a floppy disk in drive A and DOS reports that it cannot read that file. You may get one of the following messages from DOS:

```
Disk error reading drive A:
General failure reading drive A:
Read fault error reading drive A:
Sector not found error reading drive A:
Track 0 bad - disk unusable
Unrecoverable read error on drive A:
```

First, take out the disk, make sure it is inserted correctly, and close the disk drive door or lever again. Then try using the CHKDSK command on that disk. If the CHKDSK command reports that a sector on the disk is bad, RECOVER might be able to read all or part of the file by skipping over the bad spots. Suppose the file you are trying to read is SAMPLE.TXT. You would enter this command (don't do this now):

```
recover a:sample.txt
```

RECOVER would then try to read SAMPLE.TXT, part by part, ignoring the bad spots. Then it would try to rewrite the file without the bad spots, possibly allowing you to read at least some of the original SAMPLE.TXT.

Step 2: Recover an Entire Disk

If you cannot gain access to any files on a disk, then you can tell the RECOVER command to try and reconstruct the entire disk. Again, this should only be done as a last resort. Here is the command you would enter to recover all the files on the disk in drive A (don't do it now):

```
recover a:
```

Practice

1. Take a diskette with files on it that you don't need, such as the backup diskette you created in Lesson 6, and insert it into drive A. Suppose that it is a damaged disk. Execute the following command to try to get back readable information on the damaged disk:

   Type   **recover a:**
   Press   **Enter**

   Press any key when the RECOVER command asks you to do so. When it is finished, RECOVER will report how many files it recovered.

2. RECOVER is to be used only as a last resort. When it recovers files, it changes their names to FILE0001.REC, FILE0002.REC, and so on. So, you have to examine and rename the recovered files to get them into usable form again. You don't need the files you recovered on the diskette in drive A, so reformat it:

Type   **format a:**
Press   **Enter**

Lesson 8: Using the Prompt Option When Erasing Files

You have already learned how to use the ERASE (or DEL) command to remove files from a disk. If you try to erase every file on a disk or in a subdirectory, DOS will ask you if you are sure this is what you want to do before it discards the files. The ERASE command, however, does not automatically ask this question when you erase several files at once with the global file name characters * or ?. Fortunately, an optional parameter is available that lets you have DOS prompt you before erasing each file. This option is also handy for selectively erasing some files from a group of many.

Step 1: Specify the /P Parameter

Copy some files from the DOS subdirectory into your LESSONS subdirectory so that you have some files you can erase safely. Execute the following commands:

Type   **cd c:\lessons**
Press   **Enter**
Type   **copy c:\dos*.com**
Press   **Enter**

Use the DIR command to make sure that you are in the LESSONS subdirectory. Execute this command to erase the COM files from your LESSONS subdirectory with a prompt before erasing each file:

Type   **erase *.com /p**
Press   **Enter**
Type   **y**
Press   **Enter**

As Figure 11 shows, DOS will prompt you with "Delete (Y/N)?" before it actually deletes each file. For the remaining files, answer yes for some files and no for others. When the ERASE command has finished, execute this command to examine the LESSONS subdirectory:

Type   **dir**
Press   **Enter**

The files for which you answered no will still be present.

Step 2: Don't Specify the /P Parameter

To delete the remaining COM files from your LESSONS subdirectory, execute this command:

Type   **erase *.com**
Press   **Enter**

Practice   Make sure you are in your LESSONS subdirectory. Use the ERASE command with the /P parameter to tell DOS to delete every file in the subdirectory, but to prompt you first. Answer **n** for no to each prompt so that you don't erase any

Figure 11 Using the /P Parameter When Erasing Files

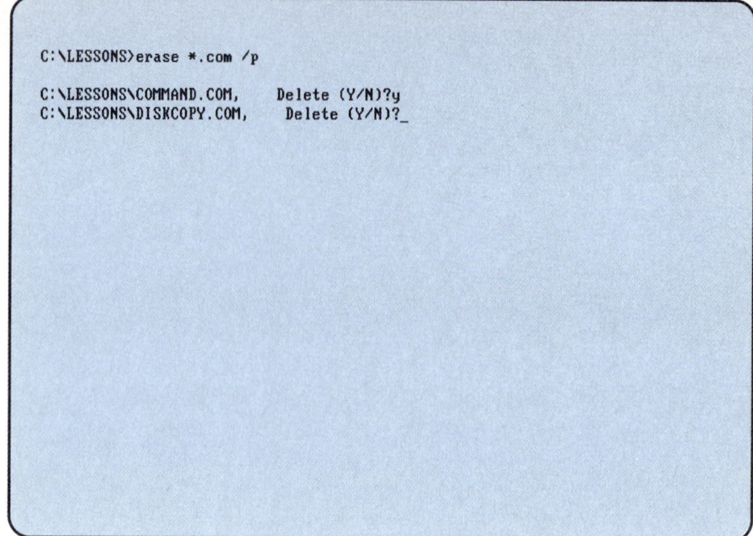

files. To be extra safe, you can make it a practice to always use the /P parameter with the ERASE or DEL command.

Lesson 9: Learning More About the COPY Command

COPY is a versatile command that can be used in several different ways. You have already learned how to use COPY to duplicate one or more files from one disk or subdirectory to another. By specifying different names for the source and the target files, you can also duplicate files in the same subdirectory.

Step 1: Copy from the Console to Create a Text File

The COPY command can create a new text file without using a word processing or text editing program. Actually, you already did this in Lesson 4, but let's go over it again.

DOS can refer to certain hardware devices as if they were files. These devices are given special file names called DOS device names. For example, CON refers to the console, or the keyboard and the screen. Similarly, PRN refers to the printer. You can use device names such as CON and PRN as if they were file names in commands such as COPY. Make sure you are in your LESSONS sub-directory and then execute this command:

```
Type   copy con sample2.txt
Press  Enter
```

This command tells DOS to take every character you now type at the keyboard and copy it into a new file named SAMPLE2.TXT. Type the following text, pressing **Enter** at the end of each line:

```
A text file contains only letters, numbers,
punctuation marks, and other symbols that
appear on the keyboard.
```

An end-of-file mark is the Ctrl-Z character; it is the last character in a text file. When you are finished entering the text, you must insert an end-of-file mark into the file by doing this:

Press   **F6**
Press   **Enter**

To see what you have done, execute these commands:

Type   **dir**
Press   **Enter**
Type   **type sample2.txt**
Press   **Enter**

Your screen should look like Figure 12.

Step 2: Use COPY to Append Files

The COPY command is sometimes used to append or combine files. Suppose you wanted to create a new file named SAMPLE3.TXT that contained the contents of SAMPLE.TXT followed by the contents of SAMPLE2.TXT. Execute this command:

Type   **copy sample.txt+sample2.txt sample3.txt**
Press   **Enter**

Any number of source files can be combined by listing their names separated by plus signs. The last file name in the COPY command is the target file that will contain the combination of the source files. If you omit the name of a target file, DOS will combine the source files and copy them to the first source file listed. To see what you have done, enter these commands:

Type   **dir**
Press   **Enter**
Type   **type sample3.txt**
Press   **Enter**

Your screen should look like Figure 13.

Figure 12 Using COPY to Create a Text File

```
C:\LESSONS>copy con sample2.txt
A text file contains only letters, numbers,
punctuation marks, and other symbols that
appear on the keyboard.
^Z
        1 File(s) copied

C:\LESSONS>dir

 Volume in drive C is HARD DISK
 Volume Serial Number is 3324-07CC
 Directory of  C:\LESSONS

 .            <DIR>       07-15-89   11:06a
 ..           <DIR>       07-15-89   11:06a
SAMPLE   TXT         29 07-15-89   11:06a
SAMPLE2  TXT        113 07-15-89   11:08a
        4 File(s)   19691520 bytes free

C:\LESSONS>type sample2.txt
A text file contains only letters, numbers,
punctuation marks, and other symbols that
appear on the keyboard.

C:\LESSONS>_
```

Figure 13 Using COPY to Append Files

```
C:\LESSONS>copy sample.txt+sample2.txt sample3.txt
SAMPLE.TXT
SAMPLE2.TXT
        1 File(s) copied

C:\LESSONS>dir

 Volume in drive C is HARD DISK
 Volume Serial Number is 3324-07CC
 Directory of  C:\LESSONS

.            <DIR>      07-15-89  11:06a
..           <DIR>      07-15-89  11:06a
SAMPLE   TXT       29 07-15-89  11:06a
SAMPLE2  TXT      113 07-15-89  11:08a
SAMPLE3  TXT      143 07-15-89  11:09a
        5 File(s)   19689472 bytes free

C:\LESSONS>type sample3.txt
This is a sample text file.
A text file contains only letters, numbers,
punctuation marks, and other symbols that
appear on the keyboard.

C:\LESSONS>_
```

Step 3: Use the /V Parameter

The COPY command has three optional parameters, /V, /B, and /A. The /V parameter tells DOS to verify that the copy has been made successfully with no errors. Each time data is written to the disk, a confirmation procedure will be performed to ensure that data can be read without error. The /V parameter is used only when making copies to disk files, not device names. Verifying a copy takes longer and is usually not necessary, but you may want to do it when copying especially important files, such as programs in which the scrambling of a single byte can cause a bug. For example, try this command:

> Type   **copy c:\command.com command.bak /v**
> Press **Enter**

You won't see any difference on the screen when the COPY command is used with the /V parameter, except that it works a little slower.

Step 4: Use the /B and /A Parameters

By default, the COPY command creates a target file that is the same type of file as the source. If you copy a text file, COPY produces a text file. Another term for text file is **ASCII file.** ASCII, which stands for American Standard Code for Information Interchange, is the most common scheme used to encode characters as numbers so that they can be manipulated by computers. A **binary file** is a file that contains programs or data that are not encoded as ASCII characters. Files with extensions of EXE and COM, for example, are binary files. If you copy a binary file, COPY normally produces a binary file.

The other two parameters of the COPY command, /B and /A, are used when the type of file you want to produce is different than the source. The /B parameter, when specified after a source file name, tells DOS to copy the entire file, including any end-of-file marks. When used with a target file name, the /B parameter tells DOS not to add an end-of-file mark to the end of the file. The /A parameter tells

DOS to treat the file as an ASCII file. If a source file name is followed by /A, only data up to and including the first end-of-file mark will be copied. If a target file name is followed by /A, an end-of-file mark will be added as the last character of the file.

In most cases, you don't have to use /B or /A. You can, however, use the /B command to view the entire contents of a binary file on your screen. First, try the following COPY command without the /B parameter:

> Type   **copy command.bak con**
> Press   **Enter**

Remember, COMMAND.BAK is a copy of COMMAND.COM, the DOS command processor, which is a binary file. When you copy it to the screen, the display will stop when the first end-of-file mark is encountered. Now, try this command to display the entire COMMAND.BAK binary file on your screen (the computer will beep quite a bit, so skip this command if you don't want to disturb others around you):

> Type   **copy command.bak /b con**
> Press   **Enter**

Don't be alarmed if your computer seems to be going crazy. All the strange characters and beeps occur because binary programming code is being displayed on the screen. Occasionally, you will see words or phrases that you can read, usually messages embedded in the command processor. It will take a couple of minutes for the entire COMMAND.BAK file to be copied to the screen, and Ctrl-Break won't stop it, so just be patient and wait.

Practice

1. Use the COPY command with the CON device name to display the contents of SAMPLE2.TXT on your screen.

2. Use the COPY command with the PRN device name to send SAMPLE2.TXT to your printer.

3. Use the COPY command with the /B parameter and CON device name to examine an EXE or COM file from the DOS subdirectory on your hard disk.

Lesson 10: Setting the VERIFY Option

In Lesson 9 you learned that the COPY command's optional /V ensures that files copied to the disk can be read without error. The VERIFY command lets you turn this option on or off whenever any files are copied to a disk, not just for a single COPY command like the /V parameter.

Step 1: Execute the VERIFY Command

To see the current setting of the VERIFY option, execute this command:

> Type   **verify**
> Press   **Enter**

The default setting of the VERIFY option is off.

Step 2: Change the VERIFY Option

You can change the current setting of the VERIFY option by following the command with ON or OFF. For example, execute these commands:

```
Type   verify on
Press  Enter
Type   verify
Press  Enter
```

 Turn the VERIFY option off again.

Lesson 11: Changing File Attributes

A **file attribute** is a characteristic of a file. DOS has several attributes that can be associated with files. The two most commonly encountered by the average user are the read-only and the archive attributes.

When a file's **read-only attribute** is turned off, the default state, it can be read, written, modified, or deleted. If the file's read-only attribute is turned on, it cannot be changed in any way. The only way to modify or delete the file is to turn the read-only attribute back off again.

The **archive attribute** indicates whether a file has been changed since it was last saved with the BACKUP command. The archive attribute is turned on whenever a file is rewritten to disk (that is, changed in some way). When the BACKUP command saves a file, its archive attribute is turned off. This is how DOS can tell if a file has been changed since you last backed it up.

Step 1: Change the Read-only Attribute

Suppose the SAMPLE.TXT file was an extremely important file that you did not want to accidentally delete. One way to help ensure that it would not be deleted would be to turn on its read-only attribute. This can be done with the ATTRIB command.

Make sure you are in the LESSONS subdirectory, and then execute this command:

```
Type   attrib +r sample.txt
Press  Enter
```

This command turns on the read-only attribute for the file SAMPLE.TXT. Now, this file cannot be changed or deleted. Try the following three commands:

```
Type   type sample.txt
Press  Enter
Type   erase sample.txt
Press  Enter
Type   dir
Press  Enter
```

As you can see from Figure 14, you can read the file, but you cannot delete it after the read-only attribute has been turned on. DOS replies with "Access denied" when you try to delete a read-only file. Entering the DIR command confirms that the file SAMPLE.TXT has not been deleted.

Figure 14 Using ATTRIB to Set the Read-only Attribute

```
C:\LESSONS>attrib +r sample.txt

C:\LESSONS>type sample.txt
This is a sample text file.

C:\LESSONS>erase sample.txt
Access denied

C:\LESSONS>dir

 Volume in drive C is HARD DISK
 Volume Serial Number is 3324-07CC
 Directory of  C:\LESSONS

.              <DIR>      07-15-89  11:06a
..             <DIR>      07-15-89  11:06a
SAMPLE   TXT        29 07-15-89  11:06a
SAMPLE2  TXT       113 07-15-89  11:08a
SAMPLE3  TXT       143 07-15-89  11:09a
COMMAND  BAK     37557 12-19-88  12:00a
        6 File(s)   19650560 bytes free

C:\LESSONS>_
```

Step 2: Change the Archive Attribute

The ATTRIB command can also be used to change the archive attribute. You could, for example, turn off the archive attribute for a file, even though it has been changed, to prevent it from being saved by the next BACKUP command. Execute the following command:

Type   **attrib -a sample.txt**
Press   **Enter**

This turns off the archive attribute for the SAMPLE.TXT file. Unless you change the file or the attribute again, it will not be saved by the next BACKUP command.

The ATTRIB command can also be used to view the current attributes of a file. Execute the following command:

Type   **attrib sample.txt**
Press   **Enter**

As Figure 15 shows, if you omit the R and A switches between the ATTRIB and the file name, DOS will report which attributes are turned on for that file. Since the read-only attribute is turned on and the archive attribute is turned off, DOS replies with only R before the full file name C:\LESSONS\SAMPLE.TXT.

You can also set both attributes at once with a single ATTRIB command. Turn the read-only attribute back off and the archive attribute back on by executing this command:

Type   **attrib -r +a sample.txt**
Press   **Enter**

Practice

1. Use the ATTRIB command to examine the file attributes of SAMPLE2.TXT.

2. Turn on the read-only attribute of SAMPLE2.TXT and then try to delete the file.

3. Turn off the read-only attribute of SAMPLE2.TXT.

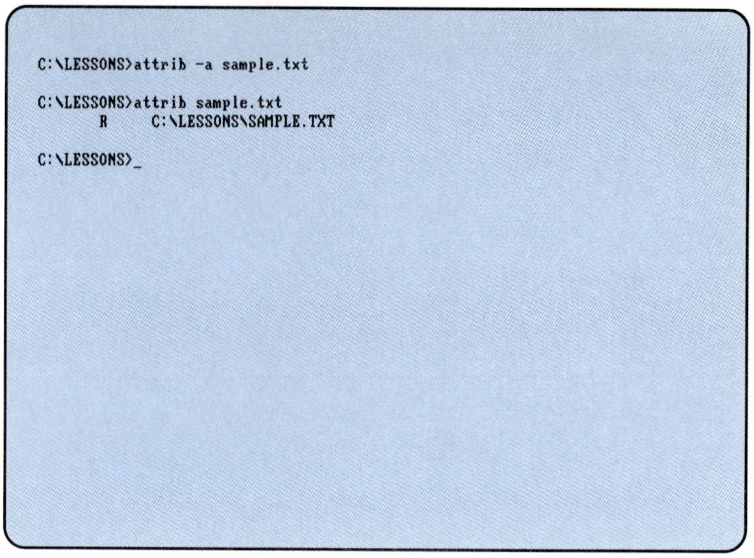

*Figure 15 Using ATTRIB to
Display a File's Attributes*

```
C:\LESSONS>attrib -a sample.txt

C:\LESSONS>attrib sample.txt
        R       C:\LESSONS\SAMPLE.TXT

C:\LESSONS>_
```

Lesson 12: Copying Groups of Files

In Chapter 2 you learned that you can copy groups of files with the COPY
command by using the global file name characters ? or * in your file specifications.
Starting with version 3.2, however, DOS included XCOPY, a more sophisticated
command for copying files. While the COPY command reads and then writes a
single file at a time, XCOPY reads as many files as it can into memory first and
then writes them. This makes XCOPY faster than COPY in some cases. In addition, XCOPY accepts more optional parameters, making it more flexible than
COPY. On the other hand, unlike COPY, XCOPY is an external command. This
means that XCOPY must be accessible on your disk if you want to use it.

Step 1: Copy a Group of Files with XCOPY

To see how XCOPY works, make sure you are in the LESSONS subdirectory on
your hard disk and put a formatted diskette in drive A. Then execute this command:

Type   **xcopy *.* a:**
Press   **Enter**

Your screen should look like Figure 16. XCOPY read all of the files in the LES-
SONS subdirectory into memory first, and then copied them to the diskette in
drive A.

Step 2: Copy Subdirectories

Unlike the COPY command, XCOPY can be instructed to copy files from all the
subdirectories in the source disk or directory. In the process, it will create new
subdirectories on the target disk if necessary. For example, change to the root
directory of your hard disk and try the following XCOPY command:

Type   **cd **
Press   **Enter**
Type   **xcopy sample.* a: /s**
Press   **Enter**

Figure 16 Using XCOPY to Duplicate a Group of Files

```
C:\LESSONS>xcopy *.* a:
Reading source file(s)...
SAMPLE.TXT
SAMPLE2.TXT
SAMPLE3.TXT
COMMAND.BAK
        4 File(s) copied

C:\LESSONS>_
```

XCOPY will look for all files with a primary filename of SAMPLE no matter what subdirectory they might be in. It will create corresponding subdirectories on the floppy disk in drive A and copy the files into the appropriate subdirectories. Execute the following two commands to see what you have done to your floppy disk:

Type   **dir a:**
Press **Enter**
Type   **dir a:\lessons**
Press **Enter**

Your screen should look like Figure 17.

Figure 17 Using XCOPY to Duplicate a Subdirectory

```
C:\>dir a:

 Volume in drive A has no label
 Volume Serial Number is 1A3F-12C9
 Directory of  A:\

SAMPLE   TXT         29 07-15-89  11:06a
SAMPLE2  TXT        113 07-15-89  11:08a
SAMPLE3  TXT        143 07-15-89  11:09a
COMMAND  BAK      37557 12-19-88  12:00a
LESSONS       <DIR>    07-15-89  11:39a
        5 File(s)    319488 bytes free

C:\>dir a:\lessons

 Volume in drive A has no label
 Volume Serial Number is 1A3F-12C9
 Directory of  A:\LESSONS

.             <DIR>    07-15-89  11:39a
..            <DIR>    07-15-89  11:39a
SAMPLE   TXT         29 07-15-89  11:06a
        3 File(s)    319488 bytes free

C:\>_
```

Step 3: Examine the Other XCOPY Parameters

Several other parameters can be used with the XCOPY command in addition to /S. The following table lists all of them.

Parameter	Action
/A	Copies only those files whose archive attribute is turned on. Does not change the archive attribute after copying.
/D:*date*	Copies only those files created or last modified on or after the specified *date*.
/E	Copies any subdirectories beneath the specified source disk or directory, even if they contain no files. This parameter, if used, must be used with /S.
/M	Same as /A, but turns off the archive attribute after copying.
/P	Prompts you for confirmation before each file is copied.
/S	Copies nonempty subdirectories beneath the specified source disk or directory.
/V	Verifies each copy to be identical to the original.
/W	Waits for you to press a key before copying files.

Practice

1. Try each of the following commands and explain exactly what they do. Answer **n** for no to each prompt to leave your diskette in drive A unchanged.

   Type **xcopy *.* a: /p /a**
   Press **Enter**
   Type **xcopy *.* a: /p /d:01-01-89**
   Press **Enter**
   Type **xcopy *.* a: /w /p /m**
   Press **Enter**

2. The XCOPY command can copy an entire diskette to another diskette, even if the source and target diskettes are different types, as long as the target diskette has enough room. For example, if you have a 5¼-inch floppy drive A and a 3½-inch floppy drive B, you would have to use XCOPY instead of DISKCOPY to duplicate a 5¼-inch diskette on a 3½-inch diskette. Even if you have only one floppy drive, you can use XCOPY to duplicate an entire diskette. Unlike DISKCOPY, however, XCOPY cannot automatically format a diskette. To copy an entire diskette with XCOPY, get an extra formatted diskette and execute the following command:

   Type **xcopy a: b: /s /e**
   Press **Enter**

   Note that this command will work even if you don't have a floppy drive B installed in your computer. DOS has the ability to "pretend" that drive A is temporarily drive B to complete such commands. It will prompt you when to insert the diskette for drive A or for drive B. Just swap the source and target diskettes in drive A. When you are finished, use DIR to examine the disk in drive A.

Lesson 13: Updating Sets of Files

Suppose you have identical copies of the file SAMPLE.TXT in various subdirectories on your hard disk and you want to update them all with a new copy of SAMPLE.TXT stored on a floppy disk. Although you cannot do this with a single COPY command, you can use a single REPLACE command. REPLACE is an external DOS command that is used to update previous versions of files.

Step 1: Prepare the Floppy Disk

Let's create an updated version of the file SAMPLE.TXT on the diskette in drive A. Then execute the following command to create a new SAMPLE.TXT:

Type   **`copy con a:sample.txt`**
Press   **Enter**

Now, do the following to add the text to SAMPLE.TXT in drive A:

Type   **`This is the new sample text file.`**
Press   **Enter**
Press   **F6**
Press   **Enter**

Step 2: Replace the Hard Disk Files

Suppose you had several copies of SAMPLE.TXT on the hard disk in different subdirectories. (You don't, but it doesn't matter for this example.) Execute the following command to replace all copies of SAMPLE.TXT on the hard disk with the new version from the floppy disk in drive A:

Type   **`replace a:sample.txt c:\ /s`**
Press   **Enter**

The /S parameter tells the REPLACE command to search through all subdirectories of the target for files to replace. To see what you have done, execute this command:

Type   **`type c:\lessons\sample.txt`**
Press   **Enter**

Your screen should look like Figure 18.

Step 3: Add Files to the Target Disk

The REPLACE command can also be used to copy files that exist on the source disk, but not on the target disk, to the target disk. Execute the following commands to move back into the LESSONS subdirectory on the hard disk and rename a few of the files:

Type   **`cd lessons`**
Press   **Enter**
Type   **`ren sample.txt part1.txt`**
Press   **Enter**
Type   **`ren sample2.txt part2.txt`**
Press   **Enter**
Type   **`ren sample3.txt example.txt`**
Press   **Enter**

Figure 18 Replacing Files on the Hard Disk

```
C:\>replace a:sample.txt c:\ /s

Replacing C:\LESSONS\SAMPLE.TXT

1 file(s) replaced

C:\>type c:\lessons\sample.txt
This is the new sample text file.

C:\>_
```

Now your LESSONS subdirectory on the hard disk contains the files PART1.TXT, PART2.TXT and EXAMPLE.TXT. The floppy disk in drive A does not contain files with these three names. Suppose you wanted to copy *only* those files with different names from C to A. Execute this command:

Type **replace *.* a: /a**
Press **Enter**

The /A is a parameter that tells the REPLACE command to add files from the source to the target, but only those that don't already exist in the target. To see the result, execute this command:

Type **dir a:**
Press **Enter**

Your screen should look like Figure 19.

Step 4: Examine the Other REPLACE Parameters

Several other parameters can be used with the REPLACE command. The following table lists all of them.

Parameter	Action
/A	Adds new files to the target instead of replacing existing files. Cannot be used with /S or /U.
/P	Prompts you for confirmation before each file is replaced.
/R	Replaces read-only files as well as regular files.
/S	Searches all subdirectories on the target disk to replace matching files. Cannot be used with /A.
/U	Replaces only those target files that are older than their matching source files. Cannot be used with /A.
/W	Waits for you to press a key before replacing or adding files.

Figure 19 Using REPLACE to Add Files

```
Adding A:\PART1.TXT

Adding A:\PART2.TXT

Adding A:\EXAMPLE.TXT

3 file(s) added

C:\LESSONS>dir a:

 Volume in drive A has no label
 Volume Serial Number is 1A3F-12C9
 Directory of  A:\

SAMPLE    TXT         35 07-15-89  11:45a
SAMPLE2   TXT        113 07-15-89  11:08a
SAMPLE3   TXT        143 07-15-89  11:09a
COMMAND   BAK      37557 12-19-88  12:00a
LESSONS       <DIR>     07-15-89  11:39a
PART1     TXT         35 07-15-89  11:45a
PART2     TXT        113 07-15-89  11:08a
EXAMPLE   TXT        143 07-15-89  11:09a
        8 File(s)      316416 bytes free

C:\LESSONS>_
```

Practice

Make sure you are in the LESSONS subdirectory on the hard disk and execute the following command to change the EXAMPLE file:

> Type **copy part1.txt+part2.txt example.txt**
> Press **Enter**

Execute this command and explain what it does:

> Type **replace *.* a: /w /p /r /u**
> Press **Enter**

Press any key to continue and answer **y** for yes to the prompt.

Lesson 14: Transferring the DOS System Files

When you format a system diskette with the /S parameter as you learned in Lesson 9 of Chapter 2, DOS copies two hidden system files to the newly formatted disk. These files, along with the command processor, COMMAND.COM, let you boot up your computer from that disk. It is also possible to format a diskette and leave space for the system files to be transferred later. This is sometimes done by individuals and companies that transfer software or data to others. It is not legal to give away or sell DOS without a license from IBM or Microsoft, so you are not supposed to distribute boot-up disks. You can, however, format a disk so that the recipient can transfer his or her own copy of DOS to that disk. The SYS command makes this possible. The SYS command is also used for upgrading to a new version of DOS. SYS, which is an external command, will not work if you are running DOS from a network.

Step 1: Format a Diskette with the /B Parameter

Execute this command to format a diskette to which DOS can be transferred later:

> Type **format a: /b**
> Press **Enter**

Insert the diskette you have been using into drive A and press the **Enter** key. When the format procedure is finished, press **Enter** to skip typing a volume label and enter **n** for no in response to the prompt asking if you want to format another disk. As you can see from Figure 20, DOS reserved 73,728 bytes for the system. The hidden system files, however, have not yet been transferred to this space.

Step 2: Transfer the Hidden System Files

To transfer the hidden system files, execute this command:

> Type   **sys a:**
> Press   **Enter**

When DOS is finished, it will display the message "System transferred," but if you examine the disk with the DIR command, no files will appear in the directory. This is because the system files are hidden.

Step 3: Copy the File COMMAND.COM

One more step is necessary in order to be able to boot up your computer from this diskette. Execute the following command to copy the DOS command processor from the root directory of your hard disk to the diskette in drive A:

> Type   **copy c:\command.com a:**
> Press   **Enter**

The diskette in drive A can now be used to boot up the computer.

Practice   1. Reboot your computer from the system diskette you just created. Enter the current date and time. Use DIR to examine the directory of your diskette. The procedure you followed in this lesson achieves the same result as using the /S parameter with the FORMAT command.

Figure 20 Using the /B Parameter with FORMAT

```
C:\LESSONS>format a: /b
Insert new diskette for drive A:
and press ENTER when ready...

Format complete

Volume label (11 characters, ENTER for none)?

     362496 bytes total disk space
      73728 bytes used by system
     288768 bytes available on disk

       1024 bytes in each allocation unit
        282 allocation units available on disk

Volume Serial Number is 283D-13CC

Format another (Y/N)?n
C:\LESSONS>_
```

2. Now, reboot your computer from the hard disk. Enter the date and time if necessary. Change the DOS prompt so it displays the current drive and directory, if it does not already do so.

Lesson 15: Comparing Files and Disks

Keeping one or more copies of important files or disks is prudent. After you make a copy of an especially important file or diskette, you might want to check it to make sure that it is identical to the original. Although errors are rare, a bit or byte can get scrambled during the copy procedure if the VERIFY option is turned off. DOS has two external commands, COMP and DISKCOMP, that compare files and diskettes, respectively. These commands can also be used if you forget whether two files or disks are identical. Note: DISKCOMP will not work if you are running DOS from a network.

Step 1: Compare Two Files

Change to your LESSONS subdirectory if you are not already there. Use the directory command to examine the files inside LESSONS. It should contain a file named COMMAND.BAK, which you created in Lesson 9. Let's see if COMMAND.BAK in the LESSONS subdirectory is identical to COMMAND.COM in the root directory of your hard disk. Execute this command:

> Type   **comp command.bak c:\command.com**
> Press   **Enter**

Your screen should look like Figure 21. The files are identical, so DOS reports that the "Files compare OK." Press **n** for no in response to the prompt asking if you want to compare more files. If the files had been different sizes or if any bytes had been different, DOS would have told you.

Figure 21 Using COMP to Compare Two Files

```
C:\LESSONS>comp command.bak c:\command.com


C:COMMAND.BAK and C:\COMMAND.COM

EOF mark not found
Files compare OK
Compare more files (Y/N) ?_
```

Step 2: Compare Two Diskettes

The DISKCOMP command is used to compare the contents of two diskettes. For example, if your computer has two floppy drives, A and B, that are the same type, put a diskette in each one and compare them with this command:

Type   **diskcomp a: b:**
Press   **Enter**

If your computer has only one floppy disk drive, like many hard disk systems, try this command instead:

Type   **diskcomp a: a:**
Press   **Enter**

DOS will then prompt you when to insert each diskette. If the two diskettes are identical, then DOS will display "Compare OK." Otherwise, "Compare error" messages will be displayed that report where mismatches were found. When it is finished, DISKCOMP will ask you if you want to compare another diskette. Type **n** for no.

Practice

1. Let's see what COMP does if two files are different. Try this command:

   Type   **comp part1.txt part2.txt**
   Press   **Enter**

   The COMP command determines immediately that the files are different sizes, so they cannot be identical. It doesn't examine them any further.

2. Now let's try comparing two files that are the same size, but different in some other way. Follow these instructions to create a file similar, but not identical, to PART1.TXT:

   Type   **copy con partx.txt**
   Press   **Enter**
   Type   **This is the old sample text file.**
   Press   **Enter**
   Press   **F6**
   Press   **Enter**

   Compare PART1.TXT with PARTX.TXT with this command:

   Type   **comp part1.txt partx.txt**
   Press   **Enter**

   Since COMP is typically used by programmers, the results are given in hexadecimal (base 16) ASCII codes. For example, the letter "n" is represented as 6E and "o" is 6F. COMP shows three differences between the two files: the letters "n e w" versus "o l d."

Lesson 16: Displaying and Changing a Volume Label

DOS calls the name of a disk the **volume label.** This name, which is optional, can be helpful when trying to identify a disk.

Step 1: Display a Volume Label

One way to see the volume label of a disk is to use the DIR command. Another way is to use the internal command VOL. Try this:

> Type   **vol**
> Press   **Enter**

DOS will display the volume label of the disk in your default drive. You can get the volume label of a disk other than the one in your default drive by specifying the disk drive letter. For example, put a formatted diskette into drive A and execute this command:

> Type   **vol a:**
> Press   **Enter**

DOS will respond with the volume label of the diskette in drive A.

Step 2: Change a Volume Label

DOS versions 4.0 and newer automatically ask you to supply a volume label whenever you format a disk. With earlier DOS versions, you can use the /V parameter to have the FORMAT command prompt you for a volume label. You can also specify a new volume label or change an existing one with the LABEL command. LABEL is an external command; it does not work if you are running DOS from a network. To see how it works, put a formatted diskette in drive A and execute this command:

> Type   **label a:**
> Press   **Enter**

DOS will report the current volume label and allow you to enter a new name, which can be up to 11 characters long.

> Type   **sample**
> Press   **Enter**

To see the new volume label of the diskette, execute this command:

> Type   **vol a:**
> Press   **Enter**

Figure 22 shows the result.

Practice

1. If you specify the new volume label right after the LABEL command, DOS won't prompt you. Try this command:

   > Type   **label a:example**
   > Press   **Enter**

   Use DIR or VOL to examine the new volume label.

2. You can also delete an existing volume label. Try the following:

   > Type   **label a:**
   > Press   **Enter**
   > Press   **Enter**
   > Type   **y**

3. VER is an internal DOS command similar to VOL. It is used to find out the version of DOS you are using, in case you don't know or forget. Try it:

Type   **ver**
Press **Enter**

Lesson 17: Displaying and Changing the Date and Time

If no AUTOEXEC.BAT file is present in the root directory of the startup disk, DOS will prompt you to enter the new date and time whenever you boot up or reboot the computer. If an AUTOEXEC.BAT file is present, DOS will not prompt you for the date and time unless the commands DATE and TIME are in AUTO-EXEC.BAT. DATE and TIME are internal commands that let you see and change the current date and time kept by the computer's real-time clock. Most microcomputers sold today have a battery that keeps the real-time clock operating even when the computer is off, so you don't need to execute DATE and TIME every time you boot up. Nevertheless, you can still use DATE and TIME to see the current date and time. In addition, DATE and TIME are sometimes needed to correct the internal clock, such as when changing to or from daylight saving time. It is important to set your computer to the correct date and time so that you know when files were created or last changed.

Step 1: Execute the DATE Command

To see the current date kept by your computer, without changing it, execute this command:

Type   **date**
Press **Enter** (2 times)

Step 2: Change the Date

One way to change the current date is to execute the DATE command without any parameters. DOS will prompt you to enter the new date. Another way to change the date is to specify the new date after the DATE command before you press Enter. For example, execute this command:

Type   `date 1-1-90`
Press   **Enter**

Now, use the DATE command without any parameters to see the date you set. Notice how DOS automatically figures out the correct day of the week.

When you specify a new date, you must use only numbers: 1–12 for the month, 1–31 for the day, and 80–79 or 1980–2079 for the year. The month, day, and year entries may be separated with hyphens (-) or slashes (/).

Step 3: Execute the TIME Command

To see the current time kept by your computer, without changing it, execute this command:

Type   `time`
Press   **Enter** (2 times)

Step 4: Change the Time

One way to change the current time is to execute the TIME command without any parameters. DOS will prompt you to enter the new date. Another way to change the time is to specify the new time after the TIME command before you press Enter. For example, execute this command:

Type   `time 14:22:13.45`
Press   **Enter**

Now, use the TIME command without any parameters to see the time you set (see Figure 23). Notice that the new time starts ticking as soon as you enter it.

When you specify a new time, you must use the 24-hour format. If you like, you can specify a new time accurate to hundredths of seconds. The command you just executed sets the time to 22 minutes, 13.45 seconds past 14 hundred hours (2 P.M.). You don't have to enter the seconds or hundredths of seconds. If the time is exactly on the hour, you don't have to enter the minutes. Any portion of the time you omit will be set to zero.

Practice

1. Use the DATE command to reset the correct date.

2. Use the TIME command to reset the correct time.

3. Check the current date and time again.

Lesson 18: Displaying a Memory Report

Starting with version 4.0, DOS includes MEM, an external command that presents a memory report. This report displays the amount of memory used and free. It can also specify the location, size, and name of each program or data area

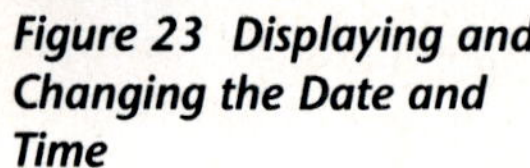

Figure 23 Displaying and Changing the Date and Time

```
C:\>date
Current date is Sun 07-16-1989
Enter new date (mm-dd-yy):

C:\>date 1-1-90

C:\>date
Current date is Mon 01-01-1990
Enter new date (mm-dd-yy):

C:\>time
Current time is 10:41:11.84a
Enter new time:

C:\>time 14:22:13.45

C:\>time
Current time is  2:22:15.09p
Enter new time:

C:\>_
```

currently loaded into memory. MEM can provide more detailed and technical information about memory usage than CHKDSK.

Step 1: Execute the MEM Command

If you don't have DOS 4.00 or newer, you cannot use MEM. Otherwise, execute this command:

Type   **mem**
Press   **Enter**

Figure 24 shows the result, although your report may have different numbers, depending on the amount of RAM installed and the programs that have been loaded in your computer.

Figure 24 Using MEM to Display a Memory Report

```
C:\>mem

    655360 bytes total memory
    655360 bytes available
    521248 largest executable program size

C:\>_
```

Step 2: Use the /PROGRAM Parameter

The MEM command has an optional parameter that will also display the programs loaded into memory. Execute this command:

> Type   **mem /program**
> Press   **Enter**

The resulting report will be longer and contain technical details concerning the location, name, and size of each program and data area in memory.

MEM has one other optional parameter, /DEBUG, that provides even more detailed information than the /PROGRAM parameter. The /DEBUG parameter presents technical facts of interest mainly to assembly language programmers, but you can still try it. Execute this command:

> Type   **mem /debug**
> Press   **Enter**

The /PROGRAM and /DEBUG parameters cannot be used at the same time.

Lesson 19: Reassigning, Joining, and Substituting Drives

DOS has three external commands that influence the use of disk drives and subdirectories, namely ASSIGN, JOIN, and SUBST. These commands can be handy when working with programs that require certain disks to be in certain drives, when programs don't allow you to specify paths, or when paths get too long. JOIN and SUBST do not work when running DOS from a network.

Step 1: Execute the ASSIGN Command

The ASSIGN command lets you change the drive letter associated with a disk drive. It is sometimes used with application programs developed before hard disks were common. A program, for example, may only work with diskette drives A and B. With ASSIGN, however, you may be able to trick the program into thinking that your hard disk is drive A. Make sure you are at the root directory of your hard disk and then execute this command:

> Type   **assign a = c**
> Press   **Enter**

To see the result, execute this command:

> Type   **dir a:**
> Press   **Enter**

DOS will present the directory of the hard disk, not the diskette in drive A. It "thinks" the hard disk is drive A, even though the DOS prompt still reports your current drive and directory as C:\ (see Figure 25).

To change all drives back to their original assignments, execute this command:

> Type   **assign**
> Press   **Enter**

Figure 25 Using ASSIGN to Change a Drive's Letter

```
C:\>assign a = c

C:\>dir a:

 Volume in drive A is HARD DISK
 Volume Serial Number is 3324-07CC
 Directory of  A:\

CONFIG   SYS        146 07-09-89   1:22p
COMMAND  COM      37557 12-19-88  12:00a
DOS          <DIR>      07-09-89   1:23p
LESSONS      <DIR>      07-12-89   4:01p
AUTOEXEC BAT        256 01-01-80  12:03a
        5 File(s)   19652608 bytes free

C:\>_
```

In practice, you should avoid using ASSIGN if at all possible because it disguises the true type of the disk drive. Microsoft suggests that you use an equivalent SUBST command instead, which we will discuss shortly, because ASSIGN may not be compatible with future versions of DOS.

Step 2: Execute the JOIN Command

The JOIN command lets you treat an entire disk as if it were a subdirectory on another disk. You can then work with files on multiple disks as if they were part of one subdirectory on one disk. Let's try an example. Make sure you are at the root directory of your hard disk. Create a new subdirectory by executing this command:

Type **md diska**
Press **Enter**

Put a formatted diskette in drive A. Then execute this command:

Type **join a: diska**
Press **Enter**

To see the result, execute these commands:

Type **join**
Press **Enter**
Type **dir diska**
Press **Enter**

Figure 26 shows the result. When the JOIN command is entered without any parameters, it displays the current drives and subdirectories that are joined. The DIR command presents the files on the floppy disk, in this case just COMMAND.COM, as if they were in the DISKA subdirectory on the hard disk.

You use the /D parameter to undo a previous JOIN command. Execute the following commands to disconnect the join and remove the DISKA subdirectory:

Type **join a: /d**
Press **Enter**

Figure 26 Using JOIN to Treat a Disk as a Subdirectory

```
C:\>md diska

C:\>join a: diska

C:\>join
A: => C:\DISKA

C:\>dir diska

 Volume in drive C is HARD DISK
 Volume Serial Number is 3324-07CC
 Directory of  C:\DISKA

COMMAND  COM     37557 12-19-88  12:00a
        1 File(s)   19650560 bytes free

C:\>_
```

Type **rd diska**
Press **Enter**

Step 3: Execute the SUBST Command

SUBST is the opposite of the JOIN command; it lets you treat a subdirectory as if it were a disk in a separate drive. For example, let's substitute the imaginary drive letter D for your LESSONS subdirectory. If you have a real disk drive D in your computer, choose a different letter. Make sure you are at the root directory of your hard disk and execute these commands:

Type **subst d: lessons**
Press **Enter**
Type **subst**
Press **Enter**
Type **dir d:**
Press **Enter**

SUBST entered without any parameters reports the substitutions that have been made. As Figure 27 shows, the subdirectory C:\LESSONS can now be referred to as simply D:.

You use the /D parameter to cancel a previous substitution. For example, execute the following command:

Type **subst d: /d**
Press **Enter**

Note that the following DOS commands do not work on drives used in the JOIN or SUBST commands: BACKUP, CHKDSK, DISKCOMP, DISKCOPY, FDISK, FORMAT, LABEL, RECOVER, RESTORE, and SYS.

Practice

The MS-DOS 4.01 *User's Reference* manual suggests that you use the SUBST command instead of ASSIGN. Repeat Step 1 of this lesson, except execute the following command instead of the ASSIGN command:

Type **subst a: c:**
Press **Enter**

Figure 27 Using SUBST to Treat a Subdirectory as a Disk

```
C:\>subst d: lessons

C:\>subst
D: => C:\LESSONS

C:\>dir d:

 Volume in drive D is HARD DISK
 Volume Serial Number is 3324-07CC
 Directory of  D:\

 .            <DIR>      07-15-89  11:06a
 ..           <DIR>      07-15-89  11:06a
 PART1    TXT        35 07-15-89  11:45a
 PART2    TXT       113 07-15-89  11:08a
 EXAMPLE  TXT       149 07-15-89  11:48a
 COMMAND  BAK     37557 12-19-88  12:00a
 PARTX    TXT        35 07-15-89   2:49p
          7 File(s)    19652608 bytes free

C:\>_
```

When you are finished examining the directory, use the SUBST command with the /D parameter to restore the original drive assignments.

Lesson 20: Learning More About the PRINT Command

PRINT is a sophisticated command that can print one or more files in the background while you continue your work with DOS. This limited multitasking ability is called **spooling.** Several PRINT parameters allow you to fine-tune this spooling capability on your computer.

Step 1: Examine the First Time PRINT Parameters

Several of the PRINT parameters may be used only the first time you execute the PRINT command after booting up. These parameters set the stage for the way PRINT will work for the rest of your DOS session. You have already used the PRINT command since you booted up, so don't try the following parameters. Just read and try to understand the explanations.

Parameter	Action
/D:*device*	Specifies the device name of the printer to be used by PRINT. The default is PRN or LPT1, the printer connected to the first parallel port on your computer. LPT2, LPT3, and COM1 through COM4 are device names of other parallel ports and serial ports to which a printer might be connected. If you don't specify the /D parameter, DOS will prompt you for the device name the first time you use the PRINT command.
/B:*size*	Sets the size in bytes of the memory buffer to be used for data to be printed. The minimum and default value is 512. The maximum value is 1634. Larger values enable PRINT to work faster, but use more memory.

/U:*ticks*	Specifies how long in clock ticks PRINT should wait before giving up for a printer that is still busy. The minimum and default value is 1. The maximum value is 255.
/M:*ticks*	Specifies the number of clock ticks it can take to print a character. The value can range from 1 to 255. The default value is 2.
/S:*time*	Specifies the time interval PRINT must wait before getting the attention of the CPU. The value can range from 1 to 255. The default value is 8.
/Q:*number*	Specifies the number of files that can be held in the **print queue,** the list of files to be printed in the background. The number can range from 4 to 32. The default number is 10.

Step 2: Print Several Files

The remaining parameters to the PRINT command can be used any time, not just the first time PRINT is executed for a given DOS session. Change to your LESSONS subdirectory on the hard disk. If you have a printer, turn it on, but take it off line. In other words, press the On Line button so that the On Line light turns off. This will simulate a busy printer. Execute the following commands:

Type	**print part1.txt**
Press	**Enter**
Type	**print part2.txt**
Press	**Enter**
Type	**print example.txt**
Press	**Enter**

Figure 28 shows the result. Each time you execute a PRINT command, the file is placed in the queue and the DOS prompt returns.

Figure 28 Placing Files in the Print Queue

```
C:\LESSONS>print part1.txt


  C:\LESSONS\PART1.TXT is currently being printed

C:\LESSONS>print part2.txt


  C:\LESSONS\PART1.TXT is currently being printed
  C:\LESSONS\PART2.TXT is in queue

C:\LESSONS>print example.txt
Errors on list device indicate that it
may be off-line. Please check it.


  C:\LESSONS\PART1.TXT is currently being printed
  C:\LESSONS\PART2.TXT is in queue
  C:\LESSONS\EXAMPLE.TXT is in queue

C:\LESSONS>_
```

Step 3: Use the /C Parameter

The /C parameter removes a file from the print queue. Execute this command:

Type **print part2.txt /c**
Press **Enter**

PART2.TXT will not be printed.

Step 4: Use the /T Parameter

To remove all the files from the print queue, use the /T parameter like this:

Type **print /t**
Press **Enter**

Step 5: Use the /P Parameter

Press your printer's On Line button. The final PRINT parameter /P adds a file to the print queue. This default option is assumed if you don't specify any parameters. For example, try this command:

Type **print example.txt /p**
Press **Enter**

Executing the above command is the same as executing this command:

Type **print example.txt**
Press **Enter**

In either case, the file EXAMPLE.TXT will be printed.

Summary

- *Using the DOS editing and function keys.* Delete, Insert, Escape, and F1 through F6 perform various editing functions on the DOS command line.

- *Setting the BREAK option.* The BREAK command changes the status of the BREAK option, OFF or ON, which controls when Ctrl-Break will cancel a program.

- *Working with subdirectories.* MD or MKDIR creates a new subdirectory, CD or CHDIR moves into a subdirectory, TREE displays the structure of a disk, and RD or RMDIR removes an empty subdirectory.

- *Using the PATH and APPEND commands.* PATH sets up a directory search path for BAT, COM, and EXE files. APPEND sets up a directory search path for all other files.

- *Changing the DOS prompt.* PROMPT followed by one or prompt codes, such as pg, changes the DOS prompt.

- *Backing up and restoring disks and files.* BACKUP backs up all or part of a hard disk onto floppy diskettes. RESTORE copies files from backup diskettes onto a hard disk.

- *Recovering files from damaged disks.* RECOVER attempts to salvage data from a damaged disk.

- *Using the prompt option when erasing files.* The ERASE (or DEL) command's /P parameter causes DOS to ask for confirmation before erasing each file.

- *Appending files and copying files to devices.* The COPY command can be used to append two or more files together. It can also be used to copy data directly to devices such as displays and printers.

- *Setting the VERIFY option.* The VERIFY command changes the status of the VERIFY option OFF or ON, which controls error checking whenever writing data to a disk.

- *Changing file attributes.* The ATTRIB command can change the status of a file's read-only and archive attributes.

- *Copying groups of files.* XCOPY is often faster and more flexible than COPY for duplicating files, subdirectories, and disks.

- *Updating sets of files.* REPLACE is used to update existing files or add new files from one disk to another.

- *Transferring the DOS system files.* If a disk has been formatted with the /B parameter, SYS can transfer the hidden DOS system files to that disk.

- *Comparing files and disks.* COMP checks two files to see if they are identical. DISKCOMP checks two diskettes to see if they are identical.

- *Changing volume labels.* LABEL can display or change the name of a disk.

- *Changing the current date and time.* DATE and TIME can display or change the current date and time kept by the computer.

- *Displaying a memory report.* MEM can present a more detailed and technical memory report than CHKDSK.

- *Reassigning, joining, and substituting drives.* ASSIGN can change the drive letter associated with a disk drive. JOIN can tell DOS to treat an entire disk as if it were a subdirectory on another disk. SUBST can tell DOS to treat a subdirectory as if it were a disk in a separate drive.

- *Printing multiple files.* PRINT can print one or more files in the background. The /P, /C, and /T parameters add or remove files from the print queue.

Key Terms

As an extra review of this chapter, try defining the following terms.

archive attribute	path
ASCII file	print queue
binary file	read-only attribute
file attribute	root directory
hierarchical	spooling
incremental backup	volume label

Multiple Choice

Choose the best selection to complete each statement.

1. Which keys would you press to repeat the previous DOS command?

    (a) F1 and then Enter
    (b) F2 and then Enter
    (c) F3 and then Enter
    (d) Escape and then Enter

2. Which key would you press to skip over a character from the previous DOS command?

    (a) Insert
    (b) Delete
    (c) Escape
    (d) F1

3. What keypresses are influenced by the BREAK command?

    (a) Alt-Break
    (b) Ctrl-Break
    (c) Alt-Num Lock
    (d) Ctrl-Num Lock

4. Which item cannot be contained in a subdirectory?

    (a) file
    (b) subdirectory
    (c) DOS external command
    (d) disk

5. Every disk has a single main directory known as the

    (a) root directory
    (b) prime directory
    (c) subdirectory
    (d) master directory

6. Which expression is a valid path?

    (a) c: hard disk lessons
    (b) a:\lessons/c:
    (c) c:\lessons\part1
    (d) c:/lessons/part1

7. Which DOS command is used to create a new subdirectory?

    (a) MD
    (b) CD
    (c) RD
    (d) TREE

8. Which DOS command displays the subdirectory structure of a disk?

    (a) MD
    (b) CD
    (c) RD
    (d) TREE

9. What must be done before you can remove a subdirectory?

    (a) execute DIR
    (b) execute TREE
    (c) delete all files in the subdirectory
    (d) delete all files in the root directory

10. Which command is used to establish a subdirectory search path for BAT, COM, and EXE files?

    (a) APPEND
    (b) PATH
    (c) TREE
    (d) SEARCH

11. Which prompt codes would you use with the PROMPT command to have the DOS prompt always display the current path?

    (a) Hello
    (b) pg
    (c) dg
    (d) vq

12. Which command would back up the entire contents of the hard disk to diskettes in drive A?

    (a) backup c: a: /s
    (b) backup c:\lessons*.* a: /s
    (c) backup a: c: /s
    (d) backup hard disk a:

13. Which command is used to salvage files from damaged diskettes?
    - (a) RESTORE
    - (b) RECOVER
    - (c) COPY
    - (d) SYS

14. Of the following commands, which is the safest to use?
    - (a) del *.*
    - (b) erase *.*
    - (c) erase ????????.*
    - (d) erase *.* /p

15. Which device name stands for the keyboard or display screen?
    - (a) CON
    - (b) PRN
    - (c) LPT1
    - (d) COM1

16. Which command appends two files to form a third?
    - (a) append file1 + file2 file3
    - (b) copy file1 + file2 file3
    - (c) xcopy file1 + file2 file3
    - (d) diskcopy file1 + file2 file3

17. Which command makes it impossible to delete the file SAMPLE.TXT?
    - (a) attrib +r sample.txt
    - (b) attrib +a sample.txt
    - (c) attrib −r sample.txt
    - (d) attrib −a sample.txt

18. Which command will read as many files as it can into memory first, before copying them?
    - (a) copy a:*.* c:
    - (b) xcopy a:*.* c:
    - (c) copy a:*.* c: /all
    - (d) mem a:*.* c:

19. Which command will copy only those files from the disk in drive A that don't already exist on the disk in drive C?
    - (a) copy a:*.* c: /a
    - (b) xcopy a:*.* c: /a
    - (c) append a:*.* c: /a
    - (d) replace a:*.* c: /a

20. What command must have been used on a diskette before you can use the SYS command to copy the DOS system files to it?
    - (a) TREE
    - (b) APPEND
    - (c) FORMAT /S or FORMAT /B
    - (d) FORMAT /V

Fill-In

1. The simplest path is _______, which represents the root directory of the default drive.

2. You can copy files into a _______ just as if it were a separate disk.

3. The _______ command tells DOS the directories to be searched for files that have extensions other than BAT, COM, or EXE.

4. The _______ command lets you change the DOS prompt.

5. Unlike COPY, the _______ command can automatically use as many diskettes as needed to save the files from a hard disk.

6. The _______ command reinstates files that have been saved with the BACKUP command.

7. The _______ parameter of the ERASE (or DEL) command tells DOS to ask for confirmation before erasing each file.

8. You can use _______ names such as CON and PRN as if they were file names in commands such as COPY.

9. The _______ parameter of the COPY command tells DOS to verify that the copy has been made successfully with no errors.

10. Another term for text file is _______ file.

11. A _______ file is a file that contains programs or data that are not encoded as ASCII characters.

12. The _______ attribute indicates whether a file has been changed since it was last saved with the BACKUP command.

13. Unlike the COPY command, _______ can be instructed to copy files from all the subdirectories in the source disk or directory.

14. The _______ command is used to update previous versions of files.

15. The _______ command is used to compare the contents of two diskettes.

16. The _______ command lets you change the name of a disk.

17. Starting with version 4.0, DOS included _______, an external command that can present a memory report more detailed than CHKDSK.

18. The ASSIGN command lets you change the drive _______ associated with a disk drive.

19. The _______ command, which is the opposite of the JOIN command, lets you treat a subdirectory as if it were a disk in a separate drive.

20. The /T parameter of the PRINT command removes all files from the print _______.

Short Problems

1. Change to your LESSONS subdirectory on the hard disk if you are not already there. Use the ATTRIB command to turn on the read-only attribute for every file in the subdirectory. Hint: you can use the global file name character * to do this with a single command. Now try to erase every file in the LESSONS subdirectory. When you are finished, turn off the read-only attributes of all the files in the LESSONS subdirectory.

2. Put a formatted floppy disk in drive A. Back up the contents of the LESSONS subdirectory using the /L parameter to create a log file. Don't specify a file name after the /L. When the BACKUP command is finished, a file named BACKUP.LOG will exist in the root directory of your hard disk. Examine this file with the TYPE command. As you can see, BACKUP.LOG lists the date and time of the backup, as well as the backup disk number and full path and name of each backed-up file.

3. You can create many interesting and useful DOS prompts with the PROMPT command. For example, try the following command:

   Type **prompt Date = $d Time = t_pg**
   Press **Enter**

   Press **Enter** a few times to see the result. When you are finished, change the DOS prompt back to the way it was.

4. Insert a formatted floppy disk into drive A. If the LESSONS subdirectory isn't your current directory, change to it. Now, use the DIR command to see a directory listing of the LESSONS subdirectory. Notice that . and .. appear as the first two entries in the listing. These are special DOS designations for your current directory and the parent of your current directory. For example,

execute the following command to see a listing of the directory immediately above your current directory, which, in this case, happens to be the root directory of hard disk C:

> Type **dir ..**
> Press **Enter**

The . designation is equivalent to *.*, meaning your entire directory. Execute this command to see how it works:

> Type **xcopy . a:**
> Press **Enter**

This command will copy all of the files in your current directory, which happens to be LESSONS, to the disk in drive A.

5. Use the COPY command to copy all the files in your DOS subdirectory to a diskette in drive A. It doesn't matter if they all won't fit. Try to time, either with a watch or by counting, approximately how long this takes. Now, turn on the VERIFY option and then repeat the same COPY operation, timing the procedure in the same way. Does turning verification on cause the COPY command to take longer? Turn off the VERIFY option when you are finished.

6. Use the DATE command to find out what day of the week July 4, 2026 will fall on.

7. Create a new subdirectory named TEXT inside your LESSONS subdirectory. Copy all files with an extension of TXT from your LESSONS subdirectory to the LESSONS\TEXT subdirectory. Use the TREE command to display the structure of the LESSONS subdirectory. Then change to the LESSONS\TEXT subdirectory.

8. Make sure you are inside the LESSONS\TEXT subdirectory. You should have the files PART1.TXT, PART2.TXT, PARTX.TXT, and EXAMPLE.TXT inside the subdirectory. Create a new EXAMPLE.TXT file with the COPY command by appending PART2.TXT to PARTX.TXT. Use the TYPE command to examine the new EXAMPLE.TXT file.

9. Erase every file inside the LESSONS\TEXT subdirectory. Use the /P parameter to have DOS prompt you before erasing each file. Answer **y** for yes each time.

10. Use DIR to confirm that the LESSONS\TEXT subdirectory is empty. Move back to its parent subdirectory, LESSONS, by using the .. designation with the CD command. Remove the LESSONS\TEXT subdirectory, but leave the LESSONS subdirectory intact. Use DIR to confirm what you have done.

BEGINNING LOTUS 1-2-3

In This Chapter

Preview

The original 1-2-3 program was conceived by Mitch Kapor, founder of Lotus Development Corporation, in 1982. By that time Kapor had already teamed up with a programmer named Jonathan Sachs, who helped develop the software. Lotus 1-2-3 was first released in the fall of 1982. One year later, its sales had reached 53 million dollars. Designed specifically for the then new IBM Personal Computer, 1-2-3 was a best-seller because of its power, flexibility, and ease of use. The second major version of 1-2-3, which was released in 1985, sold extremely well. In 1989, after a long wait by computer industry standards, Lotus finally delivered two new releases of its venerable software: Lotus 1-2-3 Release 2.2 for low-end IBM-compatible microcomputers that use the 8088 or 8086 chip, and Lotus 1-2-3 Release 3.0 for more powerful machines that use the 80286 or 80386 chip. Despite increased competition from other powerful spreadsheet packages, such as Microsoft Excel and SuperCalc5, Lotus 1-2-3 remains the best-selling spreadsheet package, with at least 65 percent of the market. In this chapter and the next two chapters, you will learn to use Lotus 1-2-3. Most of the lessons can be completed with any version of 1-2-3, Release 2.0 or newer. A few lessons address special and advanced features introduced with Lotus 1-2-3 Release 2.2 and Release 3.0.

After studying this chapter, you will know how to

- start 1-2-3.
- create a worksheet.
- use 1-2-3 menus.
- save a worksheet.
- print a worksheet.
- quit 1-2-3.
- retrieve an existing worksheet.
- get help.
- move around a worksheet.
- edit cells.
- change column widths.
- delete and insert columns and rows.
- copy and move cells.
- format cells.
- undo commands.
- use formulas.
- use functions.

Getting Started

Although Lotus 1-2-3 is a large and sophisticated software package, it is easy to learn to use for basic spreadsheet tasks. Lotus 1-2-3 might be set up several different ways at your particular computer installation. You are most likely to use the package in one of three possible arrangements:

1. On a microcomputer with two floppy drives and 1-2-3 installed on several diskettes

2. On a microcomputer with a hard disk and 1-2-3 installed in a subdirectory named 123 or 123R3 (for Release 3.0)

3. On a microcomputer connected to a local area network with 1-2-3 installed on the network file server

Insight

Which Lotus Spreadsheet Software is Right for Me?

The release of Lotus 1-2-3's new 2.2 and 3.0 versions has created an embarrassment of riches for Lotus customers.

Spreadsheet users who, in the past, automatically reached for Lotus 1-2-3 now have to decide which Lotus version to use, or whether to drop Lotus and head for Microsoft's or some other company's product.

"It's a complex and difficult decision," said one spreadsheet user. "Before, it was much simpler. Then your choices were: stay put, change to release 3.0, or go to a third product. Now, you've got four choices. It makes the decision either very complex or very easy. If all you've got is 8088 machines, it's pretty easy. For those who don't, it's much more complex. Most of us are in that boat."

Which version to use depends on the customer's microprocessor and graphics adapter support. Lotus designed release 3.0 for computers using Intel's 80286 and 80386 chips. Release 2.2 was designed for first-generation computers, which have smaller memory capabilities. But what about companies with different generations of computers?

There are other considerations as well. Version 2.2 is a direct descendant of 2.01. Release 3.0, written in C language, has a new format that prevents it from being used with existing 1-2-3 add-in packages. To further complicate matters, there is some confusion about how easy it is to upgrade from 2.2 to 3.0.

Many customers are taking a wait-and-see attitude about the new Lotus releases. Changing software is too expensive to base on a snap judgement, and in many cases, may also require an even more costly hardware upgrade.

Source: Bob Francis, "Muddy Waters," *Datamation,* July 15, 1989, pp. 31–32.

You may need some additional direction from your instructor on how to start Lotus 1-2-3, but once you get situated, you should be able to do the following lessons.

Lesson 1: Running 1-2-3

You are all ready to start working with spreadsheets, but first you must boot up your computer and run 1-2-3.

Step 1: Boot Up the Computer

If your computer is not already turned on and running DOS, boot it up as you learned to do in the Beginning DOS chapter.

Step 2: Prepare Diskette or Subdirectory for Files

The Lotus 1-2-3 software is stored on its own diskettes or in its own subdirectory on a hard disk or network. It is best to prepare a separate diskette or subdirectory for the files you will create in the following lessons. If your computer has only floppy drives, obtain a formatted diskette with room for your files and insert it into drive B. If your computer has a hard disk, create a subdirectory called LESSONS, if you don't already have one, that you can use to store your files. If you are running on a network, your instructor may have other directions for you to follow.

Step 3: Insert the System Disk or Switch to the LESSONS Subdirectory

If you have a system with only floppy drives, remove the DOS startup diskette from drive A and replace it with the Lotus 1-2-3 diskette labeled "System Disk." The diskette to hold your data files should be in drive B. Go on to Step 4.

If you have a microcomputer with a hard disk, 1-2-3 should already be installed in its own subdirectory, named 123 or 123R3 for Release 3.0 (see Appendix B, Software Installation). The following lessons assume that a path has been set up so that you can run 1-2-3 from any subdirectory and that you have a LESSONS subdirectory on the hard disk for your files. Switch to the LESSONS subdirectory with this DOS command:

> Type   **cd c:\lessons**
> Press   **Enter**

If your computer is connected to a local area network, you may have to follow other directions from your instructor before actually starting 1-2-3.

Step 4: Invoke 1-2-3

Once you are in the proper disk drive directory, running 1-2-3 is easy.

> Type   **123**
> Press   **Enter**

It will take a few moments for 1-2-3 to be loaded from the disk into memory. A screen presenting the 1-2-3 logo and copyright information will appear (see Figure 1).

Most of the Lotus 1-2-3 figures you will see in this book have been created with Release 2.2. Some figures have been created with Release 3.0 to illustrate features available only in that version of 1-2-3. Except where indicated, all of the spreadsheet lessons can be completed with any version of 1-2-3, Release 2.0 or newer, although your screen may differ slightly from the figures you see in this book.

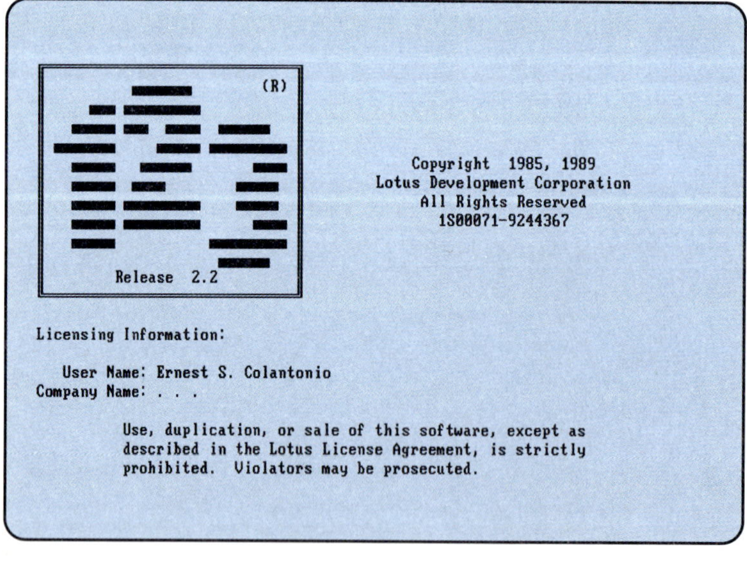

Figure 1 Lotus 1-2-3 Copyright Screen

Practice   Reboot your computer and start 1-2-3 again.

Lesson 2: Creating a Worksheet

As a simple example, let's use Lotus 1-2-3 to create a small budget worksheet. A **worksheet** is simply a table of data arranged into rows and columns. In the context of a spreadsheet program, **data** can be numbers, labels, or formulas. A **number** is a numeric quantity, such as 100, 52.34, or 0.05. A **label** is any kind of text, such as a title, heading, name, or address. A **formula** is an expression that tells the spreadsheet program to perform a calculation, such as 100 + 200.

Step 1: Examine the Worksheet Screen

After the copyright screen disappears, 1-2-3 presents the empty worksheet screen shown in Figure 2. The letters A through H across the top represent columns. The numbers 1 through 20 along the left side represent rows. Although you can see only 8 columns and 20 rows at the moment, the whole worksheet is actually much larger than this. Imagine the columns continuing out beyond the right edge of the screen and the rows continuing down below the bottom. A Lotus 1-2-3 worksheet has a maximum of 256 columns and 8,192 rows. The first 26 columns are labeled A through Z. The next 26 are labeled AA through AZ, the next 26 are labeled BA through BZ, and so on up to IV. The rows are simply numbered 1 through 8192.

Each intersection of a row and a column is called a cell. The **cell** is the basic unit of storage in a worksheet—where you put a number, label, or formula. Each cell is designated by its column letter(s) and row number. For example, A1 refers to the cell located at the intersection of the first column and the first row. This column-row designation is known as the **cell address** or **cell reference** because it uniquely identifies and locates each storage unit.

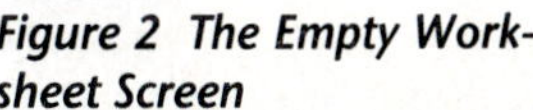

*Figure 2 The Empty Work-
sheet Screen*

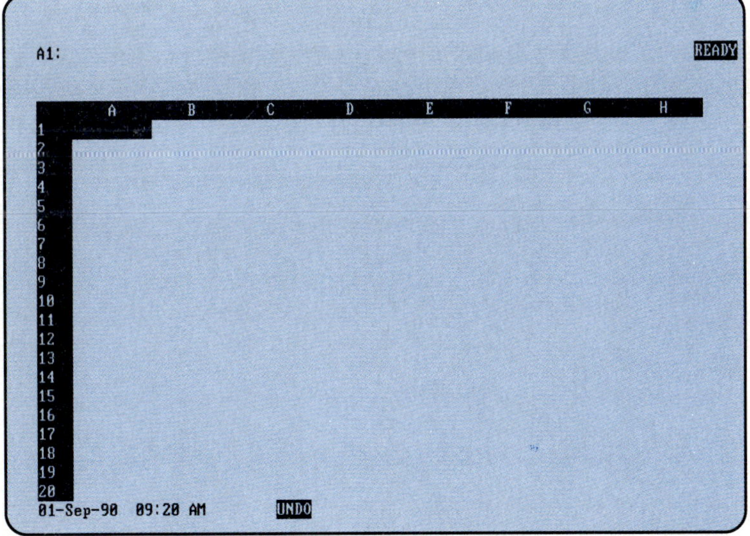

Lotus 1-2-3 can refer to 256 × 8,192 or 2,097,152 cells, but you cannot actually store data in all of these cells at once. The absolute number of cells you can fill depends on the amount of memory installed in your computer and several other factors. For example, on a microcomputer equipped with 640K of memory, you can fill around 40,000 cells with numbers before you run out of memory. Lotus 1-2-3 addresses more cells than you can possibly fill so that you can place your data in convenient locations.

As you can see in Figure 2, all of the cells are initially blank. The **cell pointer** is the highlighted bar that indicates the **current cell,** the place in the worksheet where you can enter data, perform a calculation, or initiate a command. The blinking underscore within the cell pointer is the cursor. When you start a new worksheet, A1 is the current cell.

The space at the top of the screen above the column letters is known as the **control panel.** It displays cell information, command choices, command descriptions, messages, and the mode in which 1-2-3 is operating. The address of the current cell appears in the upper left corner of the control panel. The blank space to the right of the current cell address indicates that the cell is empty. The highlighted block in the upper-right corner of the control panel is the **mode indicator,** which describes the current operating mode. Right now, the mode indicator displays READY, telling you that 1-2-3 is waiting for you to enter data or initiate a command.

Now look at the bottom of the screen. The lower left corner of the screen displays the current date and time. Lotus 1-2-3 Release 2.2 also shows the UNDO indicator, which tells you that you can use the Undo feature to cancel the last operation you performed. You will learn more about the Undo feature later in this chapter.

Step 2: Enter the Labels

Our simple budget worksheet will have text labels in column A and numbers in column C. Any text you enter that does not resemble a number or formula is assumed by 1-2-3 to be a label. To be more precise, a label is any text that does not begin with one of the following characters:

0 1 2 3 4 5 6 7 8 9 . + - ($ # @

If you want to begin a label, such as an address or phone number, with one of these characters, you must precede it with a **label prefix character.** This is a symbol, such as an apostrophe ('), that tells 1-2-3 to treat the characters that follow it as a label, not as a number or formula. You will learn more about label prefix characters later in this chapter.

To enter a label, type its characters, then press the Enter key or move the cell pointer. As you type, the characters will appear in the control panel. The characters are not actually stored in the cell until you press the Enter key or move the cell pointer. If you make a mistake before you press the Enter key or move the cell pointer, you can press the Backspace key to erase the characters, then retype them. Follow these directions to enter the labels into your worksheet:

Type   **Monthly Budget**
Press   **Down Arrow** (2 times)
Type   **INCOME**
Press   **Down Arrow** (2 times)
Type   **EXPENSES**
Press   **Down Arrow**

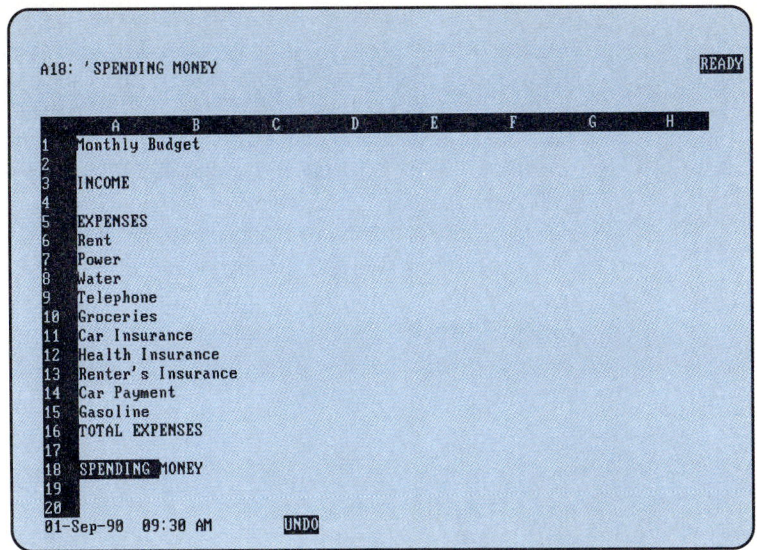

Figure 3 Labels Entered into the Worksheet

Type	**Rent**
Press	**Down Arrow**
Type	**Power**
Press	**Down Arrow**
Type	**Water**
Press	**Down Arrow**
Type	**Telephone**
Press	**Down Arrow**
Type	**Groceries**
Press	**Down Arrow**
Type	**Car Insurance**
Press	**Down Arrow**
Type	**Health Insurance**
Press	**Down Arrow**
Type	**Renter's Insurance**
Press	**Down Arrow**
Type	**Car Payment**
Press	**Down Arrow**
Type	**Gasoline**
Press	**Down Arrow**
Type	**TOTAL EXPENSES**
Press	**Down Arrow** (2 times)
Type	**SPENDING MONEY**
Press	**Enter**

Your screen should look like Figure 3.

Step 3: Enter the Numbers

Lotus 1-2-3 assumes an entry to be a number if it begins with one of the following characters:

0 1 2 3 4 5 6 7 8 9 . + - $ (

You may enter numbers without decimal points (like 10, -22, or 1234) or with decimal points (like .5, -0.12, or 11.123). You may not include spaces or commas in a number. You may precede a number with $+$ or \$, or enclose it in parentheses, but these characters will not be displayed in the worksheet. In addition to normal decimal notation, you may also enter numbers in scientific (exponential) notation. For example, $4.32E+05$ (which equals 432,000) and $-2.54E-05$ (which equals -0.0000254) are both valid number entries. Using scientific notation lets you include very large and very small numbers in your worksheet.

Entering numbers is just like entering labels; type them and press the Enter key or move the cell pointer. If you make a mistake before you press the Enter key or move the cell pointer, you can press the Backspace key to erase the number, then retype it. Follow these directions to move the cell pointer to C3, then enter the numbers into your worksheet:

Press	**Home**
Press	**Right Arrow** (2 times)
Press	**Down Arrow** (2 times)
Type	**2000**
Press	**Down Arrow** (3 times)
Type	**650**
Press	**Down Arrow**
Type	**125**
Press	**Down Arrow**
Type	**15**
Press	**Down Arrow**
Type	**75**
Press	**Down Arrow**
Type	**200**
Press	**Down Arrow**
Type	**50**
Press	**Down Arrow**
Type	**50**
Press	**Down Arrow**
Type	**15**
Press	**Down Arrow**
Type	**200**
Press	**Down Arrow**
Type	**50**
Press	**Down Arrow**

Your screen should look like Figure 4.

Step 4: Enter the Formulas

A formula is an expression that tells the spreadsheet program to perform a calculation. It can include arithmetic operators (such as $+$ and $-$), cell addresses, and functions. A **function** is a predefined formula that performs a useful operation, such as computing a sum or a square root. Lotus 1-2-3 has many functions, some of which we will discuss later in this chapter.

Our budget worksheet needs two formulas: one to compute the total expenses and the other to compute the spending money. At this point, C16 should be the current cell. Enter this formula to compute the total expenses:

Type	**@sum(c6..c15)**
Press	**Enter**

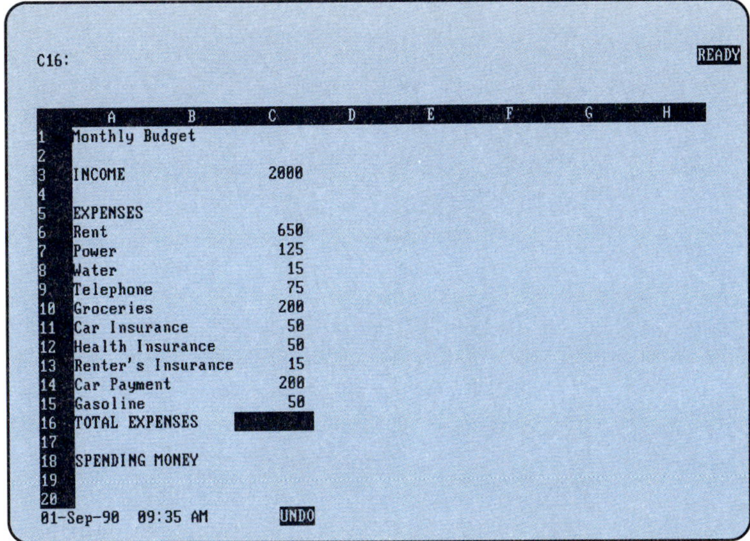

Figure 4 Numbers Entered into the Worksheet

The @ character, which must begin every function name, tells 1-2-3 that the following word is a function, not a label. The @SUM function adds the contents of a range of cells. A **range** is simply a block of adjacent cells, indicated by the address of the upper left cell, two periods, and the address of the lower right cell. The range C6..C15, for example, refers to cells C6, C7, C8, C9, C10, C11, C12, C13, C14, and C15. Note that function names and cell addresses may be entered in either uppercase or lowercase letters.

Your screen should look like Figure 5. The control panel reports that cell C16 actually contains the formula @SUM(C6..C15), but the computed result of that formula, the value 1430, is displayed in the worksheet.

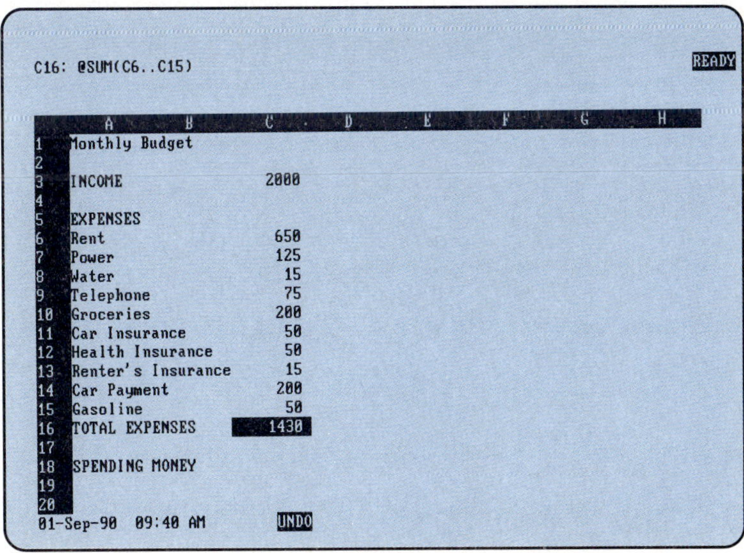

Figure 5 A Formula Entered into the Worksheet

Follow these directions to enter the other formula for this worksheet:

Press   **Down Arrow** (2 times)
Type   **+c3−c16**
Press   **Enter**

This formula tells 1-2-3 to subtract the total expenses result from the income figure. It begins with a plus sign because a formula must begin with one of these characters:

0 1 2 3 4 5 6 7 8 9 . + − (@ # $

The cell address C3 begins with a C. If you don't begin the formula with one of the above characters, 1-2-3 will assume the entry is a label and will not perform the calculation. The plus sign in front of the C3 does not change the result, it simply enables 1-2-3 to recognize the entry as a formula.

Step 5: Check and Correct Your Work

Check your screen against Figure 6 to see if you made any mistakes entering labels, numbers, or formulas. To correct a mistake, move the cell pointer with the arrow keys to the erroneous cell, retype the entry, and press the Enter key.

Practice

1. Move the cell pointer to a formula. Compare the contents of the control panel with the result you see displayed in the worksheet cell.

2. Move the cell pointer to a label. Notice the label prefix character displayed in front of the label in the control panel. The apostrophe (') is the default label prefix character automatically put in front of the label by 1-2-3. It appears in the control panel but not in the worksheet cell.

Figure 6 The Completed Worksheet

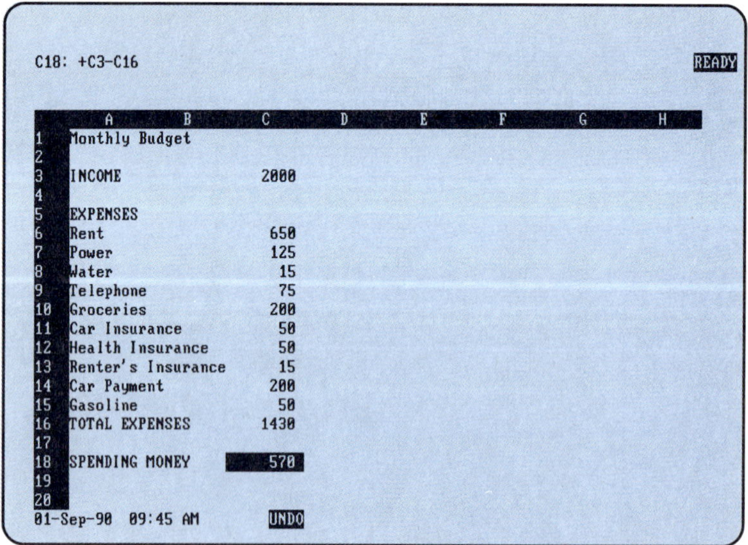

Lesson 3: Using 1-2-3 Menus

To accomplish many tasks in 1-2-3, you must select commands from menus. Commands allow you to work with, rearrange, and otherwise manipulate data stored in worksheet cells. In addition, you use commands to control the appearance, disk storage, and output of 1-2-3 worksheets. This lesson will briefly describe how to use the 1-2-3 command menus. Other lessons in this chapter and the next two chapters will cover the most important commands in more detail.

Step 1: Activate the Main Menu

Lotus 1-2-3 uses a system of pop-up menus that appear in the control panel only when activated. No menu appears in Figure 6, because 1-2-3 is in READY mode. Switch to MENU mode and display the Main menu in the control panel:

Type   /

Typing a forward slash key activates the Main menu of commands, shown in Figure 7. The mode indicator changes to MENU, and the second line of the control panel displays a list of commands. A highlighted block, known as the **menu pointer,** shows the command that will be invoked if you press the Enter key. The third line of the control panel displays information relevant to the highlighted command. In many cases this information is a list of additional options available when you invoke the highlighted command. For example, Worksheet is the command currently highlighted. If you press the Enter key, 1-2-3 will present the list of options in the third line of the control panel: Global, Insert, Delete, Column, Erase, Titles, Window, Status, Page, and Learn.

Step 2: Highlight a Command and Press Enter

One way to select a command from a menu is to position the menu pointer on the command you want and press the Enter key. For example, select the File command:

Press   **Right Arrow** (4 times)
Press   **Enter**

The menu of File commands will be activated. This method of selecting commands is often preferred by beginners because they can see information about a command on the third line of the control panel before they choose it.

Step 3: Return From a Menu

In many cases, you can return to a previous menu without executing a command. Suppose you have changed your mind about executing a command from the File menu. You can return to the Main menu from the File menu by pressing the Escape key.

Press   **Escape**

You can exit the Main menu and return to READY mode by pressing the Escape key again.

Press   **Escape**

The Main menu will disappear and the second and third lines of the control panel will be cleared.

Figure 7 The Main Menu

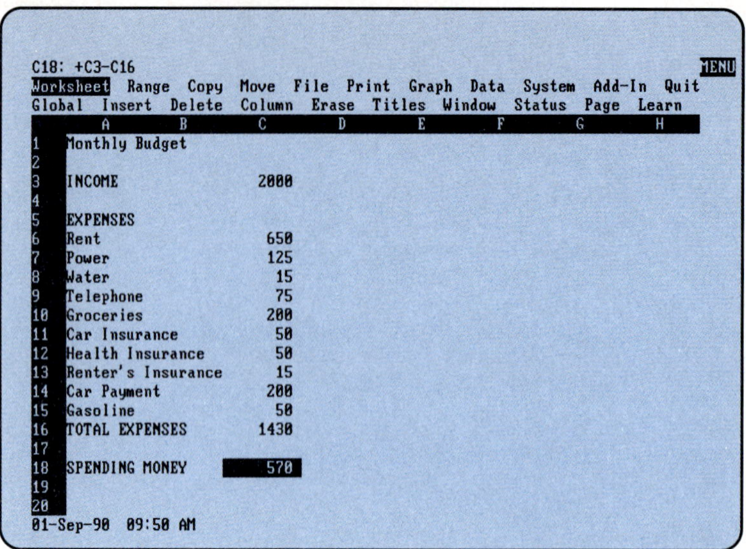

Step 4: Type the First Letter of a Command

Activate the Main menu again:

> Type   /

The second way to select a command from a menu is to type the first letter of the command. Each 1-2-3 menu is carefully designed so that every command begins with a different letter. Select the File option by typing its first letter:

> Type   **f**

Typing the first letter of a command is usually faster than moving the menu pointer and pressing the Enter key, but you don't get a chance to read the description of the command in the third line of the control panel. Users who are familiar with 1-2-3 menus often prefer to select commands this way. Now, exit the File menu and the Main menu and return to READY mode:

> Press   **Escape** (2 times)

Practice

1. Activate the Main menu.
2. Select the Print command by moving the menu pointer and pressing the Enter key, then exit the Print menu without executing a command.
3. Select the Range command by typing its first letter, then exit the Range menu and the Main menu to return to READY mode.

Lesson 4: Saving a Worksheet

The worksheet you see on the screen is held temporarily in memory. If you shut off your computer or the power goes out, the worksheet will be lost. To avoid losing your work, you must save your worksheet in a disk file. Saving a worksheet creates a more permanent copy of your work that can be later printed or retrieved and modified. You can create large worksheets a little at a time and make corrections, updates, and new versions without having to retype all of the entries.

You must save your worksheet before you leave 1-2-3 to use another application package. It is also prudent to save your worksheet every fifteen minutes or so as you work. By periodically saving your worksheet, you will guard against losing all of your work if you make a drastic mistake or a power failure occurs.

Step 1: Execute the File Save Command

The File Save command copies the current worksheet to a disk file. Execute the File Save command:

Type   **/fs**

Step 2: Enter the File Name

Lotus 1-2-3 will prompt you to enter the name of the file to save. Let's name the worksheet file BUDGET. If your computer has a hard disk and you are working from the LESSONS subdirectory, enter the file name:

Type   **budget**
Press   **Enter**

If your computer has only floppy disk drives and you want to store the worksheet on the diskette in drive B, follow these directions instead:

Press   **Escape**
Type   **b:budget**
Press   **Enter**

Lotus 1-2-3 Release 2.0 and Release 2.2 will store the worksheet in a file named BUDGET.WK1. The WK1 file name extension identifies worksheet files. Lotus 1-2-3 Release 3.0 will add the extension WK3 instead of WK1.

Practice   You can save your worksheet as many times as you like. After you name and save the worksheet the first time, 1-2-3 will remember the name, so the next time you save the worksheet you won't have to enter it again. Execute the File Save command and press Enter without typing the file name again. Lotus 1-2-3 will present a menu with three options: Cancel, Replace, and Backup. Select the Replace command to replace the file on the disk with the current worksheet. Note: Lotus 1-2-3 Release 2.0 does not present the Backup option.

Lesson 5: Printing a Worksheet

In many cases, a spreadsheet program is used to produce a finished worksheet printed on paper. Now that you have saved your worksheet, you may want to print it. If your computer is not connected to a printer, read this lesson and examine the figure without actually performing the steps.

Step 1: Execute the Print Command

The first step is to execute the Print command from the Main menu.

Type   **/p**

Step 2: Choose Printer or File

The Print command provides two options: Printer and File. Lotus 1-2-3 Release 3.0 has a few other options as well. The Printer option will send the output directly to the printer. The File option will create a text file that can be printed later or used in another application, such as a word processing package. If you have a printer, select the Printer option:

Type **p**

Step 3: Specify the Range

The program will display the Print Printer menu shown in Figure 8. Lotus 1-2-3 Release 2.2 will also present the Print Settings sheet, which shows the current values of various parameters, such as margins and page length. Before you can print a worksheet, you must tell 1-2-3 the range of cells you want to print. Select the Range option:

Type **r**

The program will prompt you to enter the print range. You can specify a range two ways. The first method is to type the range and press the Enter key. For example, to specify your entire worksheet

Type **a1..c18**
Press **Enter**

The other way to specify the range is to use POINT mode to highlight the range. To use POINT mode, move the cell pointer to the first cell in the range, type a period to anchor the cell pointer, move to the last cell in the range, then press the Enter key. If you would like to try the pointing method, follow these directions:

Type **r**
Press **Home**
Type **.**
Press **Right Arrow** (2 times)
Press **Down Arrow** (17 times)
Press **Enter**

Most 1-2-3 commands accept either of these two methods of specifying a range.

Step 4: Prepare the Printer

Make sure the printer is connected to the computer and turned on. Also, make sure that paper is loaded and aligned to the top of a new page. Finally, make sure that the printer's On Line light is lit. (If it isn't, press the On Line button.)

Step 5: Select the Go Option

To begin printing, select the Go option from the Print Printer menu:

Type **g**

The worksheet will be printed.

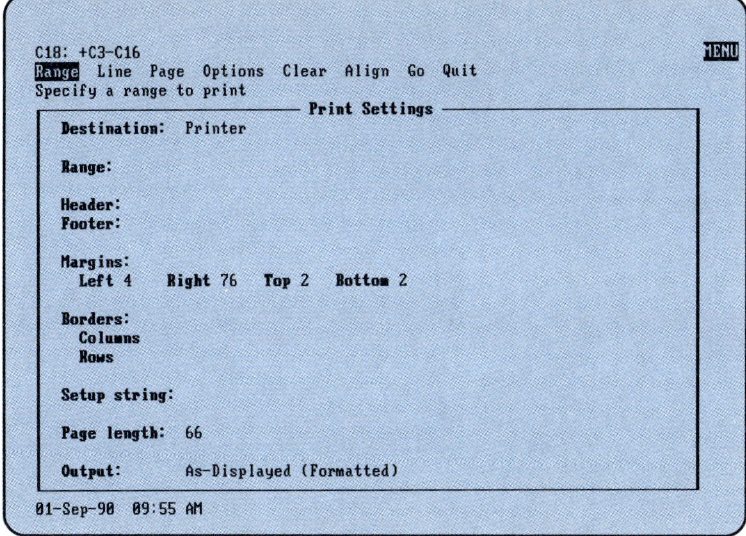

Figure 8 The Print Printer Menu and Print Settings Sheet

Step 6: Select the Page Option

If you like, you can tell 1-2-3 to have the printer advance to the top of the next page. Select the Page option from the Print Printer menu:

> Type   **p**

Step 7: Select the Quit Option

When you are finished printing, select the Quit option to exit the Print Printer menu and return to READY mode:

> Type   **q**

Practice

1. Print only this range from your worksheet: A1..A18.
2. Select the File option of the Print menu to produce a text file of your entire worksheet instead of sending it directly to the printer. Enter BUDGET as the file name. Precede the filename with B: if you have only floppy drives and want to put the file on the diskette in drive B. Lotus 1-2-3 will automatically add the file name extension PRN, indicating that it is a file to be printed.

Lesson 6: Quitting 1-2-3

You have entered, saved, and printed a worksheet. Suppose you are finished with Lotus 1-2-3 for now and want to return to DOS.

Step 1: Save the Worksheet

Although you have already saved your worksheet, you should save it again before you quit 1-2-3. This preserves the page settings created when you printed the worksheet. In addition, saving your worksheet before quitting records any changes you might have made since the previous save, and it is a good habit to form. Execute the File Save command:

Type   **/f s**
Press   **Enter**
Type   **r**

Since you have already named your worksheet the first time you saved it, you don't have to enter the file name again.

Step 2: Execute the Quit Command

Activate the Main menu and execute the Quit command:

Type   **/q**

You must confirm the quit by selecting the Yes option:

Type   **y**

The computer will exit 1-2-3 and return to DOS.

Practice

Start Lotus 1-2-3. Enter a number in cell A1. Do not save the worksheet. Execute the Quit Yes command. If you are running Lotus 1-2-3 Release 2.0, the program will immediately return to DOS. You are out of luck if you intended to save the worksheet but forgot to do so. If you are running Release 2.2 or 3.0, however, the program will display the prompt

WORKSHEET CHANGES NOT SAVED! End 1-2-3 anyway?

This warning is a welcome safety feature that tells you when you are attempting to quit without having saved your worksheet. If you really do want to save your worksheet, you can select No and then execute the File Save command. In this case, you do not want to save your worksheet, so select Yes and return to DOS.

Lesson 7: Retrieving an Existing Worksheet

Retrieving an existing worksheet is a very common procedure. You can easily examine, modify, or update a previously saved worksheet. Let's start 1-2-3 again and retrieve the BUDGET worksheet.

Step 1: Start 1-2-3

In the previous lesson, you quit 1-2-3 and returned to DOS. Start the program again:

Type   **123**
Press   **Enter**

Lotus 1-2-3 will display a new worksheet screen.

Step 2: Execute the File Retrieve Command

To load a previously saved worksheet, execute the File Retrieve command:

Type   **/f r**

Step 3: Select the File

Lotus 1-2-3 will prompt you for the name of the file to retrieve. The mode indicator will change to FILES, and the names of the worksheet files and the subdirectories in your current directory will be listed across the third line of the control panel (see Figure 9). If the file you want to retrieve is in the current directory, the easiest way to retrieve it is to use Left Arrow or Right Arrow to highlight it and press the Enter key. Alternatively, you can type the name of the file and press Enter. If you want to retrieve a file from a different disk or directory, press the Escape key twice, then enter the entire path and file name.

> Highlight   **BUDGET.WK1 (or BUDGET.WK3** for Release 3.0)
> Press   **Enter**

The worksheet will be loaded from the disk into memory and presented on the screen. The cell pointer will appear in the position it occupied when the worksheet was saved.

Practice   Change any cell in the BUDGET worksheet, but do not save the worksheet. Then execute the File Retrieve command and select the BUDGET worksheet. Lotus 1-2-3 Releases 2.0, 2.2, and 3.0 will all retrieve the file and overwrite the worksheet you have in memory without issuing a warning or confirmation prompt. You will lose the worksheet on the screen if you have not saved it whenever you retrieve an existing worksheet. Unfortunately, the designers of Lotus 1-2-3 did not add a safety feature for this situation. Always make sure you have either saved or will not need the worksheet on your screen before you retrieve an existing worksheet.

Lesson 8: Getting Help

Lotus 1-2-3 has an excellent on-line help facility that lets you retrieve information about the current command or choose from an index of topics. In many cases, using the help facility is faster and easier than consulting the printed reference manual.

Step 1: Highlight a Command

The Lotus 1-2-3 help system is **context-sensitive,** which means that it will provide information relevant to your current operation. For example, activate the Main menu:

> Type   /

The Worksheet command should be highlighted.

Step 2: Insert Help Disk If Necessary

If you are running Lotus 1-2-3 from a hard disk or a network, skip this step. If your computer has only two floppy drives and the file 123.HLP is not on the System Disk, remove the System Disk from drive A and replace it with the Help Disk.

Figure 9 The File Retrieve Command

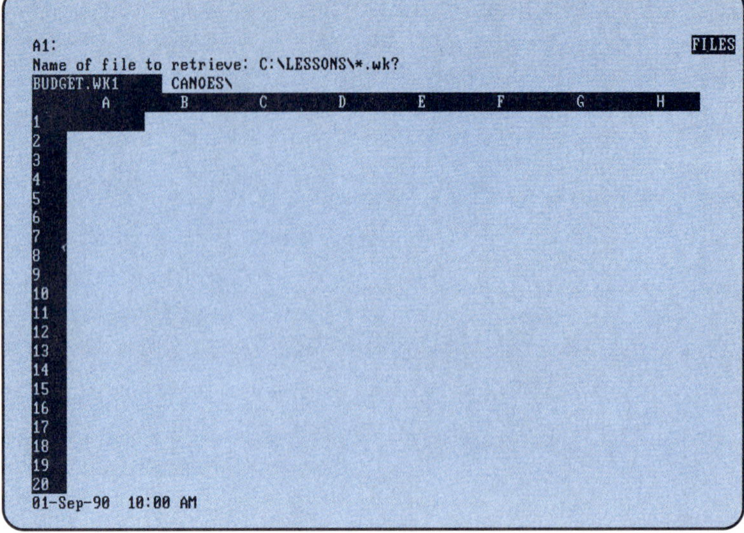

Step 3: Press the F1 Key

The help facility is activated by pressing the F1 function key.

Press   **F1**

Figure 10 shows the result. The screen provides information about the Main menu and selecting commands. The topic Worksheet Commands is highlighted. You can use the arrow keys to highlight another topic or press the Enter key to read about the highlighted topic.

Press   **Enter**

Lotus 1-2-3 will display another help screen with more detailed information about the topic you selected (see Figure 11).

Figure 10 Main Menu Help Screen

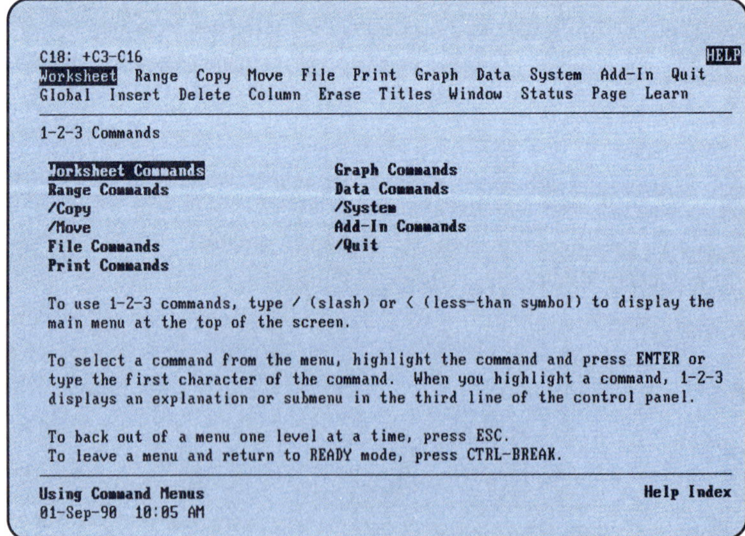

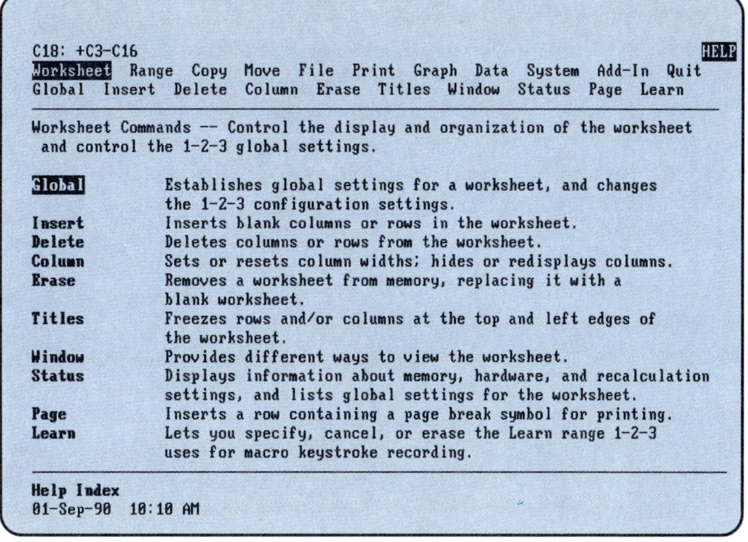

Figure 11 Worksheet Command Help Screen

Step 4: View the Help Index

You can see an index of the available help topics at any time. Highlight the Help Index topic at the bottom of the screen and press Enter:

Press   **Up Arrow**
Press   **Enter**

Figure 12 shows the Help Index. You can highlight any topic in this index and press the Enter key to see more information about it.

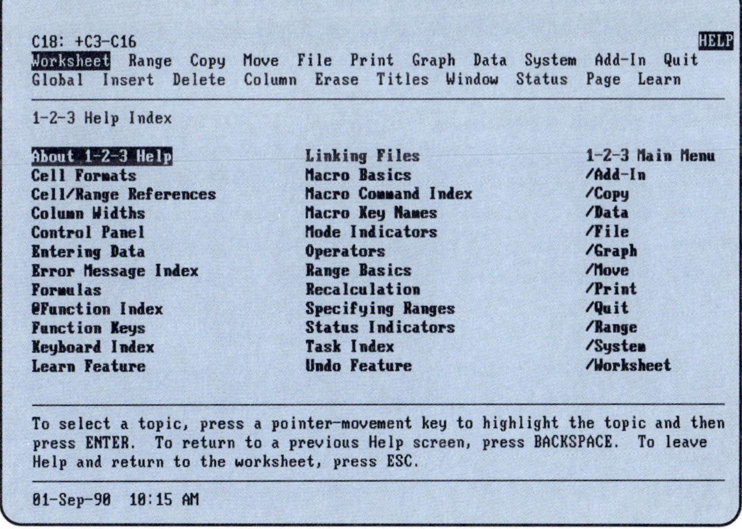

Figure 12 The Help Index

Step 5: Exit Help

When you are finished with the help facility, press the Escape key to return to what you were doing:

> Press   **Escape**

The Main menu should be on your screen with the Worksheet option highlighted. Return to READY mode:

> Press   **Escape**

If your computer has only two floppy drives, remove the Help Disk from drive A and replace it with the System Disk.

1. Activate the help facility, display the help index, and select the topic entitled "About 1-2-3 Help." Return to READY mode when you are finished.
2. Activate the Main menu and execute the File command. Activate the Help facility and read about the commands in the File menu. Return to READY mode when you are finished.

Lesson 9: Moving Around a Worksheet

Lotus 1-2-3 lets you move the cell pointer easily to any of the more than 2 million cells it can address. You have already used a few of the **pointer movement keys** that move the cell pointer. Let's examine the pointer movement keys in more detail.

Step 1: Move the Cell Pointer One Cell at a Time

The arrow keys move the cell pointer one cell at a time. Try each arrow key:

> Press   **Right Arrow**
> Press   **Left Arrow**
> Press   **Down Arrow**
> Press   **Up Arrow**

If you hold down an arrow key for more than a second, its action will be repeated about ten times a second. Try this action:

> Press   **Right Arrow** (hold for about two seconds)

The cell pointer will rapidly travel to the right. When it goes past the left edge of the screen into column I, the screen will scroll to reveal more columns. Now try rapidly moving the cell pointer down:

> Press   **Down Arrow** (hold for about five seconds)

The screen will scroll to reveal more rows when the cell pointer moves into row 21.

Step 2: Move the Cell Pointer Several Cells at a Time

Other pointer movement keys let you move the cell pointer several cells at a time. For example, try each of the following pointer movement keys:

> Press   **Home**

The Home key always moves the cell pointer to A1.

> Press   **Page Down**
> Press   **Page Up**

The Page Up and Page Down keys move the cell pointer an entire screen (usually 20 rows) up or down at a time.

> Press   **Tab** (or **Ctrl-Right Arrow**)
> Press   **Shift-Tab** (or **Ctrl-Left Arrow**)

The Tab and Ctrl-Right Arrow keys both move the cell pointer an entire screen to the right. The Shift-Tab and Ctrl-Left Arrow keys both move the cell pointer an entire screen to the left.

> Press   **End**
> Press   **Down Arrow**
> Press   **End**
> Press   **Right Arrow**
> Press   **End**
> Press   **Up Arrow**
> Press   **End**
> Press   **Left Arrow**

Pressing and releasing the End key followed by an arrow key moves the cell pointer to the next intersection of a blank cell and a nonblank cell in that direction.

> Press   **End**
> Press   **Home**

Pressing End followed by pressing Home moves the cell pointer to the lowest rightmost nonblank cell in the worksheet.

Step 3: Move to a Particular Cell

Lotus 1-2-3 also provides an easy way to move to a particular cell address. Suppose you want to move to cell AB2015.

> Press   **F5**

The F5 function key invokes the Go To feature. The program will display the prompt

```
Enter address to go to:
```

And it will suggest the current cell address. Enter the address of the cell to which you want to move:

> Type   **ab2015**
> Press   **Enter**

The cell pointer will move immediately to that cell.

Practice

1. With a single keypress, move the cell pointer to A1.
2. Move the cell pointer right two screens.
3. In the most direct manner, move the cell pointer to the lowest rightmost cell possible in a 1-2-3 worksheet, cell IV8192.

Lesson 10: Editing Cells

Suppose you make a typing error but don't discover your mistake until after you have pressed the Enter key or moved the cell pointer. Or suppose you want to modify or update the existing contents of a cell. Lotus 1-2-3 makes it easy to edit cells.

Step 1: Retype an Entry

One way to edit the existing contents of a cell is to retype the entire entry. Suppose the power bill is $130 instead of $125. Move the cell pointer to C7 and retype the entry:

Press **F5**
Type **c7**
Press **Enter**
Type **130**
Press **Enter**

Notice how the worksheet recomputes the formula results automatically. Total expenses increases by 5 and spending money decreases by 5 as soon as you change 125 to 130 for the power bill.

Step 2: Edit an Existing Entry

If an existing entry is long or complex and you don't need to change it entirely, retyping it can be tedious and can introduce errors. Fortunately, you can edit the contents of a cell without retyping the entire entry. As an example, let's change the label in cell A14 to *Car Loan Payment*. Follow these directions:

Press **F5**
Type **a14**
Press **Enter**
Press **F2**
Press **Left Arrow** (7 times)
Type **Loan**
Press **Space Bar**
Press **Enter**

First, you move the cell pointer to the cell you want to edit. Then you activate the EDIT mode by pressing the F2 key. Lotus 1-2-3 will display the existing entry in the second line of the control panel with a cursor at the end. You can use the Left Arrow, Right Arrow, Backspace, and Delete keys to move the cursor and erase characters. By default, any character you type will be inserted into the entry. To type over existing characters, you must press the Insert key. When you are finished editing the entry, press the Enter key to store it in the cell and return to READY mode. The following table summarizes the actions of certain keys in EDIT mode.

Key	*Action*
Enter	Stores entry and returns to READY mode
Backspace	Erases character to left of cursor
Delete	Erases character at cursor
Escape	Erases entire entry

Insert	Toggles insert/overwrite mode
Home	Moves cursor to first character of entry
End	Moves cursor to last character of entry
Left Arrow	Moves cursor left one character
Right Arrow	Moves cursor right one character
Tab	Moves cursor right five characters
Ctrl-Right Arrow	Moves cursor right five characters
Shift-Tab	Moves cursor left five characters
Ctrl-Left Arrow	Moves cursor left five characters
Up Arrow	Stores entry and moves up one row
Down Arrow	Stores entry and moves down one row
Page Up	Stores entry and moves up one screen
Page Down	Stores entry and moves down one screen

Step 3: Save the Worksheet

After you edit a worksheet, you should save it to preserve your changes. Execute the File Save command:

Type   **/fs**
Press **Enter**
Type   **r**

Practice

1. Use EDIT mode to change the entry in cell A11 from *Car Insurance* to *Auto Insurance*.

2. Move the cell pointer to C18. Use EDIT mode to change the formula to $(C3 - C16)$. Can you explain why this formula is equivalent to $+C3 - C16$?

Lesson 11: Changing Column Widths

The default width of columns in Lotus 1-2-3 is nine characters. Although this width is fine in many cases, you may have to change the width of a column. In the BUDGET worksheet, some of the labels in column A appear to have overlapped into column B. This overlapping does not present a problem, since column B is empty. Keep in mind, however, that the labels really are in column A. Although characters appear to be in column B on the screen, column B is still empty. You can confirm this by moving the cell pointer to cell A13 then B13 and viewing the contents of the cells displayed in the control panel. Let's widen column A so that it can hold all of the labels in the BUDGET worksheet.

Step 1: Move the Cell Pointer into the Column

Move the cell pointer to a cell in the column to be widened or narrowed. Move to cell A1:

Press **Home**

Step 2: Execute the Worksheet Column Set-Width Command

The width of a single column can be changed with the Worksheet Column Set-Width command:

Type   **/wcs**

Step 3: Enter the Width In Characters

Lotus 1-2-3 will prompt you to enter the column width, which must be between 1 and 240 characters, and it will suggest the current width of 9 characters. Change the column width to 25:

Type   **25**
Press   **Enter**

Column A will widen to 25 characters, as shown in Figure 13. Notice that the width of the column now appears in square brackets in the control panel, between the current cell address and the contents of the current cell.

Step 4: Save the Worksheet

After you modify a worksheet, you should save it to preserve your changes. Execute the File Save command:

Type   **/fs**
Press   **Enter**
Type   **r**

Practice

1. Execute the Worksheet Column Reset-Width command to change the width of column A back to the default width.

2. Execute the Worksheet Column Set-Width command to change the width of column A to 25 again.

Figure 13 Column A Widened to 25 Characters

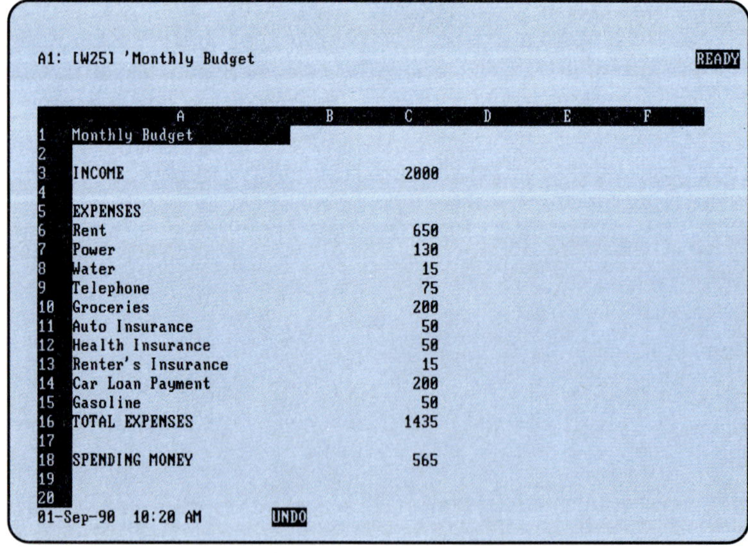

Lesson 12: Deleting and Inserting Columns and Rows

Lotus 1-2-3 provides commands for deleting and inserting columns and rows. As examples, let's delete a column and insert a row in the BUDGET worksheet.

Step 1: Delete a Column

Since you widened column A, you no longer need a blank column B. You can easily delete it. Move the cell pointer to column B and execute the Worksheet Delete Column command:

Press   **Home**
Press   **Right Arrow**
Type   **/wdc**

Lotus 1-2-3 will prompt you for the range of columns to delete, and it will suggest the current column. Since you want to delete only the current column

Press   **Enter**

The contents of column B will disappear and all the columns to the right will be shifted over to the left. The former column C is now column B. Note that the cell addresses in formulas are automatically adjusted to account for this move. For example, move to cell B16 and examine the formula to compute total expenses in the control panel:

Press   **F5**
Type   **b16**
Press   **Enter**

Before you deleted column B, the formula in C16 was @SUM(C6..B15). After you deleted column B, 1-2-3 shifted the contents of column C into column B, and it changed the formula to @SUM(B6..B15). If you examine the formula in cell B18, you will see a similar adjustment.

The process for deleting a row is similar. Move the cell pointer to the row to be removed and then execute the Worksheet Delete Row command.

Step 2: Insert a Row

Suppose you forgot to include the cable television bill in your budgeted expenses. You can easily insert a new row and then enter the data. Move the cell pointer to the row where you want the inserted row to appear, then execute the Worksheet Insert Row command:

Press   **F5**
Type   **a10**
Press   **Enter**
Type   **/wir**
Press   **Enter**

The former row 10 and all the rows below it will be shifted down. A blank row now appears as row 10. Enter the new data for this row:

Type   **Cable TV**
Press   **Right Arrow**
Type   **15**
Press   **Enter**

The new row occurs between the first and last cells in the range specified in the total expenses formula. So, the range in the formula is automatically changed to B6..B16 from B6..B15, which it was before the row was inserted. The total expenses increase by 15, and the spending money decreases by 15. Move to cell B17 to see the adjusted formula:

       Press   **F5**
       Type   **b17**
       Press   **Enter**

Your screen should look like Figure 14.

The process for inserting a column is similar. You move the cell pointer to the column where the new column is to be added, then execute the Worksheet Insert Column command.

Step 3: Save the Worksheet

After you modify a worksheet, you should save it to preserve your changes. Execute the File Save command:

       Type   **/fs**
       Press   **Enter**
       Type   **r**

Practice

1. Insert a new column B.

2. Insert a new row 13.

3. Delete the blank column B.

4. Delete the blank row 13.

Lesson 13: Copying and Moving Cells

Lotus 1-2-3 makes it easy to copy the contents of cells. The Copy command can reduce repetitive typing. As an example, let's copy a range of cells in the BUDGET worksheet. A Practice exercise will illustrate the use of the Move command, which is very similar to the Copy command.

Step 1: Execute the Copy Command

Examine your BUDGET worksheet. Suppose column B contains the numbers and formulas for a single month and you want to show another month in column C. Most of the numbers will be the same, so the easiest way to enter the data in column C is to copy the contents of column B. Execute the Copy command:

       Type   **/c**

Step 2: Specify the Source Range

Lotus 1-2-3 will prompt you to enter the range of cells to copy from. Specify the source range:

       Type   **b3..b19**
       Press   **Enter**

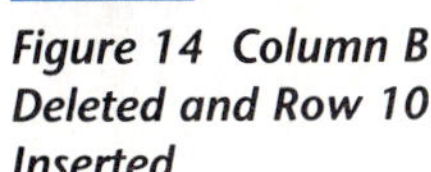

Figure 14 Column B Deleted and Row 10 Inserted

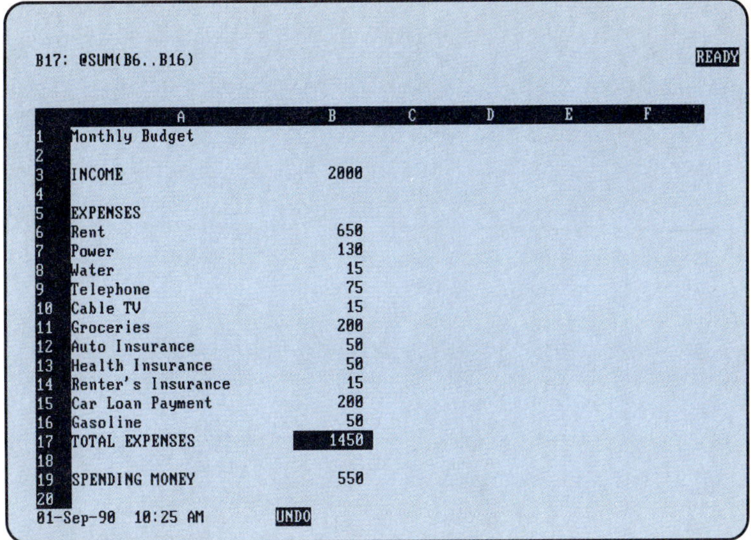

Step 3: Specify the Target Range

Next the program will prompt you to enter the range of cells to copy to. Specify the target range:

> Type   **c3..c19**
> Press   **Enter**

Lotus 1-2-3 will copy the cells from B3 through B19 to cells C3 through C19.

Step 4: Examine the Screen

Move the cell pointer to C17:

> Press   **F5**
> Type   **c17**
> Press   **Enter**

Your screen should look like Figure 15. Examine the formula in cell C17. When 1-2-3 copies formulas, it automatically adjusts the cell references. So, the formula in cell C17 sums the numbers in cells C6 through C16.

Step 5: Save the Worksheet

After you modify a worksheet, you should save it to preserve your changes. Execute the File Save command:

> Type   **/fs**
> Press   **Enter**
> Type   **r**

Practice

1. Copy the contents of cells A1 through A19 to cells D1 through D19, then delete column D.

2. The Move command is like the Copy command, except that the source cells are erased. Activate the Main menu, execute the Move command, and move

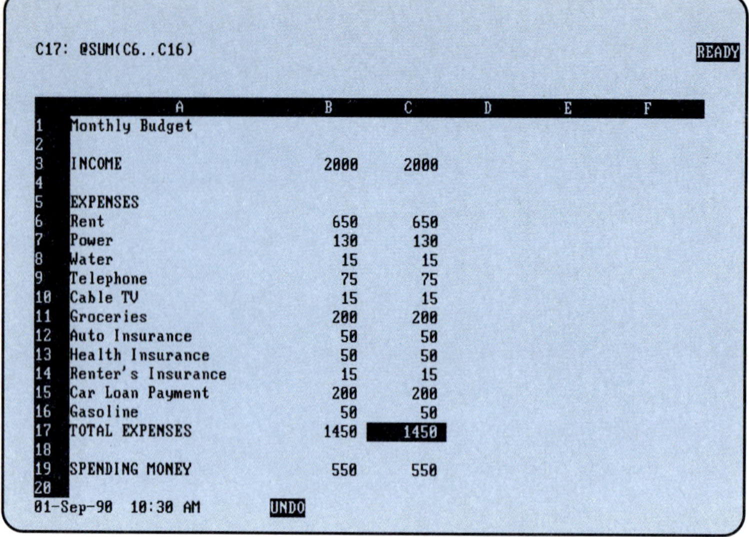

Figure 15 Cells From Column B Copied to Column C

the contents of cells C3 through C19 to cells E3 through E19, then move them back to column C.

Lesson 14: Cell Formatting

Lotus 1-2-3 offers an assortment of cell formatting options for tailoring the appearance of a worksheet. For example, you can left justify, center, or right justify labels within their columns. Numbers and formula results can be displayed as currency values, as percentages, with a fixed number of decimal places, or in scientific notation. In this lesson, you will learn how to use label prefix characters and how to format numbers as currency values.

Step 1: Left Justify a Label

The default label prefix character is the apostrophe ('), which aligns labels with the left edge of the cell. Whenever you type an entry that 1-2-3 recognizes as a label, an apostrophe is automatically inserted at the beginning. For example, move to cell A1 and examine the control panel:

Press   **Home**

The label *Monthly Budget* is preceded by an apostrophe.

In most cases, you don't have to type the apostrophe, because it will be added automatically by 1-2-3. But if a label must begin with one of these characters, you must type the label prefix character yourself:

0 1 2 3 4 5 6 7 8 9 . + - ($ # @

For example, enter a new left-justified label in cell A1:

Type   **'1991 Budget**
Press   **Enter**

Step 2: Center a Label

The caret (ˆ) label prefix character centers a label within its cell. For example, center the label *EXPENSES* in cell A5:

> Press   **F5**
> Type   **a5**
> Press   **Enter**
> Type   **ˆEXPENSES**
> Press   **Enter**

The label *EXPENSES* will be centered in cell A5.

Step 3: Right Justify a Label

The quotation mark (") label prefix character aligns a label with the right edge of its cell. For example, enter right-justified labels in cells B2 and C2:

> Press   **F5**
> Type   **b2**
> Press   **Enter**
> Type   **" Jan**
> Press   **Right Arrow**
> Type   **" Feb**
> Press   **Enter**

Step 4: Fill a Cell

The backslash (\) label prefix character fills a cell with the characters that follow it. It is often used to fill cells with hyphens (-), equal signs (=), or underscores (_) as dividing lines in a worksheet. For example, create a horizontal line of hyphens across cells A18 through C18:

> Press   **F5**
> Type   **a18**
> Press   **Enter**
> Type   **\ -**
> Press   **Right Arrow**
> Type   **\ -**
> Press   **Right Arrow**
> Type   **\ -**
> Press   **Enter**

Your screen should look like Figure 16. Note that cells A18 through C18 appear filled with hyphens, even though each cell contains only \-.

Step 5: Format a Range as Currency

Lotus 1-2-3 offers several ways to format numbers and formula results. The default format is General, which displays no trailing zeros to the right of the decimal point, displays no commas separating thousands, and uses a minus sign to indicate negative values. A common numeric format for financial worksheets is Currency. This format displays the currency symbol, separates thousands with commas, and uses parentheses to indicate negative values. Let's format the numbers in columns B and C as currency values. Execute the Range Format Currency

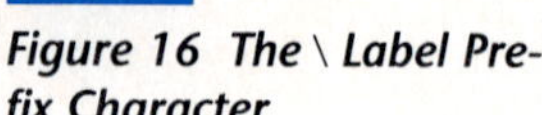

Figure 16 The \ Label Prefix Character

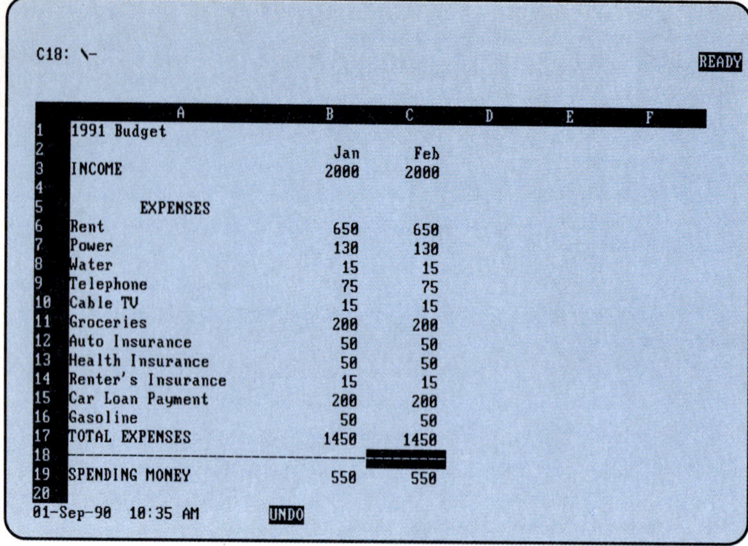

command, specify the number of decimal places as two, and then specify the range of cells to be formatted:

Type   **/rfc**
Press   **Enter**
Type   **b3..c19**
Press   **Enter**

Examine the screen. Cells B3, C3, B17, and C17 are filled with asterisks. This means that the cells are not wide enough to hold the numbers in the format you specified. Widen columns B and C:

Press   **F5**
Type   **b1**
Press   **Enter**
Type   **/wcs**
Type   **10**
Press   **Enter**
Press   **Right Arrow**
Type   **/wcs**
Type   **10**
Press   **Enter**
Press   **Home**

Your screen should now look like Figure 17.

Step 6: Save the Worksheet

After you modify a worksheet, you should save it to preserve your changes. Execute the File Save command:

Type   **/fs**
Press   **Enter**
Type   **r**

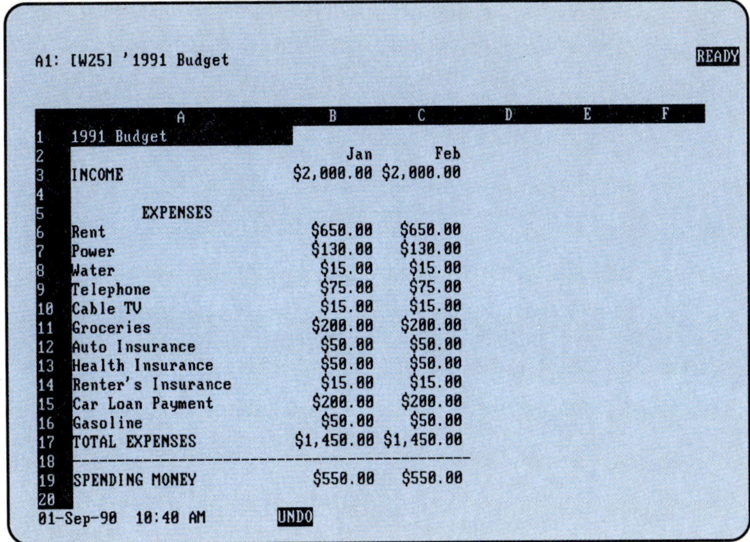

Figure 17 Values Formatted as Currency

 **Practice**

1. Move to cell B3 and examine the control panel. The cell actually contains 2000 but the value $2,000.00 is displayed in the worksheet. Changing a cell's format changes the way the number is displayed in the worksheet, not the data itself. For example, execute the Range Format Currency command and specify zero decimal places for the current cell. Enter the value 1250.25 in B3. Lotus 1-2-3 will display 1250.25 as $1,250, but it still stores the value as 1250.25 and uses the fractional part in calculations. Notice that the value in cell C19 now appears in parentheses because it is a negative value.

2. Change the format of cell B3 back to Currency with two decimal places. Enter 2000 as the value in B3.

Lesson 15: Using the Undo Feature in Releases 2.2 and 3.0

It is easy to make mistakes when using a computer. Fortunately, you can correct typing errors by retyping or editing entries. If you begin to execute a command and then change your mind, you can usually back out of the operation by pressing the Escape key. Recovering accidentally deleted data, however, can be more difficult. A good way to guard against losing data is to regularly save your worksheet to a disk file.

Lotus 1-2-3 Release 2.2 and Release 3.0 also include an Undo feature that lets you reverse the effects of the most recent operation that changed data or worksheet settings. Let's demonstrate this feature by deleting some cells and recovering them with the Undo feature. Note that the Undo feature is not available in Lotus 1-2-3 Release 2.0. If you have Release 2.0, read this lesson without performing the steps.

Step 1: Enable the Undo Feature

Lotus 1-2-3 Release 2.2 has the Undo feature turned on by default. If you see the UNDO indicator at the bottom of the screen, you know that the Undo feature is enabled. Lotus 1-2-3 Release 3.0 has the Undo feature disabled by default. Release

3.0 does not display an UNDO indicator on the screen to tell you if the Undo feature is enabled. If you are using Release 3.0, or if you are using Release 2.2 and do not see the UNDO indicator at the bottom of the screen, execute the Worksheet Global Default Other Undo Enable Quit command to turn on the Undo feature and return to READY mode:

> Type **/wgdoueq**

Step 2: Erase a Range

You have already learned how to delete entire rows or columns with the Worksheet Delete command. The Range Erase command lets you delete the contents of a range of cells. You can use the Range Erase command to erase a single cell, part of a column or row, or a block of adjacent cells in several columns and rows. Use the Range Erase command to delete the contents of cells B6 through C16:

> Type **/re**
> Type **b6..c16**
> Press **Enter**

Cells B6 through C16 will be erased.

Step 3: Use the Undo Feature

Suppose you made a mistake or changed your mind about erasing that data. To invoke the Undo feature, hold down the Alternate key and press the F4 key.

> Press **Alt-F4**

If you are using Lotus 1-2-3 Release 2.2, the data you deleted will be reinstated immediately. If you are using Lotus 1-2-3 Release 3.0, the program will ask you to confirm the Undo operation. Select the Yes option to tell the program to perform the Undo operation:

> Type **y**

Practice   The Undo feature can be used to reverse a command that changes a worksheet setting but does not delete data. For example, use the Range Format command to select the General format for cells B3 through C19, then invoke the Undo feature to reverse your action.

Lesson 16: Using Formulas

As you know, a formula is an expression stored in a cell that tells 1-2-3 to perform a calculation. You have used formulas in this chapter to sum a column of numbers and to subtract one number from another. In fact, formulas can do much more than add and subtract numbers. In this lesson, we will discuss Lotus 1-2-3 formulas in more detail.

Step 1: Create a New Worksheet

To illustrate some of the properties of formulas, let's set up a simple worksheet. First, save the BUDGET worksheet:

> Type **/fs**

Press   **Enter**
Type   **r**

Execute the Worksheet Erase Yes command to clear the worksheet screen and move the cell pointer to A1:

Type   **/wey**

Follow these directions to create a simple worksheet:

Type   **One**
Press   **Down Arrow**
Type   **Two**
Press   **Down Arrow**
Type   **Three**
Press   **Home**
Press   **Right Arrow**
Type   **100**
Press   **Down Arrow**
Type   **200**
Press   **Down Arrow**
Type   **300**
Press   **Down Arrow**

Your screen should look like Figure 18. This new worksheet is only a place for you to try out formulas for this lesson and the next lesson. You do not have to save it to a disk file when you are finished.

Step 2: Enter a Numeric Formula

Lotus 1-2-3 lets you create three basic types of formulas: numeric, string, and logical. A **numeric formula** is a mathematical expression that calculates using numeric values and produces a numeric result. Numeric formulas may include built-in functions and arithmetic operations, such as addition, subtraction, mul-

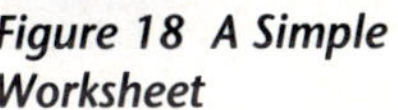

Figure 18 A Simple Worksheet

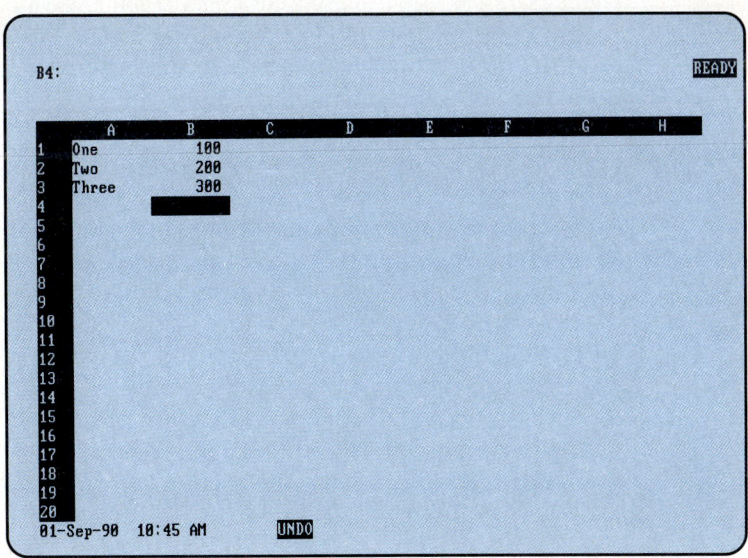

tiplication, and division. The formulas you have used so far in this chapter have all been numeric formulas. Try another numeric formula:

Type   **+b1+b2+b3**
Press   **Enter**

You should see the sum 600 displayed in cell B4.

Step 3: Enter a String Formula

A **string formula** manipulates labels. It may include the **string combination operator** (&), which joins two labels, and certain built-in functions. Although string formulas are used less frequently than numeric and logical formulas, they can be handy in worksheets that manipulate text. Move the cell pointer to C1 and enter a text formula:

Press   **Up Arrow** (3 times)
Press   **Right Arrow**
Type   **+a1&" Hundred"**
Press   **Enter**

This formula tells 1-2-3 to take the label in A1 and combine it with the label in quotation marks. The result is *One Hundred* in cell C1.

Step 4: Enter a Logical Formula

A **logical formula** compares values and produces the result of TRUE, symbolized by the value 1, or FALSE, symbolized by the value 0. Logical formulas may include certain built-in functions and logical operations, such as greater than, less than, and equal to. For example, suppose you want to know if the value in cell B3 is greater than the value in cell B1. Move the cell pointer to C2 and enter a logical formula:

Press   **Down Arrow**
Type   **+b3>b1**
Press   **Enter**

Since 300 is in B3 and 100 is in B1, the result of the logical formula is 1, or TRUE (see Figure 19). Logical comparisons can be combined with logical functions to perform different operations depending on the values in specific cells. Logical formulas make it possible for a worksheet to choose between alternative sets of computations when solving a problem.

Step 5: Try the Arithmetic Operators

An **operator** is a symbol that represents an action to be performed in a formula. An **operand** is a value on which an action is to be performed. The + operator, for example, is a symbol that represents the addition of two numbers, which are the operands. While most operators act on two operands, some operators act on only one operand. In the expression -3, for instance, the $-$ operator stands for negation, not subtraction, and acts on only one operand, the 3. Lotus 1-2-3 has three basic types of operators: arithmetic, string, and logical.

Arithmetic operators perform mathematical operations on numeric operands to produce numeric results. Let's enter a formula to illustrate each arithmetic

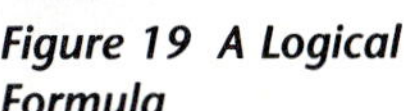

Figure 19 A Logical Formula

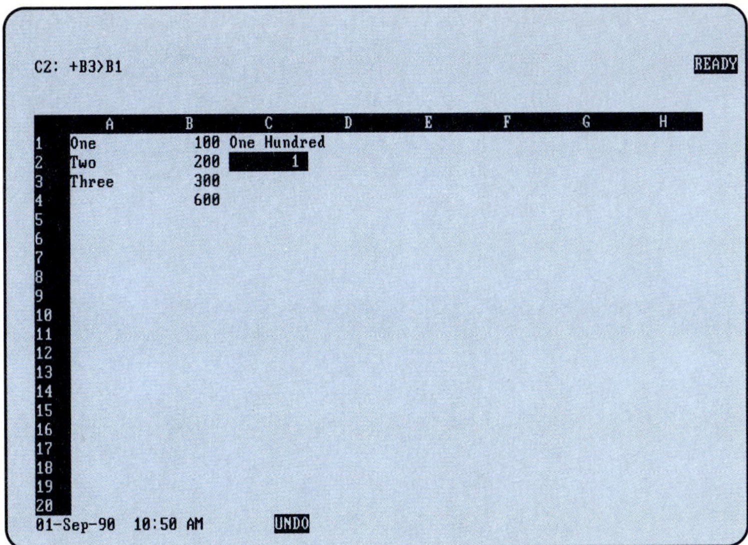

operator. After you enter each formula, examine the screen and make sure you understand the result. First, move the cell pointer to C4:

Press   **F5**
Type   **c4**
Press   **Enter**

The addition operator (+) adds two values.

Type   **25+b1**
Press   **Enter**

The subtraction operator (−) subtracts one value from another.

Type   **450−b3**
Press   **Enter**

The negation operator (−) makes a value negative.

Type   **−b1**
Press   **Enter**

The multiplication operator (*) multiplies two values.

Type   **15*b1**
Press   **Enter**

The division operator (/) divides one value by another.

Type   **+b3/b1**
Press   **Enter**

The exponentiation operator (^) takes a value to a power.

Type   **2^3**
Press   **Enter**

This formula takes 2 to the 3rd power, which is 8.

Step 6: Try the String Operator

Lotus 1-2-3 has only one string operator, the string combination operator &. Try an example of a formula that uses the string combination operator:

Type   +a1&" "&a2&" "&a3
Press   Enter

You should see *One Two Three* in the current cell.

Step 7: Try the Logical Operators

Logical operators produce the result 1 for TRUE or 0 for FALSE. Let's try an example of each logical operator. After you enter each formula, examine the screen and make sure you understand the result.

The = operator produces a result of 1 for TRUE only if its two operands are equal. Otherwise it produces 0 for FALSE.

Type   +b1=100
Press   Enter

The < operator produces a result of 1 for TRUE only if its first operand is less than its second operand. Otherwise it produces 0 for FALSE.

Type   100<b1
Press   Enter

The <= operator produces a result of 1 for TRUE only if its first operand is less than or equal to its second operand. Otherwise it produces 0 for FALSE.

Type   100<=b1
Press   Enter

The > operator produces a result of 1 for TRUE only if its first operand is greater than its second operand. Otherwise it produces 0 for FALSE.

Type   +b1>100
Press   Enter

The >= operator produces a result of 1 for TRUE only if its first operand is greater than or equal to its second operand. Otherwise it produces 0 for FALSE.

Type   +b1>=100
Press   Enter

The <> operator produces a result of 1 for TRUE only if its two operands are not equal. Otherwise it produces 0 for FALSE.

Type   +b1<>100
Press   Enter

The #NOT# operator negates a logical result. It produces 1 for TRUE if its operand was FALSE, or 0 for FALSE if its operand was TRUE.

Press   Down Arrow
Type   #not#c4
Press   Enter

The #AND# operator produces 1 for TRUE only if both of its operands are TRUE. Otherwise it produces 0 for FALSE.

Type   +c4#and#1
Press   Enter

The #OR# operator produces 0 for FALSE only if both of its operands are FALSE. Otherwise it produces 1 for TRUE.

Type   **+c4#or#1**
Press   **Enter**

Step 8: Understand the Order of Operations

When more than one operator is used in a formula, the operations are executed in a specific order. For example, try this formula:

Type   **+b1+b2/b3**
Press   **Enter**

You might expect the 100 in B1 to be added to the 200 in B2, and the result to be divided by the 300 in B3 to yield 1. In this case, however, the operations do not proceed from left to right. The division is performed before the addition, so the result is 100.6666.

You must understand the order of operations to construct formulas that execute correctly. The table below lists the Lotus 1-2-3 operators in order of priority or precedence. In other words, the ^ operator is executed first and the #AND#, #OR#, or & operator is executed last. Operators that appear on the same line in the table have equal precedence and are executed from left to right in a formula.

Order of Operations

Precedence	Operators	Operations
1	^	Exponentiation
2	–	Negation
3	* /	Multiplication and division
4	+ –	Addition and subtraction
5	= < <= > >= <>	Logical comparisons
6	#NOT#	Logical NOT
7	#AND# #OR# &	Logical AND, logical OR, and string combination

Step 9: Use Parentheses

Although it is important to understand the order of operations, you can eliminate much confusion by using parentheses in your formulas. Expressions in parentheses are evaluated first, regardless of the order of operations. When in doubt about the order of operations, use parentheses to force the order you want. For example, try this formula:

Type   **(b1+b2)/b3**
Press   **Enter**

First, the 100 in B1 is added to the 200 in B2. The sum, 300, is then divided by the 300 in B3 to yield a result of 1 (see Figure 20).

Expressions in parentheses can be nested within other parentheses. The expression inside the innermost set of parentheses is evaluated first. Evaluation

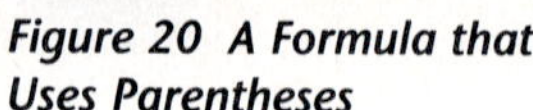

Figure 20 A Formula that Uses Parentheses

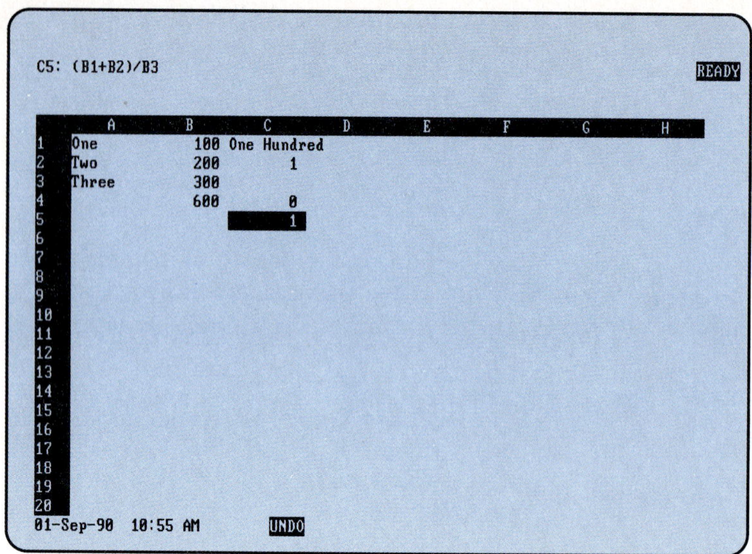

then proceeds progressively outward. Expressions within parentheses at the same level of nesting are evaluated from left to right.

Practice

1. Enter a formula to divide the result in cell B4 by 3.

2. Enter a formula to test whether the contents of cell B3 is greater than the sum of cells B1 and B2.

3. Enter a formula to add the contents of cells B1, B2, and B3 and divide the sum by 10.

Lesson 17: Using Functions

Lotus 1-2-3 functions are ready-made procedures that you can use to perform complex or common operations. For example, the @SUM function, which you have already used in this chapter, adds the contents of any range of cells. Lotus 1-2-3 provides built-in functions, like those in high-level programming languages such as BASIC or Pascal, so that users don't have to "reinvent the wheel" whenever they need to perform certain routine calculations. Functions make it easier to manipulate data in a worksheet because they provide convenience and accuracy. The built-in functions include many operations users may not know how to do on their own. For instance, do you remember how to compute a square root? Could you figure out how to compute a square root with a Lotus 1-2-3 formula? Fortunately, 1-2-3 has the @SQRT function, which will compute a square root for you.

Some functions perform operations that may be difficult or even impossible to do in any other way. For example, if you had to tally the values in 1,000 cells, you could not do it by adding the individual cells. Even if you wanted to enter all 1,000 cell addresses and plus signs, Lotus 1-2-3 would not let you, because 240 is the maximum number of characters you can enter into a cell. The @SUM function, however, lets you add up the contents of 1,000 cells as easily as 3 cells.

Lotus 1-2-3 has more than 90 different built-in functions. This lesson will introduce only a few of the most commonly used functions. You will learn more functions later. The Lotus 1-2-3 Command Summary appendix at the end of this book lists all of the Lotus 1-2-3 functions.

Step 1: Try Some Mathematical Functions

Mathematical functions compute a numeric result given one or more other numeric values. Let's try a few examples.

Type   **@abs(-25)**
Press   **Enter**

The result should be 25. The @ABS function computes the absolute value of a number. In other words, it converts a negative value to a positive value.

Type   **@int(2.667)**
Press   **Enter**

The result should be 2. The @INT function converts a value to an integer by truncating the fractional part.

Type   **@log(100)**
Press   **Enter**

The result should be 2. The @LOG function computes the base 10 logarithm of a value.

Type   **@mod(7,3)**
Press   **Enter**

The @MOD function returns the remainder (modulus) from a division operation. In this case, the result should be 1, the remainder you get when 7 is divided by 3.

Type   **@rand**
Press   **Enter**

The result could be any number between 0 and 1. The @RAND function returns a random number between 0 and 1. Random numbers are sometimes used in statistics and games.

Type   **@round(2.2468,3)**
Press   **Enter**

The result should be 2.247. The @ROUND function rounds a value to a specified number of decimal places, in this case 3.

Type   **@sqrt(9)**
Press   **Enter**

The result should be 3. The @SQRT function computes the square root of a value.

Step 2: Try Some Trigonometric Functions

Trigonometric functions are mathematical functions that deal with angles. Let's try a few examples.

Type   **@pi**
Press   **Enter**

The result should be 3.141592. The @PI function returns the value of π, the ratio of the circumference of a circle to its diameter.

    Type   `@sin(@pi/2)`
    Press **Enter**

The result should be 1. The @SIN function returns the sine of an angle assumed to be expressed in radians. Notice how functions are combined in the above formula.

    Type   `@cos(0)`
    Press **Enter**

The result should be 1. The @COS function returns the cosine of an angle assumed to be expressed in radians.

    Type   `@tan(@pi/4)`
    Press **Enter**

The result should be 1. The @TAN function returns the tangent of an angle assumed to be expressed in radians.

Step 3: Try Some Statistical Functions

Statistical functions perform calculations on lists of values. These lists may be single values, ranges, or combinations of both. Let's try a few examples. The following examples assume you still have the values 100, 200, and 300 in cells B1, B2, and B3.

    Type   `@avg(b1..b3)`
    Press **Enter**

The result should be 200. The @AVG function computes the average (or mean) of a list of values.

    Type   `@count(b1..b3)`
    Press **Enter**

The result should be 3. The @COUNT function returns the number of nonblank cells in a list of cells.

    Type   `@max(b1..b3)`
    Press **Enter**

The result should be 300. The @MAX function returns the maximum value in a list of values.

    Type   `@min(b1..b3)`
    Press **Enter**

The result should be 100. The @MIN function returns the minimum value in a list of values.

    Type   `@sum(b1,b1..b3,200)`
    Press **Enter**

The result should be 900. The @SUM function computes the sum of a list of values. This example shows how a list of values can contain individual cells, ranges, and constant values separated by commas.

Step 4: Try Some Financial Functions

Spreadsheet programs are used extensively in accounting, business, and finance. Lotus 1-2-3 provides functions for calculations concerning loans, annuities, and cash flows. Let's try a few examples.

> Type   `@pmt(9000,1%,48)`
> Press   **Enter**

The @PMT function computes the payment on a loan per payment period for a given principal amount, interest rate, and number of periods. The above formula could represent the monthly payment on a new car loan of $9,000 (the principal), at 1% per month (12% annual) interest rate, for 48 monthly payment periods. If you round the result to two decimal places, the monthly payment would be $237.

> Type   `@pv(2000,8%,10)`
> Press   **Enter**

The @PV function computes the present value of an investment, given the payment amount, discounted interest rate, and number of periods. Suppose that you have the opportunity to make an investment that will return $2,000 per year for the next ten years. To receive this fixed yearly payment or annuity of $2,000, you must invest $10,000. Is it wise to spend $10,000 today to earn $20,000 over the next ten years? You must compute the present value of the $2000 payments you will receive to decide if the investment is sound. Assume that as an alternative to this annuity, you can earn 8% investing your money in certificates of deposit. This 8% will be the discounted interest rate of the investment. The above

Real World

Temporaries Trained to Use Lotus 1-2-3

Kelly Services, one of the largest agencies of temporary workers in the United States, now provides employees who are spreadsheet literate. Because of the increase in the number of requests for temporary workers with spreadsheet skills, the agency has instituted a nationwide program to teach and certify its qualified employees in the use of programs such as Lotus 1-2-3.

"Depending on the mix of skills identified by our branch offices, we train to meet those needs," explained Carolyn Fryar, senior vice president of Kelly Services. "Software skills include setting the column width and cell display, retrieving a spreadsheet, activating calculations, sending to print, and storing a spreadsheet."

This program, the Kelly PC-Pro System for spreadsheet training, is now available in all 700 Kelly offices in the United States. Trainees receive detailed reference guides for selected spreadsheet programs and a toll-free hotline that they can call to get on-the-job help. Kelly temporaries who qualify for spreadsheet training include those who already have secretarial and word processing skills, or ledger and bookkeeping experience.

As more businesses and organizations acquire microcomputers and spreadsheet programs, their need for skilled employees grows. It seems that familiarity with spreadsheet programs is almost a necessity in today's business world.

Source: Daniel Sommer, "Kelly Trains Temps to Use Spreadsheets," *InfoWorld,* September 28, 1987, p. 48.

formula evaluates this situation. The result of 13,420.16 means that you should be willing to spend $13,420.16 now to receive $20,000 over the next ten years. Since your initial payment is only $10,000, this investment is sound.

 Type **@fv (2000, 8%, 35)**
 Press **Enter**

The @FV function computes the future value of an investment, based on a given payment, interest rate, and number of periods. Suppose you plan to deposit $2,000 at the end of each year into your Individual Retirement Account (IRA) for the next 35 years. The average rate of return on your IRA is 8% per year. How much money will you have in your IRA at the end of 35 years? The above formula answers this question. Your nest egg will be worth around $344,633 at the end of 35 years.

 Type **@term (2000, 8%, 500000)**
 Press **Enter**

The @TERM function computes the number of payment periods in the term of an investment, given a payment amount, interest rate, and future value amount. Given the scenario presented in the @FV example, how long will it take you to accumulate $500,000 in your IRA? The result of the above formula indicates that it would take a little over 39 and a half years (see Figure 21).

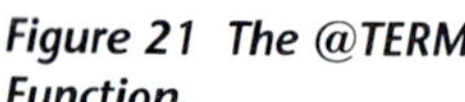
Practice

1. Calculate the square root of 65536.

2. Calculate the cosine of 2π.

3. Calculate the average of these three numbers: 25.67, 89.46, and 65.32.

4. Calculate the monthly payment on a $50,000 loan with an interest rate of 12% per year (1% per month) and a term of 30 years (360 months).

Figure 21 The @TERM Function

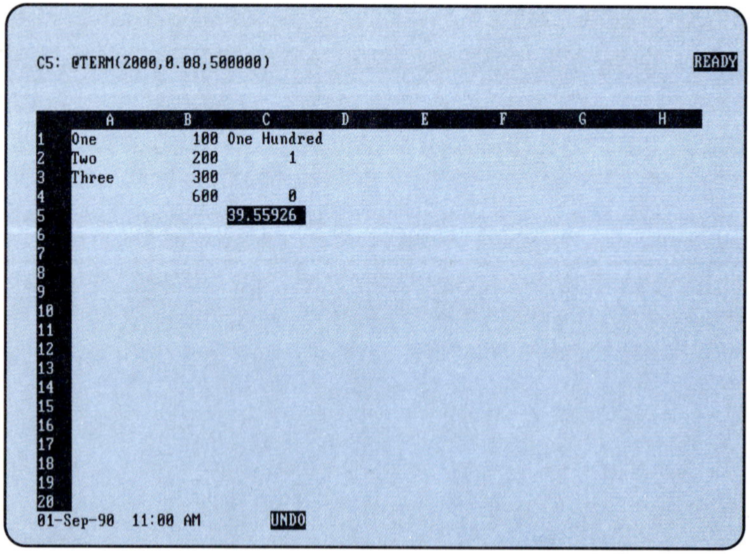

Summary

- *Starting 1-2-3.* Boot up the computer, switch to the proper disk or directory, and enter 123 from DOS.

- *Creating a worksheet.* Enter labels, numbers, and formulas into worksheet cells.

- *Using 1-2-3 menus.* Press / to activate the Main menu. Highlight a command and press Enter or type the command's first letter. Press Escape to return from a menu.

- *Saving a worksheet.* Execute the File Save command and enter the file name.

- *Printing a worksheet.* Execute the Print command, choose Printer or File, specify the range to print, and select the Go option.

- *Quitting 1-2-3.* Save the worksheet, then execute the Quit command from the Main menu.

- *Retrieving an existing worksheet.* Execute the File Retrieve command, then type or select the file name.

- *Getting help.* Press the F1 function key to activate the help facility. Press Escape to exit the help facility.

- *Moving around an existing worksheet.* The pointer movement keys include the arrow keys, Home, Page Up, Page Down, Tab, Ctrl-Right Arrow, Shift-Tab, and Ctrl-Left Arrow. Pressing End followed by an arrow key moves to the next intersection of a blank cell and nonblank cell in that direction. Pressing End followed by Home moves to the lowest rightmost nonblank cell. Pressing F5 prompts you for a cell address to go to.

- *Editing cells.* Retype an entire entry or press F2 to edit an existing entry.

- *Changing column widths.* Move to the column, execute the Worksheet Column Set-Width command, and enter the width.

- *Deleting and inserting columns and rows.* Move to the column or row and execute Worksheet Delete Column, Worksheet Delete Row, Worksheet Insert Column, or Worksheet Insert Row.

- *Copying and moving cells.* Execute the Copy or Move command, specify the source range, and specify the target range.

- *Formatting cells.* The label prefix characters include ' (left justify), ^ (center), " (right justify), and \ (fill a cell). Execute the Range Format command and select an option to format numbers and formula results.

- *Undoing commands.* Press Alt-F4 to invoke the Undo feature (not available in Lotus 1-2-3 Release 2.0).

- *Using formulas.* Three types of formulas can be used: numeric, string, and logical. The arithmetic operators are + (addition), − (subtraction and negation), * (multiplication), / (division), and ^ (exponentiation). The only string operator is &, which combines labels. The logical operators are =, <, >, <=, >=, <>, #NOT#, #AND#, and #OR#. Expression evaluation follows the order of operations unless parentheses are used.

- *Using functions.* Commonly-used mathematical functions include @ABS, @INT, @LOG, @MOD, @RAND, @ROUND, and @SQRT. Trigonometric functions include @PI, @SIN, @COS, and @TAN. Statistical functions include @AVG, @COUNT, @MAX, @MIN, and @SUM. Financial functions include @PMT, @PV, @FV, and @TERM.

Key Terms

As an extra review of this chapter, try defining the following terms.

cell	menu pointer
cell address (cell reference)	mode indicator
cell pointer	number
context-sensitive	numeric formula
control panel	operand
current cell	operator
data	pointer movement keys
formula	range
function	string combination operator
label	string formula
label prefix character	worksheet
logical formula	

Multiple Choice

Choose the best selection to complete each statement.

1. Which command do you enter to start Lotus 1-2-3 from the DOS prompt?
   - (a) START
   - (b) 1-2-3
   - (c) 123
   - (d) CALC

2. A cell is a
   - (a) worksheet row.
   - (b) worksheet column.
   - (c) column-row intersection.
   - (d) piece of data.

3. How are the columns labeled in a 1-2-3 worksheet?
   - (a) A to IV
   - (b) 1 to 256
   - (c) 1 to 8192
   - (d) A to Z

4. What are the three types of data that can be entered into worksheet cells?
   - (a) headings, text, and labels
   - (b) numbers, labels, and formulas
   - (c) sums, products, and quotients
   - (d) commands, operators, and operands

5. What is an expression that tells 1-2-3 to perform a calculation?
   - (a) cell
   - (b) address
   - (c) formula
   - (d) operand

6. Which key do you press to edit the existing contents of a cell?
   - (a) Escape
   - (b) Delete
   - (c) F1
   - (d) F2

7. Which key do you press or character do you type to activate the Main menu?
   - (a) /
   - (b) M
   - (c) Escape
   - (d) F1

8. How many cells can Lotus 1-2-3 address?
   - (a) 256
   - (b) 8192
   - (c) 10,000
   - (d) 2,097,152

9. Which label prefix character do you use to center a label within its cell?

    (a) '   (b) ^

    (c) "   (d) \

10. Which of the following numbers is not a valid 1-2-3 entry?

    (a) 0.5   (b) 100,000

    (c) 4.32E+05   (d) −11.123

11. What is a predefined formula that performs a useful operation, such as computing a sum or a square root?

    (a) command   (b) operator

    (c) function   (d) operand

12. Which of the following expressions is a range?

    (a) A1..B10   (b) +A1−B10

    (c) @RAND   (d) /wey

13. Which keys would you press or letters would you type to execute the File Save command?

    (a) Alt-F4   (b) /fs

    (c) Escape-Home   (d) \save

14. Which key(s) do you press or letters do you type to invoke the help facility?

    (a) F1   (b) F2

    (c) /h   (d) Alt-F4

15. Which key will always move the cell pointer to A1?

    (a) Escape   (b) Up Arrow

    (c) Shift-Tab   (d) Home

16. The three basic types of 1-2-3 formulas are

    (a) mathematical, statistical, and financial.   (b) numeric, string, and logical.

    (c) additive, multiplicative, and exponential.   (d) micro, mini, and macro.

17. If all of the following operators were in the same formula without parentheses, which operator would be executed first?

    (a) +   (b) −

    (c) *   (d) ^

18. Which expression evaluates to 1?

    (a) 100+200/300   (b) (100+200)/300

    (c) 1/100−99   (d) 10^1−1

19. Which operator combines two labels?

    (a) +   (b) *

    (c) &   (d) @

20. Three examples of financial functions are

    (a) @ABS, @INT, and @LOG.   (b) @AVG, @MAX, and @SUM.

    (c) @SIN, @COS, and @TAN.   (d) @PMT, @FV, and @TERM.

Fill-In

1. A worksheet is a table of _______ and _______ of entries.
2. The _______ is the basic unit of storage in a worksheet—where you enter numbers, labels, and formulas.
3. Lotus 1-2-3 can address over two _______ cells.
4. The three lines at the top of the 1-2-3 screen are known as the _______.
5. To move the cell pointer one cell at a time, you would press one of the _______ keys.
6. To move the cell pointer to a particular address, you would press the _______ key.
7. The three types of data you can enter into worksheet cells are numbers, labels, and _______.
8. You can change the existing contents of the current cell by pressing F2 to invoke the _______ mode.
9. Type _______ to activate the Main menu of commands.
10. To select an option from a menu, type its first letter, or move the menu pointer on top of it and press _______.
11. A rectangular block of one or more adjacent cells is called a _______.
12. The _______ command is just like the Copy command, except that it erases the contents of the source range.
13. The _______ copies the worksheet on the screen to a disk file.
14. Press _______ to activate the help facility.
15. _______ formulas produce either TRUE (symbolized by a 1) or FALSE (symbolized by a 0).
16. An _______ is a symbol that represents an action to be performed in a formula.
17. Expressions inside _______ are evaluated first, regardless of the order of operations.
18. As do high-level programming languages, Lotus 1-2-3 provides a set of _______ to perform certain routine calculations.
19. The _______ function truncates the fractional part of a value.
20. The _______ function computes the payment on a loan per payment period for a given principal, interest rate, and term.

Short Problems

1. If you are not already running 1-2-3, start the program. Create and print a simple multiplication table for the numbers 1 through 6. Use these numbers as your row and column labels. Enter only the value 1. All other values in the table should be calculated using formulas.
2. Create a table of the cube root, square root, square, and cube for each whole number value from 1 to 25. List the number in column A, the cube root in column B, the square root in column C, the square in column D, and cube in column E. Enter only the numbers in column A. All other values should be calculated using formulas. Hint: use the exponentiation operator.
3. Use the @RAND function and the Copy command to put random numbers between 0 and 1 into cells A1 through A10. Notice how a different random

number appears in each cell. Move the cell pointer to B1 and enter a formula using the @INT function to convert the random number in cell A1 to an integer between 1 and 6 inclusive. Hint: Try @INT(A1*6)+1. Copy the formula from B1 to cells B2 through B10. This worksheet simulates the throwing of a die ten times.

4. Use the @RAND function and the Copy command to simulate 100 coin tosses. Do this by generating random numbers in cells A1 through A100. Then convert these random numbers into either 0 (for heads) or 1 (for tails). Hint: Try @INT(A1*2) in B1 and copy this formula to cells B2 through B100. Use the @AVG function to compute the mean of the zeros and ones, which will be the probability of getting a tail. It should be near 0.5.

5. Make up twenty exam grades from 0 to 100 and enter them into cells A1 through A20. Use the @MAX function to find the highest grade and the @MIN function to find the lowest grade. Use the @AVG function to calculate the mean grade.

6. Use the @PMT function to calculate the monthly mortgage payment on a $100,000 home loan that has an interest rate of 10% per year and a term of 20 years.

7. You can calculate the number of periods to pay back a loan with the @TERM function if you use a negative value as the future value and take the absolute value of the result. Try the following formula to calculate the number of months it will take to pay back a $100,000 loan with an interest rate of 10% per year making monthly payments of $965.02:

@ABS(@TERM(965.02,10%/12, − 100000))

8. You just won $20 million in the new MegaBucks state lottery. You are given two payment options. You can receive 20 annual payments of $1 million at the end of each year, or you can receive an immediate lump sum payment of $8 million. Which option is worth more in today's dollars? Assume that if you accept the 20 annual payments of $1 million, you would invest the money at an interest rate of 8%, compounded annually. Hint: Try @PV(1000000,8%,20). The result will show that the $20 million paid over 20 years is worth $9,818,147.41 in today's dollars. Take the 20 annual payments.

9. Create a worksheet that will compute automobile gas mileage. Put the mileage when the tank is first filled in cell A1, the mileage when the tank is filled the second time in cell A2, and the number of gallons it took to refill the tank in cell A3. Enter a formula to compute the miles per gallon in cell A4.

10. Reproduce the following table in a 1-2-3 worksheet. You will need to use the Worksheet Column Set-Width and the Range Format commands to set up the worksheet to display such large numbers. Use formulas to compute the two totals.

```
ACCOUNT          THIS YEAR           LAST YEAR
------------------------------------------------------

Cash on hand   344,584,904.50      235,452,143.60
Receivables    655,473,321.08      527,004,321.97
Inventories    315,733,211.95      130,982,021.80
Real estate         894,992.20          864,389.10
Equipment      448,993,406.00      406,894,600.00
Sales          772,345,236.75      652,945,870.25

------------------------------------------------------

TOTAL
```

Long Problems

1. Create a worksheet that lists your major expenditures for the past 12 months. Include items like rent, room and board, or mortgage payments; tuition; power bills; telephone bills; health, automobile, and property insurance; travel expenses; credit card purchases; and so on. Be sure to compute both the row and column totals. Try to use the Copy command to reduce repetitive typing. Use appropriate labels and numeric formatting to improve the clarity and appearance of your worksheet.

2. Create a worksheet listing all of the courses you are taking this semester, along with the number of credit hours and the grade you expect. Also include a column showing the numerical equivalent for each grade you expect (A = 4.0, B = 3.0, C = 2.0, D = 1.0, and F = 0.0). Have your worksheet total your number of hours and your grade points and calculate your grade point average.

3. Suppose you have decided to purchase a new microcomputer system. List eight or ten components and supplies you'll need (computer, display adapter, monitor, disk drives, expansion boards, printer, cables, diskettes, paper, and so on). Enter these headings into column A and estimate an amount for each item in column B. Using ads from computer magazines or information from a local retailer, enter the actual costs for these items into column C. Enter a formula and use the Copy command to calculate the differences between your budgeted and actual costs in column D. Include column totals for each of the numeric columns, and add appropriate column headings.

4. In a small local newspaper the fee for classified advertising is a function of the price charged for the item. The fee is collected only if the item sells. The fee is 10% of the first $100.00 of the advertised price, plus 3% of the second $100.00, plus 2% of the third $100.00, plus 1% of the amount of the advertised price over $300.00. Create a worksheet that will accept the advertised price as input and calculate the advertising fee. Test your worksheet using prices of $140.00 (fee = $11.20) and $750.00 (fee = $19.50).

5. Once upon a time, a king won great acclaim from his subjects by abolishing all taxes. In their place, he told the people that they would have to place one grain of wheat in one square of a checkerboard at the end of the first year. At the end of the second year, they would owe him two grains, placed in the second square. At the end of the third year, they would owe four grains, placed in the third square, and at the end of the fourth year, eight grains in the fourth square, and so on up to the sixty-fourth square of the checkerboard. After that, they would own their land outright and wouldn't have to give up any more wheat. Update this problem using pennies instead of wheat, and produce a worksheet that shows each of the sixty-four years, the amount paid that year, and the total amount paid to date. Does this worksheet help explain the revolt that deposed the king several years later?

6. Assume you own 200 individual student apartments now renting for $110.00 a month. Since all your apartments are currently occupied, your gross is $22,000.00 per month. A real estate agent tells you your rent is way too low, but he further states that if you decide to raise the rent, you would lose one tenant for every $7.50 rent increase. In other words, you would be able to rent only 199 of the apartments at $117.50, 198 apartments at $125.00, and so on. Prepare a worksheet that will list in one column the number of apartments rented, in the second column the rent per apartment, and in the third

column the gross income for that particular combination of number rented and rent per apartment. What does your table suggest the rent should be?

7. Suppose you start a savings account that pays interest at a rate of 6% per year, and interest is paid monthly. In other words, you will receive 0.5% per month on your balance. You decide to begin a systematic savings plan in which you will deposit $10.00 per month. Create a worksheet that will show the amount of interest earned each month and the ending balance each month for a period of five years.

8. Consider the expenses of a typical traveling business person (airline tickets, automobile rental, mileage, meals, lodging, supplies, and so on). Construct a worksheet that keeps track of such expenses for each month of the year. Total all rows and columns and do a grand total.

9. Create a worksheet to maintain and balance your checkbook. Have column A contain the check number, column B the date, column C the payment or withdrawal amount, column D the deposit amount, column E an "x" if the transaction has cleared, and column F a description of the transaction. Leave a few blank rows at the top of the worksheet. In one of these cells, compute the current balance by subtracting the sum of the payments from the sum of the deposits. The first entry in the check register should be a deposit with the beginning balance. Enter at least twenty transactions into your checkbook worksheet and verify the computed balance.

10. Create a worksheet to track your income and taxes. For each month of the past year, list your gross income, federal income taxes withheld, state income taxes withheld, any other withholdings, and your net income. Then total the columns.

CHAPTER 5

INTERMEDIATE LOTUS 1-2-3

In This Chapter

Getting Started

Preview

In Chapter 4 you learned the basics of Lotus 1-2-3, the top-selling microcomputer spreadsheet package. This chapter teaches you how to create graphs and manage worksheet data bases using Lotus 1-2-3.

After studying this chapter, you will know how to

- create a bar graph.
- print a graph.
- name a graph.
- create a pie chart.
- create a line graph.
- create a stacked bar graph.
- create an XY graph.
- create a data base worksheet.
- sort a data base worksheet.
- search a data base worksheet.
- extract data from a worksheet.
- use the data base functions.

Getting Started

You've already learned how to start Lotus 1-2-3 and use its most basic features and commands. This chapter assumes you have completed the lessons and exercises of Chapter 4. Furthermore, it assumes that you have a computer with a hard disk and Lotus 1-2-3 installed on it in a subdirectory named 123 or 123R3. A DOS PATH should be set up so that you can run Lotus 1-2-3 from within any subdirectory. You should have a subdirectory named LESSONS in which to store your worksheet files.

Lesson 1: Creating a Bar Graph

VisiCalc, the first spreadsheet program, originally developed for the Apple II computer in 1979, could not produce graphs. Since the introduction of Lotus 1-2-3 for the IBM Personal Computer in 1982, however, graphics capability has been considered an essential component of any serious spreadsheet package. Lotus 1-2-3 can produce several different types of graphs from worksheet data.

Let's create a bar graph that will show a company's sales over a period of years. A **bar graph** is a chart in which numeric values are represented by evenly spaced, thick vertical lines. Bar graphs are useful for comparing different sets of data, such as the sales figures for several different years.

Step 1: Start 1-2-3

If you are not already running Lotus 1-2-3, switch to your LESSONS subdirectory and start the program:

Type **cd c:\lessons**
Press **Enter**
Type **123**
Press **Enter**

Step 2: Set Up a New Worksheet

In a spreadsheet program, a graph is created from data in a worksheet. So, you must first create the worksheet that contains the data for the graph. Widen column A to 16 characters:

Type   `/wcs16`
Press   **Enter**

Change the numeric format of the range B2 to E2 so that numbers are presented as currency values with no decimal places:

Type   `/rfc0`
Press   **Enter**
Type   `b2..e2`
Press   **Enter**

Step 3: Enter the Data

Follow these directions to enter the data for the graph into the worksheet:

Press   **Right Arrow**
Type   **1988**
Press   **Right Arrow**
Type   **1989**
Press   **Right Arrow**
Type   **1990**
Press   **Right Arrow**
Type   **1991**
Press   **Home**
Press   **Down Arrow**
Type   `Sales (millions)`
Press   **Right Arrow**
Type   **55**
Press   **Right Arrow**
Type   **115**
Press   **Right Arrow**
Type   **150**
Press   **Right Arrow**
Type   **210**
Press   **Home**

Your screen should look like Figure 1. Check your work against Figure 1 and correct any mistakes you made.

Step 4: Save the Worksheet

It is a good idea to save your worksheet in a disk file before you generate a graph. Execute the File Save command and name the worksheet file SALES:

Type   `/fs`
Type   `sales`
Press   **Enter**

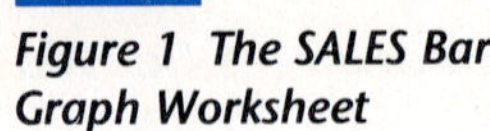

Figure 1 The SALES Bar Graph Worksheet

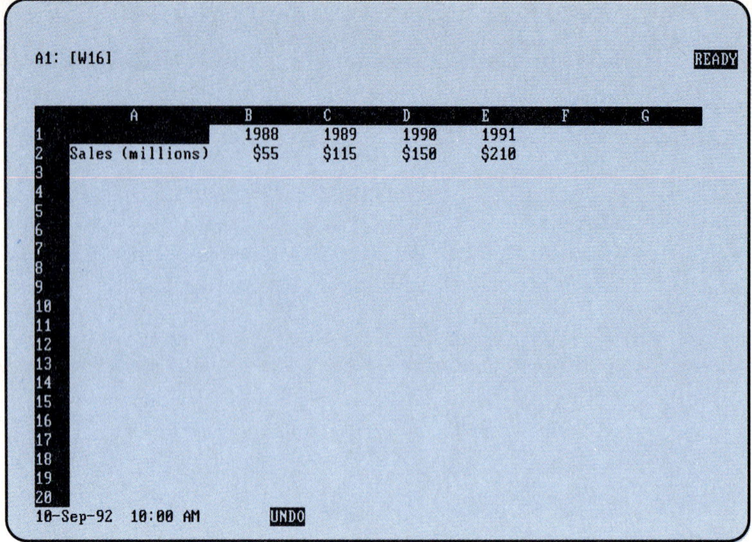

Step 5: Execute the Graph Command

To create a graph, you must execute the Graph command from the Main menu:

Type **/g**

The Graph menu will appear across the top of the screen (see Figure 2). If you are running Lotus 1-2-3 Release 2.2, the Graph Settings sheet will also appear. Release 2.0 and Release 3.0 do not display a Graph Settings sheet.

Step 6: Select the Type of Graph

Examine the third line of the control panel. Since the Type command is highlighted, the third line of the control panel displays the submenu of options available if you select the Type command. Lotus 1-2-3 Release 2.0 and Release 2.2 let you create five basic types of graphs. Lotus 1-2-3 Release 3.0 lets you create seven basic types of graphs. Select Bar as the type of graph you want to create:

Type **tb**

Step 7: Specify the X Data Range

In bar, line, and stacked bar graphs, the X data range contains the values or labels that will appear along the horizontal x-axis. In the SALES bar graph, the years should be presented along the x-axis, so select B1 to E1 as the X data range:

Type **x**
Type **b1..e1**
Press **Enter**

Step 8: Specify the A Data Range

Next you must specify the cells that contain the actual numeric data to be graphed along the y-axis. Some graphs may contain as many as six data ranges. In Lotus 1-2-3, these data ranges are specified as A, B, C, D, E, and F. For your simple

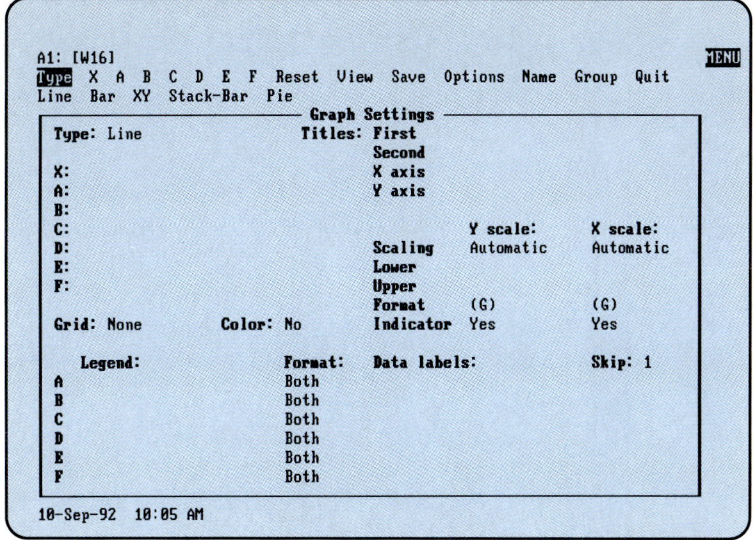

Figure 2 The Graph Menu and Graph Settings Sheet

SALES bar graph, only one data range is necessary. Specify the A data range as B2 to E2:

> Type　**a**
> Type　**b2..e2**
> Press　**Enter**

Step 9: Add Titles

Most graphs make little sense unless they have a main title and titles along the axes. Select Options, Titles, and First, and then enter the first line of the graph title:

> Type　**otf**
> Type　**Beaver Canoe Company**
> Press　**Enter**

Enter the second line of the graph title:

> Type　**ts**
> Type　**Yearly Sales of Aluminum Canoes**
> Press　**Enter**

Enter a title for the x-axis:

> Type　**tx**
> Type　**Year**
> Press　**Enter**

Enter a title for the y-axis:

> Type　**ty**
> Type　**Sales (millions)**
> Press　**Enter**

Quit the Options submenu and return to the Graph menu:

> Type　**q**

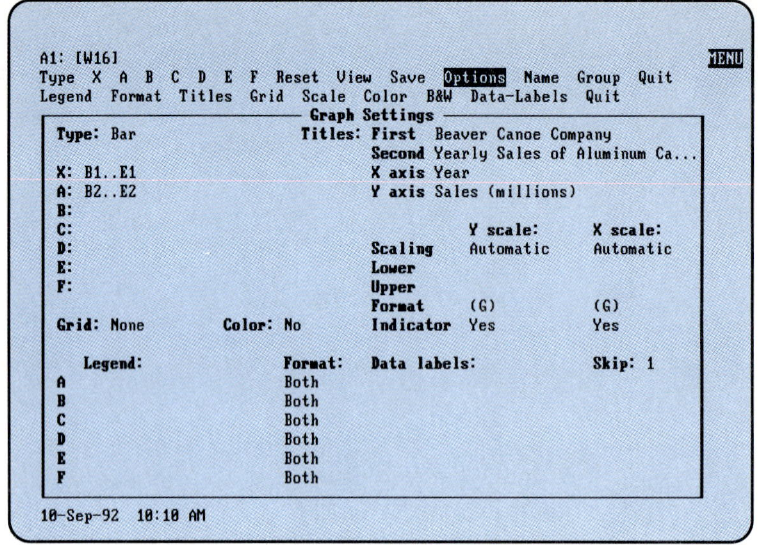

Figure 3 The Completed Graph Settings Sheet

If you are running Lotus 1-2-3 Release 2.2, the graph settings you have specified will be summarized in the Graph Setting sheet on the screen (see Figure 3).

Step 10: View the Graph

If your computer is equipped with a graphics adapter and monitor, you can view the graph you have specified. Select the View option from the Graph menu:

Type **v**

Your screen should look like Figure 4. When you are finished looking at the graph, you can press any key to return to the Graph menu:

Press **Escape**

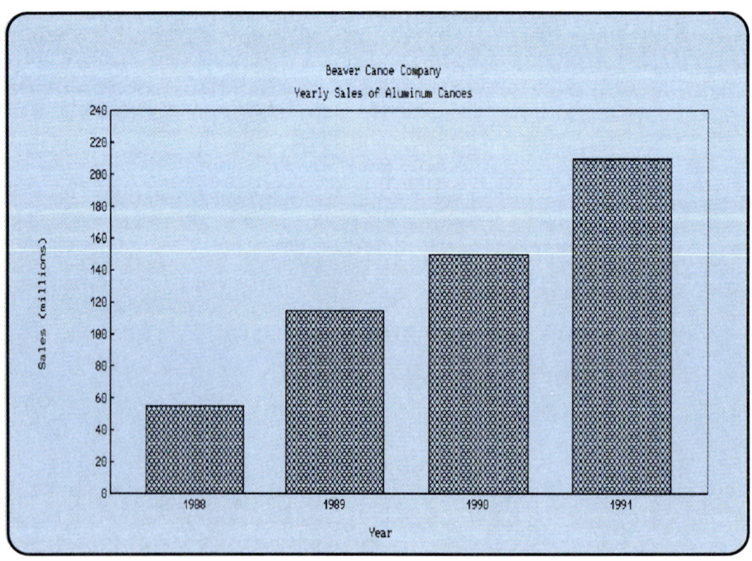

Figure 4 The SALES Graph Displayed on the Screen

Step 11: Save the Graph

Examine the Graph menu on your screen. The Save option lets you save the graph you have created in a file with a PIC extension. This type of graph file can be printed later with the Lotus PrintGraph program or loaded by another application package, such as a word processor or a graphics program that can accept Lotus PIC files. Select the Save option from the Graph menu to save your graph in a file named SALES.PIC:

> Type **s**
> Type **sales**
> Press **Enter**

Quit the Graph menu and return to READY mode:

> Type **q**

Step 12: Save the Worksheet

You have saved the graph to a file named SALES.PIC, but you must also save the worksheet to preserve the graph settings you have specified. Execute the File Save command and replace the worksheet file on the disk:

> Type **/fs**
> Press **Enter**
> Type **r**

Practice

1. When you create a graph, you must view it the first time by selecting the View option from the Graph menu. After that, you can use a shortcut from READY mode to view the graph:

   Press **F10**

   The F10 key presents the current graph on the screen. Press any key to return to READY mode.

2. Lotus 1-2-3 provides many options for altering the appearance of a graph. For example, you can add horizontal grid lines to your SALES graph to make it easier to determine the exact heights of the bars:

   Type **/goghqv**

   Press any key to return to the graph menu.

3. Save the new graph with grid lines to SALES.PIC and save the SALES worksheet as well.

Lesson 2: Printing a Graph with Release 2.0 or 2.2

If you are running Lotus 1-2-3 Release 2.0 or Release 2.2, you must use a separate program called PrintGraph to print your graphs. Skip this lesson if you are running Lotus 1-2-3 Release 3.0.

Step 1: Exit 1-2-3

Before you can start PrintGraph, you must exit 1-2-3. Make sure that you have saved your worksheet, then

> Type   **/qy**

You should see the DOS prompt on your screen.

Step 2: Start PrintGraph

To run the PrintGraph program, execute the PGRAPH command from the DOS prompt:

> Type   **pgraph**
> Press   **Enter**

The PrintGraph screen will appear (see Figure 5).

Step 3: Change the Hardware Settings

Examine the Hardware Settings on the right side of the screen. You may have to change these settings. If your computer has a hard disk, the Graphs directory should be C:\LESSONS, and the Fonts directory should be C:\123. In addition, a printer should be selected. Follow these directions to change the hardware settings if necessary:

> Type   **shg**
> Press   **Escape**
> Type   **c:\lessons**
> Press   **Enter**
> Type   **f**
> Press   **Escape**
> Type   **c:\123**
> Press   **Enter**

Figure 5 The PrintGraph Screen

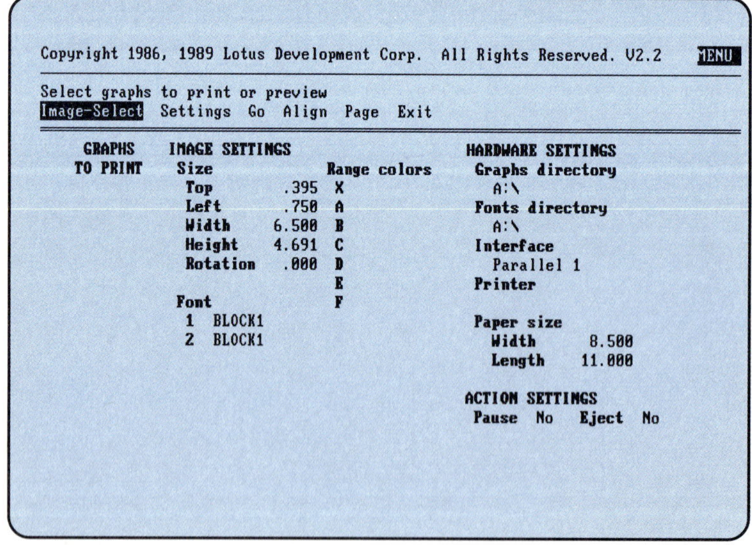

Now select the printer:

> Type   **p**

A list of the printers connected to your computer will appear, with two options for each printer: Low density and High density. Low density will produce quick, low-quality printouts. High density will produce slow, high-quality printouts. Highlight the printer and density you want to use.

> Press   **Space Bar**
> Press   **Enter**

Quit the Hardware Settings menu and the Settings menu:

> Type   **qq**

Step 4: Select the Image

Execute the Image-Select option from the Main PrintGraph menu:

> Type   **i**

A list of graph (PIC) files will be displayed on the screen.

> Highlight   **SALES**
> Press   **Space Bar**
> Press   **Enter**

Step 5: Prepare the Printer

Make sure the printer is connected to the computer and turned on. Also, make sure that paper is loaded and aligned to the top of a new page. Finally, make sure that the printer's On Line light is lit. (If it isn't, press the On Line button.)

Step 6: Select the Go Option

After you have specified all of the PrintGraph settings you want to use and have prepared the printer, select the Go option to actually print the graph.

> Type   **g**

The graph will be printed.

Step 7: Exit PrintGraph and Start 1-2-3

After the graph has been printed, exit the PrintGraph program, return to DOS, and start 1-2-3 again:

> Type   **ey**
> Type   **123**
> Press   **Enter**

Practice   Use the PrintGraph program to print the SALES graph at the other density setting. If you like, try changing some of the image settings, such as graph size, colors, and font. When you are finished experimenting with PrintGraph, exit the program and start 1-2-3 again.

Lesson 3: Printing a Graph with Release 3.0

If you are running Lotus 1-2-3 Release 3.0, you do not need to use a separate program to print out your graphs. Skip this lesson if you are running Lotus 1-2-3 Release 2.0 or Release 2.2.

Step 1: Execute the Print Printer Image Current Go Command

Printing a graph with Lotus 1-2-3 Release 3.0 is much easier than printing a graph with Release 2.0 or 2.2. You can print the current graph with the Print Printer Image Current Go command without leaving the 1-2-3 program.

Type   **/ppicg**

The graph will be produced by the printer.

Step 2: Return to READY Mode

Select the Quit option from the Print menu to return to READY mode:

Type   **q**

You can print the SALES graph to a file instead of directly to the printer, but you must use the Encoded option instead of the File option. Follow these directions to create an encoded file named SALES.ENC that can be printed later from DOS:

Type   **/pe**
Type   **sales**
Press   **Enter**
Type   **icg**
Type   **q**

To print SALES.ENC from DOS, exit 1-2-3 and execute this command:

Type   **copy sales.enc prn**
Press   **Enter**

When the printer is finished, start 1-2-3 again.

Lesson 4: Naming a Graph

If you change the graph settings in the SALES worksheet, 1-2-3 will produce a different graph. Suppose you want to create a different type of graph from the same worksheet without losing the previous graph. Fortunately, 1-2-3 lets you have several graphs associated with the same worksheet. All you have to do is name your graphs.

Step 1: Retrieve the SALES Worksheet

If the SALES worksheet is not already on your screen, retrieve it from the disk:

Type   **/fr**
Highlight   **SALES.WK1 (or SALES.WK3)**
Press   **Enter**

Step 2: View the Graph

Make sure that the current graph is the one you want to name. In this case, only one graph is associated with the SALES worksheet, but it cannot hurt to check.

> Press   **F10**

You should see the bar graph on the screen. Return to READY mode:

> Press   **Escape**

Step 3: Execute the Graph Name Create Command

To associate a name with an existing graph, execute the Graph Name Create command:

> Type   **/gnc**

Step 4: Enter a Graph Name

Lotus 1-2-3 will prompt you to enter a graph name. You can specify a name up to 15 characters long (14 characters long in Release 2.0).

> Type   **sales_bar**
> Press   **Enter**

Return to READY mode:

> Type   **q**

Step 5: Use a Named Graph

The Graph Name Use command retrieves a named graph and makes it the current graph.

> Type   **/gnu**

Lotus 1-2-3 will present a menu of graph names. Currently, only one name exists for the SALES worksheet: SALES_BAR. Select this graph:

> Highlight   **SALES_BAR**
> Press   **Enter**

The program will display the bar graph on the screen. Press any key to return to the Graph menu, then quit to READY mode:

> Press   **Escape**
> Type   **q**

Practice

If you modify a named graph after you retrieve it, and want to save the changed settings, you must use the Graph Name Create and File Save commands again. Follow these directions:

> Type   **/gnc**
> Highlight   **SALES_BAR**
> Press   **Enter**
> Type   **q**
> Type   **/fs**
> Press   **Enter**
> Type   **r**

 Lesson 5: Creating a Pie Chart

A **pie chart** represents values as wedges of a circle. Pie charts are used to show the parts of a whole. For example, a pie chart might be used to break down total sales into various categories. Let's make a pie chart for Beaver Canoe Company that shows its canoe sales at sport shows, camping stores, boat stores, department stores, and the factory outlet.

Step 1: Create the Worksheet

Let's enter the data for the pie chart in an empty area of the SALES worksheet. Move the cell pointer to A5 and enter the following data:

Press	**F5**
Type	`a5`
Press	**Enter**
Type	`Sport Show`
Press	**Right Arrow**
Type	`10`
Press	**Down Arrow**
Type	`40`
Press	**Left Arrow**
Type	`Camping Store`
Press	**Down Arrow**
Type	`Boat Store`
Press	**Right Arrow**
Type	`60`
Press	**Down Arrow**
Type	`70`
Press	**Left Arrow**
Type	`Department Store`
Press	**Down Arrow**
Type	`Factory Outlet`
Press	**Right Arrow**
Type	`30`
Press	**Enter**

The numbers you have entered represent the sales in millions of dollars at each of the outlets. Your screen should look like Figure 6. Check your work against Figure 6 and correct any mistakes you find.

Step 2: Save the Worksheet

It is a good idea to save your worksheet before you generate the graph. Execute the File Save command:

Type	`/fs`
Press	**Enter**
Type	`r`

Step 3: Execute the Graph Reset Graph Command

Since you already have a graph defined as the current graph, execute the Graph Reset Graph command to clear the settings.

Type	`/grg`

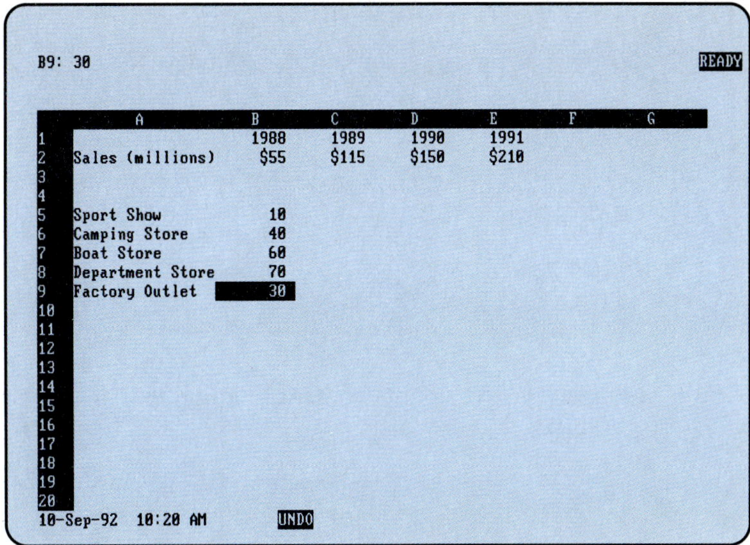

Figure 6 The Pie Chart Data

Step 4: Specify the Type Pie Option

Now tell 1-2-3 that you want to create a pie chart:

Type   **tp**

Step 5: Specify the X Data Range

In a pie chart, the X data range contains the labels for the slices of the pie. Specify the X data range as cells A5 to A9:

Type   **x**
Type   **a5..a9**
Press   **Enter**

Step 6: Specify the A Data Range

In a pie chart, the A data range contains the values that will be represented as slices. Specify the A data range as cells B5 to B9:

Type   **a**
Type   **b5..b9**
Press   **Enter**

Step 7: Add Titles

Use the Options Titles command to add a two-line title to the pie chart:

Type   **otf**
Type   **Beaver Canoe Company**
Press   **Enter**
Type   **ts**
Type   **1991 Sales to Various Outlets**
Press   **Enter**

Quit the Options submenu and return to the Graph menu:

Type   **q**

Step 8: View the Graph

Now you can view the graph you have specified. Select the View option from the Graph menu:

> Type **v**

Your screen should look like Figure 7. When you are finished looking at the graph, return to the Graph menu:

> Press **Escape**

Step 9: Save the Graph

Select the Save option from the Graph menu to save your pie chart in a file named PIE.PIC:

> Type **s**
> Type **pie**
> Press **Enter**

Step 10: Name the Graph

Since you now have two graphs associated with the SALES worksheet, you should name the pie chart. Execute the Name Create option and specify SALES_PIE as the name of the graph:

> Type **nc**
> Type **sales_pie**
> Press **Enter**

Quit the Graph menu and return to READY mode:

> Type **q**

Step 11: Save the Worksheet

You have saved the graph to a file named PIE.PIC and named the graph SALES_PIE, but you must also save the worksheet to preserve the graph settings you have specified. Execute the File Save command and replace the worksheet file on the disk:

> Type **/fs**
> Press **Enter**
> Type **r**

Practice

1. If your computer has a monochrome monitor, the pie chart you have created appears quite plain. You can, however, tell 1-2-3 to use different hatch patterns for the pie slices. You can even explode, or pull out, one or more slices for emphasis. These settings are specified by creating a B data range. Follow these directions:

> Press **F5**
> Type **c5**
> Press **Enter**
> Type **1**
> Press **Down Arrow**

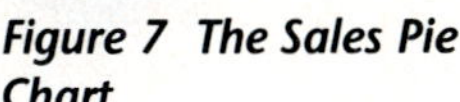

Figure 7 The Sales Pie Chart

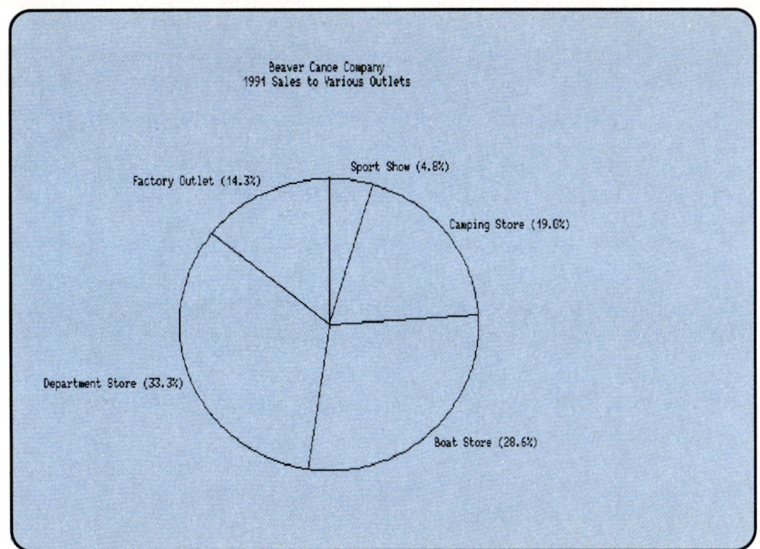

Type	**2**
Press	**Down Arrow**
Type	**103**
Press	**Down Arrow**
Type	**4**
Press	**Down Arrow**
Type	**5**
Press	**Enter**
Type	**/gb**
Type	**c5..c9**
Press	**Enter**
Type	**v**

Each slice now has a different pattern, and the Boat Store slice is exploded. Eight different hatch patterns, numbered 1 through 8, are available in Lotus 1-2-3 Releases 2.0 and 2.2. Release 3.0 has fourteen different hatch patterns. These are the numbers entered in the B data range. To explode a slice, you add 100 to the hatch pattern number in the B data range. So, the Boat Store cell in the B data range signifies hatch pattern 3 added to the 100 that indicates the slice is to be exploded from the pie.

Note that if you have a color monitor and the Graph Options Color option is set, each slice will have a different color instead of a different hatch pattern. You can select the Graph Options B&W option to display a black and white graph and see the hatch patterns.

2. Use the Name Create option to save SALES_PIE again and execute the File Save command to update the worksheet on the disk.

3. Print the new pie chart you have created.

Lesson 6: Creating a Line Graph

A **line graph** represents each data value by a point at an appropriate distance above the horizontal axis. Related points are designated by the same symbol and are connected by line segments. Line graphs are useful for plotting values that change over time. For example, the Beaver Canoe Company could use a line graph to plot the units of three canoe models sold over the past five years. Because line graphs emphasize the continuity of data over time, they are especially handy for identifying trends and making projections.

Step 1: Create the Worksheet

Let's create the line graph we just described for the Beaver Canoe Company. You can enter the data in an empty area of the SALES worksheet. Follow these directions to enter the data:

Press	**F5**
Type	**b12**
Press	**Enter**
Type	**1987**
Press	**Right Arrow**
Type	**1988**
Press	**Right Arrow**
Type	**1989**
Press	**Right Arrow**
Type	**1990**
Press	**Right Arrow**
Type	**1991**
Press	**Down Arrow**
Press	**End**
Press	**Left Arrow**
Type	**Beaver Canoe**
Press	**Right Arrow**
Type	**10000**
Press	**Right Arrow**
Type	**8000**
Press	**Right Arrow**
Type	**7000**
Press	**Right Arrow**
Type	**6500**
Press	**Right Arrow**
Type	**6000**
Press	**Down Arrow**
Press	**End**
Press	**Left Arrow**
Type	**Mohawk Canoe**
Press	**Right Arrow**
Type	**4500**
Press	**Right Arrow**
Type	**5500**
Press	**Right Arrow**
Type	**6000**
Press	**Right Arrow**
Type	**5200**
Press	**Right Arrow**
Type	**5500**
Press	**Down Arrow**
Press	**End**

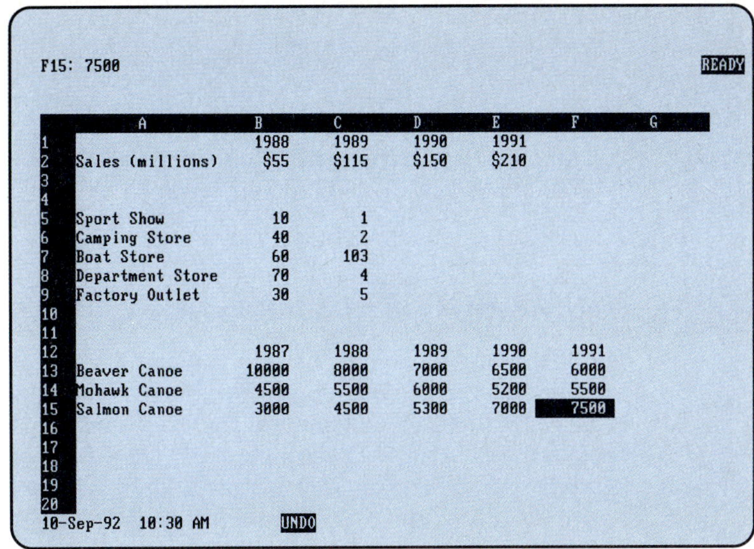

Figure 8 The Line Graph Data

Press   **Left Arrow**
Type   **Salmon Canoe**
Press   **Right Arrow**
Type   **3000**
Press   **Right Arrow**
Type   **4500**
Press   **Right Arrow**
Type   **5300**
Press   **Right Arrow**
Type   **7000**
Press   **Right Arrow**
Type   **7500**
Press   **Enter**

The numbers you have entered represent the units sold of each type of canoe for each year. Your screen should look like Figure 8. Check your work against Figure 8 and correct any mistakes you find.

Step 2: Save the Worksheet

It is a good idea to save your worksheet before you generate the graph. Execute the File Save command:

Type   **/fs**
Press   **Enter**
Type   **r**

Step 3: Execute the Graph Reset Graph Command

Since you already have a graph defined as the current graph, execute the Graph Reset Graph command to clear the settings.

Type   **/grg**

Step 4: Specify the Type Line Option

Now tell 1-2-3 that you want to create a line graph:

>Type   **tL**

Incidentally, Line is the default type of graph. If you do not select a graph type, 1-2-3 assumes you want to do a line graph.

Step 5: Specify the Data Ranges

This line graph will have four data ranges: X, A, B, and C. The X data range will contain the years 1987 through 1991. The A data range will contain the unit sales of Beaver canoes, B will contain the unit sales of Mohawk canoes, and C will contain the unit sales of Salmon canoes. The Group option from the Graph menu lets you specify several data ranges at once if they are in consecutive rows or columns. Follow these directions to specify all of the data ranges for the line graph:

>Type   **g**
>Type   **b12..f15**
>Press   **Enter**
>Type   **r**

B12 to F12 is now the X data range, B13 to F13 is the A data range, B14 to F14 is the B data range, and B15 to F15 is the C data range.

Step 6: Add Titles

Use the Options Titles command to add titles to the line graph:

>Type   **otf**
>Type   **Beaver Canoe Company**
>Press   **Enter**
>Type   **ts**
>Type   **Canoe Model Sales Comparison**
>Press   **Enter**
>Type   **tx**
>Type   **Year**
>Press   **Enter**
>Type   **ty**
>Type   **Number of Units Sold**
>Press   **Enter**

Step 7: Specify Lines and Symbols

Let's have the line graph display each point as a symbol and connect the points with lines. A different symbol will be used for each data range. Select the Format Graph Both Quit option:

>Type   **fgbq**

Figure 9 The Line Graph

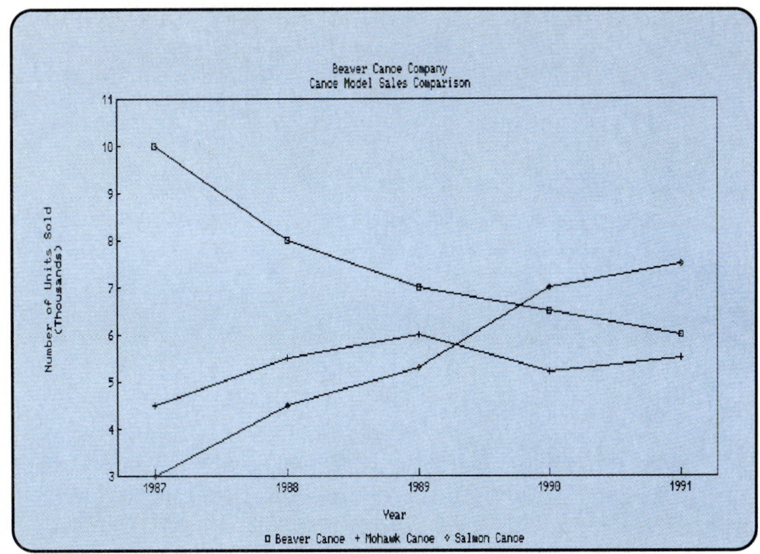

Step 8: Add a Legend

A legend identifies the data range represented by each symbol in the graph. Follow these directions to use the labels in cells A13 through A15 as the legend:

Type　**Lr**
Type　**a13..a15**
Press　**Enter**

Quit the Options submenu and return to the Graph menu:

Type　**q**

Step 9: View the Graph

Now you can view the graph you have specified. Select the View option from the Graph menu:

Type　**v**

Your screen should look like Figure 9. When you are finished looking at the graph, return to the Graph menu:

Press　**Escape**

Step 10: Save the Graph

Select the Save option from the Graph menu to save your line graph in a file named LINE.PIC:

Type　**s**
Type　**line**
Press　**Enter**

Step 11: Name the Graph

Since you now have three graphs associated with the SALES worksheet, you should name the line graph. Execute the Name Create option and specify SALES_LINE as the name of the graph:

> Type   **nc**
> Type   **sales_line**
> Press   **Enter**

Quit the Graph menu and return to READY mode:

> Type   **q**

Step 12: Save the Worksheet

You have saved the graph to a file named LINE.PIC and named the graph SALES_LINE, but you must also save the worksheet to preserve the graph settings you have specified. Execute the File Save command and replace the worksheet file on the disk:

> Type   **/fs**
> Press   **Enter**
> Type   **r**

Practice

1. You can tell Lotus 1-2-3 to label the points in the line graph with their actual values. Labeling the points lets the viewer easily see their exact values. Follow these directions to place labels above the points in the line graph:

   > Type   **/godg**
   > Type   **b13..f15**
   > Press   **Enter**
   > Type   **raqqv**

   When you are finished looking at the graph, press any key to return to the Graph menu.

2. Use the Name Create option to save SALES_LINE again and execute the File Save command to update the worksheet on the disk.

3. Print the new line graph you have created.

Lesson 7: Creating a Stacked Bar Graph

A **stacked bar graph** is a variation of the basic bar graph that shows components and total amounts for each category. For example, you could present the unit sales of the three types of canoes for five years in a stacked bar graph. Each bar would represent the total number of units sold in a year. Each bar would be divided into three stacked sections, one section for each type of canoe. Let's create such a graph. You don't have to enter the data because it already exists in the table you created for Lesson 6.

Step 1: Execute the Graph Reset Graph Command

Since you already have a graph defined as the current graph, execute the Graph Reset Graph command to clear the settings.

> Type   **/grg**

Step 2: Specify the Type Stack-Bar Option

Now tell 1-2-3 that you want to create a stacked bar graph:

Type   **ts**

Step 3: Specify the Data Ranges

This stacked bar graph will have the same four data ranges as the line graph you created in Lesson 6. Use the Group option to specify the four data ranges:

Type   **g**
Type   **b12..f15**
Press   **Enter**
Type   **r**

Step 4: Add Titles

Use the Options Titles command to add titles to the stacked bar graph:

Type   **otf**
Type   **Beaver Canoe Company**
Press   **Enter**
Type   **ts**
Type   **Five Year Unit Sales**
Press   **Enter**
Type   **tx**
Type   **Year**
Press   **Enter**
Type   **ty**
Type   **Number of Units Sold**
Press   **Enter**

Step 5: Add a Legend

A legend identifies the stack pattern that goes with each canoe model. Follow these directions to use the labels in cells A13 through A15 as the legend:

Type   **Lr**
Type   **a13..a15**
Press   **Enter**

Quit the Options submenu and return to the Graph menu:

Type   **q**

Step 6: View the Graph

Now you can view the graph you have specified. Select the View option from the Graph menu:

Type   **v**

Your screen should look like Figure 10. When you are finished looking at the graph, return to the Graph menu:

Press   **Escape**

Figure 10 The Stacked Bar Graph

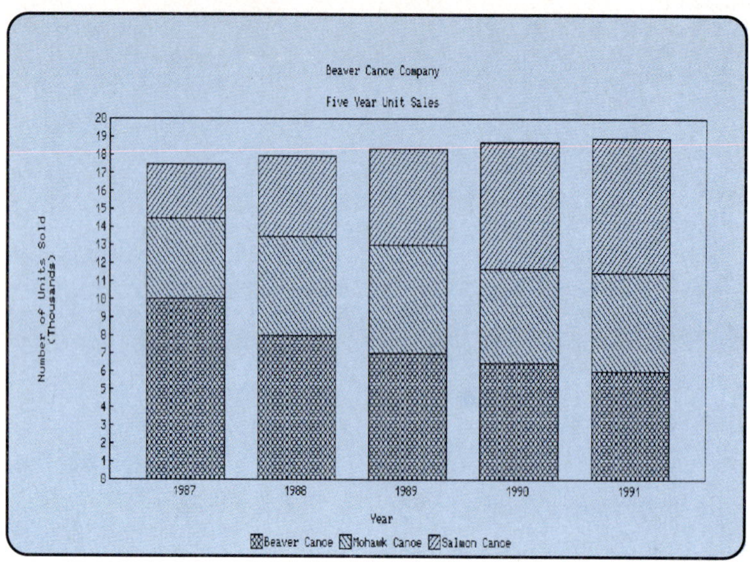

Step 7: Save the Graph

Select the Save option from the Graph menu to save your stacked bar graph in a file named STACK.PIC:

    Type   **s**
    Type   **stack**
    Press   **Enter**

Step 8: Name the Graph

Since you now have four graphs associated with the SALES worksheet, you should name the stacked bar graph. Execute the Name Create option and specify SALES_STACK as the name of the graph:

    Type   **nc**
    Type   **sales_stack**
    Press   **Enter**

Quit the Graph menu and return to READY mode:

    Type   **q**

Step 9: Save the Worksheet

You have saved the graph to a file named STACK.PIC and named the graph SALES_STACK, but you must also save the worksheet to preserve the graph settings you have specified. Execute the File Save command and replace the worksheet file on the disk:

    Type   **/fs**
    Press   **Enter**
    Type   **r**

Practice

1. You can easily create a bar graph from the same data that will show a separate bar for each canoe model. Execute the Graph Type Bar command, then view the graph you have created. This is a good example of a bar graph with multiple data ranges. When you are finished viewing the graph, change it back to a stacked bar graph, then return to READY mode.

2. Print the stacked bar graph you have created.

Lesson 8: Creating an XY Graph

An **XY graph,** sometimes called a **scatterplot,** shows the relationship between two or more variables. For example, XY graphs can be used to show correlations between sales and profits, price and the number of units sold, and per capita income and life expectancy. Let's create an XY graph that shows the relationship between the price of a canoe and the number of units sold for the Beaver Canoe Company.

Step 1: Create the Worksheet

You can enter the data for this new graph in an empty area of the SALES worksheet. Follow these directions to enter and format the data:

Type	**/rfc0**
Press	**Enter**
Type	**b20..b28**
Press	**Enter**
Press	**F5**
Type	**a19**
Press	**Enter**
Type	**"Units Sold**
Press	**Right Arrow**
Type	**"Price**
Press	**Down Arrow**
Type	**100**
Press	**Down Arrow**
Type	**200**
Press	**Down Arrow**
Type	**300**
Press	**Down Arrow**
Type	**400**
Press	**Down Arrow**
Type	**500**
Press	**Down Arrow**
Type	**600**
Press	**Down Arrow**
Type	**700**
Press	**Down Arrow**
Type	**800**
Press	**Down Arrow**
Type	**900**
Press	**Enter**
Press	**F5**

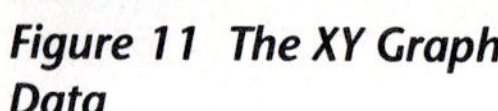

Figure 11 The XY Graph Data

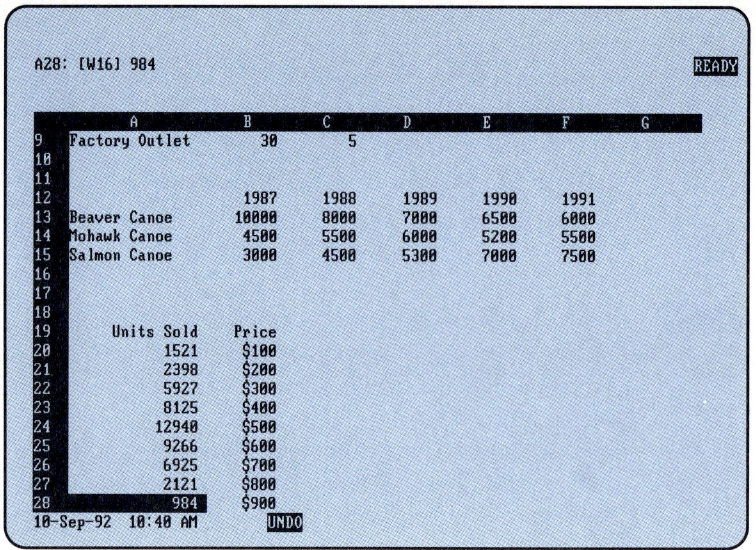

Type	**a20**
Press	**Enter**
Type	**1521**
Press	**Down Arrow**
Type	**2398**
Press	**Down Arrow**
Type	**5927**
Press	**Down Arrow**
Type	**8125**
Press	**Down Arrow**
Type	**12940**
Press	**Down Arrow**
Type	**9266**
Press	**Down Arrow**
Type	**6925**
Press	**Down Arrow**
Type	**2121**
Press	**Down Arrow**
Type	**984**
Press	**Enter**

Your screen should look like Figure 11. Check your work against Figure 11 and correct any mistakes you find.

Step 2: Save the Worksheet

It is a good idea to save your worksheet before you generate the graph. Execute the File Save command:

Type	**/fs**
Press	**Enter**
Type	**r**

Step 3: Execute the Graph Reset Graph Command

Since you already have a graph defined as the current graph, execute the Graph Reset Graph command to clear the settings.

Type   **/grg**

Step 4: Specify the Type XY Option

Now tell 1-2-3 that you want to create an XY graph:

Type   **tx**

Step 5: Specify the Data Ranges

This XY graph will have two data ranges: X and A. The X data range will contain the values for canoe prices. The A data range will contain the number of units sold at that price. Follow these directions to specify the data ranges for the XY graph:

Type   **x**
Type   **b20..b28**
Press   **Enter**
Type   **a**
Type   **a20..a28**
Press   **Enter**

Step 6: Add Titles

Use the Options Titles command to add titles to the line graph:

Type   **otf**
Type   **Beaver Canoe Company**
Press   **Enter**
Type   **ts**
Type   **Canoe Price vs. Units Sold**
Press   **Enter**
Type   **tx**
Type   **Price per Canoe (dollars)**
Press   **Enter**
Type   **ty**
Type   **Number of Units Sold**
Press   **Enter**

Step 7: Specify Lines and Symbols

Let's have the line graph display each point as a symbol and connect the points with lines. Select the Format Graph Both Quit option:

Type   **fgbq**

Quit the Options submenu and return to the Graph menu:

Type   **q**

Figure 12 The XY Graph

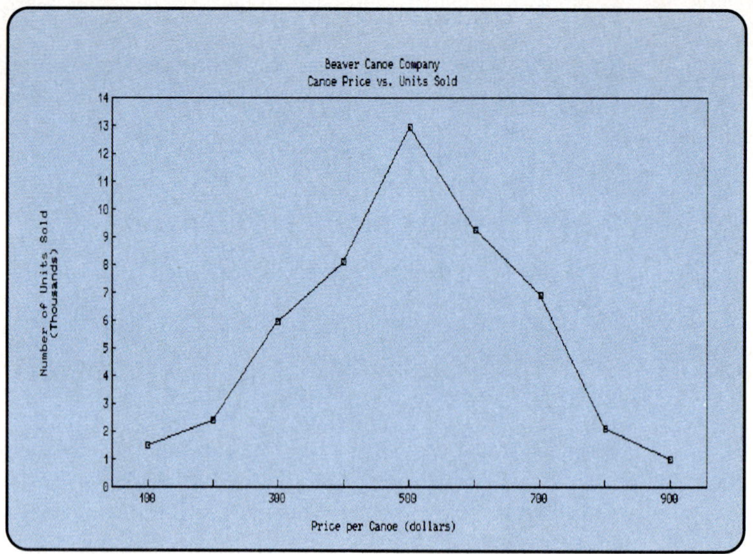

Step 8: View the Graph

Now you can view the graph you have specified. Select the View option from the Graph menu:

> Type   **v**

Your screen should look like Figure 12. This graph suggests that people buy more canoes when the price is around $500. Perhaps if they are priced too low, people will think the canoes are poorly constructed and not buy them. If they are priced too high, people cannot afford them. When you are finished looking at the graph, return to the Graph menu:

> Press   **Escape**

Step 9: Save the Graph

Select the Save option from the Graph menu to save your line graph in a file named XY.PIC:

> Type   **s**
> Type   **xy**
> Press   **Enter**

Step 10: Name the Graph

Since you now have five graphs associated with the SALES worksheet, you should name the XY graph. Execute the Name Create option and specify SALES_XY as the name of the graph:

> Type   **nc**
> Type   **sales_xy**
> Press   **Enter**

Quit the Graph menu and return to READY mode:

> Type   **q**

Step 11: Save the Worksheet

You have saved the graph to a file named XY.PIC and named the graph
SALES_XY, but you must also save the worksheet to preserve the graph settings
you have specified. Execute the File Save command and replace the worksheet
file on the disk:

    Type   **/fs**
    Press   **Enter**
    Type   **r**

Practice

1. Change the XY graph so that it displays symbols, but not line segments. Now
   change the graph to display line segments, but not symbols. Finally, change
   the XY graph so that it displays both symbols and lines again.

2. Print the XY graph you have created.

Lesson 9: Creating a Data Base Worksheet

A data base is an organized collection of one or more files of related data. A
worksheet, which stores data in a table format, can be used as a simple data
base. Although a spreadsheet package is no match for a true data base management system such as dBASE IV, you can store, sort, find, and extract data in a
worksheet. As an example, let's use Lotus 1-2-3 to set up a personal property
inventory.

Step 1: Erase the Worksheet

If the SALES worksheet is still on your screen, execute the Worksheet Erase
command to clear it from memory and start with a blank worksheet:

    Type   **/wey**

Step 2: Set Up the Worksheet for the Data Base

The data base will be a list of personal property, which you might create for
insurance purposes. Column A will hold short item descriptions, column B will
hold the purchase dates, and column C will hold the amounts paid. Column C
will also be summed, so you can maintain a property value total.
    Since column A will hold item descriptions, you should widen it. Execute the
Worksheet Column Set-Width command to widen column A to 40 characters:

    Type   **/wcs40**
    Press   **Enter**

    Column B will hold dates; widen it to 10 characters and format it to display
dates:

    Press   **Right Arrow**
    Type   **/wcs10**
    Press   **Enter**
    Type   **/rfd**
    Press   **Enter**
    Type   **b1..b100**
    Press   **Enter**

Column C will hold dollar amounts. Widen it to 11 characters and format it to display currency values:

Press   **Right Arrow**
Type   **/wcs11**
Press   **Enter**
Type   **/rfc**
Press   **Enter**
Type   **c1..c100**
Press   **Enter**

Step 3: Enter the Field Names

Each row in a data base worksheet represents a record, which contains all the data about a particular item. Each column in a data base worksheet represents a field, which contains an individual data value for each record. The first row in a data base worksheet must contain the names of the fields. Follow these directions to enter the field names:

Type   **"AMOUNT**
Press   **Left Arrow**
Type   **^DATE**
Press   **Left Arrow**
Type   **^ITEM**
Press   **Down Arrow**

Step 4: Enter the Data

Enter the data from the following table into the worksheet. The items go in column A, the date formulas go in column B, and the amounts go in column C. Note that each date is entered as a formula made up of the @DATE function. This function converts the year, month, and day numbers into a single number that 1-2-3 uses to keep track of dates. You will learn more about date numbers in the next chapter.

Personal Property Data

Item	Date	Amount
Guitar, Yamaha	@date(86,04,13)	363.50
Tent, Eureka	@date(87,06,18)	99.95
Lamp, K-Mart	@date(85,01,15)	39.97
Microwave Oven, Sears	@date(86,03,12)	386.64
Answering Machine, Panasonic	@date(88,03,17)	127.47
Backpack, L.L. Bean	@date(89,08,08)	94.50
Walkman, Sony	@date(88,03,10)	82.31
Television, Sony	@date(89,04,29)	524.75
Skis, Trak Cross Country	@date(88,01,05)	113.45
Ski Boots, Salomon	@date(88,01,05)	81.50
Telephone, AT&T	@date(87,04,15)	87.70
CD Player, Sony	@date(87,10,17)	169.00
Stereo Receiver, JVC	@date(86,10,27)	199.00
Speakers, Avid	@date(86,10,27)	156.00
VCR, Magnavox	@date(86,01,04)	318.74
Popcorn Popper, Westbend	@date(88,01,02)	22.15
File Cabinet, Sears	@date(86,11,19)	78.45

Step 5: Enter the Formula

When you use a worksheet as a data base, you can take advantage of the computational abilities of the spreadsheet program. Adding up the amounts spent on each item in the property inventory is easy.

Press   **F5**
Type   **c20**
Press   **Enter**
Type   **@sum(c2..c19)**
Press   **Enter**

If you have entered the amounts and the formula correctly, the sum will be $2,945.08. Now enter a label for the total:

Press   **Left Arrow**
Press   **Left Arrow**
Type   **"TOTAL**
Press   **Enter**

Your screen should look like Figure 13.

Step 6: Save the Worksheet

Save the worksheet in a disk file before you go on to use the data.

Type   **/fs**
Type   **property**
Press   **Enter**

The worksheet will be saved in a file named PROPERTY.WK1 (or PROPERTY.WK3 if you are using Lotus 1-2-3 Release 3.0).

Figure 13 The Completed Data Base Worksheet

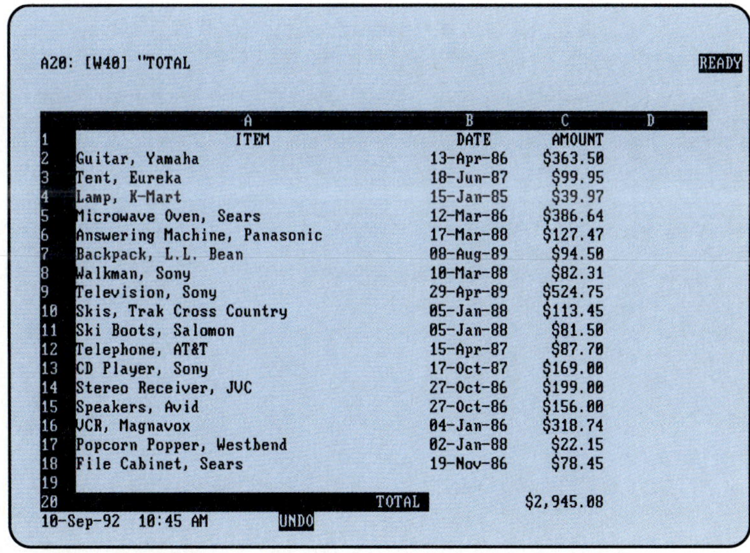

 *Practice*   Invoke the Help facility and read about the @DATE function.

Lesson 10: Sorting a Data Base Worksheet

The records in the PROPERTY data base worksheet are arranged in the order in which they were entered. Records would be easier to find if they were sorted into some predictable order. Let's tell 1-2-3 to sort the PROPERTY records by the contents of the ITEM field.

Step 1: Execute the Data Sort Command

Commands for manipulating a data base worksheet are in the Data menu. The Sort command is used to rearrange the records in a data base.

Type **/ds**

Lotus 1-2-3 will present the Data Sort menu, shown in Figure 14. If you are running Release 2.2, the program will also present the Sort Settings sheet, which displays the current settings of the Sort command.

Step 2: Specify the Data Range to be Sorted

The range to be sorted is called the data range. It should include all the records in the data base, but not the row of field names or the row with the formula for summing the AMOUNT field. Invoke the Data-Range option and specify the range of cells to be sorted:

Type **d**
Type **a2..c18**
Press **Enter**

Lotus 1-2-3 will return to the Sort menu.

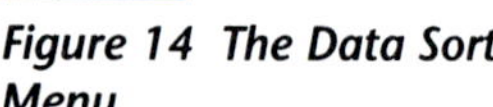 *Figure 14 The Data Sort Menu*

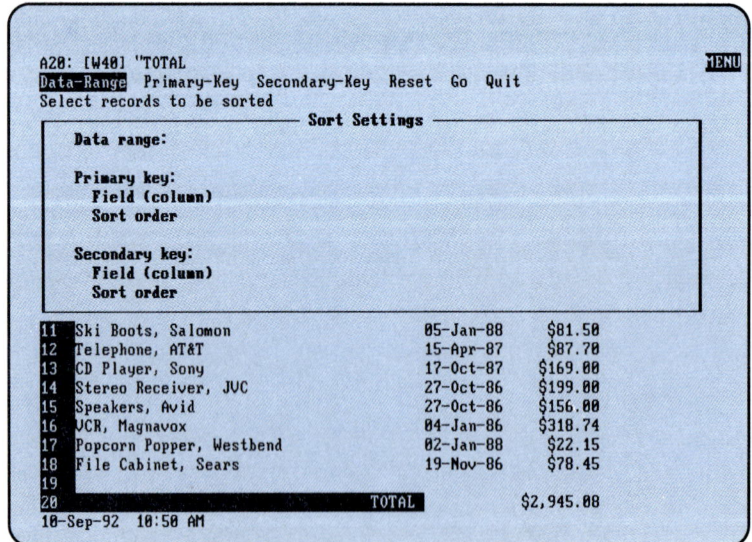

Step 3: Specify a Sort Key

A **key** is a field in a data base used to sort the records. If you want to sort the records on the basis of the contents of the ITEM field, then the ITEM field would be the key. Lotus 1-2-3 lets you specify two keys: the primary key and a secondary key. The **primary key** determines the first sort order. If you want to sort a data base on the basis of only one field, then this field is the primary key. An optional **secondary key** may be specified to determine the order of records after they are sorted first on the primary key. For example, suppose you had a mailing list data base that contained records in which several of the last names were identical. You would probably use the LAST NAME field as the primary key and the FIRST NAME field as the secondary key to sort the records. In the PROPERTY data base worksheet, you need only specify the column containing the ITEM field as the primary key.

    Type   **p**
    Type   **a1**
    Press **Enter**

Note that you could have specified any cell in the ITEM column to indicate the key.

Step 4: Specify the Sort Order

Lotus 1-2-3 will prompt you to indicate the sort order. You have two choices: descending and ascending. For text, ascending order is alphabetical order from A to Z. Specify the sort order as ascending:

    Type   **a**
    Press **Enter**

The program will return to the Sort menu.

Step 5: Execute the Sort

Now you are ready to tell 1-2-3 to sort the records. Invoke the Go option to execute the sort:

    Type **g**

The records will be rearranged on the basis of the contents of the ITEM field, as shown in Figure 15.

Step 6: Save the Worksheet

If you want to keep the data base sorted in this order, you must save it to the disk.

    Type   **/fs**
    Press **Enter**
    Type   **r**

Practice

1. Sort the PROPERTY data base worksheet by AMOUNT, with the most expensive item listed first. Do not save the worksheet when you are finished.
2. Sort the PROPERTY data base worksheet by DATE and then by AMOUNT. In other words, DATE should be the primary key and AMOUNT should be

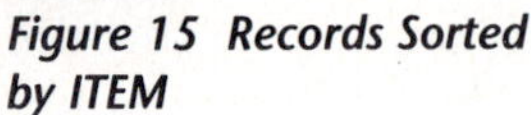

Figure 15 Records Sorted by ITEM

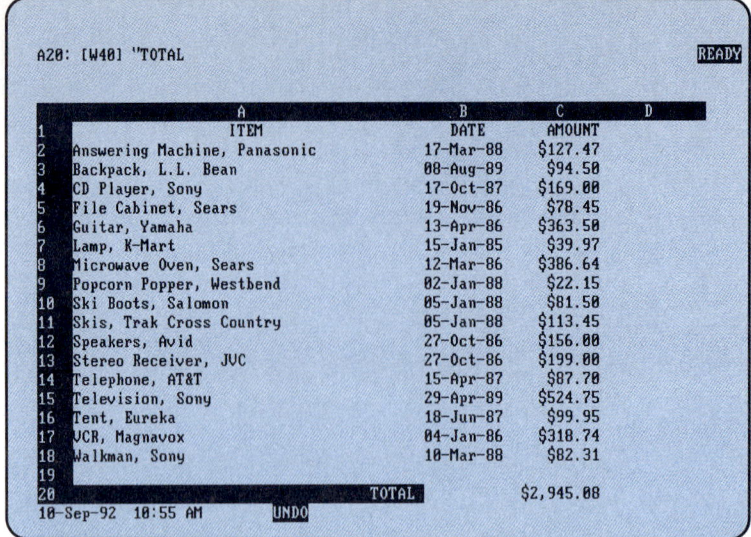

the secondary key. Arrange the records so that the oldest item is first. Within each date, list the most expensive item last. Do not save the worksheet when you are finished. Instead, retrieve the PROPERTY worksheet on the disk, which is sorted by ITEM.

Lesson 11: Searching a Data Base Worksheet

Creating a data base is a way to store and organize large quantities of information. One of the most common operations performed on a data base is searching it for one or more records. The PROPERTY data base worksheet contains only 17 records, so finding a particular record would not be difficult. Most data bases, however, have many more records. Imagine trying to find a particular record in a data base with hundreds or even thousands of records. Fortunately, Lotus 1-2-3 has a command that can locate records for you.

Step 1: Set Up the Criteria Range

Suppose you want to search PROPERTY for all items that cost $300 or more. In 1-2-3 you must set up a **query** to search a data base worksheet. The first step is to set up a range in which to enter the **criteria,** which are the search requirements. The criteria range consists of at least two rows: the first row must include one or more field names and the second row must include one or more expressions that specify the field values you want to find. To set up the criteria range, you can copy the field names from the first row to a blank portion of the worksheet. It is a good idea to copy all of the field names, even if you don't need them all at the moment, so that you can easily change the criteria later. Follow these directions to copy the field names to a blank area of the worksheet:

Press **Home**
Type   **/ca1..c1**
Press **Enter**
Type   **j1**
Press **Enter**

Figure 16 The Data Query Menu

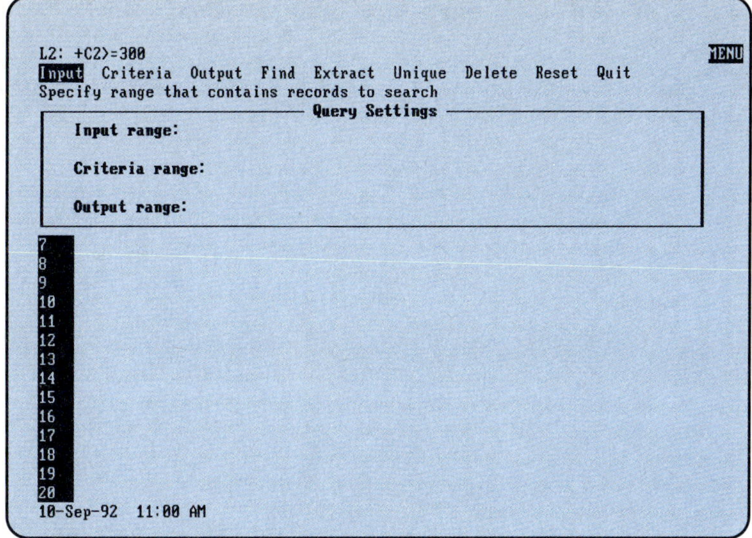

Press   **F5**
Type   **j1**
Press   **Enter**

Note that when you use the Copy command, 1-2-3 copies only the cell contents, not cell widths. Consequently, the widths of cells J1 through L1 do not match the widths of cells A1 through C1.

Step 2: Enter the Criterion

You want to search for those records with AMOUNT values equal to at least $300. In this case, the single criterion would be a logical formula that determines if a number in the AMOUNT field is greater than or equal to 300. Follow these directions to enter the criterion in the cell beneath the AMOUNT field name:

Press   **Right Arrow**
Press   **Right Arrow**
Press   **Down Arrow**
Type   **+c2>=300**
Press   **Enter**

Note that you use the cell address of the first entry in the AMOUNT field for the criterion. Lotus 1-2-3 will display 0 in cell L2 as the result of that formula because the value in cell C2 is less than 300.

Step 3: Execute the Data Query Command

To search a data base worksheet, you use options from the Data Query menu.

Type   **/dq**

Lotus 1-2-3 will display the Data Query menu. If you are running Release 2.2, it will also display the Query Settings sheet (see Figure 16).

Step 4: Specify the Criteria Range

Now you must tell 1-2-3 to use the criteria range you have set up. Select the Criteria option and specify the location of the cells that make up the criteria range:

> Type   `cj1..L2`
> Press   **Enter**

The program will return to the Data Query menu.

Step 5: Specify the Input Range

The range of cells you want to search is called the input range. Unlike the data range for a sort command, the input range must include the field names in addition to the data records. Select the Input option and specify the input range:

> Type   `ia1..c18`
> Press   **Enter**

The program will return to the Data Query menu.

Step 6: Begin the Search

Now that the criteria and input ranges have been specified, you can begin the search for the records that match your criterion. Select the Find option from the Data Query menu:

> Type   `f`

The mode indicator will change to FIND, and 1-2-3 will highlight the first record in the input range that matches the criterion in the criteria range (see Figure 17).

Step 7: Continue the Search

When 1-2-3 is in FIND mode, you simply press the Down Arrow key to advance to the next matching record.

> Press   **Down Arrow**

You can also use the Up Arrow key to see the previous record that matches the criterion.

> Press   **Up Arrow**

Keep pressing the Down Arrow key to see the rest of the records with an AMOUNT greater than or equal to $300:

> Press   **Down Arrow** (4 times)

Lotus 1-2-3 will beep if you press Down Arrow or Up Arrow when no more matching records are found.

Note that you can edit cell contents when 1-2-3 is in FIND mode. This is handy for updating only those records that match certain criteria.

Step 8: End the Search

Follow these directions to end the search and move to A1 when you are finished looking at the records:

> Press   **Enter**
> Type   `q`
> Press   **Home**

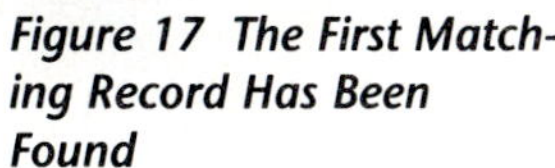

Figure 17 The First Matching Record Has Been Found

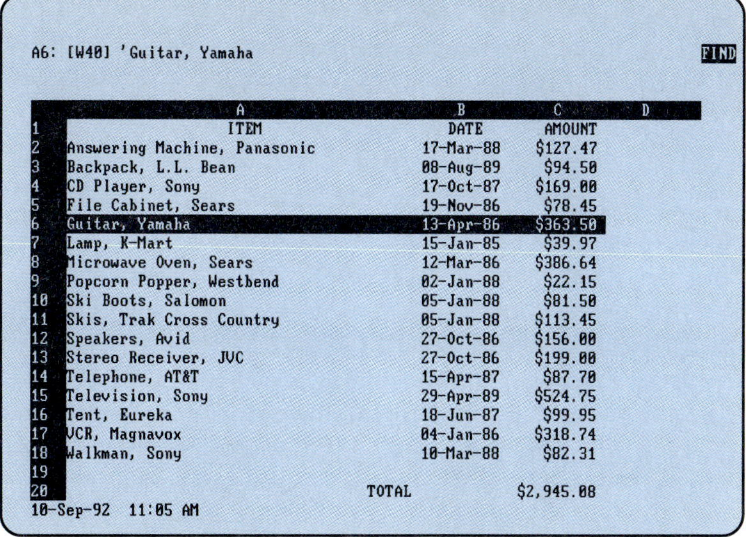

Step 9: Save the Worksheet

If you will want to use your criteria range and criterion again, you must save the PROPERTY worksheet.

Type   **/fs**
Press **Enter**
Type   **r**

Practice

1. Lotus 1-2-3 offers three special characters that can be used in criteria when searching for text: *, ?, and ~. The * (asterisk) matches any number of characters. For example, *Ski** matches *Ski lodge, Skis, Skit,* and *Skipper.* The ? (question mark) matches any single character. For example, *Ski?* matches *Skis* and *Skit,* but not *Ski lodge* and *Skipper.* The * and ? operate just like the DOS global filename characters. The ~ (tilde) matches any label except the label that follows it. For example, *~Ski* matches every label that does not begin with *Ski.* Use one of these special characters to search PROPERTY for all records that begin with *Ski* in the ITEM field.

2. Search PROPERTY for all records of items purchased after January 1, 1988.

Lesson 12: Extracting Records from a Data Base Worksheet

The Extract option of the Data Query menu lets you copy records that meet your criteria and place them in a range outside the data base. Although the term Extract implies that the records are removed from the original data base, this is not so. The Extract option merely copies the records, leaving the originals intact. This option is handy for working with a subset of a data base. For example, you could extract all records with an AMOUNT greater than or equal to $300, then print only those records.

Step 1: Specify the Criterion

In the previous lesson, you already set up the criteria range as J1 through L2 and the input range as A2 through C18. Enter the criterion again in cell L2:

Press   **F5**
Type   **L2**
Press   **Enter**
Type   **+c2>=300**
Press   **Enter**

Step 2: Set Up the Output Range

The output range is the cells where 1-2-3 will copy the records that match your criteria. The first row of the output range must contain the names of the fields that you want to extract. You do not have to extract all of the fields in the original data base. For example, you can extract only the ITEM and AMOUNT, and not the DATE. Move to a blank area of the worksheet, widen the columns, and enter the names of the fields you want to extract:

Press   **F5**
Type   **j10**
Press   **Enter**
Type   **/wcs40**
Press   **Enter**
Type   **^ITEM**
Press   **Right Arrow**
Type   **/wcs11**
Press   **Enter**
Type   **"AMOUNT**
Press   **Enter**

Step 3: Specify the Output Range

In most cases, you will not know exactly how many records 1-2-3 will find. If you specify the single row containing the field names as the output range, 1-2-3 will use as many rows as necessary for the extracted records. You should make sure you have no existing data below the row you specify. Execute the Data Query Output command and specify the output range:

Type   **/dqoj10..k10**
Press   **Enter**

The program will return to the Data Query menu.

Step 4: Extract the Records

You are now ready to extract the items and amounts of records with amounts greater than or equal to $300. Select the Extract option and then quit the Data Query menu:

Type   **e**
Type   **q**

Your screen should look like Figure 18. At this point, you could print only these records or use them for other calculations.

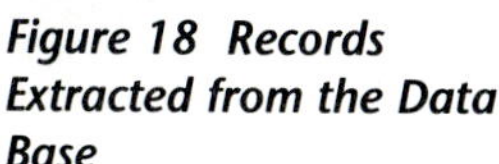

Figure 18 Records Extracted from the Data Base

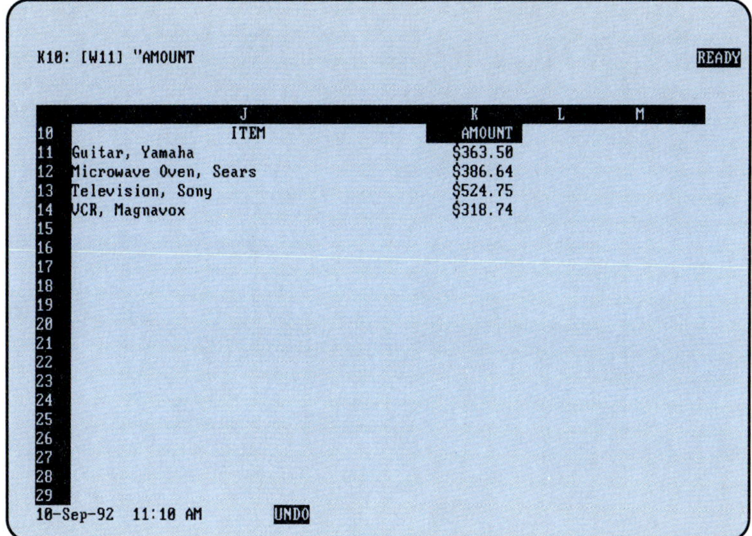

Practice   Extract the items and amounts of records with a DATE of January 1, 1988, or later. You can use the same output range.

Lesson 13: Using the Data Base Functions

Lotus 1-2-3 has a set of functions designed especially for data base worksheets. The data base functions scan a data base, select the records that match the criteria in the criteria range, then perform calculations on only the selected values. Let's briefly examine the Lotus 1-2-3 data base functions.

Step 1: Try the @DCOUNT Function

Suppose you want to know how many PROPERTY records have an AMOUNT value greater than or equal to $300. The @DCOUNT function counts the non-blank cells in a field of a data base. It considers only those records that meet the specified criteria. Follow these directions to see how @DCOUNT works:

Press   **F5**
Type   **m10**
Press   **Enter**
Type   **@dcount(a1..c18,0,j1..L2)**
Press   **Enter**

The result should be 4 (see Figure 19). The first parameter of the @DCOUNT function is the input range, which in this case is A1 to C18. The second parameter is the field number. For the data base functions, fields are numbered from the left starting at zero. In this case, it does not matter which field is checked; the 0 refers to the ITEM field. The third parameter of the @DCOUNT function is the criteria range, which is J1 to L2.

Figure 19 The @DCOUNT Function

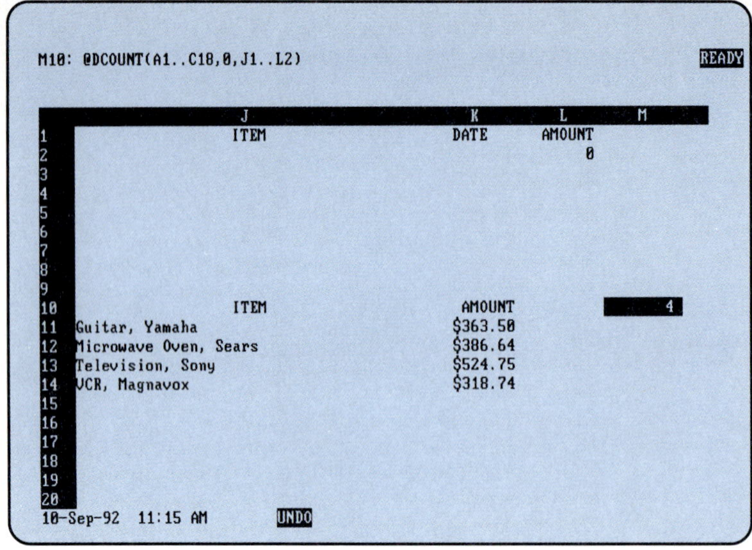

Step 2: Try the Other Data Base Functions

Lotus 1-2-3 has six other data base functions. Let's try some of them.

Type   **@davg(a1..c18,2,j1..L2)**
Press   **Enter**

The @DAVG function computes the average value of the specified field, in this case field 2, which is the AMOUNT field. It uses only those records that meet the specified criteria. Hence, the average you see is that of records with amounts greater than or equal to $300.

Type   **@dmax(a1..c18,2,j1..L2)**
Press   **Enter**

The @DMAX function returns the largest value of the specified field given the criteria.

Type   **@dmin(a1..c18,2,j1..L2)**
Press   **Enter**

The @DMIN function returns the smallest value of the specified field given the criteria.

Type   **@dsum(a1..c18,2,j1..L2)**
Press   **Enter**

The @DSUM function computes the sum of the values in the specified field given the criteria.

Two other data base functions are available in Lotus 1-2-3 for computing statistics: @DSTD and @DVAR. The @DSTD function computes the population standard deviation of the values in the specified field given the criteria. The @DVAR function computes the population variance of the values in the specified field given the criteria.

Practice   Change the criterion and use a data base function to compute the average amount of PROPERTY items that cost less than $300.

Summary

- *Creating a bar graph*. Set up the worksheet, select Bar as the graph type, and specify the data ranges.

- *Printing a graph*. Use the PrintGraph program with Lotus 1-2-3 Release 2.0 or 2.2. Execute the Print Printer Image Current Go command with Lotus 1-2-3 Release 3.0.

- *Naming a graph*. Execute the Graph Name Create command to associate a name with the current graph. The Graph Name Use command retrieves a named graph and makes it the current graph.

- *Creating a pie chart*. Set up the worksheet, select Pie as the graph type, and specify the data ranges.

- *Creating a line graph*. Set up the worksheet, select Line as the graph type, and specify the data ranges.

- *Creating a stacked bar graph*. Set up the worksheet, select Stack-Bar as the graph type, and specify the data ranges.

- *Creating an XY graph*. Set up the worksheet, select XY as the graph type, and specify the data ranges.

- *Creating a data base worksheet*. Set up the worksheet so that each column is a field and each row is a record, except for the first row, which must contain the field names.

- *Sorting a data base worksheet*. Execute the Data Sort command, specify the data range, specify one or two keys, specify the sort order, and select the Go option.

- *Searching a data base worksheet*. Set up the criteria range, enter the criteria, execute the Data Query command, specify the criteria and input ranges, and select the Find option to begin the search. Press the Down Arrow key to continue the search and the Enter key to end the search.

- *Extracting data from a worksheet*. Specify the criteria, specify the output range, and execute the Extract option from the Data Query menu.

- *Using the data base functions*. @DCOUNT, @DSUM, @DAVG, @DMIN, @DMAX, @DSTD, and @DVAR are data base functions that scan a data base, select the records that match the specified criteria, and then perform calculations on only the selected values.

Key Terms

As an extra review of this chapter, try defining the following terms.

bar graph	query
criteria	secondary key
line graph	stacked bar graph
pie chart	XY graph (scatterplot)
primary key	

Multiple Choice

Choose the best selection to complete each statement.

1. What is a chart in which numeric values are represented by evenly spaced, thick vertical lines?

   (a) bar graph
   (c) line graph
   (b) pie chart
   (d) XY graph

2. In a spreadsheet program, a graph is created from data in a

   (a) data entry form.
   (c) worksheet.
   (b) settings sheet.
   (d) separate file.

3. In bar, line, and stacked bar graphs, the X data range contains the values or labels that will appear along which axis?

   (a) horizontal
   (c) diagonal
   (b) vertical
   (d) rotational

4. After you have viewed a graph the first time with the View option from the Graph menu, which key can you press to display the current graph on the screen?

   (a) Escape
   (c) F1
   (b) Enter
   (d) F10

5. If you have Lotus 1-2-3 Release 2.0 or 2.2, what must you do to print a graph?

   (a) execute /PPICG
   (c) press Print Screen
   (b) use the PrintGraph program
   (d) press Ctrl-Alt-Del

6. Which command retrieves a named graph and makes it the current graph?

   (a) Graph Name Create
   (c) Graph Name Use
   (b) Graph Name Reset
   (d) Graph Name Delete

7. Which type of graph would you use to show the parts of a whole?

   (a) bar graph
   (c) line graph
   (b) pie chart
   (d) XY graph

8. In a pie chart, which data range contains the values that will be represented as slices?

   (a) A
   (c) C
   (b) B
   (d) X

9. In a pie chart, which optional data range can be used to specify hatch patterns and whether slices are to be exploded?

   (a) A
   (c) C
   (b) B
   (d) X

10. Which type of graph is often used to plot values that change over time as points at appropriate distances above the horizontal axis?

    (a) bar graph
    (c) line graph
    (b) pie chart
    (d) stacked bar graph

11. What graph feature identifies the data represented by each different symbol, type of line, or pattern in a graph?

    (a) legend
    (c) axis label
    (b) title
    (d) data label

12. Which type of graph shows components and total amounts for each category?
    - (a) bar graph
    - (b) line graph
    - (c) XY graph
    - (d) stacked bar graph

13. Which type of graph is often used to show the correlation between two variables?
    - (a) bar graph
    - (b) line graph
    - (c) XY graph
    - (d) stacked bar graph

14. Each row in a data base worksheet represents a
    - (a) field.
    - (b) record.
    - (c) file.
    - (d) character.

15. Each column in a data base worksheet represents a
    - (a) field.
    - (b) record.
    - (c) file.
    - (d) character.

16. The first row in a data base worksheet must contain the
    - (a) first record.
    - (b) first field.
    - (c) field names.
    - (d) record numbers.

17. Which Lotus 1-2-3 menu contains commands for manipulating a data base worksheet?
    - (a) Worksheet
    - (b) Data
    - (c) File
    - (d) Range

18. The first sort order is determined by the
    - (a) primary key.
    - (b) secondary key.
    - (b) primary record.
    - (d) secondary record.

19. In Lotus 1-2-3, what must you set up to search a data base worksheet?
    - (a) data range
    - (b) sort order
    - (c) query
    - (d) output range

20. Which function is not a data base function?
    - (a) @DSUM
    - (b) @AVG
    - (c) @DCOUNT
    - (d) @DVAR

Fill-In

1. A _______ graph is a chart in which numeric values are represented by evenly spaced, thick vertical lines.

2. Before you can create a graph, you must first create the _______ that contains the data for the graph.

3. Lotus 1-2-3 Release _______ does not require you to use PrintGraph to print out your graphs.

4. Lotus 1-2-3 lets you have several graphs associated with the same worksheet, if you _______ your graphs.

5. The Graph Name _______ command retrieves a named graph and makes it the current graph.

6. A _______ chart represents values as wedges of a circle.

7. A _______ graph is useful for plotting values that change over time.

8. A _______ bar graph is a variation of the basic bar graph that shows components and total amounts for each category.

9. A(n) _______ graph can be used to show a correlation between price and the number of units sold.

10. The _______ function converts the year, month, and day numbers into a single number that 1-2-3 uses to keep track of dates.

11. The Data _______ command is used to rearrange the records in a worksheet data base.

12. A _______ is a field in a data base used to sort the records.

13. For text, _______ order is simply alphabetical order from A to Z.

14. In 1-2-3, you must set up a _______ to search a data base worksheet.

15. In a query, the _______ range consists of at least two rows: the first row must include one or more field names and the second row must include one or more expressions that specify the field values you want to find.

16. Before you can search for records in a worksheet data base, you must specify the criteria and _______ ranges.

17. When 1-2-3 is in FIND mode, you press the _______ key to advance to the next matching record.

18. The three special characters *, ?, and ~ can be used in criteria when _______ for text.

19. The _______ option of the Data Query menu lets you copy records that meet your criteria and place them in a range outside the data base.

20. The _______ function counts the nonblank cells in a field of a data base worksheet, considering only those records that meet the specified criteria.

Short Problems

1. Retrieve the SALES worksheet you created in Lesson 1. Execute the Graph Name Use command and tell 1-2-3 that you want to use the SALES_BAR graph. Return to the Graph menu and select Options Data-Labels. For the A data range, assign B2..E2 as the range of data labels. Then select the Above option. Return to the Graph menu and view the graph. Assigning data labels in this manner presents the actual value of each bar.

2. If you are running Lotus 1-2-3 Release 2.0 or 2.2, use the PrintGraph program to print the new SALES_BAR graph. Try printing it in a different font.

   If you are running Lotus 1-2-3 Release 3.0, execute the Graph Options Advanced Text First Font command. Then select 2, 4, 5, 6, 7, or 8 to change the font of the first line of the graph title. Repeat the process for the Second and Third graph text groups, then print the graph.

3. Move the cell pointer to a blank area of the SALES worksheet below all data. Execute the Graph Name Table command and use the current cell as the range. Return to READY mode and examine the worksheet. The Graph Name Table command creates a three-column table that lists all named graphs in the worksheet, along with their graph types and titles.

4. View the SALES_PIE graph you created in Lesson 5. Modify the chart so that all slices are exploded. Save and print the new pie chart.

5. View the SALES_LINE graph you created in Lesson 6. Add horizontal and vertical grid lines to the graph. Save and print the new line graph.

6. View the SALES_STACK graph you created in Lesson 7. Add data labels above each bar for all three data ranges. Save and print the new stacked bar graph.

7. View the SALES_XY graph you created in Lesson 8. Add horizontal and vertical grid lines to the graph. Save and print the new XY graph.

8. Erase the current worksheet from the screen and retrieve the PROPERTY data base worksheet you created in Lesson 9. Make up at least ten more records and add them to the worksheet. If you add new records after the last record, you may have to change the range to include the new rows in the formula that computes the sum of the amounts.

9. Sort the PROPERTY worksheet by DATE, with the oldest item appearing first.

10. Set up a query and use a data base function to compute the average amount of PROPERTY items that cost more than $100.

Long Problems

1. Create a worksheet and bar graph to compare tape rentals of movies of various categories for the month of March for Valley Video. Use the following movie categories and numbers of rentals:

Adventure	222
Comedy	179
Foreign	65
Horror	130
Mystery	205

Be sure to create a two-line title for the graph and label both axes. Save the worksheet and print the graph.

2. Create a worksheet and multiple data range line graph to plot the sales of three computer magazines for the years 1985 to 1990. Use different symbols for each magazine, connect the points with line segments, and have 1-2-3 generate a legend. Use the following data for the numbers of thousands of magazines sold per year:

	1985	1986	1987	1989	1990
Megabytes Magazine	200	160	140	130	120
Number Cruncher	90	110	120	104	110
Hardware User	60	90	106	140	150

Be sure to create a two-line title for the graph and label both axes. Save the worksheet and print the graph.

3. Create a worksheet and pie chart to show the cost-per-unit breakdown for a Beaver Canoe. Use the following data:

Advertising	$69.99
Labor	$99.99
Materials	$219.98
Packaging	$30.00
Service	$79.99

Be sure to create a two-line title for the chart and label the pie slices. Save the worksheet and print the chart.

4. Suppose Beaver Canoe Company went public in 1988. Create a worksheet and stacked bar graph to compare the components of total capitalization. Use the following data, in millions of dollars, for each fiscal year:

	1988	1989	1990
Stockholder Equity	9	11	14
Long-Term Debt	5	4	4
Short-Term Debt	1	2	3

Be sure to create a two-line title for the graph, generate a legend, and label both axes. Save the worksheet and print the graph.

5. Create a pie chart from the 1990 data in Long Problem 4. Be sure to create a two-line title for the chart and label the pie slices. Save the worksheet and print the chart.

6. Create a worksheet and XY graph to depict the relationship between per capita income (in U.S. dollars) and male life expectancy (in years). Plot per capita income along the X axis and life expectancy along the Y axis. Use the following data:

Country	Per Capita Income	Male Life Expectancy
Afghanistan	$168	40
Australia	$9,914	70
Belgium	$9,827	69
Brazil	$1,523	61
Cambodia	$90	44
Canada	$10,193	69
Denmark	$12,956	71
Ecuador	$1,050	55
Ethiopia	$117	37
France	$7,179	70
West Germany	$11,142	67
Guatemala	$1,083	48
Haiti	$300	47
Honduras	$822	53
India	$150	52
Iran	$2,160	58
Israel	$3,332	72
Italy	$6,914	70
Jamaica	$1,340	65
Japan	$8,460	73
Kenya	$196	56
Kuwait	$11,431	67
Laos	$85	39
Libya	$6,335	51
Mexico	$1,800	62
Nicaragua	$804	51
Norway	$12,432	73
Pakistan	$280	54
Poland	$4,670	66
Singapore	$4,100	68

Country	Per Capita Income	Male Life Expectancy
Spain	$5,500	70
Sweden	$14,821	73
Turkey	$1,300	57
USSR	$2,600	64
USA	$11,675	71

Be sure to create a two-line title for the graph, connect the points with line segments, and label both axes. Save the worksheet and print the graph.

7. Retrieve the worksheet you created in Long Problem 6. Save it in a file with a different name to create a copy of the worksheet and graph. Examine the data and the printed graph. Eliminate those data points that deviate significantly from the pattern. Modify the graph so that Lotus 1-2-3 labels each point. Save the worksheet and print the graph. The moral of this problem: data can be carefully selected and graphs designed to enhance or distort the facts.

8. Create an "electronic Rolodex" with Lotus 1-2-3. Set up the columns and enter the records of a worksheet data base to hold the information you keep in your personal address book. Include fields for last name, first name, address, city, state, ZIP code, and phone number. Sort the data base by last name and then by first name. Print the worksheet when you are finished.

9. Create a data base worksheet to hold the following expense records:

No	Date	Category	Amount	Description
13	03-Mar-90	Freight	$8.75	UPS
4	09-Jan-90	Publications	$3.95	PC Magazine
1	04-Jan-90	Freight	$8.50	Federal Express
3	09-Jan-90	Freight	$2.79	Postage
15	16-Mar-90	Supplies	$5.05	Envelopes
6	14-Jan-90	Supplies	$40.98	Diskettes
20	28-Mar-90	Freight	$13.50	Federal Express
8	02-Feb-90	Software	$49.88	Reflex Plus upgrade
2	04-Jan-90	Freight	$8.50	Federal Express
10	11-Feb-90	Freight	$4.79	Postage Stamps
16	20-Mar-90	Freight	$8.50	Federal Express
11	13-Feb-90	Freight	$9.50	Federal Express
18	22-Mar-90	Publications	$19.95	Using PageMaker
14	04-Mar-90	Publications	$12.70	The Well-Connected PC
5	14-Jan-90	Publications	$3.00	CD-ROM Magazine
9	10-Feb-90	Utilities	$10.04	Telephone calls
17	21-Mar-90	Freight	$8.50	Federal Express
12	21-Feb-90	Freight	$14.50	Federal Express
19	24-Mar-90	Supplies	$35.66	Computer Paper
7	02-Feb-90	Hardware	$18.01	IBM Modem Cable

Sort the records by No or Date and sum the amounts.

10. Use the data base worksheet you created in Long Problem 9. In a blank part of the worksheet, set up queries and use the @DSUM function to compute subtotals for the following expense categories: Freight, Hardware, Publications, Software, Supplies, and Utilities.

ADVANCED LOTUS 1-2-3

In This Chapter

Preview

The previous two chapters taught you most of what the average user needs to know about Lotus 1-2-3. This chapter proceeds to more advanced spreadsheet topics, including powerful new features found in Lotus 1-2-3 Release 2.2 and Release 3.0. You may not need all of the commands and features presented in this chapter, but many of them can make your work easier, quicker, and less tedious. Learning more about Lotus 1-2-3 can help you create more complex and powerful worksheets.

After studying this chapter, you will know how to

- change worksheet settings.
- freeze titles and use windows.
- hide columns and protect cells.
- change range formats.
- use range names.
- fill a range with a sequence of numbers.
- transpose columns and rows.
- control recalculation and iteration.
- use relative, absolute, and mixed cell references.
- use additional functions.
- use macros.
- use the Release 2.2 Learn feature.
- use the Release 3.0 Record feature.
- use file linking with Release 2.2 and 3.0.
- use three-dimensional worksheets with Release 3.0.

Getting Started

You've already learned how to start Lotus 1-2-3 and use its most basic features and commands. This chapter assumes you have completed the lessons and exercises in Chapters 4 and 5. Furthermore, it assumes that you have a computer with a hard disk and Lotus 1-2-3 installed on it in a subdirectory named 123 or 123R3. A DOS path should be set up so that you can run Lotus 1-2-3 from within any subdirectory. You should have a subdirectory named LESSONS in which to store your worksheet files.

Lesson 1: Changing Worksheet Settings

Worksheet is the first option in the Main menu of Lotus 1-2-3. Selecting Worksheet activates a submenu of options for changing worksheet settings. The Worksheet Global options affect the entire worksheet. Other Worksheet options let you insert and delete columns and rows, set column widths, hide columns, erase the entire worksheet, freeze titles on the screen, split the display into windows, show the current worksheet settings, and insert page breaks into the worksheet. Let's explore some of these options.

Step 1: Start 1-2-3

If you are not already running Lotus 1-2-3, switch to your LESSONS subdirectory
and start the program:

> Type `cd c:\lessons`
> Press **Enter**
> Type `123`
> Press **Enter**

Step 2: Set the Global Format

The Worksheet Global Format command lets you specify the way numeric values
are to appear for the entire worksheet. We will discuss the various types of
formatting later in this chapter when we cover the Range Format command. For
now, let's just change the global format of the worksheet to Currency.

> Type `/wgfc`
> Press **Enter**

The default number of decimal places is two. Enter a number into any cell and
you will see it formatted as a currency value.

> Type **100**
> Press **Enter**

Step 3: Set the Global Label-Prefix

The Worksheet Global Label-Prefix command lets you set the alignment of labels
for the entire worksheet. The default label alignment is Left, which means that
the apostrophe (') is the default global label-prefix character. Suppose you want
all labels to be centered unless you explicitly specify otherwise. Set the global
label-prefix to Center, which will automatically use the caret (ˆ) as the label-prefix
character.

> Type `/wglc`

Now move the cell pointer and enter a label into any cell.

> Press **Right Arrow**
> Type **One**
> Press **Enter**

The label will be centered automatically within its cell.

Step 4: Set the Global Column-Width

You already know how to set the column width for the entire worksheet, but
let's try it once more. Use the Worksheet Global Column-Width command to set
the width of every column to 15 characters.

> Type `/wgc15`
> Press **Enter**

Every column will widen to 15 characters.

Step 5: Set the Global Default Directory

By default, 1-2-3 will search the current disk drive directory for files that you want to retrieve and it will place files that you save in that same directory. If you have a DOS PATH statement set up so that you can run 1-2-3 from within any subdirectory, you probably will not have to change this default directory setting. But suppose you want Lotus 1-2-3 to use C:\LESSONS as its default directory for saving and retrieving files, no matter which directory you are in when you start the program. Execute the Worksheet Global Default Directory command and enter the path of the directory you want 1-2-3 to use.

Type	**/wgdd**
Press	**Escape**
Type	**c:\lessons**
Press	**Enter**
Type	**q**

For the rest of your 1-2-3 session, the LESSONS subdirectory will be the default directory. If you want to make this the default directory every time you use 1-2-3, you would execute the Worksheet Global Default Update command.

Step 6: Set the Display of Zero Values

By default, 1-2-3 displays values of zero, whether they are entered as numbers or are the results of formulas. For example, move the cell pointer and enter a zero into a cell.

Press	**Down Arrow**
Type	**0**
Press	**Enter**

As you can see, $0.00 is displayed in cell B2. Suppose you want to suppress the display of zero values. Execute the Worksheet Global Zero Yes command.

Type	**/wgzy**

Examine cell B2. In the worksheet, the cell appears to be empty, but the control panel shows that the cell contains the number 0.

To turn on the display of zero values, execute the Worksheet Global Zero No command.

Lotus 1-2-3 Release 2.2 and Release 3.0 also let you display a label instead of zero values in the worksheet. For example, if you are running Release 2.2 or 3.0, try the Worksheet Global Zero Label command:

Type	**/wgzl**
Type	**(zero)**
Press	**Enter**

The label "*(zero)* will appear instead of zero values in the worksheet.

Step 7: Display the Worksheet Status

The Worksheet Status command displays information about memory use, current global settings, and various hardware options.

Type	**/ws**

Figure 1 shows the result. When you are finished examining the status screen, press any key to return to ready mode.

Press	**Enter**

Figure 2 Row 1 and Column A Frozen as Titles

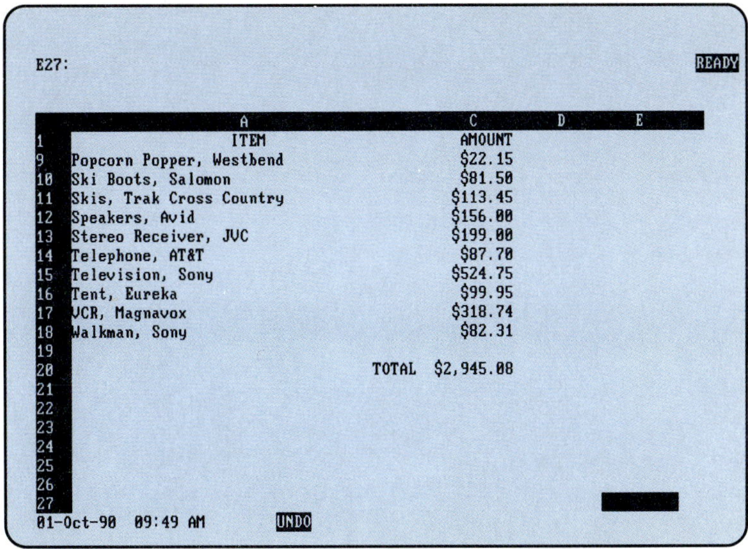

Step 4: Clear the Titles

The Worksheet Titles Clear command lets you unfreeze all existing titles.

> Type   **/wtc**
> Press **Home**

You can now move to row 1 or column A, and they will disappear when the worksheet is scrolled.

Step 5: Split the Screen Into Two Windows

The Worksheet Windows command lets you split the screen into two horizontal or vertical windows so you can view two different parts of the same worksheet. Suppose you want two horizontal windows. Move the cell pointer to the row that you want to be the top of the bottom window, say row 11, and then execute the Worksheet Window Horizontal command.

> Press **Down Arrow (10 times)**
> Type   **/wwh**

Figure 3 shows the result. The top of the second window is marked by the second column border across the middle of the screen. The top window is active and the cell pointer is in A10.

Step 6: Move Between Windows

Right now, you are in the top window. Any vertical pointer movement keys will act only within this window. For example, move the cell pointer down ten cells.

> Press **Down Arrow** (10 times)

Notice that the top window scrolls while the bottom window remains still.

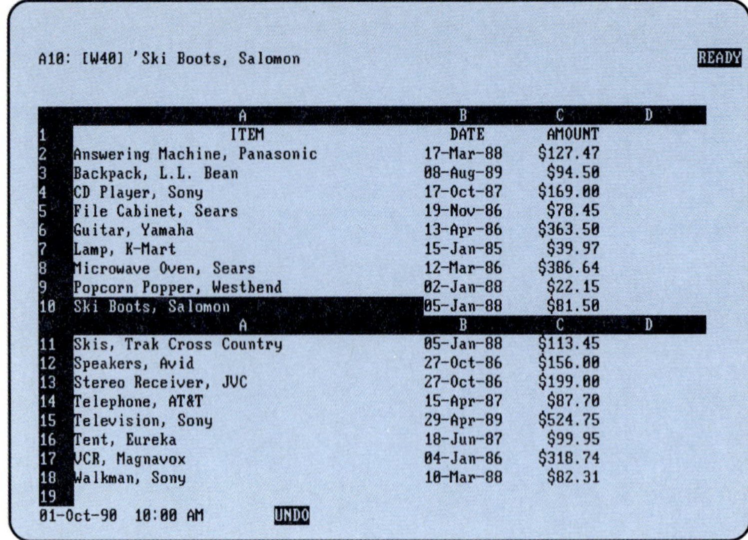

Figure 3 Two Horizontal Windows

Suppose you want to move to the bottom window. The F6 function key lets you move to the other window. Switch to the bottom window, and move the cell pointer up ten rows.

Press **F6**
Press **Up Arrow** (10 times)

This time, the bottom window will scroll while the top window remains still. Switch to the top window again and move the cell pointer to A1.

Press **F6**
Press **Home**

Step 7: Unsynchronize Windows

By default, windows are synchronized. For vertical windows, this means that the same rows are kept on the screen in both windows when you scroll up or down. For horizontal windows, this means that the same columns will remain on the screen in both windows when you scroll right or left. For example, move the cell pointer to the right.

Press **Right Arrow** (4 times)

The screen will scroll so that the same columns appear in both windows.

You can tell 1-2-3 to allow windows to scroll independently in all directions by executing the Worksheet Window Unsync command.

Type **/wwu**

Now move the cell pointer to the left in the top window.

Press **Left Arrow** (4 times)

Only the top window will scroll to the left. The bottom window will remain still.

Step 8: Clear Windows

When you are finished using windows, you can restore the screen to a single window by executing the Worksheet Window Clear command.

> Type   **/wwc**

The contents and settings of the window that was on the top or the left will expand to occupy the entire screen.

Practice

1. Freeze column A as a vertical title. Move the cell pointer to the right and see how column A always remains on the screen. When you are finished, clear worksheet titles.
2. Move the cell pointer to column B and split the screen into two vertical windows. Tell 1-2-3 to synchronize the windows. Move the cell pointer down 25 rows and see how the two vertical windows scroll together. When you are finished, clear worksheet windows and move the cell pointer to A1.

Lesson 3: Hiding Columns and Protecting Cells

Worksheets often contain sensitive data, such as salaries and grades, that you may not want anyone to see. Lotus 1-2-3 lets you hide columns without erasing the data they contain. Worksheets may also contain data that should not be changed by the average user. Lotus 1-2-3 lets you protect ranges of cells to prevent them from being changed.

Step 1: Hide a Column

Suppose you want to keep the AMOUNT values in the PROPERTY worksheet private. The Worksheet Column Hide command lets you conceal the contents of one or more columns. Move to column C and execute the Worksheet Column Hide command.

> Press   **Home**
> Press   **Right Arrow** (2 times)
> Type   **/wch**
> Press   **Enter**

Figure 4 shows the result. Column C appears to have been removed from the worksheet. In fact, it is only hidden.

Step 2: Display a Column

Now suppose you want to see the hidden column. Execute the Worksheet Column Display command and enter a cell address from the hidden column.

> Type   **/wcd**
> Type   **c1**
> Press   **Enter**

The hidden column will reappear in the worksheet.

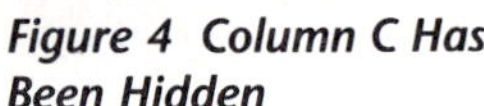

*Figure 4 Column C Has
Been Hidden*

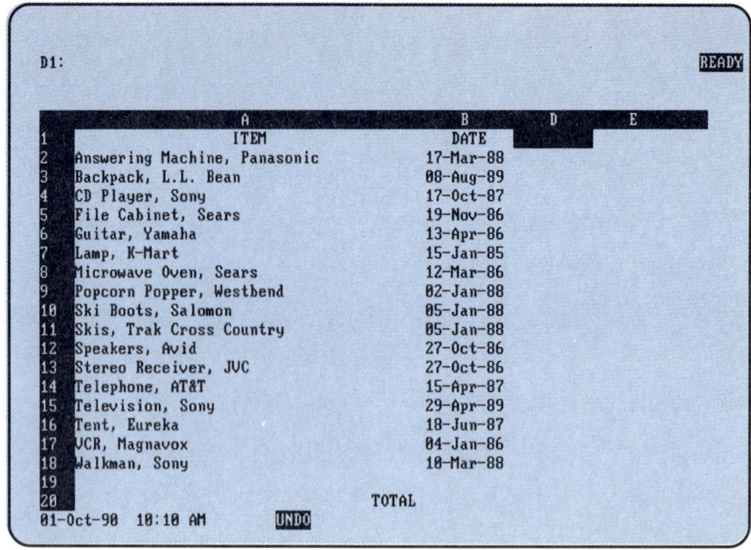

Step 3: Create a Template

A **template** is a general-purpose worksheet in which the user fills in the blanks
or changes selected entries to perform a well-defined task. The person who
creates the template enters the labels, formulas, and perhaps some constant
numbers. The person who uses the template supplies the variables. The template
generates the result. For example, you could create a template to compute the
monthly payment on a loan, given the principal, interest rate, and term. Follow
these directions to create such a template:

Type	**/wey**
Type	**/wgfc**
Press	**Enter**
Type	**/wgc15**
Press	**Enter**
Press	**Right Arrow**
Type	**'<-- Enter the amount of the loan**
Press	**Down Arrow**
Type	**'<-- Enter the annual interest rate**
Press	**Down Arrow**
Type	**'<-- Enter the term in months**
Press	**Down Arrow**
Type	**'<-- This is the monthly payment**
Press	**Left Arrow**
Type	**@pmt(a1,a2/12,a3)**
Press	**Up Arrow**
Type	**/rfga2..a3**
Press	**Enter**

The ERR message you see in cell A4 indicates a division by zero in the formula.
It will disappear as soon as numbers are entered into cells A1, A2, and A3.

Step 4: Try the Template

The template is now set up for a user to enter values in cells A1, A2, and A3. Let's try the template.

    Press **Home**
    Type   **4500**
    Press **Down Arrow**
    Type   **12%**
    Press **Down Arrow**
    Type   **24**
    Press **Enter**

The template will calculate the monthly payment to be $211.83.

Step 5: Protect the Worksheet

In this template, only cells A1, A2, and A3 should be changed by the user. The user should not change the labels or the formula. The Worksheet Global Protection Enable command prevents changes being made to all cells. The Range Unprot command can then be used to turn off protection for those cells the user is supposed to change.

    Type   **/wgpe**

Now try changing a cell.

    Type   **hello**
    Press **Enter**

Lotus 1-2-3 will beep and display the message

    Protected cell

Cancel your attempted change.

    Press **Escape**

Step 6: Unprotect Selected Cells

The template is worthless if no cells can be changed. You must use the Range Unprot command to turn off protection for cells A1 through A3.

    Type   **/rua1..a3**
    Press **Enter**

Now, try changing the amount of the loan to $9,000.

    Press **Home**
    Type   **9000**
    Press **Enter**

Cells A1 through A3 can be changed, but all other cells in the worksheet are protected.

Step 7: Save the Worksheet

Save the template you have created in a worksheet file named LOAN so that you can use it in the future.

    Type   **/fs**
    Type   **loan**
    Press **Enter**

Practice

1. The Range Protect command lets you protect one or more cells you have unprotected with the Range Unprot command. For example, suppose the interest rate will never change and you don't want users to alter it. Use the Range Protect command to prevent cell A2 from being changed. Try to change it and see what happens.

2. Protection for the entire worksheet can be turned off with the Worksheet Global Protection Disable command. Use this command to allow changes to all cells in the worksheet.

Lesson 4: Changing Range Formats

Lotus 1-2-3 lets you set the numeric format of one cell, a range of cells, or every cell in the worksheet. So far, you have used General format, which is the default, and Currency format, which is used for dollar amounts. Let's examine each of the formats you can set with the Range Format command.

Step 1: Set Up a New Worksheet

Erase the worksheet from your screen and widen all columns to 15 characters.

    Type   **/wey**
    Type   **/wgc15**
    Press   **Enter**

Step 2: Use the General Format

General format displays negative numbers with a leading minus sign, does not use commas to separate thousands, and suppresses trailing zeros after the decimal point. If the number is too large to fit within the column width, scientific notation is used to express the number. When the number of digits to the right of the decimal point exceeds the column width, 1-2-3 displays as many digits as it can. General format is the default numeric format used for all cells unless you specify otherwise. Try General format.

    Type   **General**
    Press   **Right Arrow**
    Type   **12345.678**
    Press   **Down Arrow**
    Press   **Left Arrow**

Step 3: Use the Fixed Format

Fixed format lets you specify how many decimal places to display, from 0 to 15. Values are rounded or filled out with zeros to fit the exact number of decimal places you specify. Negative numbers have a leading minus sign and commas are not used to separate thousands. Values between -1 and 1 are expressed with a leading zero before the decimal point. Enter a number and use the Range Format Fixed command with two decimal places.

    Type   **Fixed**
    Press   **Right Arrow**
    Type   **12345.678**
    Press   **Enter**

Type **/rff**
Press **Enter**
Press **Enter**
Press **Down Arrow**
Press **Left Arrow**

Notice that 12345.678 is rounded to 12345.68 to fit the Fixed format with two decimal places.

Step 4: Use the Scientific Format

Scientific format expresses numbers in exponential notation. It is useful for very large or very small numbers. A number in scientific format has three parts: the mantissa, the letter E, and the exponent. The **mantissa** is the decimal part of the number. The letter E indicates exponential format and separates the mantissa from the exponent. The **exponent** indicates the power of ten to be multiplied by the mantissa to yield the number. For example, $1.5E + 02$ is equal to 1.5×10^2 or 150. Either the mantissa or the exponent can be negative. For example, $-1.5E - 02$ is equal to -1.5×10^{-2} or -0.015. The mantissa can have up to 15 decimal places and the exponent can be any number from -99 to 99. Enter a number and use the Range Format Scientific command with two decimal places.

Type **Scientific**
Press **Right Arrow**
Type **12345.678**
Press **Enter**
Type **/rfs**
Press **Enter**
Press **Enter**
Press **Down Arrow**
Press **Left Arrow**

Notice that 12345.678 is expressed in scientific format as $1.23E + 04$ with the mantissa rounded to two decimal places.

Step 5: Use the Currency Format

You have already used Currency format, but let's try it again. Numbers are displayed with a currency symbol, such as $, thousands are separated by commas, and up to 15 decimal places can be specified. Negative values are enclosed in parentheses, a common convention in financial worksheets. However, the currency symbol and the expression of negative values in parentheses can be changed with the Worksheet Global Default Other International command. Enter a number and use the Range Format Currency command with two decimal places.

Type **Currency**
Press **Right Arrow**
Type **12345.678**
Press **Enter**
Type **/rfc**
Press **Enter**
Press **Enter**
Press **Down Arrow**
Press **Left Arrow**

The number will be rounded to two decimal places and expressed as $12,345.68.

Step 6: Use the Comma Format

Comma format is essentially the same as Currency format except it does not display the leading currency symbol. Enter a number and use the Range Format , (comma) command with two decimal places.

Type	**Comma**
Press	**Right Arrow**
Type	**12345.678**
Press	**Enter**
Type	**/rf,**
Press	**Enter**
Press	**Enter**
Press	**Down Arrow**
Press	**Left Arrow**

The number will be expressed as 12,345.68.

Step 7: Use the +/− Format

The +/− format displays a horizontal bar of plus signs or minus signs, or a period. It is used to generate crude bar graphs. The number of plus signs or minus signs equals the whole-number value of the entry rounded to the nearest integer. For example, if you enter 5 into a cell in +/− format, five plus signs will be displayed. If you enter −5 instead, five minus signs will be displayed. If the number is between −1 and 1, a period will be displayed. Enter a number and use the Range Format +/− command.

Type	**'+/−**
Press	**Right Arrow**
Type	**5**
Press	**Enter**
Type	**/rf+**
Press	**Enter**
Press	**Down Arrow**
Press	**Left Arrow**

You should see five plus signs instead of the number 5 in cell B6.

Step 8: Use the Percent Format

Percent format displays numbers as percentages with up to 15 decimal places and a trailing percent sign. In other words, a number expressed in Percent format is multiplied by 100. Enter a number and use the Range Format Percent command with two decimal places.

Type	**Percent**
Press	**Right Arrow**
Type	**0.678**
Press	**Enter**
Type	**/rfp**
Press	**Enter**
Press	**Enter**
Press	**Down Arrow**
Press	**Left Arrow**

You should see the number expressed as 67.80%.

Step 9: Use the Date and Time Formats

Lotus 1-2-3 maintains dates and times as numbers that can be used in calculations. Each day between January 1, 1900 and December 31, 2099 is assigned a sequential date number. January 1, 1900 is 1; January 2, 1900 is 2; and so on up to December 31, 2099, which is 73050. The total time in each day is represented by the number 1. The time number for midnight is 0.0; noon is 0.5; and just before midnight is 0.99999. Although these date and time numbers might seem strange, you can perform calculations with them, and 1-2-3 can easily express them in the format you are used to seeing. The Date option of the Range Format menu lets you express date numbers as dates, such as 21-Jun-90, and time numbers as times, such as 02:38:24 PM. Enter a number and use the Range Format Date 1 (DD-MM-YY) command.

Type	**Date**
Press	**Right Arrow**
Type	**33045**
Press	**Enter**
Type	**/rfd1**
Press	**Enter**
Press	**Down Arrow**
Press	**Left Arrow**

You should see the date number 33045 expressed as the date 21-Jun-90 in cell B8. Now, enter a number and use the Range Format Date Time 1 (HH:MM:SS AM/PM) command.

Type	**Time**
Press	**Right Arrow**
Type	**0.61**
Press	**Enter**
Type	**/rfdt1**
Press	**Enter**
Press	**Down Arrow**
Press	**Left Arrow**

You should see the time number 0.61 expressed as the time 02:38:24 PM in cell B9.

Step 10: Use the Text Format

Text format displays formulas in worksheet cells instead of their computed results. This format can be handy for checking formulas in a complex worksheet. Numbers in cells formatted as Text are displayed in General format. Enter a formula and use the Range Format Text command to display that formula instead of its computed result in the worksheet.

Type	**Text**
Press	**Right Arrow**
Type	**+b1+b2**
Press	**Enter**
Type	**/rft**
Press	**Enter**
Press	**Down Arrow**
Press	**Left Arrow**

You should see the formula +B1+B2 in cell B10 instead of the computed result 24691.356.

Step 11: Use the Hidden Format

Hidden format allows you to conceal the contents of one or more cells in the worksheet. The contents of a hidden cell still exist and can be viewed in the control panel unless the cell is protected and global protection is turned on. Enter a number and use the Range Format Hidden command to conceal it.

    Type   **Hidden**
    Press   **Right Arrow**
    Type   **12345.678**
    Press   **Enter**
    Type   **/rfh**
    Press   **Enter**

As Figure 5 shows, cell B11 appears to be empty in the worksheet, but its contents are visible in the control panel.

To reveal hidden cells, you can change their format to anything but Hidden. You can also use the Range Format Reset command to restore the global cell format for those cells.

Step 12: Save the Worksheet

Save the worksheet you have created in a file named FORMATS in case you want to use it again.

    Type   **/fs**
    Type   **formats**
    Press   **Enter**

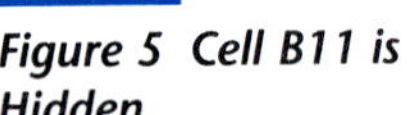

Practice   1. Change the format of cell B2 to Fixed format with 0 decimal places. Notice how the number is rounded to 12346.

2. Change the number in cell B6 to −5 and observe the result. Change the number to 0.5 and see what happens. Finally, try entering 50 into the cell. The asterisks indicate that the contents cannot fit within the specified column width. Change the number back to 5.

Figure 5 Cell B11 is Hidden

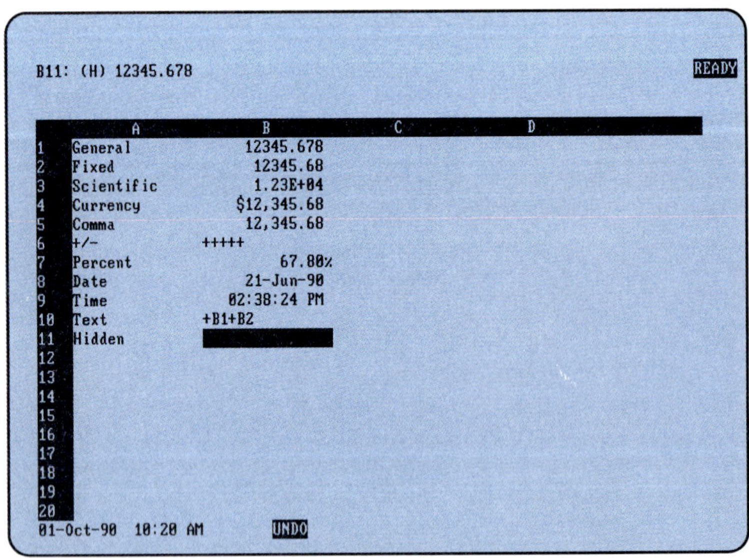

Lesson 5: Using Range Names

You have learned that a range of cells is designated like this: A1..B10. Lotus 1-2-3 also lets you assign a name to a range of cells. Range names can make it much easier to specify ranges in formulas and commands. Let's retrieve the BUDGET worksheet and see how to use range names.

Step 1: Retrieve the BUDGET Worksheet

Execute the File Retrieve command and select the BUDGET worksheet.

Type   **/fr**
Highlight **BUDGET.WK1** (or **BUDGET.WK3**)
Press   **Enter**

Step 2: Name a Range

The expenses for January are in the range B6..B16. Let's name this range. A range name can be up to 15 characters long. It should not start with a number or resemble a cell address, such as B5. A range name cannot contain spaces or any of these characters:

, ; + * - / & < > { @ #

You can, however, use the underscore (_) character in range names. Execute the Range Name Create command, enter a name, and specify the range.

Type   **/rnc**
Type   **jan_expenses**
Press   **Enter**
Type   **b6..b16**
Press   **Enter**

Step 3: Use the Range Name in a Command

Let's use the range name JAN_EXPENSES to copy the expenses from column B to column D.

Type   **/c**
Type   **jan_expenses**
Press   **Enter**
Type   **d6**
Press   **Enter**

If you don't remember or don't want to type the range name you want to use, you can press the F3 function key to display a menu of range names. For example, follow these directions.

Type   **/c**
Press   **F3**
Highlight **JAN_EXPENSES**
Press   **Enter**
Type   **e6**
Press   **Enter**

The contents of the JAN_EXPENSES range have been copied to columns D and E.

Step 4: Examine the Other Range Name Options

Activate the Range Name menu and examine the other Range Name options.

> Type   **/rn**

Figure 6 shows the Range Name menu. The Create option lets you change an existing range name as well as create a new one. The Delete option lets you remove a range name. The Labels option lets you assign range names to single-cell ranges, using the labels in adjacent cells as the range names. The Reset option deletes all range names. The Table option creates a two column table that lists all your range names and their corresponding ranges.

1. Move the cell pointer to B17 and examine the formula. Lotus 1-2-3 automatically replaced the B6..B16 in the formula with the range name JAN_EXPENSES.

2. Create range names for the February, March, and April expenses.

3. Move to an empty portion of the worksheet and execute the Range Name Table command. Return to READY mode.

Lesson 6: Filling a Range with a Sequence of Numbers

Sometimes, it is useful to fill a range of cells with a sequence of numbers. For example, suppose you wanted to number each item in your PROPERTY inventory. The Data Fill command makes it easy to generate sequences of numbers.

Step 1: Retrieve the PROPERTY Worksheet

Make PROPERTY your current worksheet.

> Type   **/fr**
> Highlight   **PROPERTY.WK1 (or PROPERTY.WK3)**

Figure 6 The Range Name Menu

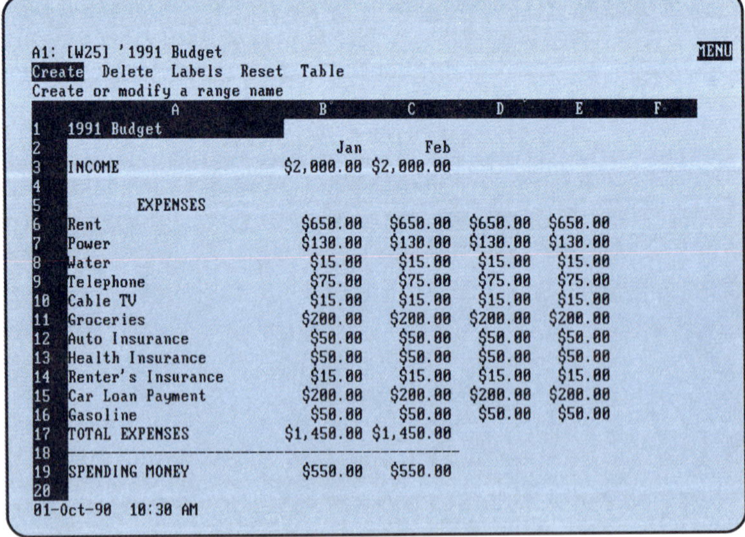

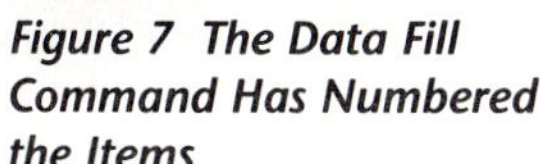

Figure 7 The Data Fill Command Has Numbered the Items

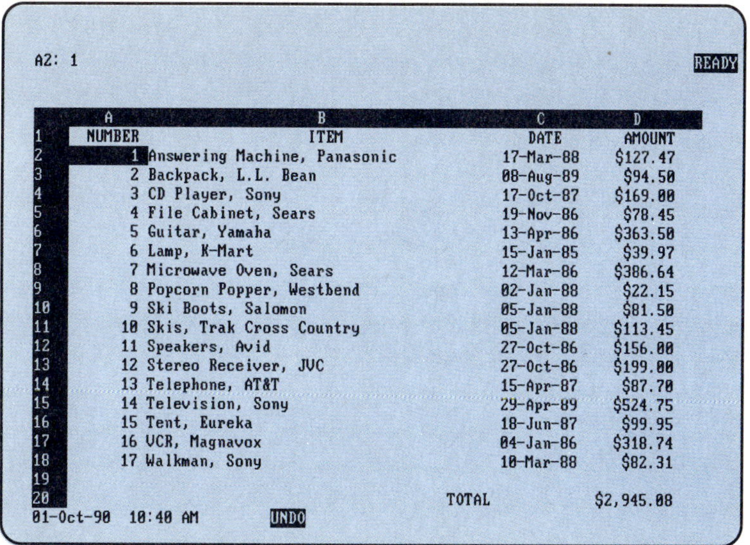

		Press	**Enter**

Press   **Enter**
Press   **Home**

Step 2: Insert a New Column A

To number the items in the first column, you must insert a new column A. Execute the Worksheet Insert Column command.

Type   **/wic**
Press   **Enter**

A new blank row A, nine characters wide, will be inserted in the worksheet. Enter a label for the column.

Type   **"NUMBER**
Press   **Down Arrow**

Step 3: Execute the Data Fill Command

We want to fill the range A2..A18 with the numbers 1 through 17. Execute the Data Fill command, specify the fill range, specify the start value, specify the step value, and specify the stop value.

Type   **/df**
Type   **a2..a18**
Press   **Enter**
Type   **1**
Press   **Enter**
Press   **Enter**
Press   **Enter**

Lotus 1-2-3 will fill the range with a sequence of numbers that starts with 1 and increases by 1 in each successive cell (see Figure 7).

Step 4: Save the Worksheet

To preserve the changes you have made, save the PROPERTY worksheet to its disk file.

    Type   **/f s**
    Press **Enter**
    Type   **r**

Execute the Worksheet Erase Yes command to clear the PROPERTY worksheet. Use the Data Fill command to load the range A1 to Z1 with the numbers 2, 4, 6, 8, 10, 12, and so on.

Lesson 7: Transposing Columns and Rows

Lotus 1-2-3 has many commands for rearranging existing data. For example, you already know how to use commands such as Move, Copy, Worksheet Insert, and Worksheet Delete. Range Trans is a more specialized command that lets you transpose data from a horizontal arrangement to a vertical arrangement, or vice versa. As an example, let's transpose a table in the SALES worksheet you created in the previous chapter.

Step 1: Retrieve the SALES Worksheet

Make SALES your current worksheet.

    Type   **/f r**
    Highlight **SALES.WK1** (or **SALES.WK3**)
    Press   **Enter**
    Press   **Home**

Step 2: Transpose a Range

The sales figures in rows 1 and 2 are arranged horizontally, with a year in each column. Let's transpose this table and make a new copy in which the sales figures are arranged vertically. Execute the Range Trans command, specify the FROM range, then specify the first cell of the TO range.

    Type   **/r t**
    Type   **a1..e2**
    Press **Enter**
    Type   **e5**
    Press **Enter**

Figure 8 shows the result. The original sales table in cells A1..E2 has been transposed and copied to cells E5..F9.

Transpose another table in the SALES worksheet. Be sure to specify a TO range in an empty part of the worksheet.

Figure 8 The Transposed Sales Table

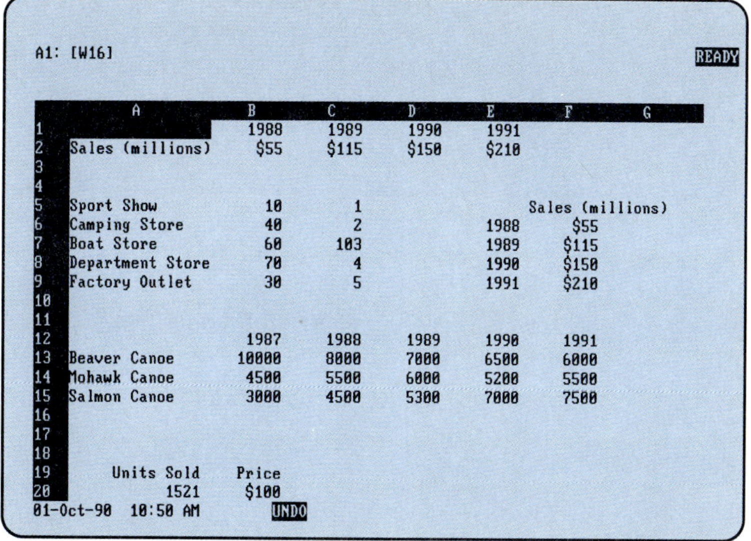

Lesson 8: Controlling Recalculation and Iteration

Spreadsheet programs are useful tools because you can easily change data and recalculate worksheets. Usually, recalculation occurs automatically, and you don't have to worry about it. In some cases, however, you must exercise control over the method and order of recalculation. Lotus 1-2-3 lets you do both.

Most formulas need only be calculated once, unless their data are changed. Some special formulas, however, may have to be recalculated many times to achieve a final result. This repeated recomputation is called **iteration.** It can also be controlled with 1-2-3.

Step 1: Set Up a New Worksheet

Erase the screen and start with a new worksheet.

Type   **/wey**

Step 2: Change the Method of Recalculation

Lotus 1-2-3 has two recalculation methods: Automatic and Manual. **Automatic recalculation** is the default method, used unless you specify otherwise. In Lotus 1-2-3 Release 2.01, automatic recalculation means that every formula in the entire worksheet is recalculated every time any cell is changed. Lotus 1-2-3 Release 2.2 and Release 3.0 use a more sophisticated type of automatic recalculation known as **minimal** or **optimal recalculation.** This feature increases speed by recalculating only those cells that have changed, and the cells that depend on them, since the worksheet was last recalculated.

Even with minimal recalculation, very large worksheets can take a long time to recalculate. The delays can be annoying. Fortunately, Lotus 1-2-3 lets you turn off automatic recalculation and use **manual recalculation** instead. When manual recalculation is turned on, the worksheet is recalculated only when you press

F9, the CALC key. For example, execute the Worksheet Global Recalculation Manual command and create a simple worksheet.

Type	**/wgrm**
Type	**100**
Press	**Down Arrow**
Type	**200**
Press	**Down Arrow**
Type	**+a1+a2**
Press	**Enter**

The formula will be calculated because it was just entered. Try changing cell A2 and see what happens.

Press	**Up Arrow**
Type	**100**
Press	**Enter**

The result in cell A3 remains 300, even though it should be 200. You must press F9, the CALC key, to tell 1-2-3 to recalculate the worksheet.

Press	**F9**

The result in cell A3 will change to 200.

Step 3: Change the Order of Recalculation

Lotus 1-2-3 can perform only one calculation at a time, so it must begin recalculating with a single cell and then proceed throughout the worksheet in some particular order. Early spreadsheet programs, such as VisiCalc, gave you a choice between two orders: column-wise and row-wise recalculation. **Column-wise recalculation** begins with cell A1 and proceeds down column A, goes on to cell B1 and proceeds down column B, and so on. **Row-wise recalculation** also starts at cell A1, but then proceeds to go across row 1, then row 2, and so on. The problem with both of these methods is that they can lead to incorrect results if you are not careful about how you set up your worksheet. For example, erase the worksheet, execute the Worksheet Global Recalculation Columnwise command, and enter the following worksheet.

Type	**/wey**
Type	**/wgrc**
Type	**100+a3**
Press	**Down Arrow**
Type	**200**
Press	**Down Arrow**
Type	**100+a2**
Press	**Enter**

As soon as you finish entering the worksheet, the formulas are calculated for the first time, and you see 100 in A1, 200 in A2, and 300 in A3. Already there is a problem. Cell A1 is supposed to contain 100 plus the value in cell A3. It should contain 400, but it contains only 100. Since the cells were evaluated in the order A1, A2, and A3, nothing was in A3 when cell A1 was originally evaluated. That is why A1 contains only 100. Now, change the contents of cell A2 to 222.

Press	**Up Arrow**
Type	**222**
Press	**Enter**

With either column-wise or row-wise recalculation, the results will be 400 in A1, 222 in A2, and 322 in A3. This is *still* not right. Cell A1 should contain 422. It now contains 400 because 1-2-3 added 100 to the formula result of 300 left in cell A3 after the previous change. Clearly, in some instances neither column-wise nor row-wise recalculation work correctly.

Lotus 1-2-3 solves this problem by using **natural recalculation** unless you specify otherwise. This method recalculates a cell only after evaluating any cells on which it depends. For example, natural recalculation would evaluate our worksheet in this order: A2, A3, then A1. Execute the Worksheet Global Recalculation Natural command and then change cell A2 back to 200.

> Type   **/wgrn**
> Type   **200**
> Press   **Enter**

The results are now computed correctly. Cell A1 displays 400, cell A2 displays 200, and cell A3 displays 300.

Although natural recalculation is best for most worksheets, Lotus 1-2-3 lets you change to column-wise or row-wise so that you can create worksheets in which you have explicit control over the order of recalculation.

Step 4: Create a Direct Circular Reference

As you have just seen, formulas can refer to cells that contain other formulas. In the previous step, cell A1 contains a formula that refers to cell A3, but A3 also contains a formula. Although this might seem unusual and perhaps even a bit confusing, it is really quite common for worksheets to contain formulas that refer to other formulas. As long as natural recalculation is used, there is seldom a problem. One potential difficulty, however, can occur. A **circular reference** results when a formula in a cell is either directly or indirectly dependent on the value in that very same cell. The most obvious example is when you use a formula that refers to the same cell in which it is stored. This is a direct circular reference. For example, move to A1 and enter the following formula.

> Press   **Home**
> Type   **100+a1**
> Press   **Enter**

Lotus 1-2-3 cannot evaluate this formula correctly. It displays the value 100 in A1 because it calculated the formula only once. The CIRC error message appears at the bottom of the screen to indicate the presence of a formula containing a circular reference. Although you could tell Lotus 1-2-3 to recalculate the formula several times, every time it would try to evaluate 100 + A1, the value in A1 would change. No matter how many times it would try, the program could not compute a final result for this formula.

Step 5: Use Iteration

Certain *indirect* circular references, however, can be resolved eventually. An absolute final answer may not be reached, but an approximate result can often be obtained by recalculating the formulas a number of times. This method is called iterative recalculation, or simply iteration, and it can be used to solve certain kinds of problems. For example, just about everyone knows what a square root is, but do you know how to calculate one? We seldom figure square roots by hand anymore because most calculators, spreadsheet packages, and programming languages have built-in functions to compute square roots. Before these tools were available, people looked up square roots in printed tables in math books. So, although you will probably never have to know how to compute a square root, let's demonstrate an interesting way to do it with 1-2-3 without using the built-in @SQRT function.

One method to compute the square root of a number is to repeatedly make better and better estimates until you finally arrive at the correct answer. Follow these directions to create a template that will simulate this method of computing a square root:

```
Type    /wey
Type    16
Press   Right Arrow
Type    '<-- Enter  the  number
Press   Down Arrow
Type    '<-- "Fudge factor"  to avoid division by 0
Press   Left Arrow
Type    0.000001
Press   Down Arrow
Type    +a4
Press   Right Arrow
Type    '<-- Contains  the  formula  +A4
Press   Down Arrow
Type    '<-- Here is  the  square  root
Press   Left Arrow
Type    @round((a3+a1/(a3+a2))/2,2)
Press   Enter
```

Obviously, the square root of 16 is not 8,000,000. By default, 1-2-3 recalculates circular references only once. Execute the Worksheet Global Recalculation Iteration command and enter 50 as the number of times to recalculate circular references. Then press the F9 key to recalculate the worksheet.

```
Type    /wgri50
Press   Enter
Press   F9
```

Figure 9 shows the result. This worksheet simulates the process of repeatedly making better square root estimates until an answer close enough to the correct answer is obtained. The formula in cell A3 displays the current result of the formula in cell A4, and the formula in cell A4 uses the current result of the formula in cell A3. This is an indirect circular reference. Each time these formulas are recalculated, the result in cell A4 gets closer to the true square root of the number in cell A1. After many iterations, a final answer is obtained.

Step 6: Save the Worksheet

Save the square root template in case you would like to use it again.

```
Type    /fs
Type    sqrt
Press   Enter
```

Practice   Use the template to compute the square roots of some numbers other than 16. For example, try 9, 81, 144, and any other numbers you like.

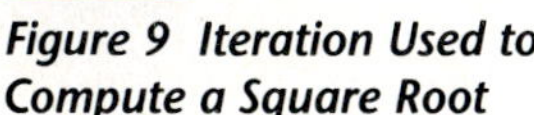

Figure 9 Iteration Used to Compute a Square Root

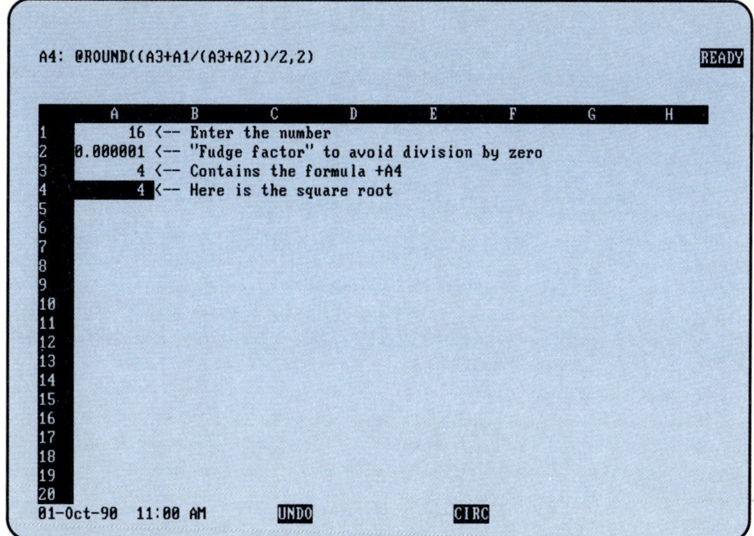

Lesson 9: Using Relative, Absolute, and Mixed Cell References

Three types of cell references can be used in a formula: relative, absolute, and mixed. A **relative reference** is a cell address that pertains to a cell's position relative to the current cell. For example, if the current cell is A3 and it contains the formula +A1+A2, the A1 in the formula refers to the cell located two cells above the formula. Lotus 1-2-3 assumes all cell references to be relative unless you specify otherwise. Relative cell references are automatically changed to reflect their new locations when they are moved or copied.

An **absolute reference** is a cell address that does not change when it is moved or copied. This type of cell address is specified by preceding the column and row designations with dollar signs. For example, the absolute reference A1 always refers to cell A1, even if a formula that contains it is moved or copied.

A **mixed reference** is half-relative and half-absolute, in which either a column or a row is absolute, but not both. For example, $A1 is a mixed reference that always means column A, but the row might be changed if this reference is copied or moved. Similarly, A$1 is a mixed cell reference that keeps the row constant.

Let's demonstrate each type of cell reference.

Step 1: Set Up a New Worksheet

Erase the screen and start with a new worksheet.

Type   **/wey**

Step 2: Use Relative References

Cell addresses without dollar signs are assumed to be relative references. For example, follow these directions to create a formula that contains relative references:

Type   **100**
Press   **Down Arrow**
Type   **200**

> Press   **Down Arrow**
> Type   **+a1+a2**
> Press   **Enter**

The cell references in the formula in cell A3 are relative references.

Step 3: Copy Relative References

The Copy command demonstrates the effect of using relative references. Copy cells A1 through A3 to column B.

> Type   **/ca1..a3**
> Press   **Enter**
> Type   **b1**
> Press   **Enter**
> Press   **Right Arrow**

Examine the formula in cell B3. The original formula was +A1+A2; it was changed to +B1+B2 when it was copied. In most cases, you want cell references to be changed in this manner when formulas are copied or moved.

Step 4: Use an Absolute Reference

In certain situations, however, you may not want a cell reference to be changed when it is copied or moved. For example, you may use a constant value, such as the current interest rate, in several formulas in different places. But you need only store the interest rate once, in a single cell. If you are going to copy or move cells containing formulas that refer to this interest rate, you should use an absolute reference for the cell containing the interest rate. Change the formula in B3 so that it contains an absolute reference to cell A1.

> Type   **+a1+b2**
> Press   **Enter**

Now change the value in B1 and see how the result of the formula in B3 remains the same because it adds A1 instead of B1 to B2.

> Press   **Up Arrow**
> Press   **Up Arrow**
> Type   **200**
> Press   **Enter**

The value displayed in cell B3 should still be 300.

Step 5: Copy An Absolute Reference

Let's see what happens when you copy a formula containing an absolute reference. Copy cells B1 through B3 to column C, then move to cell C3.

> Type   **/cb1..b3**
> Press   **Enter**
> Type   **c1**
> Press   **Enter**
> Press   **Down Arrow**
> Press   **Down Arrow**
> Press   **Right Arrow**

Examine the formula in C3 (see Figure 10). The absolute cell reference A1 was not changed, but the relative cell reference was changed to C2.

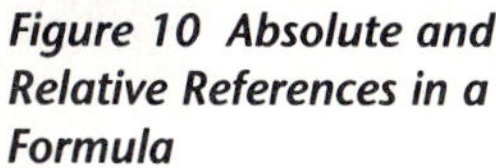

Figure 10 Absolute and Relative References in a Formula

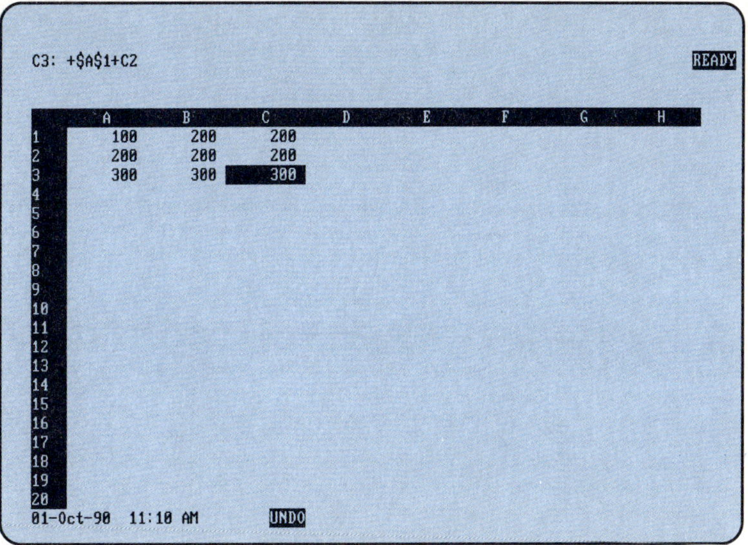

Step 6: Use Mixed Cell References

If you want part of a cell address to remain the same and part to change when you copy or move a formula, you must use a mixed reference. Let's create a small multiplication table of the numbers 0 through 5 to demonstrate the use of mixed cell references. Follow these directions to erase the worksheet and use the Data Fill command to enter the column and row headings of the multiplicands (the numbers to be multiplied):

Type   **/wey**
Type   **/dfb1..g1**
Press   **Enter** (4 times)
Type   **/dfa2..a7**
Press   **Enter** (4 times)

The numbers 0 through 5 should appear in cells B1 through G1 and A2 through A7. Move to cell B2 and enter the multiplication formula containing mixed references.

Press   **Down Arrow**
Press   **Right Arrow**
Type   **+$a2*b$1**
Press   **Enter**

When this formula is copied to the rest of the table, the $A2 mixed reference will keep column A constant, but vary the row. The B$1 mixed reference will vary the column, but keep row 1 constant. To see how these mixed references work, copy the formula in B2 to cells B3 through B7 and C2 through G7, then move to cell G7.

Type   **/c**
Press   **Enter**
Type   **b3..b7**
Press   **Enter**
Type   **/c**
Press   **Enter**

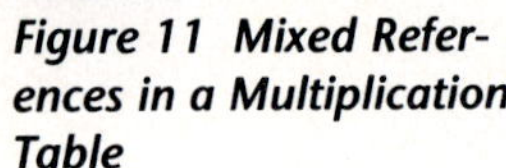

Figure 11 Mixed References in a Multiplication Table

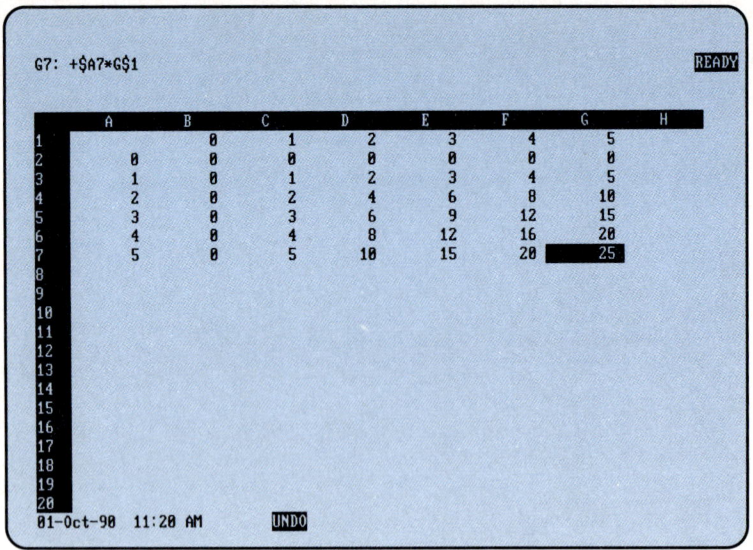

Type   **c2..g7**
Press **Enter**
Press **F5**
Type   **g7**
Press **Enter**

Your screen should look like Figure 11. The rest of the multiplication table is easily created with the Copy command, because you used mixed references to keep column A constant for the first multiplicand and row 1 constant for the second multiplicand.

Practice   See what happens if you use relative references instead of mixed references in the multiplication table. Change the formula in B2 to +A2*B1. Then copy this formula to cells B3..B7 and C2..G7. Examine some of the copied formulas and try to understand why mixed references are necessary in this case.

Lesson 10: Using Additional Functions

You have already learned to use some of the mathematical, trigonometric, statistical, and financial functions of Lotus 1-2-3. Now let's examine some of the date and time, logical, and string functions.

Step 1: Set Up a New Worksheet

Erase the screen and start with a new worksheet.

Type   **/wey**

Step 2: Try Some Date and Time Functions

Date and time functions help you work with the Lotus 1-2-3 date and time numbers. Let's try a few examples.

Type   **@date(90,12,31)**
Press **Enter**

The result should be 33238. The @DATE function returns the sequential date number, given the year, month, and day.

Press   **Down Arrow**
Type   `@day(a1)`
Press   **Enter**

The result should be 31. The @DAY function returns the day, given a date number. The @MONTH and @YEAR functions work similarly.

Press   **Down Arrow**
Type   `@time(14,10,20)`
Press   **Enter**

The result should be 0.590509, the time number for 2:10:20 PM. The @TIME function returns the 1-2-3 time number, given an hour (0-23), minute (0-59), and second (0-59).

Press   **Down Arrow**
Type   `@hour(a3)`
Press   **Enter**

The result should be 14. The @HOUR function returns the hour (0-23), given a time number. The @MINUTE and @SECOND functions work similarly.

Press   **Down Arrow**
Type   `@now`
Press   **Enter**

The @NOW function returns the full serial number for the current date and time.

Step 3: Try Some Logical Functions

Logical functions return values that are dependent on the results of conditional expressions. They essentially allow you to compare values in cells and perform different actions based on the results of those comparisons. Let's try a few examples.

Press   **Down Arrow**
Type   `@isnumber(a1)`
Press   **Enter**

The result should be 1, which stands for TRUE. The @ISNUMBER function returns 1 (TRUE) if the given value is numeric and 0 (FALSE) if it is a label. The @ISSTRING function is the opposite of @ISNUMBER.

Press   **Home**
Press   **Right Arrow**
Type   `100`
Press   **Down Arrow**
Type   `@if(b1>100,"Big","Small")`
Press   **Enter**

You should see "Small" in cell B2. The @IF function evaluates the given logical expression as TRUE or FALSE, and returns the first value if it is TRUE, or the second value if it is FALSE. Since the number in B1 is not greater than 100, the @IF function returns "Small," the second value after the logical expression.

Step 4: Try Some String Functions

String functions manipulate labels. Let's try a few examples.

> Press   **Down Arrow**
> Type   `@length(b2)`
> Press   **Enter**

The result should be 5, the number of characters in "Small," the label in cell B2. The @LENGTH function returns the length of the given string.

> Press   **Down Arrow**
> Type   `@left(b2,3)`
> Press   **Enter**

The result should be "Sma," the first three characters in the label in cell B2. The @LEFT function returns the first *n* characters in a string. The @RIGHT function works similarly, except that it returns the last *n* characters in a string. The @MID function returns *n* characters from the middle of a string, starting at the specified position.

> Press   **Down Arrow**
> Type   `@upper(b2)`
> Press   **Enter**

The result should be "SMALL." The @UPPER function converts the given string to all uppercase characters. The @PROPER function works similarly, except that it capitalizes only the first character in each word in the string.

> Press   **Down Arrow**
> Type   `@repeat("Hello ",10)`
> Press   **Enter**

The result should be "Hello" repeated ten times. The @REPEAT function repeats the given string a specified number of times.

Practice   To see how you might use @NOW, try the following formulas: @YEAR(@NOW), @MONTH(@NOW), @DAY(@NOW), @HOUR(@NOW), @MINUTE(@NOW), @SECOND(@NOW).

Lesson 11: Using Macros

A **macro** is a sequence of keystrokes and special commands that you can create to automate a task. Any task that 1-2-3 can perform can be automated with a macro. When you run a macro, 1-2-3 performs the instructions much faster than you could do them manually. Once a macro has been created, you can use it over and over again. Creating a macro takes planning and time to develop, but it can save a great deal of time in the long run. Macros are used to automate repetitive tasks, reduce keystrokes, simplify complex procedures, guide novices who are unfamiliar with 1-2-3, increase accuracy, and ensure consistency in a worksheet. Let's start with a simple macro that will automatically enter labels into a worksheet.

Step 1: Plan the Macro

A macro is a sequence of keystrokes that you can store, name, and play back over and over again. The first step in creating a macro is to decide what you want it to do. Suppose you want to create a macro that will enter the names of the months of the year across the columns. To plan the macro, think of how you would do this procedure manually. First, you would type *January* and press the Right Arrow key. Then you would type *February* and press the Right Arrow key. After entering the twelve months in this fashion, you would move the cell pointer down to the beginning of the next row. For now, clear the current worksheet and widen all columns to 12 characters.

> Type **/wey**
> Type **/wgc12**
> Press **Enter**

Step 2: Enter the Macro Definition

Before you can use a macro, you must define it. This definition tells 1-2-3 what keystrokes to execute when you run the macro. A macro definition is basically a series of labels stored in an empty part of the worksheet. Usually, a macro definition is stored in cells far below or to the right of the area the actual worksheet is expected to occupy. For this example, move the cell pointer to A100.

> Press **F5**
> Type **a100**
> Press **Enter**

You may type the label entries of a macro definition in any column of cells. Furthermore, you may type more than one macro instruction in any cell, as long as you don't try to enter more than 240 characters in a single cell. Every cell entry in a macro definition must be a label; numbers and formulas will be translated when the macro is run. The entries in a macro definition may consist of any characters you can type on the keyboard. In addition, keys that perform actions instead of displaying characters can also be included in macro definitions. These special keys are specified by entering a symbol or a name enclosed in braces ({ and }). For example, to include a Right Arrow keystroke in a macro definition, you would enter {right}. The following table shows the macro instructions for some common keys.

Macro Instructions for Common Keys

Key	Macro Instruction
Enter	˜(the tilde character)
Down Arrow	{down}
Up Arrow	{up}
Left Arrow	{left}
Right Arrow	{right}
Home	{home}
End	{end}
Page Up	{pgup}
Page Down	{pgdn}
Ctrl-Right Arrow	{bigright}

Macro Instructions for Common Keys (continued)

Key	Macro Instruction
Ctrl-Left Arrow	{bigleft}
F2	{edit}
F5	{goto}
Escape	{esc}
Backspace	{bs}
Delete	{del}

Now, follow these directions to enter the definition of a macro that will enter the months of the year across the columns.

Type	^January {right}
Press	Down Arrow
Type	^February {right}
Press	Down Arrow
Type	^March {right}
Press	Down Arrow
Type	^April {right}
Press	Down Arrow
Type	^May {right}
Press	Down Arrow
Type	^June {right}
Press	Down Arrow
Type	^July {right}
Press	Down Arrow
Type	^August {right}
Press	Down Arrow
Type	^September {right}
Press	Down Arrow
Type	^October {right}
Press	Down Arrow
Type	^November {right}
Press	Down Arrow
Type	^December {down}
Press	Down Arrow
Type	{end} {left}
Press	Enter

Step 3: Name the Macro

Before you can use a macro, a range name must be assigned to the cells that hold the macro definition. This range name will serve as the macro name. Two types of macro names can be used: a backslash followed by a single letter (such as \A or \M) or a name of up to 15 characters (such as HEADING or MONTHS). The type of name you choose determines how you run the macro. (Note: Lotus 1-2-3 Release 2.01 allows only macro names that consist of a backslash and a single letter.) Follow these directions to name your macro \M:

Type	/rnc
Type	\m

Figure 12 The Completed Macro Definition

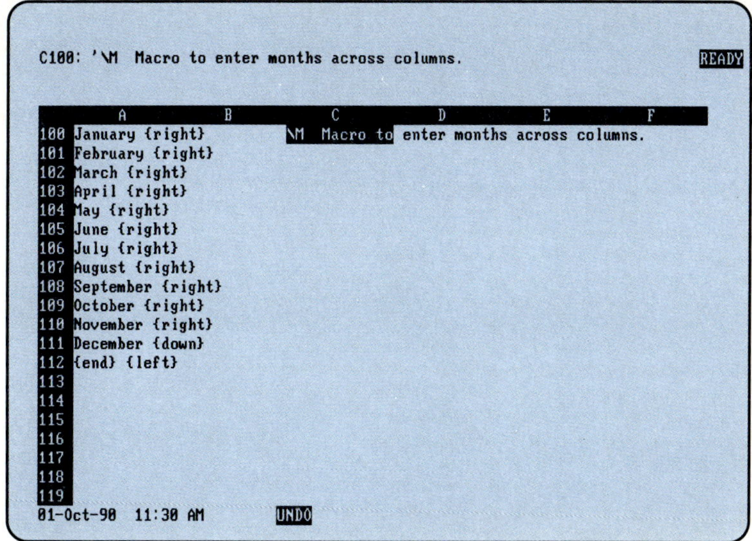

Press   **Enter**
Type   **a100..a112**
Press   **Enter**

Step 4: Document the Macro

It is a good idea to enter the macro name and a brief description beside the macro definition to document the macro for yourself and other users. Complex macros may also have a brief comment beside each macro instruction. Follow these directions to document your macro:

Press   **F5**
Type   **c100**
Press   **Enter**
Type   **'\M Macro to enter months across columns.**
Press   **Enter**

The completed macro is shown in Figure 12.

Step 5: Run the Macro

Now you can use the macro you have created. A macro named with a backslash and a letter is invoked by holding down the Alternate key and typing the letter. Move to cell A2 and run the macro:

Press   **Home**
Press   **Down Arrow**
Press   **Alt-M**

Wasn't that fun? All twelve month labels are entered automatically and the cell pointer returns to the beginning of the next row. Try it again:

Press   **Alt-M**

Your screen should look like Figure 13. You can use the \M macro in any row and as many times as you like.

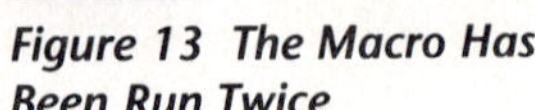

Figure 13 The Macro Has Been Run Twice

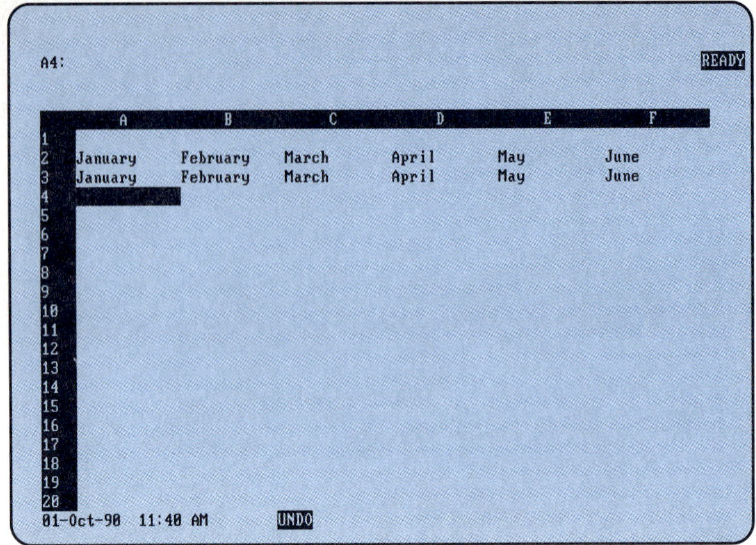

Note: a macro with a long name, such as HEADING or MONTHS, created with Lotus 1-2-3 Release 2.2 or 3.0, is run by pressing Alt-F3, the RUN key, to display a menu of macro names. You then highlight the name of the macro you want to run and press the Enter key.

Step 6: Save the Worksheet

To save the macro you have created, you must save the worksheet.

Type   **/f s**
Type   **months**
Press   **Enter**

Practice   Modify the \M macro so that it always moves the cell pointer to A1 when it is finished entering the months. Test the modified macro to make sure it works correctly.

Lesson 12: Using the Learn Feature with Release 2.2

Lotus 1-2-3 Release 2.2 has an easier way to create macros. (If you are not running Lotus 1-2-3 Release 2.2, just read this lesson without performing its steps.) The **learn feature** lets you have 1-2-3 record your keystrokes as you perform the task you want to automate in order to generate the macro definition. Let's use this method to create a macro to enter today's date in the current cell. This lesson assumes that the global column width has been set to 12 characters.

Step 1: Specify the Learn Range

The **learn range** is the single-column range of cells in your worksheet where 1-2-3 will record your keystrokes and create the macro definition. Since you cannot always be certain how many cells your macro will require, you should reserve more cells than you think you might need. The date macro should require no more than five cells. Execute the Worksheet Learn Range command and specify cells A50 to A55 as the learn range.

Type	`/wlr`
Type	`a50..a55`
Press	**Enter**

Step 2: Turn On the Learn Feature

You must turn on the learn feature so that 1-2-3 knows what keystrokes to record. First, make sure that the cell pointer is not in the learn range. Alt-F5, the LEARN key, is used to turn on the learn feature.

Press	**Alt-F5**

The LEARN indicator will appear at the bottom of the screen.

Step 3: Perform the Task

To record the macro, you perform the task you want to automate. Follow these directions to enter the @NOW function and format the current cell as a date:

Type	`@now`
Press	**Enter**
Type	`/rfd1`
Press	**Enter**

Note that the keystrokes you execute are performed as they are recorded in the learn range.

Step 4: Turn Off the Learn Feature

After you have executed the keystrokes you want to automate, you must turn off the learn feature. Alt-F5, the LEARN key, also turns off the learn feature.

Press	**Alt-F5**

The LEARN indicator will disappear from the bottom of the screen.

Step 5: Name the Macro

The macro definition must be named before you can use it. Move to the learn range:

Press	**F5**
Type	`a50`
Press	**Enter**

Notice cells A50 and A51 are filled with the keystrokes you executed while the learn feature was turned on. Remember that the ~ (tilde) character symbolizes the Enter key. Execute the Range Name Create command to name the macro \D:

Type	`/rnc`
Type	`\d`
Press	**Enter**
Type	`a50..a51`
Press	**Enter**

Step 6: Document the Macro

Move to cell B50 and enter the macro name and a brief description.

Press   **Right Arrow**
Type   `'\D Macro to enter today's date.`
Press   **Enter**

Your screen should look like Figure 14.

Step 7: Run the Macro

Move to cell A5 and run the new macro.

Press   **F5**
Type   **a5**
Press   **Enter**
Press   **Alt-D**

Today's date number will be entered into cell A5 and the cell will be formatted as a date.

Modify the macro definition so that the cell is formatted to display only the day and month. Hint: use date format number 2.

Lesson 13: Using the Record Feature with Release 3.0

Lotus 1-2-3 Release 3.0 has a feature similar to the Learn feature of Release 2.2 for easily creating macros. (If you are not running Lotus 1-2-3 Release 3.0, just read this lesson without performing its steps.) The **record feature** lets you create a macro by copying keystrokes saved in the **record buffer,** a 512-byte area of

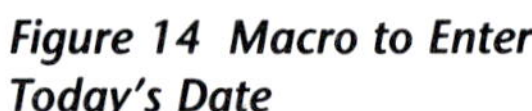

Figure 14 Macro to Enter Today's Date

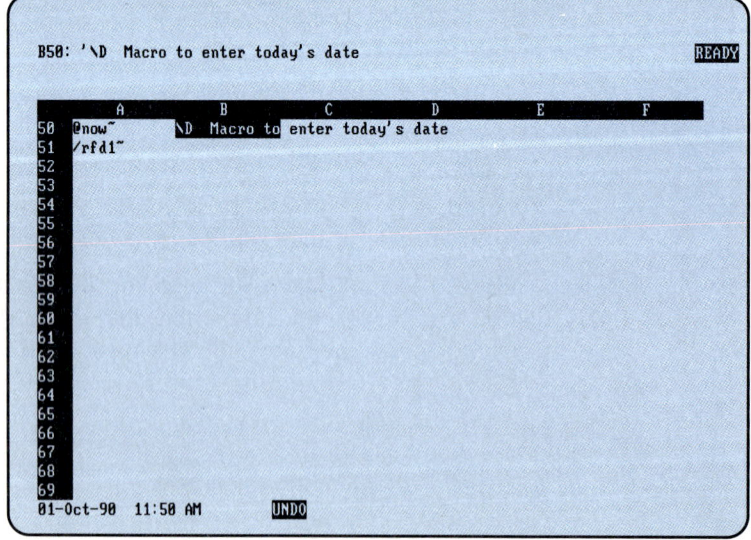

memory in which Lotus 1-2-3 Release 3.0 stores your most recent keystrokes. Let's use this method to create a macro to enter today's date in the current cell. This lesson assumes that the global column width has been set to 12 characters.

Step 1: Erase the Record Buffer

Press Alt-F2, the RECORD key, and select the Erase option to clear the current contents of the record buffer.

    Press   **Alt-F2**
    Type   **e**

Step 2: Perform the Task

Move the cell pointer to the cell where you want to start the task, and execute the keystrokes you want to automate.

    Type   **@now**
    Press   **Enter**
    Type   **/rfd1**
    Press   **Enter**

Today's date number will be entered in the current cell and it will be formatted as a date.

Step 3: Copy the Keystrokes from the Record Buffer

The next step is to copy the keystrokes you just executed from the record buffer to the range in which you want to store the macro definition. Let's store the macro definition in cell A50. Press the RECORD key, select the Copy option, highlight the keystrokes in the buffer, and specify the destination cell.

    Press   **Alt-F2**
    Type   **c**
    Press   **Home**
    Press   **Tab**
    Press   **End**
    Press   **Enter**
    Type   **a50**
    Press   **Enter**

The recorded keystrokes will be copied into cell A50.

Step 4: Name the Macro

The macro definition must be named before you can use it. Move to the cell containing the macro definition and name it \D:

    Press   **F5**
    Type   **a50**
    Press   **Enter**
    Type   **/rnc**
    Type   **\d**
    Press   **Enter**
    Press   **Enter**

Step 5: Document the Macro

Move to cell B50 and enter the macro name and a brief description.

    Press   **Right Arrow**
    Type   `'\D Macro to enter today's date.`
    Press   **Enter**

Step 6: Run the Macro

Move to cell A5 and run the new macro.

    Press   **F5**
    Type   `a5`
    Press   **Enter**
    Press   **Alt-D**

Today's date number will be entered into cell A5, and the cell will be formatted as a date.

 Modify the macro definition so that the cell is formatted to display only the day and month. Hint: use date format number 2.

Lesson 14: Linking Worksheets with Releases 2.2 and 3.0

Lotus 1-2-3 Releases 2.2 and 3.0 include a linking feature that allows you to use values from other worksheets in your current worksheet. (If you are running Lotus 1-2-3 Release 2.01, just read this lesson without performing its steps.) Linking is often used to consolidate data from a number of worksheets in a summary worksheet. As an example, let's create a worksheet that uses values from three other worksheets.

Step 1: Create the Three Sales Worksheets

Suppose a business has offices in three cities: New York, Chicago, and Los Angeles. Sales figures from each office are kept in separate worksheets. Follow these directions to create the three sales worksheets:

    Type   `/wey`
    Type   `/wgc12`
    Press   **Enter**
    Type   `/wgfc`
    Press   **Enter**
    Type   `New York`
    Press   **Right Arrow**
    Type   `Sales`
    Press   **Down Arrow**
    Type   `99600`
    Press   **Enter**
    Type   `/fs`
    Type   `ny`
    Press   **Enter**

Type	**/wey**
Type	**/wgc12**
Press	**Enter**
Type	**/wgfc**
Press	**Enter**
Type	**Chicago**
Press	**Right Arrow**
Type	**Sales**
Press	**Down Arrow**
Type	**88466**
Press	**Enter**
Type	**/fs**
Type	**ch**
Press	**Enter**

Type	**/wey**
Type	**/wgc12**
Press	**Enter**
Type	**/wgfc**
Press	**Enter**
Type	**Los Angeles**
Press	**Right Arrow**
Type	**Sales**
Press	**Down Arrow**
Type	**90800**
Press	**Enter**
Type	**/fs**
Type	**la**
Press	**Enter**

Step 2: Create the Summary Worksheet

Now create a worksheet that will summarize the sales figures from New York, Chicago, and Los Angeles.

Type	**/wey**
Type	**/wgc12**
Press	**Enter**
Type	**/wgfc**
Press	**Enter**
Type	**Sales Summary**
Press	**Down Arrow**
Type	**New York**
Press	**Down Arrow**
Type	**Chicago**
Press	**Down Arrow**
Type	**Los Angeles**
Press	**Down Arrow**
Type	**TOTAL**
Press	**Right Arrow**
Type	**@sum(b2..b4)**
Press	**Up Arrow**

Step 3: Enter Linking Formulas

You create a link between two files by entering a linking formula in the current worksheet that refers to a cell in the other worksheet file. The cell in the other worksheet is called the source cell and the cell in the current worksheet is called the target cell. Once the two files are linked, 1-2-3 copies the value from the source cell to the target cell. A linking formula must have the following format:

> +<<*file name*>>*cell reference*

For example, follow these directions to enter the linking formulas into the summary worksheet:

Type	**+<<la.wk1>>b2**
Press	**Up Arrow**
Type	**+<<ch.wk1>>b2**
Press	**Up Arrow**
Type	**+<<ny.wk1>>b2**
Press	**Enter**

Note: if you are running Lotus 1-2-3 Release 3.0, you should enter LA.WK3, CH.WK3, and NY.WK3 as the worksheet file names.

Your screen should look like Figure 15. Cell B2 contains the sales figure from cell B2 in the worksheet file NY.WK1, cell B3 contains the sales figure from cell B2 in the worksheet file CH.WK1, and cell B4 contains the sales figure from cell B2 in the worksheet file LA.WK1. The formula in cell B5 computes the sum of these values from three different worksheets.

Step 4: Save the Summary Worksheet

Save the summary worksheet in a disk file.

Type	**/fs**
Type	**summary**
Press	**Enter**

Figure 15 Linking Formulas in the Summary Worksheet

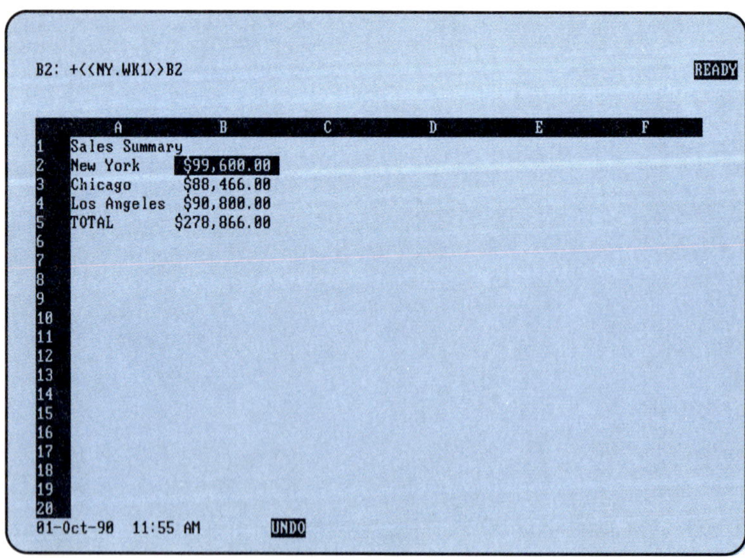

Retrieve NY.WK1, change the sales figure, and save the updated file. Then retrieve SUMMARY.WK1 and see the result. If the source files are changed, values in target cells are automatically updated when the target file is retrieved.

Lesson 15: Using Three-Dimensional Worksheets with Release 3.0

Three-dimensional worksheets carry linking to its logical extreme: every cell in a worksheet can be linked to corresponding cells in other worksheets. A third dimension creates a kind of "super-worksheet" that is like a stack of conventional worksheets. Perhaps the easiest way to envision a three-dimensional worksheet is as a sequence of pages, each of which is a table of rows and columns. Lotus 1-2-3 Release 3.0 lets you create such multiple-sheet worksheet files. (If you are not running Lotus 1-2-3 Release 3.0, just read this lesson without performing its steps.) Let's create a simple three-dimensional worksheet.

Step 1: Set Up a New Worksheet

The worksheets we will create will hold sales figures for two different years and a summary statement. First, clear your current worksheet and set up the first sales worksheet.

Type	**/wey**
Type	**/wgc12**
Press	**Enter**
Type	**/wgfc**
Press	**Enter**
Type	**Sales 1989**
Press	**Down Arrow**
Press	**Down Arrow**
Press	**Right Arrow**
Type	**^Jan-Mar**
Press	**Right Arrow**
Type	**^Apr-Jun**
Press	**Right Arrow**
Type	**^Jul-Sep**
Press	**Right Arrow**
Type	**^Oct-Dec**
Press	**Right Arrow**
Type	**^TOTAL**
Press	**End**
Press	**Left Arrow**
Press	**Left Arrow**
Press	**Down Arrow**
Type	**Sales**
Press	**Right Arrow**
Type	**4200**
Press	**Right Arrow**
Type	**5000**
Press	**Right Arrow**

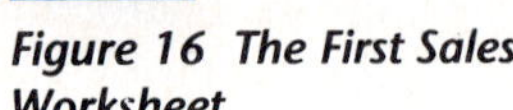

Figure 16 The First Sales Worksheet

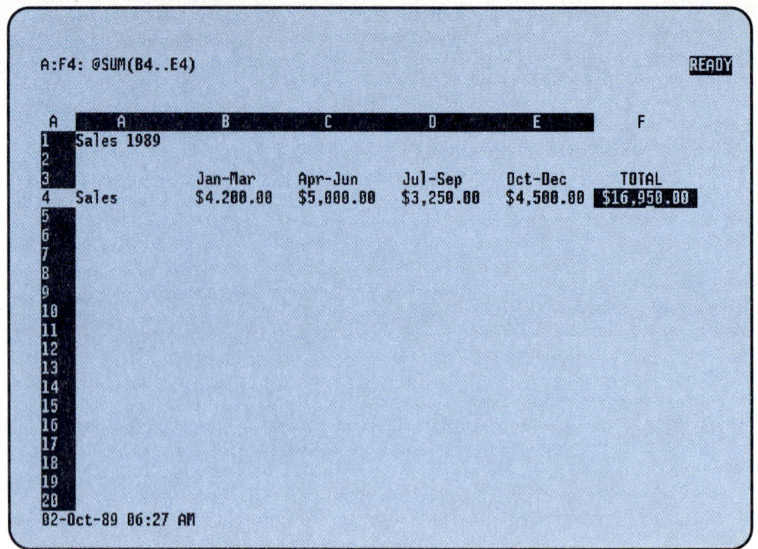

Type   **3250**
Press   **Right Arrow**
Type   **4500**
Press   **Right Arrow**
Type   **@sum(b4..e4)**
Press   **Enter**

Your screen should look like Figure 16.

Step 2: Add New Worksheets to a File

Lotus 1-2-3 always starts with a single worksheet on the screen. You can add up to 255 additional worksheets, depending on how much memory is installed in your computer. When multiple worksheets are loaded into memory, you can work with any one of them or with several at the same time. You can move between multiple worksheets like flipping pages in a notebook. Worksheets are designated by letters. The first worksheet is A, the second is B, and so on up to IV. Examine the upper left corner of the control panel. The full address of the current cell is A:F4, which means row 4 of column F of worksheet A.

You are going to add two new worksheets to the file. The second worksheet will hold the sales figures for 1990, and the third worksheet will summarize the first two worksheets. Execute the Worksheet Insert Sheet After 2 command to add two new worksheets after the current worksheet.

Type   **/wisa2**
Press   **Enter**

Worksheet B will appear on the screen.

Step 3: Change to Perspective View

Lotus 1-2-3 lets you display three consecutive worksheets on your screen at the same time stacked in an upward slope. Execute the Worksheet Window Perspective command.

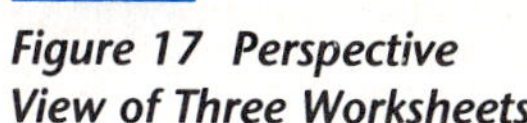

**Figure 17 Perspective
View of Three Worksheets**

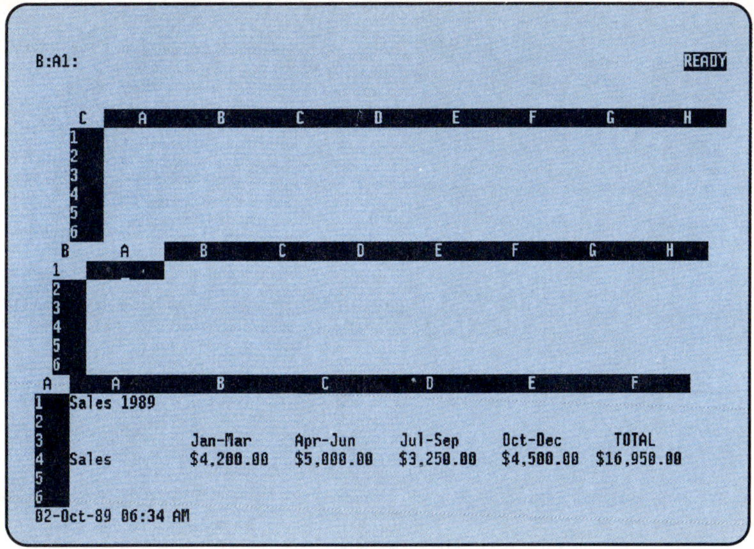

Type   **/wwp**

Your screen should look like Figure 17.

Step 4: Move Among Worksheets

Right now, worksheet B is your current worksheet. Several keys allow you to
move among the multiple worksheets you have loaded. Move to the previous
worksheet:

Press   **Ctrl-PgDn**

Move to the next worksheet:

Press   **Ctrl-PgUp**

Use the GOTO key to move to a particular cell in a particular worksheet:

Press   **F5**
Type   **c : d4**
Press   **Enter**

Move to cell A:A1:

Press   **Ctrl-Home**

Step 5: Format Worksheets Simultaneously

In many cases, you want all of the worksheets in the same file to be formatted
the same way. You could format each worksheet individually, but by using GROUP
mode, you can format all of the worksheets at once. When you turn on GROUP
mode, 1-2-3 changes the format of all the worksheets in the file to match the
format of the current worksheet. Make sure A is your current worksheet and
execute the Worksheet Global Group Enable command.

Type   **/wgge**

The GROUP indicator will appear at the bottom of the screen and worksheets B and C will be formatted like worksheet A. The global column width is now 12 and the global format is Currency for all three worksheets. The GROUP mode remains turned on until you disable it, and the worksheets will continue to format simultaneously.

Step 6: Copy Between Worksheets

You can easily create the second and third worksheets by copying the first worksheet, then making any necessary modifications. To copy the contents of worksheet A to the other two worksheets, specify a three-dimensional range that includes the worksheet letter. For example, execute the following Copy command to duplicate the contents of worksheet A in worksheets B and C.

```
Type   /c
Type   a:a1.a:f4
Press  Enter
Type   b:a1..c:f4
Press  Enter
```

The contents of worksheet A will be copied to worksheets B and C.

Step 7: Modify Worksheet B

Worksheet B will contain the sales figures for 1990. Follow these directions to make the necessary modifications:

```
Press  Ctrl-PgUp
Press  Home
Type   Sales 1990
Press  Down Arrow (3 times)
Press  Right Arrow
Type   4750
Press  Right Arrow
Type   5200
Press  Right Arrow
Type   5050
Press  Right Arrow
Type   6100
Press  Right Arrow
```

The TOTAL sales for 1990 should be $21,100.00.

Step 8: Modify Worksheet C

Worksheet C will summarize the figures in worksheets A and B. Instead of numbers, worksheet C will contain formulas that sum cells in worksheets A and B. Follow these directions to create the summary worksheet.

```
Press  Ctrl-PgUp
Press  Home
Type   Sales Summary 1989 – 1990
Press  Down Arrow (3 times)
Press  Right Arrow
Type   @sum(a:b4..b:b4)
```

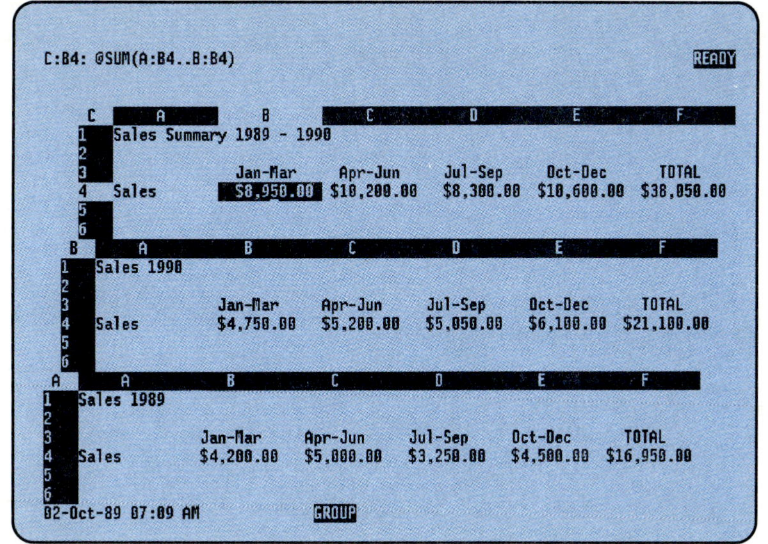

Figure 18 The Completed Summary Worksheet

Press **Enter**
Type **/c**
Press **Enter**
Type **c4..f4**
Press **Enter**

Figure 18 shows the result. Worksheet C summarizes worksheets A and B.

Step 9: Save the File

You must save the file to preserve the worksheets you have created.

Type **/fs**
Type **three_d**
Press **Enter**

All three worksheets will be saved in the file THREE_D.WK3.

Practice Print all three worksheets at the same time by specifying a three-dimensional print range.

Summary

- *Changing worksheet settings.* The Worksheet Global options affect the entire worksheet. You can change the format, label-prefix, column width, default directory, and the display of zero values. You can also display the worksheet status and insert page breaks.

- *Freezing titles and using windows.* The Worksheet Titles command lets you keep certain rows, columns, or both always on the screen. The Worksheet Windows command lets you split the screen into two horizontal or vertical windows.

- *Hiding columns and protecting cells.* The Worksheet Column Hide command lets you conceal the contents of one or more columns. The Worksheet Global

Protection Enable command prevents changes from being made to any cells. The Range Unprot command can then be used to turn off protection for selected cells.

- *Changing range formats.* The Range Format command lets you set Fixed, Scientific, Currency, Comma, General, $+/-$, Percent, Date, Text, and Hidden formats for one or more cells.

- *Using range names.* The Range Name Create lets you assign names to ranges to be used in commands and formulas.

- *Filling a range with a sequence of numbers.* The Data Fill command lets you fill a range of cells with a sequence of numbers.

- *Transposing columns and rows.* The Range Trans command lets you rearrange columns as rows or rows as columns.

- *Controlling recalculation and iteration.* The Worksheet Global Recalculation command lets you specify Natural, Columnwise, Rowwise, Automatic, or Manual recalculation. It also lets you set the iteration count for circular references.

- *Using relative, absolute, and mixed cell references.* Relative references change when cells are copied or moved. Absolute references, indicated by a $ in front of both the column letter and row number, always refer to the same address, even if they are copied or moved. Mixed references are half-relative and half-absolute.

- *Using more functions.* Date and time functions include @DATE, @DAY, @MONTH, @YEAR, @TIME, @HOUR, @MINUTE, @SECOND, and @NOW. Logical functions include @ISNUMBER, @ISSTRING, and @IF. String functions include @LENGTH, @LEFT, @RIGHT, @MID, @UPPER, @PROPER, and @REPEAT.

- *Using macros.* Plan the macro, enter the macro definition, and name the macro. Macros named with a \ (backslash) and a letter are run by holding down the Alternate key and typing the letter.

- *Using the Release 2.2 Learn feature.* Lotus 1-2-3 Release 2.2 lets you create a macro definition by specifying the learn range, pressing Alt-F5 to turn on the learn feature, and executing the actions to be automated.

- *Using the Release 3.0 Record feature.* Lotus 1-2-3 Release 3.0 lets you create a macro definition by copying keystrokes saved in the record buffer.

- *Using file linking with Release 2.2 and 3.0.* Lotus 1-2-3 Release 2.2 and 3.0 let you use values from other worksheets in your current worksheet.

- *Using three-dimensional worksheets with Release 3.0.* Lotus 1-2-3 Release 3.0 lets you create multi-page worksheets in a single file.

Key Terms

As an extra review of this chapter, try defining the following terms.

absolute reference	exponent
automatic recalculation	iteration
circular reference	learn feature
column-wise recalculation	learn range

macro
mantissa
manual recalculation
minimal (optimal) recalculation
mixed reference
natural recalculation

record buffer
record feature
relative reference
row-wise recalculation
template

Multiple Choice

Choose the best selection to complete each statement.

1. What options affect the entire worksheet?
   - (a) Worksheet Global
   - (b) Range Format
   - (c) File Save
   - (d) Data

2. What command lets you set the alignment of labels for the entire worksheet?
   - (a) Worksheet Global Format
   - (b) Worksheet Global Column-Width
   - (c) Worksheet Global Label-Prefix
   - (d) Worksheet Global Protection

3. Which command lets you freeze rows or columns or both on the screen so you can see them even if you scroll the worksheet?
   - (a) Worksheet Global Zero
   - (b) Worksheet Titles
   - (c) Worksheet Window
   - (d) Worksheet Page

4. Which command lets you split the screen horizontally or vertically?
   - (a) Worksheet Global Zero
   - (b) Worksheet Titles
   - (c) Worksheet Window
   - (d) Worksheet Page

5. Which command lets you conceal the contents of one or more columns?
   - (a) Worksheet Global Protection
   - (b) Worksheet Global Default
   - (c) Worksheet Column Hide
   - (d) Range Format Text

6. A general-purpose worksheet in which the user fills in the blanks or changes selected entries to perform a well-defined task is called a
   - (a) macro.
   - (b) iteration.
   - (c) template.
   - (d) circular reference.

7. The Worksheet Global Protection Enable command prevents changes being made to
   - (a) all cells.
   - (b) selected cells.
   - (c) cells marked with the Range Prot command.
   - (d) no cells.

8. Which Range Format would you use to display a number this way: 25,246.00?
   - (a) Fixed
   - (b) Scientific
   - (c) Currency
   - (d) , (comma)

9. Which Range Format would you use to generate crude bar graphs?
   - (a) General
   - (b) +/−
   - (c) Percent
   - (d) Text

10. In a Lotus 1-2-3 time number, the total time in each day is represented by the number
    - (a) 1.
    - (b) 12.
    - (c) 24.
    - (d) 360.

11. Which command would you use to enter the numbers 1 to 100 in cells A1 to A100?

      (a) Copy   (b) Move

      (c) Data Fill   (d) Range Format

12. What is the default method of recalculation?

      (a) Automatic   (b) Manual

      (c) Column-wise   (d) Row-wise

13. What is the default order of recalculation?

      (a) Automatic   (b) Natural

      (c) Column-wise   (d) Row-wise

14. A formula either directly or indirectly dependent on the value in the same cell results in a(n)

      (a) manual recalculation.   (b) circular reference.

      (c) absolute reference.   (d) iteration.

15. Which term describes the repeated recalculation of formulas containing circular references?

      (a) minimal recalculation   (b) automatic recalculation

      (c) iteration   (d) absolute reference

16. A cell address that does not change when it is moved or copied is called a(n)

      (a) relative reference.   (b) absolute reference.

      (c) mixed reference.   (d) circular reference.

17. The cell address A\$1 is an example of a(n)

      (a) relative reference.   (b) absolute reference.

      (c) mixed reference.   (d) circular reference.

18. Which function returns the full serial number for the current date and time?

      (a) @DATE   (b) @TIME

      (c) @NOW   (d) @HOUR

19. What key(s) would you press to execute a macro named \B?

      (a) Alt-B   (b) Ctrl-B

      (c) Shift-B   (d) F5

20. Which of the following expressions is a valid linking formula that refers to cell B5 from the worksheet file NY.WK1?

      (a) +B5<<NY.WK1>>   (b) +(NY.WK1)B5

      (c) +<<NY.WK1>>B5   (d) B5{NY.WK1}

Fill-In

1. The Worksheet _______ options affect the entire worksheet.

2. The Range Format _______ command displays formulas in worksheet cells instead of their computed results.

3. Range _______ can make it much easier to specify ranges in formulas and commands.

4. Lotus 1-2-3 Release 2.2 and 3.0 use _______ recalculation to increase speed by recalculating only those cells that have changed, and the cells that depend on them, since the worksheet was last recalculated.

5. A(n) _______ reference results when a formula in a cell is either directly or indirectly dependent on the value in that very same cell.

6. Certain indirect circular references can be eventually resolved through _______.

7. Lotus 1-2-3 assumes all cell addresses to be _______ unless you specify otherwise.

8. The cell address A1 is an example of a(n) _______ reference.

9. If you want part of a cell address to remain the same and part to change when you copy or move a formula, you must use a(n) _______ reference.

10. The _______ function returns the sequential date number, given the year, month, and day.

11. The _______ function evaluates the given logical expression as TRUE or FALSE, and returns the first value if TRUE, or the second value if FALSE.

12. The _______ function lets you repeat the given string a specified number of times.

13. A _______ is a sequence of keystrokes and special commands that you can create to automate a task.

14. In a macro definition, the macro instruction _______ performs the same action as pressing the Right Arrow key.

15. A macro named with the _______ and a letter is executed by holding down the Alternate key and typing that letter.

16. To facilitate the creation of macros, Lotus 1-2-3 Release 2.2 has the _______ feature and Release 3.0 has the _______ feature.

17. The range of cells containing a macro definition must be _______ before the macro can be run.

18. In Lotus 1-2-3 Release 2.2 and 3.0, you can create a _______ between two files by entering a formula in the current worksheet that refers to a cell in the other worksheet file.

19. One way to envision a three-dimensional worksheet is as a sequence of _______, each of which is a table of rows and columns.

20. In Lotus 1-2-3 Release 3.0, multiple worksheets in the same file are designated by _______, like columns.

Short Problems

1. Erase the current worksheet from the screen. Change the Worksheet Global Format to Fixed with two decimal places, the Worksheet Global Label-Prefix to Center, and the Worksheet Global Column-Width to 12 characters.

2. Retrieve the PROPERTY worksheet. Freeze the first row as a horizontal title. Then try scrolling the worksheet down.

3. Split the screen at row 11 into two horizontal windows. Switch to the other window and scroll the worksheet down. When you are finished, clear worksheet windows.

4. Turn on worksheet global protection. Try changing the contents of a cell. When you are finished, disable global protection.

5. Erase the current worksheet from the screen. Change the range format of cells A1 through A5 to scientific notation with two decimal places. Then enter the following numbers into cells A1 through A5: 156,000,000, $-25,200$, 0.000000381, -0.000000000752, and 4,321,123,321.

6. Erase the current worksheet from the screen. Fill cells A1 through A4095 with only even numbers from 2 through 8190.

7. Erase the current worksheet from the screen. Enter the names of the months of the year in columns B through M, then transpose these names into cells A2 through A13.

8. Retrieve the SQRT worksheet. Enter the formula @SQRT(A1) into cell A10 to check the iterative square root calculation method against the built-in SQRT function. Calculate the square root of 123456. Enter other values to try to "stump" the iterative method. Now try an obviously invalid value of -1 and see what happens.

9. Retrieve the MONTHS worksheet you created in Lesson 11. Modify the \M macro so that it enters the names of the months down a column instead of across a row. Run the macro to make sure it works correctly.

10. If you have Lotus 1-2-3 Release 2.2 or 3.0, retrieve the SUMMARY worksheet you created in Lesson 14 to demonstrate linking. You may want to see the list of linked files when you are working on a summary worksheet. Fortunately, Lotus 1-2-3 lets you do this. Execute the File List Linked command. Press the Enter key when you are finished viewing the list.

Long Problems

1. Suppose you are an instructor who uses 1-2-3 to track your students' grades. You want to post the final grades without displaying the students' names, only their social security numbers. Create the following grades worksheet and hide the names column. Then print the worksheet.

Name	SSN	Grade
Abel	324-32-9974	A
Alexander	322-93-2854	B
Banks	495-89-9832	C
Becker	123-93-8237	A
Calhoon	324-58-9245	D
Carver	258-11-3848	B
Crawford	429-29-2847	C
Daily	199-23-9382	A
Davis	342-21-9284	C
Diamond	415-28-3018	B
Eaton	321-45-8294	B
Edwards	312-29-9285	A

2. A company uses Lotus 1-2-3 to store employee salary information. Create the following worksheet and hide the salary column. Enter a formula in cell C1 to sum the salaries. Although cells may be hidden, they can still be referenced in formulas.

Name	Salary
Abel	$32,500.00
Alexander	$25,000.00
Banks	$30,000.00
Becker	$45,000.00

```
Name            Salary

Calhoon         $25,000.00
Carver          $20,000.00
Crawford        $35,000.00
Daily           $45,000.00
Davis           $25,000.00
Diamond         $32,250.00
Eaton           $20,000.00
Edwards         $35,000.00
```

3. Enter the following worksheet. Then transpose the columns and rows.

```
Year    Sales

1987    $32,500.00
1988    $25,000.00
1989    $30,000.00
1990    $45,000.00
1991    $25,000.00
```

4. Indirect circular references and iteration are sometimes used in business calculations. For example, suppose you want to calculate a bonus that is ten percent of net profit, and net profit is defined as gross profit minus the bonus. Create a worksheet that contains the following data and formulas:

```
  A                 B

1 Gross Profit      $1,000.00
2 Bonus             10%*B3
3 Net Profit        +B1-B2
```

Set the Worksheet Global Recalculation Iteration to 50 and recalculate the worksheet to get final answers. The Bonus should be $90.91 and the Net Profit should be $909.09.

5. Create an addition table for the numbers 0 through 5. Enter the numbers 0 through 5 in cells B1 through G1 and cells A2 through A7. Enter a formula that adds the column and row header using mixed references. Use the Copy command to fill out the rest of the table.

6. Create a formula using the @NOW and @DATE functions to calculate the number of days since you were born.

7. Create a macro to widen all columns to 12 characters, set the worksheet global label prefix to Center, and enter the names of the days of the week in columns A through G. If you have Lotus 1-2-3 Release 2.2, use the Learn feature. If you have Lotus 1-2-3 Release 3.0, use the Record feature.

8. Create a macro to format the current cell to display the time in Lotus standard long form (for example 10:22:05 AM) and then enter the time of day.

9. If you have Lotus 1-2-3 Release 2.2 or 3.0, create a separate worksheet for each of the following income statements from different cities. Use formulas to compute the Income figures. Then create a summary worksheet that uses linking to import and sum the Income figures from the three cities.

Boston

Net Sales	$12,000.00
Expenses	$7,350.00
Income	$4,650.00

St. Louis
Net Sales $11,000.00
Expenses $6,050.00
Income $4,950.00

San Diego
Net Sales $15,000.00
Expenses $9,250.00
Income $5,750.00

10. If you have Lotus 1-2-3 Release 3.0, create a multiple-worksheet file that puts each of the following income statements in a separate worksheet. Use formulas to compute the Income figures. Add another worksheet to summarize the data from the three income statements. Save and print your multiple-worksheet file.

Income Statement 1989
Net Sales $10,000.00
Expenses $6,350.00
Income $3,650.00

Income Statement 1990
Net Sales $13,000.00
Expenses $8,050.00
Income $4,950.00

Income Statement 1991
Net Sales $16,000.00
Expenses $10,250.00
Income $5,750.00

Selecting a System

More and more people are buying microcomputers for business and home use. Most companies already have at least one microcomputer, and they are continually acquiring more. Schools at all levels have been purchasing microcomputers for both students and faculty. It's been estimated that at least 20% of all U.S. households will ultimately have some type of microcomputer. Just as most of you will eventually purchase stereo systems, video systems, other high-tech home appliances, and automobiles, it's likely that in the near future you may be investing in a computer system, too. Perhaps you won't be buying a computer for your home, but you might still be involved in the process of selecting a system for your school or work. This appendix offers some guidelines that can help both individuals and organizations in their process of computerization.

Computers are complicated equipment. Although their prices have been steadily dropping, computers still represent a substantial investment for most people. With so many different computer models and an overwhelming array of software packages on the market, unless you're wealthy or are already a computer expert, purchasing a system is no trivial task. The choices you make can have profound effects on the quantity and quality of work you will accomplish with your computer. To make good choices, you need to have a plan.

Selecting a computer system is somewhat like selecting a stereo system or automobile. If you buy on irrational impulses, you risk regretting your decision for years to come. If, on the other hand, you follow a well-thought-out, step-by-step selection process, chances are good that you'll end up with an economical labor-saving system. One such approach involves six basic steps:

1. Learn about computers.
2. Define your needs.
3. Select the software.
4. Select the hardware.
5. Purchase the system.
6. Install the system.

 ## Step 1: Learn About Computers

You need not be a computer scientist to effectively select and use computers. Some basic knowledge, however, can help a great deal. The first step in selecting a system is to become familiar with the capabilities and limitations of computers. In other words, you need to know what computers can and cannot do for you. The chapters in this book are designed to provide you with an understanding of the capabilities and limitations of microcomputers.

Of course, this book can by no means cover all relevant microcomputer topics. Although learning more is not absolutely required, the more you do know the better prepared you'll be to take advantage of what computers have to offer. Fortunately, there are many opportunities for you to learn more about computers. Some of the possibilities include books, periodicals, organizations, shows, courses, conferences, and workshops.

Books

An astonishing number of computer books are available in local bookstores, libraries, and computer stores. Some are quite technical, but many others have been written especially for novices. Some of the most common books you'll find are "How to" books that cover specific computer models or software packages. Others teach programming in certain languages or deal with the philosophical and sociological aspects of using computers. You can even buy books that discuss how to select a computer system.

Periodicals

In 1975, only two magazines were devoted solely to microcomputers. Today, hundreds of microcomputer newspapers, newsletters, and magazines are available. Although books can cover topics in great detail, they're usually somewhat out of date by the time they actually hit the shelves. Newspapers, newsletters, and magazines reveal what's happening in the marketplace *now*. They frequently contain reviews and in-depth evaluations of hardware and software products. Periodicals also contain informative articles and columns that answer questions and provide tips from other computer users. They are crammed with ads from manufacturers, retailers, and mail-order outfits. Many owners have at least one subscription to a microcomputer periodical. Some of the more popular publications include *A+*, *BYTE*, *Infoworld*, *Macworld*, and *PC Magazine*.

In addition to traditional periodicals printed on paper, *disk magazines* have been gaining popularity recently. These publications are issued on floppy disks and are aimed at users of particular computer models. They uniquely provide subscribers with tested programs for business, education, entertainment, and home use.

Organizations

Computer users, it seems, are a very sociable lot. At regular intervals, thousands of folks gather in societies, clubs, and user groups to share computer experiences, help solve each others' problems, and trade software. Although most people don't join such organizations until after they purchase a computer system, joining before buying can be advantageous. Many user groups are centered around a particular computer model or type of popular software. Group members can usually offer advice on where to get the best deals. Joining a computer organization may even qualify you for certain group discounts off the retail prices of selected hardware and software products. Once you have your system, a computer organization can put you in contact with people who have the same hardware and software. These colleagues can be an invaluable source of information because it's likely that they've already solved problems you might be having as a beginning user.

Computer organizations offer fellowship, support, general information, and answers to those tricky questions not answered in any manuals. Many groups have been established since the advent of microcomputers in the mid-1970s. For example, more than 850 groups in the United States serve Apple computer users. Some groups have remained local, small, and dedicated to one particular type of computer, like the Champaign-Urbana, Illinois Apple II Users Group with its 40 or so members. Other groups have grown immense and wield a good deal of influence over the microcomputer industry. The Boston Computer Society, for instance, was founded in 1977 by Jonathan Rotenberg when he was thirteen years old. Today, with about 24,000 members, it's perhaps the nation's largest microcomputer users group. The Boston Computer Society has its own magazine, *Computer Update*, sponsors around 100 monthly events, and has approximately 40 special-interest subgroups, each of which publishes its own newsletter.

Shows

Every year, computer shows are held in various cities across the United States. These events may be sponsored by individual entrepreneurs, manufacturers, retail stores, magazine publishers, or other associations that deal with computers. Although many shows specifically target manufacturers and retailers, others are open to the general computer-buying public. They are typically held in large exhibit halls, with booth space rented to hardware manufacturers, software manufacturers, dealers, distributors, retailers, computer clubs, publishers, and any other organizations that want to sell or advertise products. Admission is often charged. Besides exhibiting new products and services, many shows also offer short talks, seminars, and classes for attendees, frequently given by well-known computer personalities. These shows may last several days and attract thousands of people who come from all over the country.

Computer shows can offer the following opportunities:

- *See new products.* Manufacturers often introduce products at computer shows, so it may be an early chance to see what's new in the market. Furthermore, most shows exhibit a wider variety of products than you can usually find in the typical computer store. It's easy to collect all kinds of brochures, product descriptions, advertisements, and other handouts.
- *Try out products.* Many computer show exhibits are specifically designed to let you "test drive" hardware and software products. This may be your only chance to get hands-on experience with an item before you actually buy it.
- *Buy products.* Frequently, computer shows allow exhibitors to sell their products directly to consumers. At some shows, you can buy anything from a single diskette to an entire microcomputer system. Prices are generally less than retail and it's possible to get some good bargains at computer shows, especially as closing time nears.
- *Learn more.* As we mentioned before, many computer shows sponsor lectures and seminars. Subjects may include very specific topics, such as how to use a particular feature of a software package, or more general matters, such as the role of microcomputers in our society.

- *Meet people.* Computer shows offer excellent opportunities to come into contact with other people who have similar interests. You may meet just one person at a booth looking for the same product, or you may discover an entire users group that you want to join. The people you meet can offer advice, answer questions, and share some of their computer experiences with you.
- *Talk to manufacturers.* Since many hardware and software manufacturers send representatives to computer shows, you may get an opportunity to ask questions, get more information, or even complain about a particular product.

Courses

For people who seek a more structured approach to learning about computers, a wide variety of formal courses is offered to both students and the general public. Traditional educational institutions, like high schools, community colleges, and universities, hold classes aimed primarily at those seeking diplomas. Many community colleges and university continuing education and extension services also offer computer courses for non-degree students. Classes range from simple, non-technical introductions for novices to in-depth studies for those pursuing computer careers. Alternative learning centers, such as those affiliated with local churches, libraries, and park districts, often conduct classes taught by computer experts in their spare time. Although such courses may be less academic than those run by traditional educational institutions, they may be more accessible to the general public. Computer stores often teach courses about particular hardware and software products, but these courses may be limited to customers. Several proprietary (for-profit) schools also offer computer-related coursework. Many accredited home study schools as well as colleges and universities have correspondence courses that teach computer subjects by mail. Finally, some private individuals offer computer courses too. Before you enroll in any course, however, be sure to investigate it thoroughly to determine just what is being offered and how much it will cost.

Conferences and Workshops

Many organizations offer conferences and workshops covering particular computer topics. Some of these events are expensive, intensive training sessions aimed specifically at computer professionals. Others are less technical and attract novice computer users. They typically last from several hours to several days, and are held in various cities across the country.

Step 2: Define Your Needs

Once you have a general picture of what microcomputers can do, you can begin to examine how you might use one. It's important to carefully consider exactly what you want to do with a computer before you purchase anything. Of course, you probably can't anticipate every possible use you'll find for your computer once you get it, but you should have some clearly stated, specific reasons for investing in a system. A good approach is to make a list. Write down, in order of importance, all of the uses you expect to have for a computer. At this stage, try not to think too much about costs, but keep your ideas realistic. As a sample, your list might look something like this:

1. *Word Processing*. For term papers, reports, class notes, and letters.
2. *Record Keeping*. For addresses, phone numbers, personal property inventory, bank account numbers, credit cards, and tax-deductible expenses.
3. *Calculating*. For bills, budgets, and income taxes.
4. *Education*. For math review, foreign language study, college entrance test review, and learning about computer programming.
5. *Entertainment*. For fun with computer games and simulations.

This list is probably fairly typical of the uses a student or other individual might have for a computer at home or school. A business, however, might have a more specific list of computer needs, especially if it is computerizing for the first time, or perhaps considering replacing an existing system. A small business, for example, might have the following uses for a microcomputer system:

1. *General Ledger*. To keep track of financial records and produce reports, such as balance sheets and profit and loss statements, that summarize the financial status of the firm.
2. *Accounts Receivable*. To keep track of the money owed to the company and when payments are due.
3. *Accounts Payable*. To keep track of money the company owes to its suppliers.
4. *Payroll*. To calculate each employee's gross pay, withhold taxes, subtract deductions, print paychecks, and maintain necessary payroll records.
5. *Inventory*. To monitor the goods on hand and make sure enough are in stock for production and customer requests.
6. *Mailing List*. To prepare direct mailing of ads and notices.
7. *Word Processing*. To create letters, reports, newsletters, and memos.
8. *Personnel Files*. To hold information for insurance, retirement, and governmental regulations.

Step 3: Select the Software

Now comes perhaps the most difficult step in acquiring a computer system: selecting the software. First of all, from the user's standpoint, software is much more important than hardware. Software is what makes the computer accomplish useful work. Without programs, computer hardware is utterly worthless. It's likely that you'll pay much more for all the software you'll eventually buy than the hardware. If you have a stereo system, this probably doesn't surprise you, since most people have more money invested in records, tapes, or compact discs than they originally paid for the stereo components. Shopping for software is also more difficult than shopping for hardware, because there is so much more software on the market than hardware. Some software companies sell only by mail, so it may be difficult to obtain information about their programs. A thorough evaluation of software requires using it in your own particular situation for a substantial amount of time. This may be difficult, if not impossible, to do by running a program at a single sitting in your local computer store. Finally, because software usually has a smaller profit margin than hardware, computer salespeople may not be as enthusiastic or helpful about selling a program as they would an entire computer system.

All those difficulties aside, it really is possible, even for novices, to make good software selections. First, go back to your list of computer uses. For each item, come up with at least three different software packages. Here you'll need some of those learning resources we talked about previously. Perhaps the best source of possible selections may be people you know from school, work, clubs, user groups, or computer shows. See if you can arrange to try a potential software selection for an extended period of time. Perhaps a friend or relative has a computer and software you can use. If your school has a computer lab, you may be able to use it at times when classes aren't in session. Many school labs have software you can check out and run on a computer at your own pace.

Probably the best source of information comparing various software packages are computer magazines. Most have reviews of new software products; some even devote entire issues to comparing all the major competitors in a particular application. The publications extensively test each package by using it for a pre-determined set of activities, and then quantitatively rate how each one does. Often, the reviewers will conclude with one or more "editor's choices," and give their reasons for selecting these packages as the best of the lot. Scanning the magazine stands and going through back issues in the library are excellent ways to find out more about specific application packages.

As you begin to compile your list of potential software selections, make your own evaluations and rank the packages, if possible. As you talk to people and read product reviews, note the following characteristics of good software:

- *Competent*. Capable of performing an important job well.
- *Easy to Learn*. Can be mastered with moderate effort in a reasonable amount of time.
- *Easy to Use*. Intrudes as little as possible between the user and getting the job done.
- *Tolerant*. Gently and sensibly handles errors made by the user.
- *Layered*. Simple and self-evident on the outside for beginners, and progressively more complex and powerful as internal features are mastered.
- *Flexible*. Can be adapted to handle variations in its basic task.
- *Compatible*. Works well with other software by using standard conventions and being able to share files.
- *Well-Documented*. Comes with clearly written, correct instruction and reference manuals designed with both novices and experts in mind.
- *Supported*. Backed by its manufacturer, which conscientiously fixes errors, provides updated versions, and answers users' questions.
- *Reasonably-Priced*. Provides value comparable to its cost.

Once you complete this process, you'll have a list of computer uses ordered according to your priorities, within which will be sublists of potential software packages ranked by preference. You're not ready to buy anything yet, and you haven't singled out the exact packages you'll eventually get, but you have a pretty good idea of the field of contenders.

Step 4: Select the Hardware

By seriously considering software first, the selection of hardware is much easier. The idea is to choose hardware that can run the software packages you've selected. This helps you put together a system that really matches your needs.

Computer

Some of the software packages you've selected have versions that run on different computers, but many will only work on a single machine. This is where you begin to determine the most important hardware decision facing you: which computer to get. Although there are hundreds of different companies making microcomputers, the great majority of machines fit into one of just a few categories. Today, these categories are IBM and IBM-compatible computers, Apple Macintoshes, Apple II computers, and all others. This is not to belittle all those "other" computers. There are quite a few great machines with large numbers of devoted users. However, there's no doubt that the microcomputers in the first three categories far outnumber all the rest, especially in businesses, offices, and schools.

IBM and IBM-Compatible Computers   IBM is the recognized leader in the microcomputer industry. They sell more microcomputers than any other single manufacturer. People who prefer other computers may not concede that IBM sells the "best" computers, but the fact remains that they sell the most. Although IBM no longer manufactures members of its original Personal Computer line (PC Jrs, PCs, PC Portables, XTs, and ATs), millions of these machines remain in use and some dealers are still selling new ones. The current IBM Personal System/2 line of computers improves on the previous models while still being able to run all the old software. IBM computers tend to be solidly-built, reliable machines that have been traditionally popular in the business world. Even though IBM computers might be a bit more expensive than comparable machines from other manufacturers, they have been getting more price-competitive lately. It's been said that "no manager ever got fired for buying IBM."

A true **IBM-compatible** computer is one that can run all the software and accept all the expansion boards and peripheral units that IBM microcomputers can use. Because IBM chose standard parts, published detailed design descriptions in technical references, and used an operating system designed and also sold by Microsoft, it was relatively easy for other manufacturers to produce compatible computers. Although there may still be some exceptions, most IBM-compatibles produced today do a very good job of mimicking the way IBM computers work. Many such "clones" offer more advanced features at a significantly lower price than IBM computers. Some IBM-compatible manufacturers, such as COMPAQ, have become highly-respected microcomputer industry leaders in their own right. Many well-established computer and electronic companies, like Tandy and Zenith, have expanded their lines to include IBM-compatible machines. In addition, quite a few mail-order firms, such as Dell Computer Corporation and Northgate Computer Systems, sell IBM-compatibles that they construct themselves from standard components. In fact, many more IBM-compatibles are sold today than IBM microcomputers.

Although IBMs and IBM-compatibles have their critics, selecting such computers has many advantages. American businesses have over $80 billion invested in IBM and IBM-compatible computers. This includes over 72 million software and hardware products, and hundreds of millions of hours of training. Books, magazines, and user groups devoted solely to IBM-compatible computers abound. Chances are good that you can find experts nearby to help you if you have problems. Most IBM and IBM-compatible systems can be easily expanded if you need to add more capabilities later.

Apple Macintosh Computers   In the early days of IBM microcomputers, many people considered them to be powerful and expandable, but not particularly easy to set up and use. Apple, building on their great success with the Apple II line, decided to address these concerns and build a computer "for the rest of us." In 1984, Apple introduced the Macintosh. Easy to learn and fun to use, the Macintosh has changed the way people perceive computers. Today's models preserve the philosophy of simplicity, yet have become more powerful and expandable. The Macintosh is becoming increasingly popular in businesses, especially for word processing, graphics, and desktop publishing applications. Many individuals and schools are also purchasing Macintoshes in ever greater numbers. Hundreds of software packages and a variety of optional peripherals are now available for this machine.

Apple II Computers   The original Apple II computer was introduced in 1977. Since then, several million of the Apple II family (including the Apple II+, Apple IIe, Apple III, Apple IIc, and Apple IIGS) have been sold. These computers have done very well in elementary and secondary schools. The Apple II's share of sales in this market is currently around 50%, although some schools are turning more toward Macintoshes and low-cost IBM-compatibles. Apple II computers have also been quite popular as home computers and were common in businesses before the introduction of the IBM Personal Computers. At least 10,000 software packages run on Apple II computers and a wide variety of expansion devices and peripherals are available. Although this family of computers is not as powerful and fast as Macintoshes and IBM-compatibles, they are still viable machines with a large number of devoted users.

Memory

In the early days of microcomputers, RAM was expensive and most machines could have no more than 64K. This situation has changed dramatically. Many microcomputers now have the potential to use up to 4 gigabytes of RAM, and memory chips are less expensive. For many people, the memory that comes with the computer will be sufficient for most of their needs. For example, most IBM microcomputers now come with at least 640K standard and all Macintoshes come with at least one megabyte installed. On other machines, you'll have to make sure you get enough memory to run the application packages you've selected. Since most software manufacturers state how much memory is required for their programs, figuring out how much memory to buy should be fairly simple. If you can, try to choose a computer system that can accept more RAM than you may initially need. Then if you later purchase software that requires more memory, you can add more RAM to upgrade your system.

Disk Drives

When it comes to secondary storage, you have several choices to make. The first one is whether you need the high capacity and rapid data access of a hard disk. This depends on the types of applications you'll run and the quantity of data you'll be working with. Some application packages require a hard disk. Others don't actually require one, but would work much better and faster with a hard disk. If the application programs you run and the data files you'll work with won't each fit on a single floppy disk, you probably need a hard disk. If you're not sure if you want to invest the extra few hundred dollars in a hard disk, make sure that you get a computer system that can accommodate a hard disk if you decide to add one later.

The other most common secondary storage decisions involve what kind and how many floppy drives to get. The 5¼-inch diskette drives are still more common, less expensive, and use less expensive floppies than 3½-inch drives. However, many computers, like the Macintosh and IBM Personal System/2 computers, come with only 3½-inch disk drives standard. Most software is now distributed on either type of disk. Each type of floppy drive has its advantages, but your major concern should be whether you can trade diskettes with colleagues, co-workers, and friends. It's best to get the same type of diskette drives as people with whom you'll be frequently exchanging programs and data. If you do get a hard disk, one floppy drive will probably be sufficient. However, if you often need to copy entire diskettes, it might be worth investing in two drives. In systems without hard disks, having two floppy drives is the most practical arrangement.

Display

With some computers, you have no choice as to what kind of display to get. The Apple Macintosh Plus and Macintosh SE, for example, come with a built-in 9-inch monochrome graphics display. On most computers, however, you have a choice among several alternatives. Older and less-expensive computers give you a choice among monochrome text, monochrome graphics, and color graphics monitors. Many newer microcomputers, like the IBM Personal System/2 series, support only graphics monitors, but you do have a choice between monochrome and color. To complicate matters more, many computers can accept several different display adapters, each of which may support several video modes.

To resolve your display dilemma, first look at your software selections. If you want to run software that uses graphics, you'll need a graphics display. On the other hand, if you're *positive* that you'll only be working with text, you may want to opt for a less expensive monochrome text monitor. Although in most cases color is not absolutely necessary, many people find that color monitors are more pleasant to work with, despite the added expense. If you are planning to use software that manipulates detailed graphics, you'll need a high-resolution display. As with most hardware selections, try to choose a system that can be upgraded later, if possible. Your needs may expand and prices may fall to a point where you would like to invest in a more sophisticated display. It's much easier and less expensive to replace a display adapter and monitor than an entire computer system.

Printer

Literally hundreds of microcomputer printers are on the market. Before you choose a particular model, you must first decide on what type of printer you need. Most microcomputer users have 9-pin dot-matrix printers. These printers can do graphics and can print fairly rapidly in draft mode, yet also have a more attractive, but much slower, near-letter-quality mode. If you will be printing letters on bond or letterhead paper, be sure to look for models that can easily accept single sheets as well as the fan-fold, pin-feed computer paper most dot-matrix printers use. For true letter quality, you might want to get a daisy-wheel printer. These printers produce text that looks just like that from typewriters, but they are quite slow. Applications that produce very high-quality text and graphics may require a 24-pin dot-matrix printer or perhaps even an expensive laser printer. Before you make your final decision on any printer, be sure to see samples of the text and graphics it can produce. Also consider the cost of supplies like paper, ribbons, toner cartridges (for laser printers) and additional typefaces.

Other Peripherals

A wide range of optional peripheral devices can be connected to a microcomputer. In your selection of a system, you should try to choose initially only those devices that will be absolutely necessary. You can always add more peripherals later, provided that you've chosen a system that can be expanded. If you'll be accessing remote computers, you'll need to select a modem. Many graphics applications require the use of a mouse. Some computer games use joysticks or trackballs. Examine your software selections carefully to make sure that you understand exactly what hardware devices are necessary.

Specifications and Benchmarks

In the preceding sections, we've briefly described the hardware you need to select. But, how do you pick the exact models to buy? Just as in making software selections, one method is to look carefully at what people around you have purchased. Some experts have even suggested that you get a system exactly like another one you have access to, perhaps at school, work, or a friend's. This way, you can become familiar with the components before you buy, and after you get your system, you have access to an exact duplicate in case your system isn't working. Although it definitely helps to have access to a similar system, if you only buy what someone else has, you're depending a great deal on their judgment, which may or may not be better than your own.

Another method of selecting hardware is to read reviews published in computer and consumer magazines. Just like software reviews, hardware reviews compare and evaluate actual products. For computers, hardware reviews can provide in-depth information about how they are constructed and how they work. For devices like displays, printers, and modems, reviews can compare models quantitatively and tabulate their features. Be forewarned, however, that these reviews are often saturated with specifications and benchmarks.

Specifications are a detailed list of the exact components, options, and capabilities of a particular hardware device. Microcomputer specifications typically list the manufacturer, exact size, microprocessor, coprocessors, system clock speed, amount of standard RAM, total possible RAM, amount of ROM, disk drives and capacities, number and type of expansion slots, number and type of interfaces, retail list price, and many other details. Sometimes, specifications include measures of performance. For example, many printer specifications include the number of characters printed per second. Although specifications can be one way to compare different devices, they may be misleading. Performance measurements are often made under ideal conditions. So, a printer advertised at 200 characters per second, may not actually be that fast when printing a document from your word processor, especially if it contains underlining, boldface, and italics.

A **benchmark** is an objective, reproducible measure of hardware or software performance, typically the amount of time it takes to run a standard program or process a particular set of data. Just like specifications, benchmarks are one way to compare hardware, but they can also be misleading. For example, a common benchmark for computer performance is one cycle of a calculation known as the *Sieve of Eratosthenes*. This is a method of finding prime numbers (numbers only evenly divisible by themselves and 1) that has been adapted to computers. Although benchmarks such as these may be useful for measuring the time required for certain very specific kinds of computer operations, they provide little or no information about ease of use, reliability, maintainability, the amount of manufacturer support for a product, or other equally important attributes. Sometimes, magazines like *BYTE* and *PC Magazine* develop their own benchmarks for reviewing products. Although these benchmarks are designed to measure performance under typical conditions, they may still not reflect how fast your software will run on your machine. Benchmark results, like specifications, should be taken with a grain of salt.

Step 5: Purchase the System

After selecting your hardware, you may have to go back and modify your list of software packages so that you have ones that will all run on the machine you've chosen. Before you even think of buying anything, you should have a fairly complete list of the exact software and hardware products you'll need. Since most product reviews and ads contain prices, you should also have a good notion of how much all this will cost. This is the time to look at your budget and make some realistic choices. You may not be able to afford all the software packages and optional peripherals you want to get. Fortunately, some of these purchases can be postponed. If you've listed your selections by priority, you can initially buy only those most essential items.

When to Buy

For many people, the most disconcerting circumstances of microcomputer shopping are the rate at which technology advances and how quickly prices can drop. Computer newspapers and magazines are filled with rumors, educated guesses, and pre-release previews about new products and upgrades to existing ones. Most manufacturers, it would seem, are constantly on the verge of releasing a computer, peripheral, or software package that will render every preceding product hopelessly obsolete. Even worse, what you pay $4,000 for this year may cost less than $1,000 two years from now. This perpetual anticipation can immobilize some potential computer shoppers.

Unfortunately, you must simply accept the facts that whichever hardware and software you choose, prices will drop and new versions will be released. There may be some prudence in waiting one or two months if a product is about to be released that will truly meet your needs. However, production often lags behind the demand for new products and it's sometimes best not to be one of the first owners of a brand-new piece of hardware or software. New technology, such as automobiles, stereos, hardware, and software, frequently has unsuspected flaws. It's nearly impossible to detect all of the potential problems in a complex product that's being rushed out of the factory into a highly competitive marketplace. Although it's tempting to be one of the first to get the latest hardware or software, you may wind up as a guinea pig whose complaints contribute to the design of Version 2.0.

In most cases, the time to buy is *now*. If you truly need a computer, you probably can't afford to wait months for the release and delivery of a brand-new product. A great deal of hardware and software is currently available that will provide years of valuable service, even if new versions are released after your purchase. Assuming you've done your homework and selected a system that fulfills your requirements, it shouldn't matter that less expensive, more powerful alternatives will eventually be released. Even if your computing needs grow, you can most likely expand your current system later. Someday, you may even want to select a completely new system, but in the meantime you will have a computer that can help you now.

Where to Buy

Nowadays, computer hardware and software can be purchased from a variety of sources. The outlet you select often depends upon such factors as how much you know about computers, how much money you want to save, how soon you need a system, whether you're buying a well-established brand name product, and whether you're buying hardware or software. You can purchase a computer system from computer stores, department stores, school stores, manufacturers, mail-order firms, and used equipment dealers.

Computer Stores   Local retail outlets that specialize in computers, such as Computerland and Radio Shack Computer Centers, are the traditional source of hardware and software products for many shoppers, especially novices. Salespeople are usually knowledgeable and can help a great deal in putting together a system that meets your needs. Most computer stores can also service your hardware should it need repair after the purchase. Many items are in stock or can be ordered and obtained in a few days. Unfortunately, many computer stores sell only a few brands. Although the brands tend to be from a select group of well-established manufacturers, your choices may be somewhat limited at a computer store. Items are usually sold at retail list prices, but there may be occasional sales or discounts given to certain groups of people. It may cost a bit more to buy a computer or peripheral device at a computer store, but dealers are nearby, accessible, and stand behind the hardware they sell.

Despite the additional cost, it often makes sense to buy hardware from a computer store. There is less advantage, however, to buying brand name software from a computer store. Software doesn't break down in the sense that hardware does, so a computer store technician can't repair a program. For most software packages, any problems or questions you have must usually be taken directly to the manufacturer. Although computer store salespeople may be able to answer some of your software questions, they simply can't be experts on every program they sell. In many cases, brand name software can be purchased for less from other sources.

Department Stores   Sometimes, retail department stores like Sears, Target, and Service Merchandise sell computers and software. List prices are usually discounted and you can get items immediately if they are in stock. Unfortunately, department store salespeople may not be very knowledgeable about computers. Furthermore, each store typically only carries a single computer brand. In most cases, service after the sale may only be obtained from the original manufacturer. However, if you're fairly knowledgeable about computers and a local department store has exactly what you want, you may be able to get a good bargain.

School Stores   If you're a student, faculty, or staff member of a college or university and in the market for a computer system, you may be in luck. Many schools have special deals with computer hardware and software manufacturers enabling them to offer products to qualified buyers at substantial savings. Hardware and software may be sold through a university bookstore, student union, educational consortium, or local computer center at discounts of up to 50% for students, faculty, and staff. Computer manufacturers like Apple, IBM, Hewlett-Packard, and Zenith often make deals with schools to sell their equipment at very low prices. In many cases, sales agents are knowledgeable and schools may also have their own service centers.

Manufacturers   Sometimes, there's no dealer in the area that sells the computer you want. Or, you may qualify for a volume discount by wanting to purchase a number of systems all at once. In such situations it may be advantageous to go directly to the manufacturer of a particular hardware or software product. Unless you're purchasing in volume, you'll probably pay the list price and it may take several days or weeks for the item to be shipped to you. However, at least you know that you're going directly to the source and eliminating the middleman. Some large manufacturers, like IBM, may even have a local office through which you can purchase products and get equipment serviced after the sale.

Mail-Order Firms   In the past, computer mail-order firms have had a somewhat less than prestigious reputation. With very few exceptions, that reputation is no longer justified. In fact, the seventh largest domestic microcomputer manufacturer, Dell Computer Corporation, is strictly a mail-order firm. This particular company even offers an optional next-day, on-site service contract for most major metropolitan areas and unlimited access to technicians over toll-free phone lines. Although most mail-order firms may not be this accommodating, a great many individuals, schools, and businesses buy computer hardware and software through the mail. Mail-order buying can save you money, and, in this day of overnight package delivery, can also be very convenient.

Still, the rule is "let the buyer beware" when it comes to mail-order purchasing. Ordering hardware over the phone can be daunting to computer novices. Many mail-order firms put together their own computers from standard components. These computers can be fantastic machines, but unless you know exactly what you're doing, it's probably best to stick to established brand names. Although, as we said, some mail-order firms offer repair service, most of them don't. Many advertise technical support over the phone, but it can sometimes be difficult to get through and have your questions answered politely, quickly, and accurately. Make sure that any mail-order firm you do choose has been in business for awhile.

Buying brand name software through the mail, however, offers several advantages. Discounts are usually substantial and the package you get in the mail is identical to what you would get from your local computer store or directly from the manufacturer. Large mail-order firms may have many items in stock and can often deliver them the next day via an overnight carrier for a modest extra charge.

Used Equipment Dealers   A recent market study showed that most people buying new computers have owned at least one computer before. What's happening to all those computers that are being replaced? Some are winding up at used computer dealers. As the microcomputer industry ages, more and more used computer stores are opening. Sometimes you can find real bargains at such stores but, like buying a used car, purchasing a pre-owned computer or hardware component can be somewhat risky. Many of the machines in used computer stores are obsolete. They may still be quite useful, but it might be difficult to get parts, service, and software for computers no longer in production. If, on the other hand, a used computer is being sold because its owner simply upgraded to a more powerful system, there may be no reason not to buy it as long as it's been thoroughly tested and guaranteed by the dealer.

Step 6: Install the System

You've chosen and purchased your software and hardware. The system was delivered today and now it's at home still in the boxes. What do you do? Well, first open all the boxes and get out the instructions. Make sure all the components, cables, disks, and other items are there. Follow the directions and set up the machine. Some computers come with tutorial programs you can run to teach you the basics of using the hardware and running the operating system. Besides being entertaining, these tutorials are usually quite informative and well worth the time. Once you feel comfortable with the fundamentals, you can follow the instructions to install your software on your computer. Don't be surprised if you have problems or if things don't work exactly as the tutorials and manuals indicate. Reread the instructions and try again. If you're still having problems, call your dealer or the manufacturer's customer service department. If you still can't get your system running, you may have an honest-to-goodness defect and will have to return your system.

Once you do get your system up and running, try out all of the hardware and software components as soon as possible. Read your warranties and mail in the cards that register you with the manufacturers as a new owner. Not only will this validate your warranties, it will also put you on mailing lists so that you can get information about new versions and upgrades. At this time you might be thinking about insurance and service contracts. If your computer system represents a substantial investment to you, and you come to need it on a daily basis, you'll want make sure that it's insured and that you can get it repaired if it breaks down.

Finally, consider the surroundings in which you set up your system. A sturdy, roomy table or desktop and a well-designed, comfortable chair are musts if you expect to use your computer system for hours at a time. Keep your system clean and free from dust, spills, food crumbs, and other foreign materials. Try to keep any cooling vents unobstructed so that your system won't overheat. Unplug your hardware when not in use and try not to run it during electrical storms. Computer equipment, like other electronic devices, can be easily damaged or even destroyed by electrical surges caused by lightning or other power line disturbances. It might be prudent to plug all of your equipment into a **surge protector**. This is a relatively inexpensive device with a main switch, several electrical sockets, and circuitry to rapidly cut off power when a voltage surge occurs. Careful installation of your computer system can help ensure its reliability and usefulness for years to come.

SOFTWARE INSTALLATION

Most operating systems and application packages must be **installed** on your computer before you can use them. This typically involves running a special installation or setup program included with the software. Installation programs often create a new subdirectory on your hard disk, copy the files from the floppy disks included with the package to that subdirectory, and let you specify what kind of hardware you have. At most school microcomputer labs, this has already been done for you by the attendants. If you own a computer, however, you will probably have to install any new software you purchase yourself. The documentation that comes with the software should explain, step-by-step, how to run the installation program and answer any questions that may be asked about your hardware and software. Let's briefly go over the steps necessary to install the software discussed in this book: PC-DOS and MS-DOS Version 3.30, IBM DOS 4.00, MS-DOS 4.01, Lotus 1-2-3 Release 2.01, Lotus 1-2-3 Release 2.2, and Lotus 1-2-3 Release 3.0.

PC-DOS and MS-DOS Version 3.30

MS-DOS 3.30 and PC-DOS 3.30 are very similar. The MS-DOS package comes with two manuals entitled *MS-DOS User's Guide* and *MS-DOS User's Reference*. The first one contains the instructions for installing the system. The package can be purchased on either 3½-inch, 720K floppy disks, or 5¼-inch, 360K floppy disks. The 5¼-inch package comes with two disks, one labeled *Startup* and the other *Operating*.

Although the DOS 3.30 *Startup* diskette can be copied to another diskette to routinely boot up the computer from drive A, many people install the operating system on their hard disk C, if they have one. To install DOS 3.30 on a hard disk, follow these steps:

1. Insert the DOS 3.30 Startup disk into drive A.

2. Turn on the computer. If it is already on, press **Ctrl-Alt-Del** to reboot.

3. If the hard disk is not formatted (e.g., if you have a brand new computer), enter **format c: /s**. WARNING: Do not use this command if your hard disk is already formatted, or you will lose all files stored on it.

4. If the hard disk is already formatted with a previous version of DOS, enter **sys c:** instead of using the FORMAT command.

5. Enter **copy command.com c:** to copy the command processor to the hard disk.

6. If a subdirectory named DOS already exists on the hard disk, enter **del c:\dos*.*** to delete its contents. If such a subdirectory does not exist, enter **md c:\dos** to create it.

7. Enter **copy *.* c:\dos** to copy all the files from the Startup diskette to the DOS subdirectory on the hard disk.

8. Take the Startup diskette out of drive A, replace it with the Operating diskette, press **F3**, and press **Enter** to repeat the previous command and copy all of the files from the Operating diskette to the DOS subdirectory on the hard disk.

9. Remove the diskette from drive A, store all your original DOS diskettes in a safe place, and press **Ctrl-Alt-Del** to reboot your computer from the hard disk with DOS 3.30.

10. Enter **path c:\;c:\dos;** to set up the search paths for the root directory and the DOS subdirectory. You can add other search paths on the end of this command if you like. Ideally, this path command should be put in your AUTOEXEC.BAT file.

IBM DOS Version 4.00

The IBM DOS 4.00 package comes with two short manuals entitled *Getting Started with Disk Operating System Version 4.00* and *Using Disk Operating System Version 4.00*. The first one contains the instructions for installing the system. The package can be purchased on either 3½-inch, 720K floppy disks or 5¼-inch, 360K floppy disks. You should get the package with disks that match your floppy drive A. The 3½-inch package comes with two disks, one labeled *Install* and the other *Operating*. The 5¼-inch package comes with five disks labeled *Install*, *Select*, *Operating 1*, *Operating 2*, and *Operating 3*.

Although DOS 4.00 can be installed on floppy disks to boot up the computer from drive A, most people install the operating system on their hard disk C, if they have one. To install DOS 4.00 on a hard disk, follow these steps:

1. Insert the DOS 4.00 Install disk into drive A.

2. Turn on the computer. If it is already on, press **Ctrl-Alt-Del** to reboot.

3. After the copyright screen appears, press **Enter** and follow the instructions given by the installation program, which is called Select.

4. When you are finished with the installation program, remove the DOS floppy disk from drive A, store all your DOS disks in a safe place, and press **Ctrl-Alt-Del** to reboot your computer from the hard disk with DOS 4.00.

MS-DOS Version 4.01

The MS-DOS 4.01 package comes with three manuals entitled *MS-DOS User's Guide*, *MS-DOS User's Reference*, and *MS-DOS Shell User's Guide*. The first one contains the instructions for installing the system. The package can be purchased on either 3½-inch, 720K floppy disks or 5¼-inch, 360K floppy disks. You should get the package with disks that match your floppy drive A. The 3½-inch package comes with two disks, one labeled *Install* and the other *Operating*. The 5¼-inch package comes with six disks labeled *Install, Select, Operating 1, Operating 2, Operating 3,* and *Shell*.

Although MS-DOS 4.01 can be installed on floppy disks to boot up the computer from drive A, most people install the operating system on their hard disk C, if they have one. To install MS-DOS 4.01 on a hard disk, follow these steps:

1. Insert the MS-DOS 4.01 Install disk into drive A.

2. Turn on the computer. If it is already on, press **Ctrl-Alt-Del** to reboot.

3. After the copyright screen appears, press **Enter** and follow the instructions given by the installation program, which is called Select.

4. When you are finished with the installation program, remove the DOS floppy disk from drive A, store all your DOS disks in a safe place, and press **Ctrl-Alt-Del** to reboot your computer from the hard disk with MS-DOS 4.01.

Lotus 1-2-3 Release 2.01

When you purchase Lotus 1-2-3 Release 2.01, you get three softcover manuals entitled *Getting Started, Tutorial,* and *Reference*. Also included are various keyboard guides and a quick reference card. The 5¼-inch package contains six floppy disks:

- *System Disk.* This disk holds the actual 1-2-3 program, along with a program called Lotus that lets you switch between 1-2-3 and the other programs included with it.
- *PrintGraph.* This disk holds a separate program called PrintGraph that allows you to print your 1-2-3 graphs. Depending on your printer's ability, this program lets you control colors, fonts, and the layout of your graphs.
- *Utility Disk.* This disk contains the Install program that lets you set up 1-2-3 to use a printer and display graphs, and the Translate program that lets you transfer data between 1-2-3 and other application packages.
- *Install Library Disk.* This disk contains files used by the Install program to set up 1-2-3 to run with various monitors and printers.
- *A View of 1-2-3.* This disk holds View, an onscreen tutorial program to help you learn about 1-2-3.
- *Backup System Disk.* This is simply a backup copy of the System Disk, in case you damage or lose the original.

To install Lotus 1-2-3 on a hard disk, follow these steps:

1. Turn on your computer.

2. Type **md \123** and press **Enter** to create a new subdirectory named 123 on your hard disk.

3. Type **cd \123** and press **Enter** to switch to the subdirectory you've just created.

4. Insert the System Disk into drive A.

5. Type **copy a:*.*** and press **Enter.**

6. After the contents of the floppy disk have been copied into the 123 subdirectory, remove the disk from drive A.

7. Repeat Steps 4 through 6 for all the remaining floppy disks included with the package, except the Backup System Disk.

8. Type **install** and press **Enter.**

9. Press **Enter** after reading the introductory screen.

10. The Install program displays the Main menu on the screen. Press **Enter** to select the First-Time Installation option from the menu and follow the directions to answer questions about your monitor and printer.

11. When you finish the First-Time Installation, select the Exit Install option.

12. Put your original Lotus 1-2-3 floppy disks away in a safe place.

Lotus 1-2-3 Release 2.2

When you purchase Lotus 1-2-3 Release 2.2, you get two softcover manuals entitled *Reference* and *Setting Up 1-2-3, Tutorial, Quick Start, and Sample Applications*. Also included are various keyboard templates and two booklets: *Upgrader's Handbook* and *Quick Reference*. The 5¼-inch package contains twelve floppy disks:

- *System Disk*. This disk holds the actual 1-2-3 program, along with a program called Lotus that lets you switch between 1-2-3 and the other programs included with it.
- *Help Disk*. This disk holds the on-line help facility, which lets you get information about a topic while you are using 1-2-3.
- *PrintGraph Disk*. This disk holds a separate program called PrintGraph that allows you to print your 1-2-3 graphs. Depending on your printer's ability, this program lets you control colors, fonts, and the layout of your graphs.
- *Install Disk*. This disk holds the Install program that lets you set up 1-2-3 to use a printer and display graphs.
- *Install Library Disk*. This disk contains files used by the Install program to set up 1-2-3 to run with various monitors and printers.
- *Translate Disk*. This disk holds the Translate program that lets you transfer data between 1-2-3 and other application packages.
- *Sample Files Disk*. This disk holds worksheet files that you use while following instructions in the Tutorial, Quick Start, and Sample Applications sections of the manual.
- *Always Setup Disk*. This disk holds the Always spreadsheet publishing add-in program, which lets you format worksheets and graphs.
- *Always Disk 1* through *Always Disk 4*. These disks contain font files and device driver files for Always.

To install Lotus 1-2-3 Release 2.2 on a hard disk, follow these steps:

1. Turn on your computer.

2. Insert the System Disk in drive A and close the door.

3. Type **a:** and press **Enter** to switch to the disk in drive A.

4. Type **init** and press **Enter** to start the Initialization program.

5. Follow the directions to complete the Initialization program, recording your name and company's name on the System Disk.

6. Type **c:** and press **Enter** to switch back to the hard disk.

7. Type **md \123** and press **Enter** to create a new subdirectory named 123 on your hard disk.

8. Type **cd \123** and press **Enter** to switch to the subdirectory you've just created.

9. Make sure the System Disk is in drive A.

10. Type **copy a:*.*** and press **Enter.**

11. After the contents of the floppy disk have been copied into the 123 subdirectory, remove the disk from drive A.

12. Repeat Steps 9 through 11 for the remaining floppy disks included with the package, except the Allways disks.

13. Type **install** and press **Enter.**

14. Press **Enter** after reading the introductory screen.

15. The Install program displays the Main menu on the screen. Press **Enter** to select the First-Time Installation option from the menu and follow the directions to answer questions about your monitor and printer.

16. When you finish the First-Time Installation, select the Exit Install option.

17. Put your original Lotus 1-2-3 floppy disks away in a safe place.

Lotus 1-2-3 Release 3.0

Lotus 1-2-3 Release 3.0 can run only on IBM-compatible computers that have an 80286, 80386, or 80486 microprocessor, a hard disk drive, and at least one megabyte of memory. When you purchase Lotus 1-2-3 Release 3.0, you get a three-ring manual entitled *Reference* and four booklets: *Setting Up, Tutorial, Upgrader's Handbook,* and *Quick Reference.* Also included are various keyboard templates. The 5¼-inch package contains four high density (1.2-megabyte) floppy disks:

- *1-2-3 System Disk.* This disk holds the actual 1-2-3 program.
- *Install Disk.* This disk holds the Install program that lets you set up 1-2-3 on your computer.
- *Drivers Disk.* This disk contains files used by the Install program to set up 1-2-3 to run with various monitors and printers.
- *Font Disk.* This disk holds the various fonts available in 1-2-3 Release 3.0.

To install Lotus 1-2-3 Release 3.0, follow these steps:

1. Turn on your computer.

2. Insert the Install Disk in drive A and close the door.

3. Type **a:** and press **Enter** to switch to the disk in drive A.

4. Type **install** and press **Enter** to start the Install program.

5. Follow the directions to complete the Install program.

6. Put your original Lotus 1-2-3 floppy disks away in a safe place.

COMMAND SUMMARIES

MS-DOS Version 4.01

DOS Keys

Keypress	Description
Ctrl-Alt-Del	Reboots DOS.
Ctrl-Break	Cancels a command.
Ctrl-PrtSc	Echoes to the printer.
Enter	Processes a command.
Esc	Cancels the current line.
Pause	Pauses screen scrolling (Enhanced keyboards).
Ctrl-Num Lock	Pauses screen scrolling (PC and AT keyboards).
Print Screen	Prints the contents of the screen (Enhanced keyboards).
Shift-PrtSc	Prints the contents of the screen (PC and AT keyboards).
F1	Retypes one character from the previous command.
F2	Retypes previous command up to the specified character.
F3	Retypes all of the previous command.
F4	Deletes previous command up to the specified character.
F5	Saves current command as if it were the previous command.
F6	Inserts an end-of-file code (Ctrl-Z).
Del	Skips over a character from the previous command.
Ins	Switches insert/overwrite mode in the command line.
>	Redirects output.
>>	Redirects and appends output.
<	Redirects input.
|	Pipes output.

DOS Commands

These conventions are used in the list of DOS commands that follows.

Command Format Conventions	
[ ]	optional command switch or parameter, such as [/a]
or	either/or choice, such as DEL **or** ERASE
...	optional repetition of the previous item as necessary
italics	name or value you must enter, such as the following:
drive:	disk drive name, such as A: or B:
path	directory name, such as \WP\LETTERS\WORK
filename	file name, including extension, such as JIM.DOC
pathname	path plus a *filename*, such as \WP\LETTERS\WORK\JIM.DOC
(Internal)	indicates an internal (resident) DOS command.
(External)	indicates an external (transient) DOS command.
(No Network)	indicates a command that does not work over a network.

You can specify a drive and/or path before any external command in the table below.

DOS Command	Formats and Description
APPEND	APPEND [/x] [/e] [;] **or** APPEND [*drive:*]*path*[;[*drive:*][*path*]...] **or** APPEND [*path*] [/x:[off **or** on]] [/path:[off **or** on]] Specifies the paths to be searched for files with extensions other than BAT, COM, and EXE. (External) /x Searches for BAT, COM, and EXE files, too. /e Stores appended paths in the DOS environment. /path If on, searches for files in the appended paths even if the files have drive or path prefixes.
ASSIGN	ASSIGN [*x* [=] *y*] ... Reassigns a disk drive letter to another drive. (External)
ATTRIB	ATTRIB [+r **or** -r] [+a **or** -a] [*drive:*]*pathname* [/s] Changes a file's read-only or archive attribute. (External) +r Turns on read-only attribute. -r Turns off read-only attribute. +a Turns on archive attribute. -a Turns off archive attribute. /s Processes files in subdirectories.
BACKUP	BACKUP [*drive1:*][*path*][*filename*] [*drive2:*] [/s] [/m] [/a] [/f:*size*] [/d:*date*] [/t:*time*] [/L:[[*drive:*][*path*]*filename*]] Backs up one or more files from one disk to another. (External)

DOS Command	Formats and Description
BACKUP *(continued)*	/s Backs up subdirectories. /m Backs up only changed files. /a Adds files without erasing backup disks. /f: Formats target disks if necessary; *size* indicates type of disk (160K, 180K, 320K, 360K, 720K, 1.2M, or 1.44M) /d: Backs up only those files modified on or after *date*. /t: Backs up only those files modified on or after *time*. /L: Makes a backup log entry in the specified file.
BREAK	BREAK [off **or** on] Turns Ctrl-Break off or on for certain operations. (Internal)
CD or CHDIR	CD **or** CHDIR [*path*] Switches between subdirectories or displays the current directory. (Internal)
CHCP	CHCP [*nnn*] Displays or changes the current code page, where *nnn* is the code page. (Internal)
CHKDSK	CHKDSK [*drive:*][*pathname*] [/f] [/v] Displays a disk and memory status report and checks for errors. (External) (No Network) /f Fixes lost cluster chains on the disk. /v Displays the name of every file on the disk.
CLS	CLS Clears the screen. (Internal)
COMMAND	COMMAND [*drive:*][*path*] [*device*] [/e:*nnnnn*] [/p] [/c *string*] Starts a new command processor. (External) /e: Specifies the environment size, where *nnnnn* is the size in bytes. /p Keeps the secondary command processor in memory. /c Performs the commands specified in *string* and then returns to the primary command processor.
COMP	COMP [*drive:*][*pathname1*] [*drive:*][*pathname2*] Compares the contents of two sets of files. (External)
COPY	COPY [*drive:*]*pathname1* [*drive:*][*pathname2*] [/v] [/a] [/b] **or** COPY [*drive:*]*pathname1* [/v] [/a] [/b] [*drive:*][*pathname2*] **or** COPY *pathname1* + *pathname2* ... *pathnameN* Duplicates one or more files. Also appends files. (Internal)

DOS Command	Formats and Description	
COPY *(continued)*	/v /a /b	Turns on the verify switch. Copies ASCII files. Copies binary files.
CTTY	CTTY *device* Changes the console (terminal) to another device. (Internal)	
DATE	DATE [*mm-dd-yy*] Displays or sets the date. (Internal)	
DEL or ERASE	DEL **or** ERASE [*drive:*] *pathname* [/p] Removes one or more files from a disk. (Internal) /p Prompts user before each deletion.	
DIR	DIR [*drive:*][*pathname*] [/p] [/w] Lists the files on a disk or in a subdirectory. (Internal) /p Pauses after each screen. /w Displays a wide listing.	
DISKCOMP	DISKCOMP [*drive1:*] [*drive2*] [/1] [/8] Compares two diskettes. (External) (No Network) /1 Compares just the first sides. /8 Compares just the first 8 sectors of each track.	
DISKCOPY	DISKCOPY [*drive1:*] [*drive2:*] [/1] Duplicates an entire floppy disk. (External) (No Network) /1 Copies only one side.	
DOSSHELL	DOSSHELL Starts the DOS Shell. (Batch File)	
EXE2BIN	EXE2BIN [*drive:*]*pathname1* [*drive:*]*pathname2* Converts EXE files to BIN or COM files. (External)	
EXIT	EXIT Exits the COMMAND.COM program. Also, returns to the DOS Shell from the DOS prompt. (Internal)	
FASTOPEN	FASTOPEN [*drive:*[= *n*][...]] /x **or** FASTOPEN [*drive:*[= (*n*,*m*)][...]] /x **or** FASTOPEN [*drive:*[= ([*n*],*m*)][...]] /x Speeds up disk access by storing directory and file names and locations in a memory cache. (External) (No Network) *n* The number of files FASTOPEN will work with (10–999). *m* The number of file extent entries (1–999). /x Puts the cache in expanded memory.	
FDISK	FDISK Partitions a hard disk. (External) (No Network)	
FIND	FIND [/v] [/c] [/n] "*string*" [[*drive:*][*pathname*] ...] Searches for a text string in one or more files. (External)	

DOS Command	Formats and Description
FIND *(continued)*	/v Displays all lines *not* containing the string. /c Displays only the number of lines that contain the string. /n Precedes each line with its line number in the file.
FORMAT	FORMAT *drive:* [/1] [/4] [/8] [/n:*sectors*] [/t:*tracks*] [/v[:*label*]] [/s] **or** FORMAT *drive:* [/1] [/b] [/n:*sectors*] [/t:*tracks*] **or** FORMAT *drive:* [/v[:*label*]] [/f:*size*] [/s] Prepares a disk for use. (External) (No Network) /1 Formats only one side. /4 Formats a 360K disk in a 1.2M drive. /8 Formats 8 sectors per track. /n: Specifies the number of sectors. /t: Specifies the number of tracks. /v: Specifies the disk name (volume label). /b Leaves room for the DOS hidden system files. /s Creates a bootup disk. /f: Specifies the disk size (160K, 180K, 320K, 360K, 720K, 1.2M, 1.44M)
GRAFTABL	GRAFTABL [*xxx*] **or** /status **or** [?] Enhances the display of graphics characters on a Color Graphics Adapter. (External) *xxx* The code page id number. /status Displays the active character set. ? Displays instructions for using GRAFTABL.
GRAPHICS	GRAPHICS *type* [*profile*] [/r] [/b] [/lcd] [/printbox:*id*] Allows printing of graphics screens. (External) /r Prints black on the screen as black on the page. /b Prints the background in color. /lcd Uses aspect ratio of LCD screens. /printbox Selects the printbox size.
JOIN	JOIN [*drive: drive:path*] **or** *drive:* /d Treats a disk drive as if it were a subdirectory. (External) (No Network) /d Unjoins a previous JOIN.
KEYB	KEYB [*xx*[,[*yyy*],[[*drive:*][*path*]*filename*]]] [/ID:*nnn*] Loads a keyboard-translation table for a country, where *xx* is a two-letter country code and *yyy* is the code page that defines the character set. (External) /ID: Specifies the keyboard in use to be *nnn*.
LABEL	LABEL [*drive:*][*label*] Creates or changes a disk's name (volume label). (External) (No Network)

DOS Command	Formats and Description
MD or MKDIR	MD **or** MKDIR [*drive:*]*path* Creates a new subdirectory. (Internal)
MEM	MEM [/program **or** /debug] Displays a memory report. (External) /program Displays programs in memory. /debug Displays technical information.
MODE	MODE [*device*] [/status] **or** MODE LPT*n*[:][*c*][,[*l*][,*r*]] **or** MODE LPT*n* [cols = *c*] [lines = *l*] [retry = r] **or** MODE COM*m*[:]*b*,[,*p*[,*d*[,*s*[,*r*]]]] **or** MODE COM*m* baud = *b* [data = *d*] [stop = *s*] [parity = *p*] [retry = r] **or** MODE *display, n* **or** MODE [*display*], *shift* **or** MODE CON[:] [cols = *m*] [lines = *n*] **or** MODE CON[:] rate = *r* delay = *d* **or** MODE *device* codepage prepare = ((*yyy*)[*drive:*][*path*]*filename*) **or** MODE *device* codepage select = *yyy* **or** MODE *device* codepage refresh **or** MODE *device* codepage [/status] **or** MODE LPT*n*[:] = COM*m*[:] Establishes settings for various input/output devices. See the *MS-DOS User's Reference* for detailed information. (External)
MORE	MORE < *source* **or** *source*	MORE Accepts input and presents it one screen at a time as output. (External)
NLSFUNC	NLSFUNC [[*drive:*][*path*]*filename*] Specifies country-specific language and code page. (External)
PATH	PATH [*drive:*[*path*][;[*drive:*][*path*]...] **or** PATH [;] Tells DOS where to search for BAT, COM, and EXE files, or displays the current path. (Internal)
PRINT	PRINT [/d:*device*] [/b:*size*] [/u:*value1*] [/m:*value2*] [/s:*timeslice*] [/q:*qsize*] [/t] [*drive:*][*pathname*] [/c] [/p] Prints a text file. (External) /d: Specifies the device name. /b: Specifies the size of the internal buffer in bytes. /u: Specifies the number of clock ticks PRINT will wait for a printer. /m: Specifies the number of clock ticks PRINT can take to print a character. /s: Specifies the timeslice for background printing.

DOS Command	Formats and Description

PRINT *(continued)*

/q:	Specifies the number of files allowed in the print queue.
/t	Deletes all files in the print queue.
/c	Removes the preceding file and all following files from the print queue.
/p	Adds the preceding file and all following files to the print queue.

PROMPT

PROMPT [[*text*][$*character*]...]
Changes the format of the DOS prompt. (Internal) The *character* may be one of the following:

q	The = character.
$	The $ character.
t	The current time.
d	The current date.
p	The current directory.
v	The DOS version number.
n	The default drive.
g	The > character.
l	The < character.
b	The | character.
—	The Enter key.
e	The Escape key.
h	The Backspace key.

RD or RMDIR

RD **or** RMDIR [*drive:*]*path*
Removes an empty subdirectory. (Internal)

RECOVER

RECOVER [*drive:*][*path*]*filename* **or**
RECOVER *drive*
Reconstructs damaged files or disks. (External) (No Network)

RENAME or REN

RENAME **or** REN [*drive:*][*path*]*filename1 filename2*
Changes the name of one or more files. (Internal)

REPLACE

REPLACE [*drive:*]*pathname1* [*drive:*][*pathname2*] [/a] [/p] [/r] [/s] [/w] [/u]
Updates a set of files. (External)

/a	Adds new files to the target instead of replacing existing ones.
/p	Prompts user before replacing each file.
/r	Replaces read-only files.
/s	Searches all subdirectories.
/u	Replaces only older files.
/w	Prompts user before beginning.

RESTORE

RESTORE *drive1:* [*drive2:*][*pathname*] [/s] [/p] [/b:*date*] [/a:*date*] [/e:*time*] [/L:*time*] [/m] [/n]
Restores files backed up with the BACKUP command. (External)

/s	Restores subdirectories.
/p	Prompts the user before restoring read-only files or files that have been changed.

DOS Command	Formats and Description
RESTORE *(continued)*	/b: Restores only files modified on or before *date*. /a: Restores only files modified on or after *date*. /e: Restores only files modified at or earlier than *time*. /L: Restores only files modified at or later than *time*. /m Restores only files modified since the last backup. /n Restores only files that no longer exist on the target disk.
SELECT	SELECT menu Installs DOS. SELECT is usually executed by inserting the MS-DOS Install diskette in drive A and pressing Ctrl-Alt-Del. (External)
SET	SET [*string* = [*string*]] Displays or changes the contents of the DOS environment. (Internal)
SHARE	SHARE [/f:*space*] [/L:*locks*] Permits file sharing and locking on network systems. (External) /f: Specifies the storage space used to record file sharing information. /L: Specifies the number of locks to allow.
SORT	[*source*]	SORT [/r] [/ + *n*] **or** SORT [/r] [/ + *n*] *source* Accepts input, arranges it in order, and writes it out. (External) /r Reverses the sort (Z–A, 9–0). / + *n* Sorts the file according to the character in column *n*.
SUBST	SUBST [*drive*: *drive*:*path*] **or** SUBST *drive*: /d Treats a subdirectory as if it were a disk drive. (External) (No Network) /d Cancels a previous substitution.
SYS	SYS *drive*: Installs hidden system files on a properly formatted disk. (External) (No Network)
TIME	TIME [*hour*:*minute*[:*second*][.*centisecond*]]] Displays or sets the time of day. (Internal)
TREE	TREE [*pathname*:] [/f] [/a] Displays the directory structure of a disk. (External) /f Displays the names of the files in each directory. /a Uses only characters that can be output on any display or printer.

DOS Command	Formats and Description
TYPE	TYPE [*drive:*]*filename* Displays a text file on the screen. (Internal)
VER	VER Displays the DOS version number. (Internal)
VERIFY	VERIFY [off **or** on] Turns verification off or on when copying files. (Internal)
VOL	VOL [*drive:*] Displays the disk name (volume label). (Internal)
XCOPY	XCOPY [*drive:*]*pathname* [*drive:*][*pathname*] [/a] [/d:*date*] [/e] [/m] [/p] [/s] [/v] [/w] **or** XCOPY *drive:*[*pathname*] [*drive:*][*pathname*] [/a] [/d:*date*] [/e] [/m] [/p] [/s] [/v] [/w] Duplicates files faster and more flexibly than COPY. (External)

/a	Copies files that have their archive bit set.
/d:	Copies files modified on or after *date*.
/e	Copies subdirectories, even if they are empty.
/m	Same as /a, but turns off archive bit.
/p	Prompts user before copying each file.
/s	Copies subdirectories, unless they are empty.
/v	Turns on the verify switch.
/w	Waits before copying files.

Batch File Command	Formats and Description
CALL	CALL [*drive:*][*path*]*batchfile* [*argument*] Invokes *batchfile* from within the current batch file. The *argument* is the command in the current batch file that will be run following *batchfile*. (Internal)
ECHO	ECHO [off **or** on **or** *message*] Turns screen messages off or on, or displays *message*. (Internal)
FOR	FOR %%c in *set* do *command* **or** FOR %c in *set* do *command* Sets up a repeating loop in a batch file to perform a command for a set of files. The character *c* represents a variable name, the *set* is a set of files, and the *command* is a DOS command or program. (Internal)
GOTO	GOTO [:]*label* Transfers execution in a batch file to the line after *label*. (Internal)

Batch File Command	Formats and Description
IF	IF [not] errorlevel *number command* **or** IF [not] *string1* = = *string2 command* **or** IF [not] exist *filename command* Executes a command based on the result of a condition. (Internal)
PAUSE	PAUSE [*message*] Temporarily suspends the execution of a batch file until the user presses a key. (Internal)
REM	REM [*comment*] Identifies a batch file comment or remark. (Internal)
SHIFT	SHIFT Sets up more than nine batch file parameters. (Internal)

CONFIG.SYS Command	Formats and Description
BREAK	BREAK = [off **or** on] Turns Ctrl-Break off or on for certain operations.
BUFFERS	BUFFERS = *n*[,*m*] [/x] Sets the number of disk buffers. *n* The number of disk buffers (1–99). *m* The maximum number of sectors that can be read or written in one input/output operation (1–8). /x Sets the maximum number of disk buffers to 10,000 or the largest number of buffers that will fit in memory, whichever is less.
COUNTRY	COUNTRY = *xxx*[,[*yyy*][,[*drive:*]*filename*]] Changes country-specific information. *xxx* The country code. *yyy* The code page for the country. *filename* The file containing country information.
DEVICE	DEVICE = [*drive:*][*path*]*filename* [*argument*] Installs a device driver.
DRIVEPARM	DRIVEPARM = /d:*number* [/c] [/f:*factor*] [/h:*heads*] [/i] [/n] [/s:*sectors*] [/t:*tracks*] Defines parameters for block devices such as disk and tape drives. /d: Specifies the physical drive number (0–255). /c Indicates that the drive can sense if its door has been opened. /f: Specifies the device type or form factor (0–7).

CONFIG.SYS Command	Formats and Description
DRIVEPARM *(continued)*	/h: Specifies the maximum head number (1–99). /i Specifies an electrically-compatible 3½-inch disk drive. /n Specifies a nonremovable block device. /s: Specifies the number of sectors per track (1–99). /t: Specifies the number of tracks per side (1–999).
FCBS	FCBS = x,y Allows access to file control blocks. x The number of files that can be open at one time. y The number of files that DOS cannot close automatically.
FILES	FILES = x Specifies the maximum number of open files (x).
INSTALL	INSTALL = [*drive*:][*path*]*filename* [*parameters*] Installs RAM-resident features. The *filename* must be FASTOPEN.EXE, KEY.EXE, NLSFUNC.EXE, or SHARE.EXE.
LASTDRIVE	LASTDRIVE = x Specifies the last accessible drive, where x is the drive letter (A–Z).
REM	REM *comment* Allows a comment or remark to be entered in the CONFIG.SYS file.
SHELL	SHELL = [*drive*:][*path*]*filename* [*parameters*] Begins execution of the top-level command processor.
STACKS	STACKS = n,s Supports the dynamic use of data stacks. n The number of stacks (0–64). s The size of each stack (0–512).

Lotus 1-2-3 Release 2.2

Lotus 1-2-3 Keys

Keypress	Description
/	Activates the Main menu.
Enter	Completes an entry.
Backspace	Erases preceding character.
Delete	Deletes character at cursor.
Insert	Switches INSERT/OVERWRITE mode.
Escape	Exits a menu; erases entry in control panel.
Home	Moves to cell A1.
Left Arrow	Moves left one cell.
Right Arrow	Moves right one cell.
Up Arrow	Moves up one cell.
Down Arrow	Moves down one cell.
Ctrl-Left Arrow	(BIG LEFT) Moves left one screen.
Shift-Tab	Moves left one screen.
Ctrl-Right Arrow	(BIG RIGHT) Moves right one screen.
Tab	Moves right one screen.
Page Up	Moves up one screen.
Page Down	Moves down one screen.
End, Right Arrow	Moves right to intersection of a blank and a nonblank cell.
End, Left Arrow	Moves left to intersection of a blank and a nonblank cell.
End, Up Arrow	Moves up to intersection of a blank and a nonblank cell.
End, Down Arrow	Moves down to intersection of a blank and a nonblank cell.
F1	(HELP) Activates the help facility.
Alt-F1	(COMPOSE) Creates international and graphics characters.
F2	(EDIT) Changes to EDIT mode.
Alt-F2	(STEP) Turns on STEP mode, which executes macros one step at a time for debugging.
F3	(NAME) Displays a menu of range names.
Alt-F3	(RUN) Displays a menu to select the name of the macro to run.
F4	(ABS) Changes the type of cell addressing.
Alt-F4	(UNDO) Cancels the previous change.
F5	(GOTO) Moves to a particular cell address.
Alt-F5	(LEARN) Turns macro learn feature on and off.
F6	(WINDOW) Switches to other split-screen window.
F7	(QUERY) Repeats most recent Data Query command.
F8	(TABLE) Repeats most recent Data Table command.
F9	(CALC) Recalculates all worksheet formulas.
F10	(GRAPH) Displays the most recently specified graph.

Lotus 1-2-3 Release 2.2 Menu Commands (Levels 1 and 2)

Command	Description
/WG	Worksheet Global Specifies the default settings applied to all cells for items such as numeric format, label alignment, column width, recalculation method, cell protection, and the display of zero values.
/WI	Worksheet Insert Adds blank rows or columns to an existing worksheet.
/WD	Worksheet Delete Removes rows or columns from an existing worksheet.
/WC	Worksheet Column Specifies settings for column width and column hiding.
/WE	Worksheet Erase Completely erases the entire worksheet.
/WT	Worksheet Titles Freezes rows and/or columns so they can always be seen.
/WW	Worksheet Window Allows use of two horizontal or vertical windows.
/WS	Worksheet Status Displays information about memory, global settings, and hardware.
/WP	Worksheet Page Inserts a printer page break into the worksheet.
/WL	Worksheet Learn Specifies the learn range where macro instructions will be stored in LEARN mode.
/RF	Range Format Sets the numeric format for a range of cells.
/RL	Range Label Aligns existing labels in a range of cells.
/RE	Range Erase Removes the contents of a range of cells.
/RN	Range Name Creates or deletes cell range names.
/RJ	Range Justify Rearranges words in a column to fit within a specified width.
/RP	Range Protect Prevents changes and deletions to a range of cells.

Command	Description
/RU	Range Unprotect Allows changes and deletions to a range of cells.
/RI	Range Input Restricts cell pointer movement to unprotected cells.
/RV	Range Value Converts formulas to their computed values in a range of cells.
/RT	Range Transpose Reorders a range of cells, switching rows and columns.
/RS	Range Search Locates strings in labels and/or formulas within a specified range.
/C	Copy Creates a copy of existing cell contents.
/M	Move Moves a range of cells to another place in the worksheet.
/FR	File Retrieve Loads a worksheet from a disk into memory.
/FS	File Save Copies a worksheet from memory to a disk file.
/FC	File Combine Copies, adds, or subtracts values from one worksheet to another.
/FX	File Xtract Extracts and saves part of one worksheet in another file.
/FE	File Erase Removes one or more files from a disk.
/FL	File List Displays the names of files on a disk.
/FI	File Import Imports data from a text file into the worksheet.
/FD	File Directory Changes the current disk drive directory.
/FA	File Admin Recalculates linked formulas, shares files on a network, or creates a table of information about the files on a disk.
/PP	Print Printer Sends a worksheet directly to the printer.
/PF	Print File Sends a worksheet to a file to be printed later.

Command	Description
/GT	Graph Type Specifies the type of graph to be created.
/GX	Graph X Specifies the range of cells for the X-axis labels.
/GA	Graph A Specifies the first range of cells to be used as data for the graph.
/GB–/GF	Graph B–Graph F Specify additional data ranges.
/GR	Graph Reset Cancels graph settings.
/GV	Graph View Displays the current graph on the screen.
/GS	Graph Save Stores the current graph in a disk file so it can be printed later.
/GO	Graph Options Specifies various options for enhancing a graph's appearance.
/GN	Graph Name Creates, uses, deletes, or resets a graph name.
/GG	Graph Group Specifies all graph data ranges at once, when the X and A through F data ranges are in consecutive columns or rows of a range.
/GQ	Graph Quit Exits from the Graph submenu.
/DF	Data Fill Enters a sequence of numbers into a range of cells.
/DT	Data Table Tabulates the effects of changing values in formulas.
/DS	Data Sort Rearranges rows of cells in a specified order.
/DQ	Data Query Searches for, copies, extracts, or removes specified rows of cells.
/DD	Data Distribution Creates a frequency distribution of the values in a range of cells.
/DM	Data Matrix Multiplies and inverts matrices of cells.
/DR	Data Regression Fits a line to a set of data points.

Command	Description
/DP	Data Parse Breaks up long labels into individual cell entries.
/S	System Allows the use of DOS commands while working with 1-2-3.
/AA	Add-In Attach Loads an add-in program, such as Allways, into memory.
/AD	Add-In Detach Removes an attached add-in program from memory, freeing the memory it occupied.
/AI	Add-In Invoke Activates an attached add-in program.
/AC	Add-In Clear Removes all attached add-in programs from memory, freeing the memory they occupied.
/AQ	/Add-In Quit Returns to READY mode from the Add-In menu.
/Q	Quit Ends 1-2-3 and returns to DOS.

Lotus 1-2-3 Functions

Function	Format and Description
@@	$@@(location)$ Returns the contents of the cell at *location*.
@ABS	$@ABS(x)$ Calculates the absolute value of x.
@ACOS	$@ACOS(x)$ Calculates the arc cosine of x.
@ASIN	$@ASIN(x)$ Calculates the arc sine of x.
@ATAN	$@ATAN(x)$ Calculates the arc tangent of x.
@ATAN2	$@ATAN(x,y)$ Calculates the four-quadrant arc tangent of y/x.
@AVG	$@AVG(list)$ Averages the values in *list*.
@CELL	$@CELL(attribute,range)$ Returns information about an *attribute* for the first cell in *range*.

Function	Format and Description
@CELLPOINTER	@CELLPOINTER(*attribute*) Returns information about an *attribute* for the current cell.
@CHAR	@CHAR(*x*) Returns the character that corresponds to Lotus International Character Set code *x*.
@CHOOSE	@CHOOSE(*offset*,*list*) Returns value or string in *list* specified by *offset*.
@CLEAN	@CLEAN(*string*) Removes control characters from *string*.
@CODE	@CODE(*string*) Returns the Lotus International Character Set code for the first character in *string*.
@COLS	@COLS(*range*) Counts columns in *range*.
@COS	@COS(*x*) Calculates the cosine of *x*.
@COUNT	@COUNT(*list*) Counts the nonblank cells in *list*.
@CTERM	@CTERM(*interest*,*future-value*,*present-value*) Calculates the number of compounding periods for an investment *present-value* to grow to a *future-value*, given a fixed periodic *interest* rate.
@DATE	@DATE(*year*,*month*,*day*) Calculates the date number for *year*, *month*, and *day*.
@DATEVALUE	@DATEVALUE(*string*) Calculates the date number for a *string* that looks like a date.
@DAVG	@DAVG(*input*,*field*,*criteria*) Averages value in a *field* of a data base (*input* range) that meet criteria in *criteria* range.
@DAY	@DAY(*date-number*) Calculates the day of the month in *date-number*.
@DCOUNT	@DCOUNT(*input*,*field*,*criteria*) Counts nonblank cells in a *field* of a data base (*input* range) that meet the criteria in *criteria* range.
@DDB	@DDB(*cost*,*salvage*,*life*,*period*) Calculates depreciation allowance of an asset using the double-declining balance method.
@DMAX	@DMAX(*input*,*field*,*criteria*) Finds the largest value in a *field* of a data base (*input* range) that meets the criteria in *criteria* range.

Function	Format and Description
@DMIN	@DMIN(*input,field,criteria*) Finds the smallest value in a *field* of a data base (*input* range) that meets the criteria in *criteria* range.
@DSTD	@DSTD(*input,field,criteria*) Calculates the population standard deviation of values in a *field* of a data base (*input* range) that meet the criteria in *criteria* range.
@DSUM	@DSUM(*input,field,criteria*) Sums values in a *field* of a data base (*input* range) that meet the criteria in *criteria* range.
@DVAR	@DVAR(*input,field,criteria*) Calculates the population variance of values in a *field* of a data base (*input* range) that meet the criteria in *criteria* range.
@ERR	@ERR Returns the error value.
@EXACT	@EXACT(*string1,string2*) Returns 1 (true) if *string1* and *string2* are the same; returns 0 (false) otherwise.
@EXP	@EXP(*x*) Calculates the value of *e* (2.718282) raised to the power *x*.
@FALSE	@FALSE Returns the logical value 0 (false).
@FIND	@FIND(*search-string,string,start-number*) Returns the number of the first occurrence of *search-string* in *string*, beginning with *start-number*.
@FV	@FV(*payments,interest,term*) Calculates the future value of a series of equal *payments*, given a periodic *interest* rate and number of payment periods (*term*).
@HLOOKUP	@HLOOKUP(*x,range,row-offset*) Returns the contents of the cell in *row-offset* of the horizontal lookup table (*range*).
@HOUR	@HOUR(*time-number*) Calculates the hour (0–23) in *time-number*.
@IF	@IF(*condition,x,y*) Evaluates *condition* and returns *x* if *condition* is 1 (true), *y* if *condition* is 0 (false).
@INDEX	@INDEX(*range,column-offset,row-offset*) Returns the value in the cell located at *column-offset* and *row-offset* in *range*.
@INT	@INT(*x*) Returns the integer portion of *x*, without rounding.

Function	Format and Description
@IRR	@IRR(*guess,range*) Calculates the internal rate of return for a series of cash flows in *range*, based on the percentage *guess*.
@ISAAF	@ISAAF(*name*) Returns 1 (true) if *name* is a defined add-in @function; otherwise it returns 0 (false).
@ISAPP	@ISAPP(*name*) Returns 1 (true) if *name* is an attached add-in @function; otherwise it returns 0 (false).
@ISERR	@ISERR(x) Returns 1 (true) if x is the value ERR; otherwise it returns 0 (false).
@ISNA	@ISNA(x) Returns 1 (true) if x is the value NA; otherwise it returns 0 (false).
@ISNUMBER	@ISNUMBER(x) Returns 1 (true) if x is a value or a blank cell; otherwise it returns 0 (false).
@ISSTRING	@ISSTRING(x) Returns 1 (true) if x is a string; otherwise it returns 0 (false).
@LEFT	@LEFT(*string,n*) Returns the first n characters in *string*.
@LENGTH	@LENGTH(*string*) Counts the characters in *string*.
@LN	@LN(x) Calculates the natural logarithm (base e) of x.
@LOG	@LOG(x) Calculates the common logarithm (base 10) of x.
@LOWER	@LOWER(*string*) Converts all letters in string to lowercase.
@MAX	@MAX(*list*) Returns the largest value in *list*.
@MID	@MID(*string,start-number,n*) Returns n characters from *string*, beginning with the *start-number* position.
@MIN	@MIN(*list*) Returns the smallest value in *list*.
@MINUTE	@MINUTE(*time-number*) Calculates the minute (0–59) in *time-number*.
@MOD	@MOD(x,y) Returns the remainder (modulus) of x/y.

Function	Format and Description
@MONTH	@MONTH(*date-number*) Calculates the month (1–12) in *date-number*.
@N	@N(*range*) Returns the entry in the first cell of *range* as a value.
@NA	@NA Returns the value of NA (Not Available).
@NOW	@NOW Calculates the date and time numbers that correspond to the current date and time.
@NPV	@NPV(*interest,range*) Calculates the net present value of a series of future cash flows (*range*), discounted at a fixed, periodic *interest* rate.
@PI	@PI Returns the value of π (pi), calculated at 3.1415926536.
@PMT	@PMT(*principal,interest,term*) Calculates the payment needed to pay off a loan (*principal*), given the *interest* rate and number of payment periods (*term*).
@PROPER	@PROPER(*string*) Capitalizes the first letter of each word in *string*.
@PV	@PV(*payments,interest,term*) Calculates the present value of a series of equal *payments*, discounted at a periodic *interest* rate and given a number of payment periods (*term*).
@RAND	@RAND Generates a random number between 0 and 1.
@RATE	@RATE(*future-value,present-value,term*) Calculates the periodic interest rate necessary for the investment *present-value* to grow to *future-value*, given the number of compounding periods (*term*).
@REPEAT	@REPEAT(*string,n*) Repeats *string n* times.
@REPLACE	@REPLACE(*string1,start-number,n,string2*) Replaces *n* characters in *string1* beginning at *start-number* from *string2*.
@RIGHT	@RIGHT(*string,n*) Returns the last *n* characters from *string*.
@ROUND	@ROUND(*x,n*) Rounds the value *x* to *n* decimal places.
@ROWS	@ROWS(*range*) Counts the number of rows in *range*.

Function	Format and Description
@S	@S(*range*) Returns the entry in the first cell of *range* as a label.
@SECOND	@SECOND(*time-number*) Calculates the seconds (0–59) in *time-number*.
@SIN	@SIN(*x*) Calculates the sine of x.
@SLN	@SLN(*cost,salvage,life*) Calculates the straight-line depreciation allowance of an asset for one period.
@SQRT	@SQRT(*x*) Calculates the square root of x.
@STD	@STD(*list*) Calculates the population standard deviation of the values in *list*.
@STRING	@STRING(*x,n*) Converts the value x to a string with n decimal places.
@SUM	@SUM(*list*) Calculates the sum of the values in *list*.
@SYD	@SYD(*cost,salvage,life,period*) Calculates the sum-of-the-years'-digits depreciation allowance of an asset for a specified *period*.
@TAN	@TAN(*x*) Calculates the tangent of x.
@TERM	@TERM(*payments,interest,future-value*) Calculates the number of payment periods in the term of an investment necessary to accumulate *future-value*, given *payments* of equal value, when the investment earns a periodic *interest* rate.
@TIME	@TIME(*hour,minute,second*) Calculates the time number for *hour, minute,* and *second.*
@TIMEVALUE	@TIMEVALUE(*string*) Calculates the time number for a *string* that looks like a time.
@TRIM	@TRIM(*string*) Removes the leading, trailing, and consecutive spaces in *string*.
@TRUE	@TRUE Returns the logical value 1 (true).
@UPPER	@UPPER(*string*) Converts all letters in *string* to uppercase.
@VALUE	@VALUE(*string*) Converts the number entered as *string* to its numeric value.

Function	Format and Description
@VAR	@VAR(*list*) Calculates the population variance of the values in *list*.
@VLOOKUP	@VLOOKUP(*x*,*range*,*column-offset*) Returns the contents of the cell in *column-offset* of the vertical lookup table *range*.
@YEAR	@YEAR(*date-number*) Calculates the year, an integer from 0 (1900) to 199 (2099), in *date-number*.

GLOSSARY

absolute reference   a cell address that does not change when it is moved or copied

access arm   a mechanical extension in a disk drive that moves the read-write head toward or away from the center of the disk

account   a file containing financial information

accounting package   software that manages an organization's finances

accounts payable   the accounting subsystem that records the purchases of goods and services from each vendor

accounts receivable   the accounting subsystem that records all sales of goods and services

action line   in dBASE III PLUS, the line above the status bar that shows the command generated by the current Assistant operation

active cell   see *current cell*

Ada   a powerful, comprehensive high-level programming language applicable to a wide range of problems

adapter   see *expansion board*

address   a unique identifying number for a storage location in memory

address file   see *secondary merge file*

aggregate operator   see *summary operator*

alias   in dBASE, a number, letter, or name that refers to a work area or data base file

allocation unit   in DOS, a group of contiguous sectors, also known as a cluster

alphanumeric characters   letters, numbers, and punctuation marks

alternate operating environment   see *windowing environment*

American Standard Code for Information Interchange (ASCII)   the code used by most microcomputers for representing text in binary form

application   see *application software*

application generator   see *fourth generation language*

application package   see *application software*

application software   a program or set of programs that applies the computer to useful tasks like helping you write letters, figure taxes, maintain mailing lists, and draw charts

Applications Generator   in dBASE, an easy-to-use tool for creating a customized data base system without programming

archive attribute   the file attribute that indicates if a file has been changed since it was last saved with the DOS BACKUP command

artificial intelligence (AI)   a field of study combining aspects of computer science, mathematics, philosophy, psychology, and linguistics whose main goal is to mimic human learning and decision making

ascending order   the arrangement of numbers from smallest to largest, and of text alphabetically from A to Z

ASCII file   see *text file*

assembler   a program that translates assembly language instructions into the binary numbers of machine language

assembly language   a programming language that substitutes meaningful abbreviations for the numerically coded instructions of a machine language

Autokey macro   A VP-Planner Plus macro created by recording keystrokes

automated vision   a type of software that allows computers to distinguish and interpret images from optical sensors

automatic hyphenation   a word processing feature that uses a set of built-in rules to split words at the ends of lines when necessary without confirmation from the user

automatic recalculation   the ability of a spreadsheet program to immediately update the entire worksheet whenever the contents of a cell are changed

background   in OS/2, where an application that does not have control of the physical console is running

backup   an extra copy of vital programs or data; to make such a copy

balance sheet   a report that summarizes the assets, liabilities, and capital of a business

bar graph   a chart in which numeric values are represented by evenly spaced, thick vertical lines

BASIC   (Beginners' All-purpose Symbolic Instruction Code) a simple, interactive programming language originally designed to teach students about computer programming

Basic Input/Output System (BIOS)   on some computers, the hardware interface that controls physical components such as disk drives, monitor, keyboard, and printer

batch file a text file that lists operating system commands to be performed automatically when the name of the batch file is entered

batch processing using batch files to reduce several frequently used operating system commands to just one command to save time and effort

batch processing commands a special set of internal DOS commands, such as CALL and ECHO, that add power and flexibility to batch files

benchmark an objective, reproducible measure of hardware or software performance

Bernoulli box see *Bernoulli disk drive*

Bernoulli disk drive a secondary storage device that combines the advantages of both floppy and hard disk drives

billing the accounting subsystem that prepares and records invoices

binary file a file that contains programs or data that are not encoded as ASCII characters

binary point the period that separates the whole part from the fractional part of a mixed binary number

bit the basic unit of data processing; a single binary digit, 0 or 1, off or on

bit-mapped see *pixel-based*

bits per second (bps) unit of modem transmission speed

block a contiguous section of text—can consist of a single character up to an entire document

booting up initially loading and executing the operating system

border palette a menu of line thicknesses used to draw lines and outline shapes

branching altering the order in which batch file commands are executed using IF and GOTO commands

briefcase computer see *laptop computer*

browse to casually scan the records of a data base

bug an error or problem in a computer program

built-in dictionary an automatic proofreading feature that looks for spelling errors

bus a set of wires and connectors that link the CPU to memory and other computer components

bus network a topology in which each workstation is connected to a single cable running past all the workstations

byte a contiguous group of eight bits; the amount of memory it takes to store a single character or a numeric quantity from 0 to 255

C a concise, yet powerful programming language frequently used for the development of system software and application packages

cache an intermediary storage place

calculated field a field that contains the result of an expression instead of a value entered directly in a data base file

capture to gather incoming data from a host computer and save it in a disk file

carrier sense multiple access (CSMA) a protocol that requires each network workstation to listen before sending messages or data

catalog in dBASE, a list of files

cathode ray tube (CRT) a display that uses an electronic gun to paint images on a phosphor-coated glass screen

cell the box at the intersection of a row and a column in a worksheet

cell address a designation that specifies a cell's exact location within a worksheet

cell pointer the highlighted cell that marks the current location in a worksheet

cell reference see *cell address*

central processing unit (CPU) the part of a computer that performs calculations, logic, and control operations

chaining executing a batch file as the last command in another batch file

chamfer a CAD feature that joins two lines with another straight line

character formatting specifying the way individual letters or words are presented

charting program a program that produces graphs, plots, and charts from data entered directly or imported from a spreadsheet or data base file

chassis a metal and plastic frame that houses all of the internal components of a computer

child file the more specific file in a relation that contains the information to be looked up by the parent file

chip see *integrated circuit chip*

circular reference the result of a formula in a cell being either directly or indirectly dependent on the value in that very same cell

clicking moving the mouse pointer on top of an item to be selected and briefly pressing and releasing the mouse button

clipboard a temporary storage area for copying data

clone a computer that works just like, or very similar to, another computer

coaxial cable a center conductor surrounded by a shield or wire braid, used for cable television and local area networks

COBOL a high-level programming language introduced in 1960 especially for business data processing

code in WordPerfect, a hidden formatting indicator generated when you press a key such as Enter or Tab, or execute a command that changes a document's appearance, such as Center or Bold

code page a conversion table that tells DOS how to translate data stored as numeric values into letters, numbers, punctuation, and other symbols to be displayed or printed

color graphics monitor a monitor that can display both text and graphics in more than one color

column a field in an SQL table

column-wise recalculation the order of worksheet recalculation that begins with cell A1 and proceeds down column A, goes on to cell B1 and proceeds down column B, and so on

combining   see *merging*

command   a directive that is issued to a program

command-line interface (CLI)   a user interface, such as DOS without the DOS Shell, that presents a prompt and accepts commands instead of using menus, icons, and windows

comment out   temporarily shut off a command in a program or batch file by inserting a comment in front of it on the same line

communications package   software that lets a computer transfer messages, programs, and data to other computers

communications parameters   the settings that specify the technical details of how a computer will communicate with another computer

communications server   a network workstation that lets users communicate with computers outside the network via serial ports and a high-speed modem

compact disc read-only memory (CD-ROM)   an optical disk drive that allows access to previously recorded data, but not storage of any new data

compiler   a program that translates high-level language instructions into machine language

complex instruction set computer (CISC)   a microprocessor, such as the Intel 80486 or Motorola 68040, that incorporates many relatively slow instructions especially designed for high-level languages

computer   an electronic device that performs calculations and processes data into information

computer-aided design (CAD)   a type of software package for drafting complex plans, blueprints, models, schematics, and other detailed drawings of parts, mechanisms, and buildings

computer-aided engineering (CAE)   a system that allows engineers to simulate and test their designs on a computer before they are built

computer-aided manufacturing (CAM)   a system in which a computer controls the machines that make or assemble products

computer-assisted instruction (CAI)   a system that uses computers to teach students at their own pace

computer graphics   the presentation of images such as figures, charts, graphs, maps, diagrams, and other pictures on a display screen

computer-managed instruction (CMI)   a system that uses computers to help with school administrative tasks

computer matching   a technique that involves comparing records in various data bases to identify individuals who meet overlapping sets of criteria

computer virus   a hidden program that secretly copies itself from disk to disk and across networks, often causing mischief or outright destruction of data

computerized axial tomography (CAT or CT)   a computer-controlled, three-dimensional X-ray machine

context-sensitive   the ability of a help facility to display information specifically relevant to the current activity

Control Center   the menu system of dBASE IV

control panel   the space on the screen that displays cell information, menus, messages, and the operating mode

coprocessor   integrated circuit chip designed to perform a specialized task for the main microprocessor

copy-and-paste   a word processing operation in which a section of text is reproduced in another location

copy-protection   a way to prepare diskettes so that it is difficult or impossible to copy them with ordinary operating system commands

CP/M   a single-user, single-tasking generic microcomputer operating system sold by Digital Research

criteria   requirements that a record must fulfill to be retrieved by a search or query

Critical Path Method (CPM)   a scheduling method that focuses on the sequence of critical activities that must be performed to complete a project

crosshair   two lines that intersect on the screen to indicate the current cursor position

current cell   the cell marked by the cell pointer, where you can enter data or initiate commands

cursor   a small, blinking underscore or box that marks the position where characters will appear on the screen when typed

cut-and-paste   a word processing operation in which a section of text is moved from one location to another

daisy-wheel printer   a printer with solid, raised characters embossed on the ends of little arms arranged like the spokes of a wheel, for producing slow, but letter-quality output

data   numbers, text, pictures, and sounds that are to be processed into information; in a spreadsheet program, data can be numbers, labels, or formulas

data base   an organized collection of one or more files of related data

data base management package   software that lets you organize large quantities of information, such as mailing lists and inventories

data bus   the pathway connecting the microprocessor to memory

data encryption   a security method that encodes information so that it can be read and changed only by authorized users who know the password

data entry form   a listing of each field in a record, accompanied by an empty box for each field's contents

debug   to remove the errors from a computer program

debugger   a program that helps to detect errors in software under development

decision support system (DSS)   a computer system that helps managers make decisions by applying statistical models and mathematical simulation

dedicated server   a network workstation reserved solely as a file, printer, or communications server

dedicated word processor   a microcomputer system expressly designed and solely used to prepare, store, and print documents

de facto **standard**   a standard that emerges from many manufacturers voluntarily making products that will work together

default   predefined settings for certain features (margins, line spacing, column widths, etc.) that a software package uses automatically if the user does not explicitly establish settings

default drive   the disk drive where DOS will look for programs and data files unless otherwise specified

delete   to remove, erase, or destroy one or more pieces of information

delimiter   a space, comma, semicolon, equal sign, or tab

descending order   the arrangement of numbers from largest to smallest, and of text alphabetically from Z to A

desk accessory   a utility program that provides commonly used desk functions such as a calculator, calendar, or address book

desktop computer   the most common type of microcomputer, small enough to fit on top of a table or desk

desktop organizer   see *desk accessory*

desktop publishing   using a computer and laser printer to produce near-typeset-quality documents

desktop publishing package   software that combines the results of word processing and graphics to produce near-typeset-quality documents

device controller   a set of chips or a circuit board that operates a piece of computer equipment such as a disk drive, display, keyboard, mouse, or printer

device driver   a file that contains the programming code needed to attach and use a special device, such as a nonstandard disk drive, memory board, mouse, monitor, or printer

digitizer   see *graphics tablet*

direct access medium   storage medium, such as magnetic disk, that allows data items to be retrieved in any order

direct-connect modem   see *external modem*

directory   a list of the files stored on a disk; another term for subdirectory

disk   a medium used by computers to store information, consisting of one or more flat surfaces on which bits are recorded magnetically or optically

disk backup utility   a program that facilitates making backup copies of a hard disk on floppy disks

disk buffer   an area of memory DOS uses to temporarily hold data being read from or written to a disk

disk caching utility   a program that reserves part of memory as an intermediary storage place to speed up the retrieval of frequently used software and data

disk copying utility   a program that specializes in duplicating files and disks, especially those that are copy protected

disk drive   a computer system component that reads and writes programs and data on disks

diskette   see *floppy disk*

Disk Operating System (DOS)   see *PC-DOS*

disk optimizing utility   a program that makes secondary storage devices operate more efficiently

display   output screen on which the computer presents text and graphic images

display adapter   a circuit board or set of chips that controls a monitor

display-only field   see *read-only field*

document   the paper output of a word processor

documentation   the user manual or technical information about a computer or software package

document file   a collection of text created by a word processing program in such a way that the text includes embedded formatting codes

DOS   a generic name for PC-DOS and MS-DOS

DOS Compatibility Box   see *DOS Session*

DOS environment   a special area of memory, like a scratch pad for DOS, that some programs use to hold variables, values, and text

DOS prompt   a symbol that identifies the current default drive and indicates that DOS is waiting for a command

DOS Session   the special environment in OS/2 that can run a single DOS application at a time

DOS shell   a menu-driven addition to DOS that helps manage disk files and directories

DOS Shell   the DOS shell developed by IBM and Microsoft and included with DOS versions 4.0 and newer

dot-matrix printer   a common type of printer that constructs character images by repeatedly striking pins against the ribbon and paper

dot pitch   the distance between the illuminated centers of any two adjacent dots on a display screen

dot prompt   the dBASE command-line interface

dot prompt command   a dBASE command entered in response to the dot prompt and not selected from a menu

double clicking   pressing and releasing a mouse button twice in rapid succession

downloading   transferring a file from a host computer to your computer

draft mode   the fastest print mode in which low-quality characters are formed by a single pass of the printhead

dragging   holding down the mouse button while moving the mouse—used to pull down menus, outline parts of a picture, move selections, and stretch objects

drive specifier   a disk drive letter immediately followed by a colon

edit   to make changes in a file

electronic mail (E-mail)   a way to send and receive messages with a computer

electronic typewriter   an electric typewriter with a built-in microprocessor

Encapsulated PostScript (EPS) file   a graphics file containing gray-shade information that can be imported and printed by page layout programs that use the PostScript language

encryption   a method of protecting sensitive data by scrambling it so that it cannot be read without the proper key

end user   see *user*

endnote   a numbered comment or explanation similar to a footnote, except that it appears at the end of the document instead of at the bottom of each page

erasable optical disk drive   a disk drive that uses optical disks that can be written to and read from any number of times

ergonomics   the science of designing objects so that they can be most easily, effectively, comfortably, and safely used by people

example variable   in dBASE IV, a place holder for the value of a field entered in the link field to link two data base files

expansion board   a circuit board that plugs into an expansion slot

expansion card   see *expansion board*

expansion slot   an internal connector that allows you to plug an additional circuit board into the motherboard; an extension of the bus

expert   an experienced computer user

expert system   a computer program that contains both a collection of facts and a list of rules for making inferences about those facts

expert system shell   microcomputer software that contains an inference engine and lets nonprogrammers set up expert systems by supplying (1) their own facts to create knowledge bases and (2) rules to create rule bases

exponent   in scientific notation, the number indicating the power of ten to be multiplied by the mantissa

exporting   writing data in a format that can be accepted by a different program

extension   the second part of a DOS file's name

external command   a DOS command that is kept in disk storage and temporarily loaded into memory only when needed or specifically requested

external modem   a modem built into its own separate housing

fiber-optic cable   glass filaments that transmit data in the form of extremely rapid pulses of light generated by lasers, used for high-speed local area networks

field   a group of related characters in a data base record; a single data item, such as a number, character, word, or phrase

field template   in dBASE, a representation of the width and contents of a data field to be displayed in a form

file   a collection of information kept in secondary storage and loaded into primary memory when needed by a program; in a data base, a group of related records

file attribute   a characteristic of a file, such as read-only or archive

file compression utility   a program that squeezes files into less disk space by eliminating waste and redundant data

file control block (FCB)   a data structure used by early versions of DOS to manage open files

file conversion utility   a program that modifies files from one application so that they can be used by another application

file locking   allowing only one person or program to use the same file at the same time on a network

filename   the primary part of a DOS file's name

file recovery utility   a program that can reinstate accidentally erased files, restore reformatted hard disks, or perform other useful file operations

file server   a network workstation used to store shared program and data files on a large-capacity, high-speed hard disk

file sharing   allowing two or more people or programs to use the same file at the same time on a network

file skeleton   a graphic representation of a data base file

file specification   the combination of a disk drive specifier, a filename, and an extension

file transfer utility   a program that can move data among different types of computers

fillet   a CAD feature that joins two lines to create a rounded corner

film recorder   a graphics output device that turns screen images into 35-mm slides

filter   a DOS command (FIND, MORE, or SORT) that normally reads input from the keyboard, changes it in some way, and then displays it as output on the screen

filter condition   in dBASE, an expression that determines which records are to be selected for a view

Finder   a part of the Apple Macintosh operating system that allows users to run application programs, set up disks, and organize, copy, and delete files

firmware   low-level, system software stored in ROM chips, such as the BIOS

first line indent   a format in which only the first line of the paragraph is moved in from the left margin

fixed currency format   a worksheet format in which two places are to the right of the decimal point, thousands are separated by commas, and each number is preceded by a dollar sign

fixed disk drive   see *hard disk drive*

fixed-point number   a number whose decimal or binary point is in a fixed place in relation to the digits

flat-file data base manager   a program that works with one file of structured data at a time

floating-point number   a number in which the position of the decimal or binary point can vary

floor model   a powerful, expensive microcomputer with a system unit larger than that of the typical desktop computer and designed to accommodate more add-in hardware components

floppy disk   an inexpensive, flexible magnetic medium for storing computer programs and data that can be removed from the disk drive when not in use

floppy disk drive   a disk drive that accepts floppy disks

font   a set of letters, numbers, punctuation marks, and other symbols with a consistent appearance

footer one or more lines of text printed at the bottom of every page

footnote a numbered comment or explanation at the bottom of a page

foreground in OS/2, where the application that has control of the physical console is running

form a screen or printout that shows the fields of an individual record

formatting initializing a disk so that files can be stored on it

formula an expression that instructs a spreadsheet program to perform calculations or other manipulations on numbers, labels, or the contents of cells

FORTRAN one of the first high-level programming languages, designed to fulfill the computational needs of scientists, engineers, and mathematicians

fourth generation language (4GL) the most abstract type of programming language, designed to make it as easy as possible for users to tell a computer what to do

free-form data base manager a program designed to handle narrative text and irregular pieces of data, such as paragraphs, pages, articles, notes, discussions, and instructions

full-duplex a communications mode in which the characters sent to the host computer are echoed back to the terminal's screen

function a ready-made procedure that performs tedious, complex, or often-used computations or other manipulations

function keys on an IBM-compatible computer, the keys on the left side or top of the keyboard labeled F1 through F10 or F12, used to perform common operations

game adapter a circuit board or set of chips that allows the use of joysticks or trackballs

Gantt chart a horizontal bar graph that shows the major tasks of a project, when each task must be performed, and how long each task will take to perform

general ledger the main listing of the accounts of a business

generic operating system an operating system that can be adapted to almost any type of computer

gigabyte (G) 1,073,741,824 bytes

global pertaining to or acting upon an entire document, spreadsheet, or data base file

global delete the ability to remove all those records that meet certain criteria

global filename character the * (which matches any group of characters) or the ? (which matches any single character) used in a DOS file specification to indicate names with one or more characters in common

global modify the ability to change all those records that meet certain criteria

global search and replace changing a word or phrase automatically throughout an entire document

graphical user interface (GUI) a sophisticated, easy-to-use system that includes pull-down menus, icons, windows, and a simulated desktop

graphics any kind of graphs, plots, drawings, and other images not restricted to text characters

graphics adapter a display adapter that can produce graphics

graphics-based windowing environment a windowing environment that can work with programs that display pictures and characters of all different sizes, styles, and fonts

graphics package software that can produce graphs, plots, drawings, pictures, or charts

graphics tablet a flat surface on which the user draws with a stylus, pen, or some other pointing device

greeking representing text too small to be distinguished by tiny characters or shaded bars to show its position on a page

grid criss-crossed lines used to keep objects lined up with each other on the screen; a visual aid for placing objects in a drawing

hacker a hardware designer or programmer with an obsession for computing

half-duplex a communications mode in which the characters sent to the host computer are not echoed back to the terminal's screen

hand-held computer the smallest type of microcomputer, smaller than a paperback book and weighing less than a pound

handle a little black square on the boundary of a selected object, used to drag or resize the object

hanging indent a format in which all lines of a paragraph except for the first are moved in from the left margin

hard disk a circular platter of rigid aluminum or glass covered with a thin magnetic coating for storing computer programs and data

hard disk drive a disk drive that contains one or more hard disks

hard hyphen a hyphen created by pressing the - key

hard page break in WordPerfect, a division between two pages that is manually generated by pressing Ctrl-Enter

hard return in WordPerfect, a new line or paragraph begun by pressing the Enter key

hard space in WordPerfect, a blank created by pressing the Space Bar

hardware the physical components of a computer system

Hayes-compatible modem a modem that operates like a Hayes Smartmodem

head crash the result of a disk drive's read-write head colliding with a minute obstruction or hitting the surface of a disk

header one or more lines of text printed at the top of every page

headword in WordPerfect, a word that can be looked up in the thesaurus

hexadecimal system base 16 number system

hidden column a worksheet column that exists and contains data, but is not displayed or printed

hidden file a special file used by DOS or some other program that does not appear in the disk directory

hierarchical a method of organizing files into rank-ordered groups

high-level language an abstract programming language that facilitates the expression of complex data processing operations

host computer the computer being called by another computer

hypermedia the nonsequential organization and presentation of information, including graphics, audio, and video

hypertext the nonsequential organization and presentation of information with a computer

hyphenation the division of certain words at the ends of lines to improve the appearance of text

IBM-compatible a microcomputer that works just like, or in some ways better than, an IBM microcomputer, and can run the same software

icon a small pictorial symbol that represents a file, a file folder, an action to be performed, or a program to be run

importing reading and, if necessary, translating data originally created with some other program

income statement a report that summarizes the revenues and expenses of a business for a given period of time

incremental backup a backup procedure that copies only those files that have been changed since the last backup

indenting moving text away from the margin toward the center of the page

index file a file that contains record numbers listed in a particular order

indexing a way to reorder the records of a data base without actually duplicating the data in a new file or rearranging the actual records in the original file

information a more organized and useful form of input data

ink-jet printer a printer with a mechanism for squirting tiny droplets of ink to form text and graphics on paper

input any data or information entered into a computer

insertion point another term for *cursor*; where text is inserted with a word processing package

insert mode a typing mode in which all characters typed at the current cursor location push aside existing text to the right

installed when a software package is copied to a hard or floppy disk and set up to be run

instruction set a limited collection of low-level tasks a computer can do with a single instruction

integrated circuit chip a thin slice of semiconductor material, such as pure silicon crystal, impregnated with carefully selected impurities, commonly used in computers and many other electronic devices

integrated software a software package that includes word processing, spreadsheet, data base, graphics, and communications capabilities

intelligent recalculation see *smart recalculation*

interface a connection between a computer's CPU and an external device operated under its control

internal command an essential or frequently used DOS command that is kept in memory

internal modem a modem built onto an expansion board or directly onto the motherboard

interpreter a program that translates and runs one high-level language instruction at a time as it is entered into a computer

interrupt a signal that suspends the current program to tell the CPU that some critical event has occurred

inventory control the accounting subsystem that tracks products and materials on hand

invoice a bill sent to a customer

iteration a way to obtain an approximate result to an indirect circular reference in a worksheet by recomputing the formulas a number of times

journal a chronological listing of transactions

joystick a vertical lever that can be tilted in any direction to control a cursor or steer a simulated vehicle

justified a type of text alignment in which text is flush to both the left and right margins

key a field used to sort or index the records of a data base

keyboard the primary input device with which you enter data and tell a computer what to do

keyboard macro see *macro*

keyboard template a plastic or cardboard guide that fits over or near the function keys on the keyboard listing the most common keyboard commands

kilobyte (K) 1,024 bytes

knowledge-based system see *expert system*

label in a DOS batch file, a place for a GOTO command to branch to; in a spreadsheet program, any kind of text, such as a heading, title, name, address, or note in a worksheet cell

label macro a macro created by entering the labels that represent the keystrokes to be performed when the macro is run

label prefix character a special character (', ^, ", \) that tells the program that the following item is a label and not a number or formula, and indicates how to align labels within cells or if a character is to be repeated within a cell

laptop computer a full-fledged microcomputer squeezed into a 4- to 15-pound housing smaller than most briefcases

laser printer a high-quality printer that uses tightly focused beams of light to transfer images to paper

layer   a CAD feature like a transparent overlay sheet that can be created separately and superimposed on top of other layers

learn feature   in Lotus 1-2-3, a way to create a macro by recording keystrokes

learn mode   an easy-to-use method of defining a macro by recording keystrokes

learn range   in Lotus 1-2-3, the single-column range of cells where keystrokes will be recorded for a macro definition

left indent   a format in which all lines of a paragraph are moved in from the left margin

letter-quality   like the output of a good electric typewriter

light pen   a rod used to point at or draw on a computer display screen

line editor   a simple program that can only work with a single line of text at a time

line graph   a plot that represents each data value by a point at an appropriate distance above the horizontal axis and connects the points by line segments

line height   in WordPerfect, the distance between lines of printed text

link field   a common field that connects two data base files

linker   a program that combines the output files of programming language translators into a single executable program file

liquid crystal display (LCD)   a flat-panel screen that presents black characters against a grey background, commonly used in watches, clocks, calculators, and hand-held and laptop microcomputers

load   to copy a program or data file from disk into memory

local area network (LAN)   several microcomputers connected together within the same building, or nearby buildings, to share hardware, software, and data

locked cell   see *protected cell*

logged   the current disk drive or directory

logical formula   in a worksheet, a formula that compares values and produces a result of 1 for true or 0 for false

logical operator   in dBASE, an operator (.AND., .OR., or .NOT.) that modifies the true or false result of one or two conditions

log-in   to enter the assigned group name, user name, and password to gain access to a system

Lotus Access System   a program called Lotus that lets you start 1-2-3 or any of the other programs that come with the Lotus 1-2-3 package

machine language   the only programming language that can be directly used by a computer, consisting of binary numbers that represent CPU instructions, memory addresses, and data

machine learning   a method by which computers can program themselves, through trial and error, to accomplish a particular task

macro   a sequence of keystrokes that can be recorded, stored, and replayed

magnetic disk   a semipermanent storage medium that can be erased and written over and over again

magnetic resonance imaging (MRI)   a medical scanning method that produces high-quality cross-sectional pictures of the body without X-rays or other radiation

magnetic tape   a long strip of thin plastic covered with a magnetic coating

magnetic tape drive   a secondary storage device that uses magnetic tape to hold programs and data

mail-merge   a word processing or data base feature that lets you combine a master document with a data file of names and addresses to create personalized form letters

mainframe   a big, powerful, fast, expensive computer

management information system (MIS)   a computer system that provides managers with the information they need to do their jobs more effectively

mantissa   in scientific notation, the decimal part of the number that is to be multiplied by the power of ten indicated by the exponent

manual hyphenation   a hyphenation method that requires you to confirm the splitting of each word as you scroll through the document

manual recalculation   a feature that causes the formulas in a worksheet to be recalculated only when explicitly directed to do so

many-to-many link   a type of link that connects multiple records to other multiple records in data base files

master document   a document containing text and special commands to be mail-merged with a data file

master index file   the index file that specifies the order in which all records will be displayed unless otherwise specified

megabyte (M)   1,048,576 bytes

megahertz (MHz)   a unit of frequency equal to one million cycles per second

memo marker   in dBASE IV, an indicator that appears in a record to show if the associated memo field contains any text

memory   a computer's internal storage for temporarily holding programs and data

memory-resident   a type of program that allows a user to temporarily suspend an activity and switch to another one under a single-tasking operating system such as DOS

memory variable   in dBASE, a place in RAM that temporarily holds a data value

menu   a list showing options available in a program

menu bar   a list of the names of pull-down menus across the top of the screen

menu pointer   the highlighted block that shows the command that will be invoked if you press the Enter key

merging   combining two worksheets into one

message line   in dBASE, a line near the bottom of the screen that displays messages

Micro Channel Architecture   the high-performance bus (underlying circuit) design of IBM's Personal System/2 Models 50 through 80 microcomputers

microcomputer　a small computer that uses a single microprocessor chip as its central processing unit

microcomputer standard　a generally accepted set of rules by which hardware and software operate

microprocessor　a central processing unit made up of a single integrated circuit chip

million instructions per second (MIPS)　a unit of computer performance that represents the execution of computer instructions

minicomputer　a medium-sized computer that simultaneously serves several users or controls complex equipment

minimal recalculation　a spreadsheet program feature that increases speed by recalculating only those cells that have changed, and the cells that depend on them, since the worksheet was last recalculated

mixed reference　a cell address that is half-relative and half-absolute, in which either a row or column is absolute, but not both

mnemonic　an easy-to-remember abbreviation for a computer operation, such as ADD

mode indicator　the highlighted block in the upper right corner of the control panel that describes the current operating mode, such as READY or MENU

modem　a device that allows a computer to transmit and receive programs and data over ordinary phone lines

modem cable　a cable that connects an external modem to a serial interface socket at the back of a computer

modular phone jack　a socket that accepts the little plastic plug on the end of a telephone cord

monitor　a computer display screen (see *display*)

monochrome graphics monitor　a single-color screen that can display both text and graphics

monochrome text monitor　a single-color screen that displays sharply-defined characters, but no graphics

motherboard　the main circuit board of a computer

mouse　an input device consisting of a small box with one or more buttons that is slid across the tabletop to manipulate objects on the screen, draw, and select menu options

MS-DOS　see *PC-DOS*

multidimensional spreadsheet　a spreadsheet program that allows every cell in a worksheet to be connected to corresponding cells in other worksheets

MultiFinder　an addition to the Apple Macintosh operating system that allows some multitasking capabilities and lets users run application programs, set up disks, and organize, copy, and delete files

multifunction board　an expansion board that includes several add-on options, such as memory, a real-time clock, a game adapter, a display adapter, and serial and parallel interfaces

multiple index file　in dBASE IV, a file with an extension of MDX that can contain up to 47 separate indexes of a data base file

multiprocessing　the ability to run several programs simultaneously by using more than one processing unit

multiscan monitor　a monitor that can change its resolution to match a number of different display adapters

multitasking　the ability to run more than one program concurrently

natural language processing　getting computers to understand portions of ordinary human languages such as English

natural recalculation　the order of worksheet recalculation that updates a cell only after evaluating any cells on which it depends

navigation line　in dBASE, a line near the bottom of the screen that lists some of the available keystrokes

near letter-quality (NLQ)　a dot-matrix print mode that produces attractive output by having the printhead make two or more passes over each character

nesting　in DOS, using the CALL command to invoke one batch file from within another batch file without ending the first batch file

NETBIOS (Network Basic Input/Output System)　low-level programs that send and receive data to and from the network adapter

network　computers connected to share hardware, software, and data

network adapter　a sophisticated expansion board that connects a microcomputer to a local area network

network interface　the adapter and connector that link a workstation to a network

network media　the cables that connect network workstations

network server　a network workstation that handles special chores

network software　a set of programs, mostly on the file server, that moves data and messages between the workstations and servers, and controls the sharing of files and hardware devices

network workstation　an ordinary microcomputer used to run software, transfer files, and send messages on a network

neural network　a type of computer or a software simulation loosely modeled after the interconnection of neurons, or nerve cells, in the human brain

newspaper-style columns　text that continues from the bottom of one column on the left to the top of the next column to the right on the same page

nonprocedural language　see *fourth generation language*

novice　a beginning computer user

null-modem cable　a cable for directly connecting the serial ports of two computers

number　a numeric quantity, such as 100, 52.34, or 0.05

numeric formula　in a worksheet, a mathematical expression that calculates using numeric values and produces a numeric result

numeric keypad　on an IBM-compatible computer, the area on the right side of the keyboard arranged like the number keys on a calculator

object code   software that has been translated into machine language

object-oriented   a package that lets you create and manipulate images made up of only discrete geometric objects such as lines, curves, rectangles, ovals, irregular outlines, polygons, and text

octal system   base 8 number system

one-to-many link   a type of link that connects a single record in one file to multiple records in one or more other files

one-to-one link   a type of link that connects a single record in one file to a single record in another file

on-line   connected to and controlled by the computer

on-line help   information about how a program works that you can display on the screen, without your having to look it up in a printed reference manual

on-line information service   a service that allows computers equipped with a modem to retrieve vast quantities of information and communicate with other users

on-line reference   a program such as a spelling checker, thesaurus, or user manual that you can use while running another program

open style   in WordPerfect, a style that has just a beginning code, often used to set formats for an entire document

operand   a number on which an operation is to be performed

operating system   a set of programs that controls a computer's hardware and manages the use of software

operation code (opcode)   the part of a machine language instruction that indicates which operation is to be performed

operator   a symbol that represents an action to be performed in a formula, such as + or *

optical disk drive   a secondary storage device that uses a laser to read or write data on a plastic disk

optimal recalculation   see *minimal recalculation*

orphan   the first line of a paragraph that appears at the bottom of a page

OS/2   a single-user, multitasking operating system, developed by IBM and Microsoft, for IBM and IBM-compatible microcomputers that use the Intel 80286, 80386, and 80486 microprocessors

output   any information produced by the computer; the computer's responses to your input

overwrite mode   a typing mode in which characters typed at the current cursor location replace existing characters

packet-switching network   see *public data network*

page break   a division between two pages

page description language   a specialized computer programming language for defining the size, format, and position of text and graphic elements on a printed page

page formatting   specifying the general organization of an entire page of text

page layout software   a package for arranging text and graphics on pages before they are printed

painting program   a pixel-based program for producing pictures on a computer screen

paired style   in WordPerfect, a style that has a beginning and ending code

palette   the total number of colors to choose from in a particular video mode

pan   a CAD feature that lets you move the viewing window up, down, left, or right

paragraph formatting   specifying the appearance of individual blocks of text

parallel columns   text that continues in the same column on the next page

parallel interface   a connection that transmits data, an entire byte at a time, between a computer and an external device, such as a printer

parallel port   see *parallel interface*

parameter   an entry that designates possible alternate actions

parent file   the more general file in a relation that looks up the information in the child file

parity   a method of error checking used to help ensure that all of the data bits of a character were received correctly after a transmission

partition   a separate section of a hard disk that may contain its own operating system

Pascal   a general-purpose, high-level language originally designed to teach students the principles of good programming

patent   an exclusive right to produce or sell an invention for a given time

path   a drive specifier followed by a list of subdirectory names, separated by backslashes, that describes the route to a particular subdirectory

pattern palette   a menu of patterns that can be used with drawing tools to create objects and to fill in enclosed areas on the screen

payroll   the accounting subsystem that maintains personnel information, generates paychecks, computes tax withholdings, and creates summary reports of employee earnings

PC-DOS   a single-user, single-tasking operating system developed by Microsoft for IBM microcomputers

pel   see *pixel*

personal computer   see *microcomputer*

physical console   the display and keyboard

pie chart   a graph that represents values as wedges of a circle, used to show the parts of a whole

piping   a DOS feature, symbolized by the | (vertical bar), that takes the output of one command, which would normally go to the display screen, and feeds it as input to another command

pixel   picture element; a tiny dot on a computer display

pixel-based   a package that has control over every dot on the screen

plotter   an output device that uses one or more pens to draw on paper

point   a typographical measure equal to about 1/72-inch

pointer movement keys keys that you press to move the cell pointer

polling a protocol in which a controlling workstation sends messages to other workstations on the network, asking each one in turn if it has any messages or data to transmit

pop-up menu a list of options that appears on the screen only when a user issues a special command

pop-up utility see *desk accessory*

portable computer a microcomputer about the size of a small suitcase, designed to be moved, but not used, in transit

positron emission tomography (PET) a medical scanning technique that produces images by detecting positively charged particles emitted from radioactive substances injected into the bloodstream

PostScript a page description language for high-resolution printers and typesetters

power supply a refined source of electrical power for a computer that contains a transformer to lower and regulate the voltage level

power user see *expert*

Presentation Manager the graphical user interface of OS/2

primary file in WordPerfect, the text of a form letter containing special mail-merge codes

primary key the field on which records are sorted first

primary storage a computer's internal memory

print buffering see *print spooling*

printer a device for producing permanent copies of computer output on paper

printer setup string a group of special control codes directing the printer to turn on such options as compressed print

print queue a list of files to be printed in the background

print server a network workstation used to control a printer shared by other workstations on a network

print spooler a utility program that reduces or eliminates waiting for a printer to produce documents

print spooling the ability to print one document while working on another

procedure file see *batch file*

ProDOS a single-user, single-tasking proprietary operating system for the Apple II family of microcomputers

program a sequence of step-by-step instructions that tell a computer what to do

Program Evaluation and Review Technique (PERT) a scheduling method for tasks whose completion times are difficult to estimate

programmable data base manager a relational or flat-file data base manager that includes its own programming language or works with a standard programming language such as BASIC, C, COBOL, FORTRAN, or Pascal

programmer a person who creates computer programs

programming language a set of symbols and rules that direct the operations of a computer

project management software a package that helps to formally plan and control complex undertakings

prompt a symbol or statement that indicates the computer is waiting for a response from the user

proportional spacing allotting different amounts of space for different characters

proprietary hardware or software, with tightly controlled patents or copyrights, that cannot be legally duplicated without being licensed by the originator

proprietary operating system an operating system designed specifically for a single model or line of computers

protected cell a cell that cannot be altered, deleted, or moved unless its protection is first turned off

protocol a set of rules that govern how computers communicate

public data network a way to call a distant communications service from a local telephone number

pull-down menu a list of options that appears when the list's title or symbol is selected from the top of the screen

query a search for records that meet one or more specific criteria; in dBASE, a set of instructions to retrieve, display, organize, or edit data

Query-by-Example (QBE) a highly interactive query language that makes it easy for a user to extract information from a data base

query file in dBASE III PLUS, a special type of file that filters a data base to display or print only those records that meet specific criteria

query language a specialized set of commands for rearranging or extracting data from data bases

QuickDraw laser printer a laser printer designed especially for Apple Macintosh computers as a lower-cost alternative to PostScript printers

RAM cache a part of memory specially reserved for data that must be frequently retrieved

RAM disk an area of memory that is set up to simulate a disk drive

RAM resident see *memory resident*

random access memory (RAM) storage in which all addresses are equally accessible; the portion of a computer's primary storage used to hold programs and data temporarily

range a block of adjacent cells in a worksheet, indicated by the address of the upper left cell, two periods, and the address of the lower right cell

read-only attribute the file attribute that determines if a file can be written, modified, or deleted

read-only field a data base field whose contents can be viewed but not altered

read-only memory (ROM) permanent primary storage that is encoded with programs and data at the factory, retains its contents when the power is turned off, and can be read and used but never erased, changed, or augmented

read-write head   a tiny electromagnet on a disk drive's access arm that can create or erase minuscule magnetic spots on the disk directly below

real number   see *floating-point number*

real-time clock   a built-in clock that keeps the date and time-of-day for a computer

record   an array of related fields that contains all the data about a particular person or object

record buffer   in Lotus 1-2-3 Release 3.0, a 512-byte area of memory that stores the most recent keystrokes

record feature   in Lotus 1-2-3 Release 3.0, a way to create a macro by copying keystrokes saved in the record buffer

record locking   preventing the deletion or modification of an individual record currently being used by another person on the same network

record number   a unique number assigned to each record in a data base file

record pointer   in dBASE, an invisible pointer that keeps track of the current record

redirection   changing the normal source or destination of information processed by a DOS command by using the >, <, or >> symbols

redirector   a layer of software that acts as a traffic controller for the data and messages transmitted over a network

reduced instruction set computer (RISC)   a microprocessor that has a relatively small number of simple instructions that all execute very quickly

reformatting   erasing and reinitializing a previously formatted disk

register   a storage compartment inside the CPU for temporarily holding numbers that are currently being manipulated

relate   to link two or more data base files

relational data base   a data base that includes two or more files with at least one field in common

relational data base manager   a program that allows you to create, maintain, reorganize, and print structured data from more than one file at a time

relational operator   a symbol or word that specifies how items are to be compared

relative reference   a cell address that pertains to a cell's position relative to the current cell, and changes when the cell is moved or copied

replace   a word processing feature used to automatically substitute one word or phrase for another throughout a document

replaceable parameter   a special code inserted into a batch file that allows the user to pass information to the batch file while it is running

report   a printed listing of the contents of a data base

report band   in dBASE IV, a logical piece of a report design

resident routine   see *internal command*

resolution   the sharpness of a display screen

ring network   a topology in which each workstation is connected to a single cable that runs past all of the workstations, with the two ends of the central cable hooked together

robot   a computer-controlled machine that performs mechanical tasks

root directory   the main directory on every DOS disk

row   a record in an SQL table

row-wise recalculation   the order of worksheet recalculation that begins with cell A1 and proceeds across row 1, then row 2, and so on

ruler guide   in a page layout program, a dotted line that helps keep text and graphics aligned

ruler line   a line that shows the positions of the margins and tab stops

rules   dividing lines placed to separate columns and offset blocks of text

running head   the same title printed on every page

sans serif   a kind of plain typeface without serifs

scanner   an input device that can read text and/or graphics from paper and enter it directly into the computer

scatterplot   see *XY graph*

scroll bar   an on-screen tool used to allow movement within a document, usually found in word processing packages with graphics interfaces

scrolling   the upward movement of text on a display screen

search   a word processing feature used to locate a name or topic within a document

secondary key   the field on which records are sorted second, after the primary key

secondary merge file   in WordPerfect, the data file that contains the names and addresses for a mail-merge

secondary storage   storage that supplements primary storage by providing a place to keep programs and data when they are not needed

sector   a division of a disk track

semiconductor   a substance that conducts electricity poorly at low temperatures, but well at high temperatures, and is used to make integrated circuit chips

sequential access medium   storage medium, such as magnetic tape, on which data items can be retrieved only in the order in which they were recorded

serial interface   a connection that transmits bytes of data, one bit at a time, between a computer and an external device, such as a modem

serial port   see *serial interface*

serif   a kind of typeface that has lines crossing and finishing off the main strokes of the characters

service program   low-level program in the BIOS or DOS that can be invoked by other software to perform hardware-related tasks

shared word processor   a word processing system on a large, multiuser computer

single-tasking   the simplest type of operating system that accommodates a single user and runs a single program at a time

site license   permission to make copies of software for internal use at a reduced fee for each copy

slide show program   a program that allows you to present a sequence of pictures on a computer screen, either automatically timed or directly controlled

Small Computer System Interface (SCSI)   a connection that provides high-speed access to peripheral devices such as hard disks

smart recalculation   the ability of a spreadsheet program to automatically update only those cells, if any, that are affected when a new entry is made

snaking columns   see *newspaper-style columns*

snap   a CAD feature that automatically aligns objects to the nearest grid lines

soft hyphen   a hyphen generated by the auto-hyphenation feature

soft page break   a division between two pages automatically generated by the word processing software

soft return   a new line begun by the word wrap feature

soft space   an extra blank generated by a word processing program to justify text

software   a program or set of programs that tells a computer system what to do

software licensing   a legal agreement in which a program is not actually sold, but licensed to a user with limits on what can be done with the program

software piracy   the practice of illegally copying software

sorting   arranging items in some particular order

Soundex search   a search technique that finds words that sound like the specified word

source   a disk or file to be copied

source code   software in an assembly language or a high-level language before it is translated into machine language

specifications   a detailed list of the exact components, options, and capabilities of a particular hardware device

speech synthesizer   an output device that either mimics human speech or constructs it out of prerecorded sounds

spelling checker   see *built-in dictionary*

spooling   multitasking technique that prints files in the background while the computer is used for other work

spreadsheet   see *worksheet*

spreadsheet package   software that helps you manipulate tables of numbers

stack   a data structure used by the CPU, operating system, or application program as a temporary storage area

stacked bar graph   a variation of the basic bar graph that shows components and total amounts for each category by dividing each bar into sections

stackware   information systems created with the Hypertalk language of Apple's Hypercard program

star network   a topology in which an individual cable is run from a central server to each workstation

startup directory   the disk drive and directory automatically used to store and retrieve worksheet files unless otherwise specified

static menu   a list of options that usually remains on the screen in a fixed position

status bar   in dBASE, a line near the bottom of the screen that displays information about the operation you have chosen

status line   in WordPerfect, the line at the bottom of the screen that displays messages and warnings

stop bits   bits that mark the end of an individual data character transmission

string combination operator   the & (ampersand), which joins two labels

Structured Query Language (SQL)   a standardized language for extracting information from a relational data base

style   in WordPerfect, a collection of formatting codes and possibly text that can be created, saved, and inserted into documents to automate formatting and provide a consistent appearance to documents

style sheet   a collection of formatting instructions that can be saved in a file and applied to different documents

subdirectory   a group of files on a disk organized under a single name

submenu   a menu that is activated by selecting an option from a higher-level menu

summary operator   in dBASE IV, an operator for performing operations in view queries such as SUM, AVERAGE, and COUNT

supercomputer   an extremely fast mainframe

supermicro   see *workstation*

supermini   a powerful minicomputer with capabilities similar to those of some mainframes

surge protector   a device that rapidly cuts off the electricity when a voltage surge occurs

switching drives   telling DOS to use a different disk drive as the default

symbolic addressing   the assignment of meaningful names, such as TOTAL, to computer memory locations

system board   see *motherboard*

system call   see *service program*

system clock   a crystal, oscillating several million times per second, that synchronizes the internal operations of the microprocessor and other computer components

system prompt   see *DOS prompt*

system software   the software that handles the many details of managing a computer system

system unit   in many microcomputers, the box that houses the central processing unit, control circuitry, expansion boards, memory, and disk drives

table   a screen that displays a record in each row and a field in each column; the basic component of an SQL data base

tag   in dBASE IV, the name of an index in a multiple index file

target   a disk or file copy to be created

telecommute   to work at home using a microcomputer or a terminal connected to a computer at the office

teleconference   an electronic forum that allows computer users who share special interests to communicate and hold on-line meetings

template   a general-purpose, ready-made worksheet in which the user fills in the blanks or changes selected entries

terminal   a computer input/output station consisting of a keyboard and a display

terminal emulation   a communications software feature that lets you use a microcomputer as a computer terminal

text area   in WordPerfect, the area on the screen where you enter text and edit a document

text-based windowing environment   a windowing environment that uses only the standard character set built into the computer and that cannot work with graphics programs

text file   a file, also known as an ASCII file, that contains only ordinary letters, numbers, and punctuation marks

time-sharing   an operating system that rapidly switches among several users at fixed intervals of time

token-passing   a protocol that uses a control signal called a token that determines which workstation is allowed to transmit messages or data

tool palette   a menu of icons for drawing, adding text, moving about, and selecting parts of a picture created with a painting or drawing program

topology   the way hardware components are arranged in a network

touch screen   an input device built into or over a display screen that uses infrared light beams or an electrically conductive surface to identify the position of a finger as it points to the screen

track   a ring on a disk where data can be stored

trackball   a box that contains a protruding ball that can be freely rotated in any direction and is often used as an alternative to a mouse

trademark   a legal protection for creative expression, usually limited to a word, phrase, or graphic symbol representing a company or product

transient routine   see *external command*

Transputer   a special microprocessor that can be connected with other Transputers to construct a fast, powerful multiprocessing computer

twisted-pair wire   two wires that have been partially wrapped around each other, used for ordinary telephone lines and inexpensive local area networks

typeface   see *font*

ultrasound scanner   a medical imaging device that uses very high-frequency sound waves

undo   a feature that lets you cancel your most recently performed operation

UNIX   a multiuser, multitasking generic operating system originally developed at AT&T's Bell Laboratories

update query   in dBASE IV, a query used to add, modify, or delete data in a data base file

uploading   transferring a file from your computer to a host computer

upwardly compatible   the ability of a new software product to handle every official command that worked with previous versions of it

user   a person who runs software on a computer to accomplish some task

user friendly   easy-to-learn; can be used by people who don't have a lot of computer experience

user interface   how a user directs the actions of software and how the software responds to these requests

utility   a small, specific program that adds handy features to a particular operating system or application package

value-added network   see *public data network*

very high level language   see *fourth generation language*

video mode   a combination of screen resolution and number of colors that can be used at one time

view   in dBASE, an arrangement of data on the screen

view file   in dBASE III PLUS, a file that displays data from two or more data base files

view query   in dBASE IV, a set of instructions that displays selected data on the screen

view skeleton   in dBASE IV, a graphic representation of the fields that will be displayed by the view query

virtual console   a simulated display and keyboard used by programs that run in the background under OS/2

voice recognition system   an input device that can recognize a finite number of isolated sounds, words, and phrases

volume label   in DOS, the name of a disk

widow   the last line of a paragraph that appears at the top of a page

wildcard character   in WordPerfect and dBASE, the * (which represents any group of characters) or the ? (which represents any single character) used in search and replace operations

what-you-see-is-what-you-get (WYSIWYG)   a feature in which a document is printed on paper exactly as it appears on the screen

window   a boxed-in area on the screen that shows the activity of a particular software program

windowing environment   system software that lets you divide your screen into a number of different boxes and run a separate program in each one

word processing   a common computer application that allows you to produce documents, such as letters and reports, with a computer

word processing package   a software package used to create, enter, edit, format, store, and print documents

word wrap   a word processing feature that automatically begins new lines when necessary without the user having to press the Enter key (carriage return)

work area   in dBASE, a place in memory that holds an open data base file

worksheet a table of columns and rows of numbers, text labels, and formulas used in a spreadsheet package for the manipulation of numerical, financial, and accounting data

workstation a small, yet powerful computer generally used by only one person at a time, traditionally used by scientists and engineers for drafting, design, and map-making

write once, read many (times) (WORM) an optical disk drive that allows users to record data once, and then only read it thereafter

write-protection a diskette feature that can be used to prevent the contents from being erased or altered

write-protect notch a small rectangle cut out of one side of a 5¼-inch diskette that can be covered with a gummed tab to write-protect the disk

write-protect switch a tab on a 3½-inch diskette that can be slid to open a little hole in the disk's plastic case, thereby write-protecting the disk

XY graph a plot that shows the relationship between two or more variables

PHOTO CREDITS

Chapter 1
2 IBM; 3 IBM; 4 Intel; 5 Memorex; 6 Seagate Technologies;
7 IBM; 8 IBM; 10 Hewlett-Packard; 11 Hewlett-Packard

Chapter 2
8 IBM.

MS–DOS® 4.01

Key	Ctrl	Shift	Alt
F1	Retype one character from previous command		
F2	Retype previous command up to specified character		
F3	Retype all of previous command		
F4	Delete previous command up to specified character		
F5	Save current command as previous command		
F6	Insert End-of-file code Ctrl-Z		
F7			
F8			
F9			
F10			

Ctrl-Alt-Del	Reboot	Enter	Process cmd.
Ctrl-Break	Cancel	Esc	Cancel line
Ctrl-Print Screen	Echo	Del	Skip char.
Print Screen	Print	Ins	Toggle insert

D.C. Heath

Lotus 1–2–3® R. 2.2

Key	Ctrl	Shift	Alt
F1	HELP	COMPOSE	
F2	EDIT	STEP	
F3	NAME	RUN	
F4	ABS	UNDO	
F5	GOTO	LEARN	
			Alt
F6	WINDOW		
F7	QUERY	APP1	
F8	TABLE	APP2	
F9	CALC	APP3	
F10	GRAPH	APP4	

/	Main menu	Home	Go to A1
Enter	Process entry	Ctrl←	Left screen
Esc	Exit menu	Ctrl→	Right screen

D.C. Heath

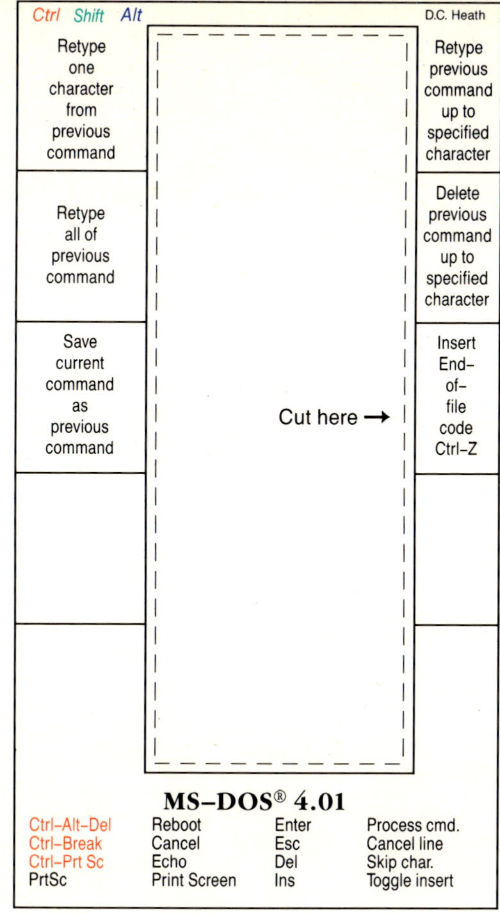

Ctrl Shift Alt · D.C. Heath

Retype one character from previous command	Retype previous command up to specified character
Retype all of previous command	Delete previous command up to specified character
Save current command as previous command	Insert End-of-file code Ctrl-Z

Cut here →

MS–DOS® 4.01

Ctrl-Alt-Del	Reboot	Enter	Process cmd.
Ctrl-Break	Cancel	Esc	Cancel line
Ctrl-Prt Sc	Echo	Del	Skip char.
PrtSc	Print Screen	Ins	Toggle insert

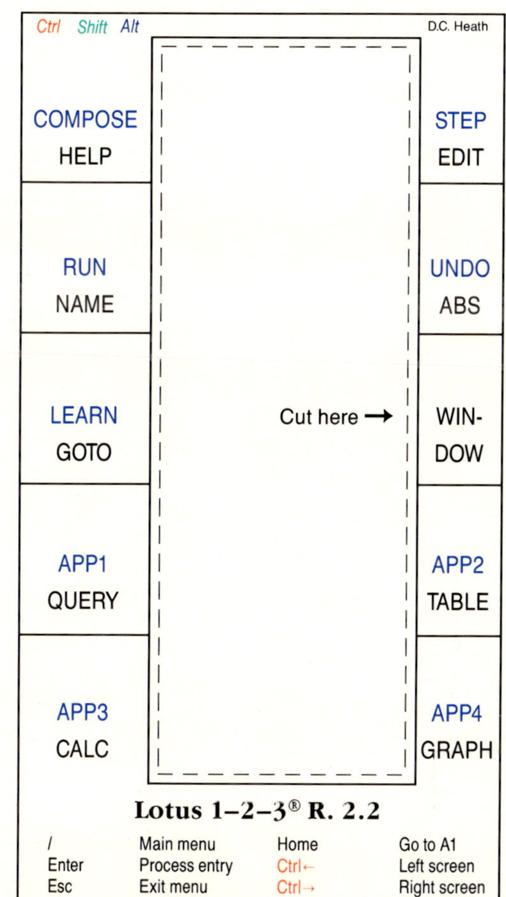

Ctrl Shift Alt · D.C. Heath

COMPOSE / HELP	STEP / EDIT
RUN / NAME	UNDO / ABS
LEARN / GOTO	WIN-DOW
APP1 / QUERY	APP2 / TABLE
APP3 / CALC	APP4 / GRAPH

Cut here →

Lotus 1–2–3® R. 2.2

/	Main menu	Home	Go to A1
Enter	Process entry	Ctrl←	Left screen
Esc	Exit menu	Ctrl→	Right screen